AS Level for OCR

Applied Business

Rob Dransfield • Dave Needham

www.heinemann.co.uk
✓ Free online support
✓ Useful weblinks
✓ 24 hour online ordering

01865 888058

Heinemann Educational Publishers
Halley Court, Jordan Hill, Oxford OX2 8EJ
Part of Harcourt Education

Heinemann is a registered trademark of
Harcourt Education Limited

First published 2005

10 09 08 07 06 05
10 9 8 7 6 5 4 3 2 1

British Library Cataloguing in Publication Data is available
from the British Library on request.

10-digit ISBN: 0 435 40116 5
13-digit ISBN: 978 0 435401 16 0

Edited by Rosalyn Bass
Designed by Lorraine Inglis
Typeset and illustrated by Saxon Graphics Ltd, Derby
Original illustrations © Harcourt Education Limited, 2005
Cover design by Wooden Ark Studio
Printed in Great Britain by The Bath Press Ltd
Cover photo © Getty
Picture research by Ginny Stroud-Lewis

Acknowledgements
Every effort has been made to contact copyright holders of material reproduced
in this book. Any omissions will be rectified in subsequent printings if notice is
given to the publishers.

Websites
Please note that the examples of websites suggested in this book were up to
date at the time of writing. It is essential for tutors to preview each site before
using it to ensure that the URL is still accurate and the content is appropriate.
We suggest that tutors bookmark useful sites and consider enabling students to
access them through the school or college intranet.

Contents

Acknowledgements   vi

Introduction   vii

UNIT 1

CREATING A MARKETING PROPOSAL   1

Introduction   1
1.2.1   Marketing objectives   2
1.2.2   Functional areas of a business and their supporting role   10
1.2.3   Market research   13
1.2.4   The marketing mix   33
1.2.5   Presentational skills   49
1.2.6   How to judge potential success   51
Resources   53

UNIT 2

RECRUITMENT IN THE WORKPLACE   55

Introduction   55
2.2.1   Job roles   56
2.2.2   The recruitment process   59
2.2.3   The selection process   73
2.2.4   The induction process   80
2.2.5   Employee motivation   84
2.2.6   The legal dimension   93
2.2.7   Research   94
2.2.8   How to judge effectiveness   96
Resources   99

UNIT 3

UNDERSTANDING THE BUSINESS ENVIRONMENT   101

Introduction   101
3.2.1   Business ownership   102
3.2.2   Sources of finance   109
3.2.3   Budgeting and budgetary control   114
3.2.4   Break-even analysis   120
3.2.5   Cash-flow forecasts and statements   126
3.2.6   Importance of accurate record keeping and technology   130
3.2.7   Analysis of the current market position   137
3.2.8   Economic conditions and market conditions   142
3.2.9   Ethical, legal, social, political and environmental factors   148
3.2.10 Stakeholders   153
Resources   163

| | UNIT 4 | **THE IMPACT OF CUSTOMER SERVICE** | **165** |

Introduction 165
4.2.1 Definition of a customer 166
4.2.2 Definition of customer service and its importance to any
business 169
4.2.3 Customer needs and their potential power 179
4.2.4 How businesses gather information on customer needs
and the issues surrounding the storage of this information 185
4.2.5 Impact that legal and ethical issues can have on the
provision of customer service 191
4.2.6 Implications for maintaining a high level of customer
service on staff and senior management 197
4.2.7 Assessing the quality and effectiveness of customer service 203
Resources 206

UNIT 5 **ICT PROVISION IN BUSINESS** **209**

Introduction 209
5.2.1 How ICT is used by businesses 210
5.2.2 Forms ICT provision can take 219
5.2.3 The benefits/drawbacks of introducing ICT provision 238
5.2.4 Contingency planning 244
5.2.5 Research 247
5.2.6 Presentational skills 247
5.2.7 How to judge viability 250
Resources 252

UNIT 6 **RUNNING AN ENTERPRISE ACTIVITY** **253**

Introduction 253
6.2.1 Setting aims and objectives 254
6.2.2 Building and developing an effective team 260
6.2.3 Time management 267
6.2.4 Required resources 270
6.2.5 Need for regular meetings 273
6.2.6 Possible constraints 277
6.2.7 Research and analysis 279
6.2.8 Potential future changes to the enterprise activity 282
Resources 284

UNIT 7	FINANCIAL PROVIDERS AND PRODUCTS	285
	Introduction	285
	7.2.1 Customers of financial services	286
	7.2.2 Financial service providers and products	292
	7.2.3 Research into the financial services market	309
	7.2.4 Constraints affecting the provision of financial services	317
	7.2.5 Potential effect of future changes to customer circumstances	320
	Resources	322

UNIT 8	UNDERSTANDING PRODUCTION IN BUSINESS	323
	Introduction	323
	8.2.1 The role of the production department	324
	8.2.2 Operational efficiency	331
	8.2.3 Organising production	335
	8.2.4 Ensuring quality	339
	8.2.5 Stock control	345
	8.2.6 Health and safety	348
	8.2.7 Research into production	349
	8.2.8 Potential production improvements	350
	Resources	352

Glossary	353
Index	358

Acknowledgements

The authors and publishers are grateful to those who have given permission to reproduce material.

Every effort has been made to contact copyright holders of material reproduced in this book. Any omissions or errors will be rectified in subsequent printings if notice is given to the publishers.

Text acknowledgements

Anything Left-Handed, www.anythingleft-handed.co.uk – page256

Association of British Insurers – pages 295, 303

Building Societies Association – page 294

Call Centre Association – page 190

Camelot Group. Lottery ticket reproduced with the kind permission of Camelot Group plc, Operator of the National Lottery. The 'Crossed Fingers' logo is a registered trademark owned by The National Lottery Commission – page 222

Charity Commission, www.charitycommission.gov.uk/supportingcharities/ccebank.asp – page 304

Dibb, Sally et al., Marketing Concepts and Strategies, Boston: Houghton Mifflin, 2001 – page 33

Euromonitor International – page 139

The Football Association. Extract © The Football Association Limited 2002–04. All Rights Reserved – page 192

Institute of Customer Service – page 194

London Stock Exchange – page 297

Manchester United – page 257

Microsoft PowerPoint® is a registered trademark of Microsoft Corporation in the United States and other countries

Microsoft product screenshots reprinted with permission from Microsoft Corporation

Mintel – page 218

Moneyfacts – the UK's largest selling professional financial monthly. For subscription details: www.moneyfacts.co.uk or 0870 2250 100 – page 316

NatWest – page 290

Nielsen Media Research – page 42

Research Machines plc – page 36

Shipley, D., Pricing Objectives in British Manufacturing Industry, Journal of Industrial Economics, vol.29, no. 4 – page 36

The Sunday Times – page 85

TDC – page 187

Tesco – pages 151, 178, 298, 334, 335

Vodafone – page 192

World Advertising Research Centre/DIMS – page 43

Crown copyright material is reproduced under Class Licence No. C02W0005419 with the permission of the Controller of HMSO and the Queen's Printer for Scotland.

Photo Acknowledgements

The Advertising Archives – pages 219, 294

Alamy – pages 134, 138

Alamy Images/ACE STOCK LIMITED – pages 58, 249

Alamy Images/Allan Ivy – page 4

Alamy Images/Andy Bishop – page 174,

Alamy Images/Ashley Cooper – page 185

Alamy Images/David Hoffman Photo Library – page 86

Alamy Images/David Moore – page 45

Alamy Images/Motoring Picture Library – page 344

Alamy Images/Peter Arnold Inc./Oldrich Karasek – page 41

Alamy Images/Photofusion Picture Library – pages 15, 183(b)

Alamy Images/Popperfoto – page 89

Alamy Images/Robert Harding Picture Library Ltd/Glynn Genin – page 101

Alamy Images/The Photolibrary Wales – page 105

Art Directors and Trip/Peter Kaplan – page 49

Art Directors/Helene Rogers – pages 225(b)

Bic company – page 332(a)

Corbis rf – pages 187, 221

Corbis/Jacques M. Chenet – page 254

Corbis/Reuters/John Gress – page 172

Debbie Rowe – page 199

Empics/PA – pages 7, 156, 255, 327

Getty – pages 24, 75, 147

Getty Images/Manchester United – page 257

Getty Images/Stone +/Javier Pierini – page 273

Getty Images/Stone/Michael Rosenfeld – page 332(b)

Getty Images/Stone/Robert E. Daemmrich – page 315

Getty Images/The Image Bank – page 88

Getty Images/The Image Bank/Kay Chernush – page 325

Getty Images/The Image Bank/Luis Castaneda Inc – pages 242, 323

Getty Images/Tim Graham – page 309

Ginny Stroud-Lewis – pages 8, 92, 108, 139, 183(a), 287

Harcourt Education /Gareth Boden (Photos) – pages 220, 223, 225(a), 226

Harcourt Education/Peter Morris (UK SCHOOLS) – page 300

Harcourt Index – page 320

Harcourt Index/Photodisk Getty Images – page 165, 211, 212

Hoffmans Photos – page 303

Photodisk (photos) – page 222

Robin Hammond/Guzelian – page 343

Rosabeth Moss Kanter – page 92

Shout/John Callan – pages 201

Introduction

Welcome to your GCE Applied Business course. The term 'Applied Business' is used to describe your course because it is focused not just upon learning about business organisations but also upon finding out and investigating how people within such organisations behave and make decisions. The OCR qualification aims to 'encourage candidates to develop skills, knowledge and understanding in realistic business contexts, such as discovering problems and opportunities faced by local businesses and/or developing an enterprise activity'.

Your learning will involve using theory and finding out how that theory relates to all of the decisions and activities that are taken by people within organisations at a variety of different levels. You will undertake a range of investigative portfolio activities that enable you to apply your understanding and use of theory to problems, issues and activities that make your course both theoretical and practical. This provides you with a first-hand opportunity to learn within and outside a classroom about many of the important activities and functions that people in business are involved with by undertaking many of these functions yourself. In this way your course is closely 'work related' and is designed to give you a much deeper and more meaningful understanding of the sort of activities that people in business are involved with, so that you gain both knowledge and experience.

The OCR Applied Business qualification is flexible because it provides you with a real choice about which parts of the qualification you want to undertake. Just like the more traditional A levels, the Applied GCE adopts the AS and A2 structure of GCEs.

For the AS Double Award candidates must take Units 1, 2, 3 and 4, plus two other units from units 5, 6, 7 and 8. All these units are covered in this book and they are:

Unit 1: Creating a Marketing Proposal (Internally Assessed)
Unit 2: Recruitment in the Workplace (Internally Assessed)
Unit 3: Understanding the Business Environment (Externally Assessed)
Unit 4: The Impact of Customer Service (Externally Assessed)
Unit 5: ICT Provision in a Business (Internally Assessed)
Unit 6: Running an Enterprise Activity (Internally Assessed)
Unit 7: Financial Providers and Products (Internally Assessed)
Unit 8: Understanding Production in Business (Internally Assessed).

In this course you will complete both external and internal assessments in the form of portfolio work. The external assessment will relate to a business scenario to provide an appropriate context for the vocational element of your studies. For the internally-based portfolio assessments you will be asked to undertake realistic activities that relate to a vocational scenario, each of which you will be able to undertake in tandem with your learning within each unit. Following the dialogue and undertaking the activities in this book will help you to prepare for all of your assessment activities.

Teachers should refer to the OCR specifications for full details on the requirements for internal and external assessments. There is also sample assessment material available from OCR.

Throughout this book key words or concepts are highlighted in bold. These are also listed in the glossary at the back of the book.

Enjoy your Applied Business course. By succeeding with your course you are opening up avenues so that you can either go into the workplace or go into higher education following your course.

Dave Needham
Rob Dransfield

UNIT 1

Creating a marketing proposal

This unit contains six elements:

1.2.1 Marketing objectives

1.2.2 Functional areas of a business and their supporting role

1.2.3 Market research

1.2.4 The marketing mix

1.2.5 Presentational skills

1.2.6 How to judge potential success

Introduction

If you have been stopped in the shopping mall 'just to answer a few questions' or heard a TV advertisement which says 'nine out of ten **customers** preferred...', you have seen some aspects of **marketing**. You may have wondered how a supermarket decides which products to promote or place on the top or bottom shelf. These are all very visible parts of a highly skilled and sophisticated marketing process which interacts with all the other functions of a business.

It is very easy to take our lifestyle and the range of products and choices that we see or think about every day for granted. When we go into shops there is a huge variety of goods on view and we have to make a range of decisions that relate not just to our needs but also our income. At the same time, we are constantly offered a range of service

opportunities to match our lifestyle. It is clear that all of the people and organisations offering so many different opportunities not only show a good understanding of us as **consumers** and how our thoughts, perceptions and minds work, but they must also have undertaken widespread and precise **market research** to find out about our needs.

At the heart of this process of understanding customers is the need for organisations to find out what their customers require, make appropriate **investments** and bring **resources** together to provide goods or services for their customers. This whole process requires considerable preparation and planning, the starting point of which is the creation of a marketing proposal.

As you study this unit, you will produce a marketing proposal to launch a new product or service of your choice within the context of your chosen business. The proposal will be presented to an informed audience in the form of an oral presentation.

Your oral presentation will focus on your proposal of a **marketing mix** for your new product or service based on your own research and analysis of gathered data.

Finally, you will show evidence of reasoned judgements as you discuss the likely success of your marketing proposal for your new product or service.

1.2.1 Marketing objectives

Marketing is about understanding the customer and ensuring that products and services match existing and potential customer needs. Marketing is also about looking at ways of influencing the behaviour of customers.

Marketing is essential to the success of any business. Its primary aim is to enable businesses to meet the needs of their actual and potential customers, whether for **profit** or not. If a business's marketing is to be successful, it must:

* understand consumer needs

* understand and keep ahead of the competition

* communicate effectively with its customers to satisfy customer expectations

* co-ordinate its functions to achieve marketing aims

* be aware of constraints on marketing activities.

One of the key components of marketing, therefore, is understanding customer wants and needs. Marketing is the process through which Jaguar is able to identify the kinds of cars

people will want to buy in the near future and the features that should be built into those cars. Marketing helps Reebok anticipate changes in consumers' preferences for trainers, and helps digital television formats such as Freeview and Sky Television to identify the types of channels viewers will want to watch in the future.

Marketing objectives are an essential part of the **marketing plan** as they provide direction for activities to follow. Without clear objectives it is difficult to evaluate what a marketing plan is trying to achieve or whether a plan has been successful. It is usual to translate marketing objectives into quantifiable 'result areas', such as **market share**, market penetration or growth rate of sales. Some of these may be further broken down into specific sales volumes, value goals or geographical targets. Marketing objectives may have a time frame and direction. They also provide a basis for evaluation. Marketing must ensure that organisational activities are co-ordinated in such a way that marketing objectives are met.

When an organisation makes a mission statement it is setting a direction for everything that the business does. It is from this mission that decision-takers around the organisation set their own objectives for their particular area of activity. So, if an organisation has a mission to become a global player in aromatherapy oil, marketers within the organisation will know and understand that when they set their business objectives they need to set objectives that help the business to become a global player.

Marketing objectives create a direction for marketing activity. In this way marketing objectives are a starting point from which marketing activities follow. Before an organisation participates in any activity its owners and managers must think about what their marketing objectives will be. It is from these objectives that activities across the whole organisation will develop.

For example, as a business evolves, managers across the organisation need to know how their part of the business is serving the needs of customers. So, somebody involved in operation management or human resources will want to know how well their activities are helping the business to meet the needs of customers or keeping the business ahead of the competition. If they are involved in operations they will want to know that the quality of products is high enough to meet customer needs. Human resource managers will want to know whether staff are trained well enough to carry out activities that help the business stay ahead of the competition and so on.

When writing marketing objectives it is possible to use the SMART approach to writing objectives. This is that marketing objectives must be:

SPECIFIC – the objectives need to relate to the issues and markets in which the organisation is involved.
MEASURABLE – this helps managers to evaluate whether they have been successful in achieving marketing objectives.
ACHIEVABLE – marketing objectives must be realistic. For example, setting sales targets that are too high would create too many pressures upon a business and might damage rather than help the business.

REALISTIC – objectives must relate to the business and its activities and not be too fanciful.
TIMELY – planning for objectives involves identifying when and how they may be achieved.

The following marketing objectives help us to understand how organisations pursue *business activities*.

Understanding consumer needs

It is important to discover the needs of consumers to ensure that quality goods and services are produced. Being human, all customers are different, but only a few businesses (a tailor, for example, or a firm of architects) can provide products specifically designed for each individual customer. Most marketing activities are therefore designed to meet the needs of groups of customers within a market.

Theory into practice

Think of a product on offer that is all about technology and is not focused sufficiently upon meeting the needs of customers. Are there still some of these products around? Think equally about products that are all about sales and perhaps lack some market orientation. Finally, think of products that you feel are really well marketed and are clearly focused upon customer needs. Why is this so? What makes them so unique?

Selling low-value products cheaply and in volume

For many years, Marks & Spencer had been a British institution, supported by their faithful customers. The products were a benchmark of British quality – dependable and decent – and stood as a British emblem. However, people increasingly started to think that a lot of their merchandise was dull and out of touch with changing fashions.

During the 1980s, M&S were probably propped up by good fortune. Men's and women's fashions in the 1980s were based on the older styles of the 1940s and, as more women entered the workforce, the ready-made meal became accepted as a comfort food. At the time, the alternatives to M&S were probably not attractive enough, but then George at Asda, designers at Debenhams, Zara,

Next and Gap changed the fashion world with new merchandise every three weeks instead of M&S's twice-yearly collections. The most fashion conscious of women suddenly became those women in their thirties and forties. They had money, knew about fashion and wanted to make an effort.

During the 1990s, M&S, emphasised 'value' rather then price, and this provided them with an enviable position in the high street. However, it was during this time they also got so hung up on quality they forgot about style and fashion. With inappropriate styles, sales fell and even their food halls lost customers.

In recent years M&S have got into branding, including the launch of their Per Una fashion brand which was formed as a joint venture between M&S and George Davies, the designer.

The future of M&S largely depends upon how well their designers are able to push through improvements to core products and win back the confidence of the British public. It is argued today that M&S's biggest problem is public perception, and their solution to change such perceptions is through the process of branding.

1 To what extent were the problems encountered by M&S a failure to understand their customers?
2 Describe how M&S could use their marketing objectives to improve the way in which they operate. In order to answer this, cross-reference your answer to the marketing objectives within this section.

Understanding and keeping ahead of the competition

As organisations develop their marketing proposal, senior managers need to think about how to understand their customers and keep ahead of competition. All organisational activities take place in an environment where there is some element of risk. For example, last year a firm might have sold 40,000 fridges to a market in Italy. Who is to say that they will sell the 50,000

they plan to sell this year? They may suddenly find new competitors in this market with a much better product than they currently produce, and which is being sold at a lower price. Italy may go through a cold spell or there may be problems in the economy that reduce the likelihood that people will change their fridge.

A key objective for many organisations is to use market research to provide an invaluable source of information to help organisations make decisions and develop new and existing products

Connecting the washer to the Web

Ariston have developed a washing machine that can communicate with the Internet using its own mobile phone. The margherita2000.com washing machine will be able to send breakdown reports for repair and download new washing cycles from its own website. The householder will also be able to control the washing machine remotely either by using a mobile phone or by logging on to the machine's own website.

The key achievement of this machine is that it is the first of a range of web-connected devices in the home that will be able to talk to each other using a new open communications system called – WRAP – WebReady Appliances Protocol. In the first years of the new century Ariston hope to follow up the launch of the washing machine with a dishwasher, fridge and then an oven.

1   To what sort of audience might the margherita2000 appeal?
2   What sort of market research questions might product planners ask before launching this type of product?
3   What sort of marketing objectives would marketers have had for Ariston's new washing machine?

---

to enable them to keep ahead of their competitors. For example, it could help them to:

* identify their competitors
* improve their knowledge of consumers and competitors so that changing trends can be identified
* use trends to forecast activities
* monitor their market position and develop plans
* improve their competitive advantage.

The need to be innovative and enterprising when identifying opportunities

Marketing is a discipline that involves all of the activities that an organisation engages in. As managers create their marketing proposal, they will be concerned about how to appear innovative and enterprising as well as how to develop new business opportunities for their organisation.

A new product may be one which:

* replaces an old product
* opens up a new market
* broadens an existing market.

It may involve an innovation, a technological breakthrough or simply be a line extension based upon a modification. It is often said that only about 10 per cent of new products are really new. In fact, in order to be enterprising and meet marketing objectives, it is often possible to turn old products into new products simply by finding a new market for them.

There are six distinct stages in the development process for new products. These stages illustrate that by introducing new products organisations are being innovative and enterprising. They are:

* Step 1: Ideas
* Step 2: Screening of ideas
* Step 3: Marketing analysis
* Step 4: Product development
* Step 5: Testing
* Step 6: Launch and commercialisation.

As new products go through each of these stages there is a mortality rate (see Figure 1.1).

Step 1: Ideas

All new products start from ideas. These ideas may be completely new or simply be an update of an existing product. Ideas may come from:

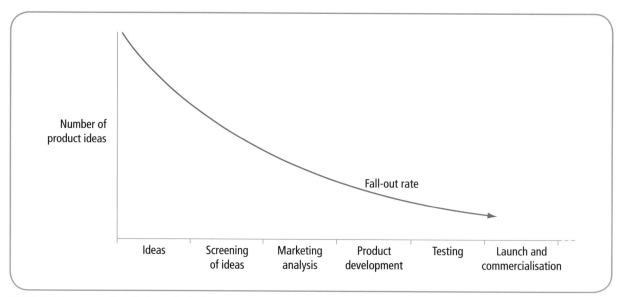

FIGURE 1.1 *Mortality (fall-out) during the new product development process*

Research and development – product development and market research working together. Technological breakthroughs and innovations from research are very important.

Mindstorming – involving a few people developing ideas from words and concepts.

Suggestions box – case incentives may encourage employees to contribute their own ideas.

Sales force – working close to customers, the sales force understands their needs and requirements.

Forced relationships – sometimes one or more products can be joined together to form new product concepts. For example, shampoo and conditioner.

Competitors – monitoring the actions of competitors may provide a rich source of new ideas.

Step 2: Screening of ideas

Once ideas have been generated it is important to screen the ideas likely to be successful and reject the rest. Considerations may include how well the product fits in with others in the product range, the unique elements of any idea that make it competitive, the likely demand for the product and whether or not it could be manufactured economically.

Step 3: Marketing analysis

Once the ideas have been screened, further marketing analysis begins. This involves a thorough analysis of the product's market potential. This type of research helps to identify the market volume (units that could be sold) as well as the value of sales expected. It may also help to identify market potential.

Step 4: Product development

Having come through the test of marketing analysis it is now time to translate the idea or product concept into a product. Design, innovation and the uses of technology are very important in product development. An assessment of packaging and branding may also be involved.

Step 5: Testing

Testing is a vital stage in the product development process. It may involve identifying valuable information through further market research which helps to fine-tune the venture. Test marketing may comprise testing on part of a consumer market or trialling the product to ensure that it meets the required standards.

Step 6: Launch and commercialisation

The launch is the most important day in the life of a product – it is finally revealed to customers. A common technique is to provide sneak glimpses of new products before they are launched.

Communicating effectively with customers to satisfy their expectations

From the very beginning, human beings have used hand signals, vocal patterns, symbolic drawings and facial expressions for the purpose of communicating some form of message to one another. Today, the exchange of information is a sophisticated process that produces subtle messages and that uses emerging technologies, such as the Internet and digital television.

An effective network of communications is essential for any form of promotional activity. It enables an organisation not only to communicate with its customers and satisfy their expectations but also to build an image with the world at large. Such an image will help others to form a judgement about what the organisation stands for and will influence their dealings with it.

For marketing purposes, communication of products and services contributes to the persuasion process which encourages consumers to avail themselves of whatever is on offer. The various tools used to communicate effectively with customers to satisfy their expectations fall within 'the promotional mix'. The promotional mix might include:

* Advertisements – messages sent via the media which are intended to inform or influence the people who read them.

* Direct mail – personally addressed advertising sent through the mail.

* Public relations – non-personal communications using the media.

* Sales promotions – techniques designed to increase sales, such as money-off coupons, samples and competitions.

* Sponsorship – the financing or partial funding of a project, event or activity in order to gain consumer awareness or media coverage.

* Product presentation – improving a **brand**'s visibility through packaging, the use of labels, merchandising and branding.

* Direct selling – making sales with an emphasis upon the importance of salesmanship.

Dealing with internal / external constraints that may hamper marketing activities

Internal constraints

Internal constraints relate to the resource capabilities of an organisation, such as costs. For example, an organisation might identify potential customers, but how capable is it of meeting their needs? It might not have the resources to do so.

For example, in recent years Coca-Cola has developed a global presence. It has been able to do this by ploughing more money into long-term investment. Coca-Cola invests 70 per cent of its profits and achieves a staggering rate of growth.

When a company wants to develop new products or services it needs the resources to finance expansion. The bigger the scale of the development projects, the more resources are required. Sometimes companies finance expansion by selling off existing assets, for example, ICI has moved into higher value-added chemical products, such as components for lip-glosses and eye shadow. To finance this move it sold off a number of its existing heavy chemical plants which had no long-term profit potential.

In addition to financial resources, business organisations need the skills and know-how for a range of marketing activities. Increasingly, companies rely on buying in expertise from outside the organisation.

External constraints

External constraints involve a series of factors, within the business environment in which an organisation operates, that limit its activities. These will include:

* Consumers – if an organisation is not market-focused or if consumers are not interested in a product, then it will be difficult to market.

* Competitors – it may be difficult to market a product for which a competitor already has an advantage.

* Economy – in a period of economic recession when consumers have falling incomes, it may be difficult to market a luxury product.

* The law – there may be a number of laws that constrain the activities of a business and make it difficult for it to do well.

CASE STUDY

Scenario

Daniel and his younger brother George are experienced market traders, working in various markets across south-east London. They are self-motivated entrepreneurs whose main aim in life is to become millionaires. As small businessmen, they do not always find life easy!

Dan was recently offered the opportunity to buy some of the latest videos, which were claimed to be 'kosher'. This is a big opportunity to expand the business, with an up-to-date consumer product that will bring the customers in. The great benefit would be that if customers were interested in the videos, Daniel could offer them a deal with some quick-boiling kettles he bought a few months ago that he has had trouble getting rid of. The kettles look smart but take 15 minutes to boil.

Daniel's problem is that neither he nor George has the money to buy the videos. He is wondering about selling off the van to provide him with the capital, but that would mean buying an alternative form of transport such as 'company mopeds', although this might have the alternative benefit of allowing them to start some courier work.

Another idea Daniel has to expand the business is to use George's expertise in

information technology to set up training courses. Although George was very good with computers, he has not used one for five years and feels that if Daniel is going to do this, they need to buy in help from another person.

1 What a) internal, and b) external constraints make life more difficult for Daniel and George?
2 What might be a better business plan for them?

The market-focused company will fully research all of these constraints and try to find solutions that enable it to turn weaknesses into strengths and threats into opportunities.

1.2.2 Functional areas of a business and their supporting role

Functional areas

An organisation needs to be sure about its capability, a key part of which is not just the marketing systems and activities, but also the support provided by the functional areas across the business to the process of marketing. For example:

Having appropriate marketing objectives. Organisations need to identify marketing objectives that realistically provide them with opportunities to meet the business plans that they have developed.

Structuring the organisation to support marketing objectives. It is important that the functional areas of an organisation enable marketers to achieve their business objectives.

Organisations depend upon their departments to support marketing activities. By developing and focusing upon marketing objectives each part of an organisation is brought together through a process of interdependence to work to meet the same ends. Even though many of the departments do very different things, they are still working on the same objectives.

Departmentalisation is the process by which certain activities or sections of an organisation are grouped logically and assigned to managers. The way in which this is done depends on the aims of the organisation. Departments are the most usual way in which organisations break down into structures that perform particular tasks

Structuring an organisation to meet its marketing objectives

within an organisation. It is important that they work closely together to co-ordinate the different ways in which they meet customer needs. The departments/activities which an organisation engages with will vary from one business to another.

Marketing

The marketing department is responsible for identifying, anticipating and satisfying consumer requirements profitably. Marketing is not just about sales, promotion or market research. As we have seen it has an important role in setting objectives that create a base for an organisation's business plan, which then affects all of the organisation.

Marketing, like all departments, will have a **budget** to work to, and will work closely with research and development to ensure that new product offers match customer needs and requirements. Marketing must also work with production and operations to ensure that the variety, choice, needs and requirements of customers are met. It needs to ensure that the finance department invests in promotional activities and other activities that help to communicate products and services to customers. Customer service is part of the product offer available for customers, and needs to be co-ordinated alongside other marketing activities.

Finance

The Finance department keeps records of events as they occur and will be responsible for producing the annual financial accounts. Management accounts will be responsible for co-ordinating plans across business organisations, including budgets and targets for achievement. In meeting customer needs they will have a vital role in ensuring that each department within the business organisation has the resource capability to meet customer needs. For example, operations need the capability to manufacture or produce goods or services to meet the number of orders coming from customers. In order to support the activities across the organisation, decisions taken by the finance team would involve allocating budgets to support the activities of each department. Marketing departments must work within the budget specified by the finance department and this can often dictate the type of marketing activities a company will use. The amount of money allocated to marketing a product may depend on the amount of **revenue** a product is likely to generate. For example, Coca-Cola may spend millions on sponsorship, television and radio to promote their products while a smaller company may only spend thousands to market their orange juice. At the same time, finance must be involved with investment decisions that are taken for new products and services.

Customer service

Customers are the most important people for any organisation and are the natural resource upon which an organisation depends. Increasingly, organisations are becoming more customer focused and adding more value to their goods by focusing upon developing relationships with customers through the quality of customer service they provide. Customer service helps to provide repeat business and provides the base for an organisation to achieve its marketing objectives.

In many ways the actions of those involved in customer service are part of the product on offer from an organisation.

Customer service needs to provide feedback to the marketing and production functions to ensure that customer needs are fully met. Those involved in customer service will find out about quality issues and be able to report back to quality assurance who in turn will work with production. Customer service will have a budget that enables it to undertake a range of activities focused upon customer needs.

Operations / production

Operations/production involves the activities necessary to produce a good or service that satisfies a customer. It is often argued that this part of the business is the most difficult to carry out. It involves getting the quality of the good or service just right and it usually employs the largest amount of capital, assets, labour and other factors of production.

Operations have to be customer focused. Although ideally it would be easier for those involved in operations to provide customers with fewer choices and less added value with their own timescale, this would directly conflict with marketing objectives that focus upon meeting customers needs.

It is sometimes said that operations is the 'sharp end' of a business organisation. They are there to ensure that customer needs are met through the quality of goods or services they provide. This might mean 'overtime' for staff during a particular week to ensure that goods are delivered on time or rescheduling production lines to provide for greater variety and choice. To meet the demands put upon this part of the business, operations needs to be appropriately financed with a budget that enables it to do so.

Research and development

New products and innovations taking place around an organisation must match information from market research and be focused upon customers if they are to be successful. Research and development can be very expensive and, while it is going on, the products that are being researched are not generating income. For example, Sony and Nintendo are competitors in the highly lucrative games market. Millions of pounds are invested in research and development and testing with key markets before a games console can be produced and sold to consumers. Research and development needs considerable support from finance to ensure that good quality development can take place. Researchers also need to work with operations to find out whether new product developments can be manufactured at an efficient cost as well as meeting customer service requirements.

Quality assurance department

Some people argue that quality is one of the most important factors in determining demand for many goods and services as consumers often search for quality rather than value. The quality assurance department has a huge influence upon how well marketing objectives are met, by trying to ensure that the quality of products or services meet customer expectations. If quality is not good, the reputation and 'how customers think' about the organisation will dip. This could influence an organisation's market position and cause it to lose business to competitors.

Human resources

Within the **human resources department**, managers will be responsible for **recruitment** and for training staff across the organisation. The success of this recruitment and training process will determine that the right people are in appropriate positions and are able to deal with customer-focused situations within their professional lives. For example, customer service individuals need to understand customer needs and be able to deal with queries on a day-to-day basis.

Human resource management will also be involved in keeping employees focused upon the tasks of the business. This includes keeping individuals motivated so that they feel happy with their role.

Administration and ICT

Information and communication technology have a huge impact upon how well customer needs are met. If a major system goes down, it may be difficult for the organisation to process a payment or provide a customer with appropriate access to information. Increasingly as e-commerce and e-business activities have a larger influence upon supplying goods and services for customers in the right place at the right time, information and

The potential impact of poor customer service upon marketing objectives

communication technology activities have become all the more critical.

All of the above departmental activities are likely to be linked in more than one way through a range of information technologies. For example, they may all be accessing the same systems and be able to see what orders are on the order book and how that relates to operational needs over the next few weeks. For human resources this might mean employing more people; for operations it could mean greater variety and choice in meeting customer needs; and for quality assurance it might mean looking at procedures that help operations produce larger batch runs with greater efficiency and with better quality.

1.2.3 Market research

Business activities are competitive, with producers constantly entering and leaving the market and consumer preferences providing signals for the development of different products and services. Whereas some organisations will succeed and achieve or surpass their marketing objectives, others will inevitably not perform as well.

Market research is that vital link in the chain between buyers and suppliers. It enables those who provide goods and services to keep in touch with the needs and wants of those who buy the services.

The American Market Research Association defines market research as:

Theory into practice

It has been said that 'a problem well defined is a problem half solved'. How might this relate to the context of market research?

Theory into practice

Imagine that your school or college wanted to develop two new courses that would either encourage new students to enter or persuade existing students to stay longer. What information would be helpful before any decisions are made? How might they go about collecting this information?

The systematic gathering, recording and analysis of data about problems related to the marketing of goods and services.

Defining a market

A market is made up of actual or potential buyers of a product and the sellers who offer goods to meet buyers' needs. The market for computers is composed of existing owners and prospective buyers of computers, as well as companies such as Apple Macintosh who manufacture them, Microsoft who develop software and Time who distribute them within the marketplace. A market requires a process of exchange between buyers and sellers.

Interaction between buyers and sellers is based upon the notion of the marketing mix. The marketing mix provides a useful way of looking at the marketplace for products. As we shall see later in this chapter, organisations need to create a successful mix of:

* the right product or service
* sold in the right place
* at the right price
* using the most suitable form of promotion.

FIGURE 1.2 *Process of exchange between buyers and sellers*

Positioning a product or service in a segment within the market

Remember that the simplest and most important principle of marketing is that marketing and its related activities should be designed to serve the customers. Serving customer needs with goods and services that do so more precisely than those of an organisation's competitors has become more important than ever. Whereas in the past, in many markets, all customers were treated to a similar diet of goods and services, organisations now recognise that groups of consumers have different needs, wants and tastes, for example, not every person likes the same make of motor car or has the same taste in clothes.

Instead of trying to serve all customers equally, an organisation may focus its efforts on different parts of the total marketplace. Within the total marketplace it is possible to group customers with similar characteristics and divide the market into parts. This is known as market segmentation. **Market segments** are groups of customers with similar needs and characteristics. The task is to produce and supply different products to suit these segments.

Mass marketing

If you attempt to market a single product to the whole population, this is sometimes called **undifferentiated** or **mass marketing**. A single marketing mix is offered to the whole marketplace. In other words, all potential customers are treated as if they have similar characteristics. This may be a relatively cheap way of tackling marketing, but its weakness is that it ignores individual differences.

Theory into practice

Does any market today exist where segmentation does not take place?

Niche marketing

When it is not possible to satisfy all of its customers' needs with a uniform product, an organisation will use market segmentation to divide consumers into smaller segments consisting of buyers with similar needs or characteristics.

Market segmentation uses differentiated marketing plans to tailor separate products to different sectors of the market. For example, the market for cars has many segments such as economy, off-road, MPV, luxury, high performance, etc. This approach recognises that in order to be successful and hit consumer needs, it is necessary to understand the needs of different groups of consumers and meet them in different ways (see Figure 1.4).

In fact, some organisations simply exist to serve highly specialised market segments. They deliberately choose to compete in one segment and develop the most effective mix for that market. This is known as concentrated marketing. For example, Morgan serves the specific needs of customers who like a car from the past, and Jaguar cars are associated with luxury market segments. Similarly, quality fashion retailers today increasingly use brand names to position themselves in particular parts of a market. A disadvantage is that if sales of a product decline in that segment, the lack of diversification means that this may affect the performance of the organisation.

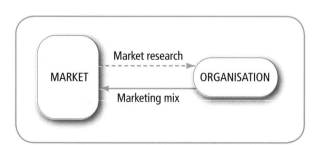

FIGURE 1.3 *Undifferentiated marketing*

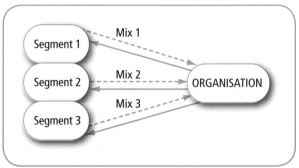

FIGURE 1.4 *Niche marketing*

The World Wide Web

It could be argued that one of the great things about the World Wide Web is that it allows small organisations to identify and reach niche markets, sometimes almost as well as large organisations. Most marketers know that 20 per cent of buyers consume 80 per cent of product volume. If you could identify that key 20 per cent and find others like them, you could sell much more product with less effort. The Web enables organisations to do this and makes it easier to enter markets that are well segmented.

Even large companies have embraced niche marketing, by continuing to refine and target their product offerings to more specific buyer groups. For example, we only have to look at the car market to see how many different models are offered by large organisations and the huge number of variants they offer both in terms of the extras they put on them as well as colours and options.

1 **How does the Web provide business opportunities for smaller organisations?**
2 **What is niche marketing?**
3 **To what extent has marketing become increasingly focused upon niches?**

There are three elements to segmentation:

1 *Market segments*. Market segments are groups of customers with similar needs and characteristics. The task is to produce and supply different products to suit these segments.

2 *Targeting*. Once segments have been identified, organisations have to identify one or more segments which has a need which can best be met by the organisation. This is known as **targeting** and may involve mass, niche or concentrated marketing.

3 *Positioning*. Even though parts of the market are divided into segments and organisations have worked out which ones to target, buyers within each segment will not have identical needs. The position is how the product is perceived in the minds of customers. Repositioning involves moving the product away from its current position in the market to another part of the market, where it might compete more effectively. Perhaps the most famous example in recent years is Skoda, who have moved away from a low-cost, low-reliability position in the market to become a well-respected high-value brand.

Investigating consumer attitudes

Consumer attitudes are their beliefs, and they represent how they view the world. It is important to understand such attitudes as there is a relationship between consumer attitudes and their behaviour. For example, by understanding consumer attitudes it is possible to develop products or services that consumers are more receptive to and positive about. It is also possible to advertise or promote goods or services to individuals in a way that encourages them to be receptive.

Market research in action on the high street

FIGURE 1.5 *Buyer behaviour may be influenced if consumer attitudes are known*

Interviewing is one way of finding out about consumer attitudes. It is then possible to link consumer attitudes with the products and services they buy.

Different attitudes can be categorised under the following headings:

Stability of attitude. Some individuals constantly change their attitudes, which results in unstable buyer behaviour patterns.

Conflict of attitude. More than one attitude may be applicable in a certain situation, so the resulting consumer behaviour might need a compromise between conflicting aims.

Strength of attitude. The strength with which an attitude is kept may determine behaviour, with strongly-held attitudes less likely to change.

Elapsed time. Since attitudes are dynamic, the longer the time between the measurement of the attitude and the behaviour, the more likely it is that the relationship between the two will break down.

Situational factors. In some cases the situations individuals find themselves in may preclude action, e.g. they have no money or the retailer is not open.

Monitoring usage

Having anticipated customer needs and attempted to meet them, it is important to verify how well-satisfied customers are. Organisations want happy

> ### Key terms
>
> **Customer service** might be defined as a reactive approach to resolving problems. It takes place after sales and is intended to solve any problems that occur in an efficient and customer-friendly way.
>
> **Customer care** is a collective approach to resolving potential problems before they occur. It attempts to anticipate problems and deal with them before they happen, within the context of the notion that 'prevention is better than cure'.

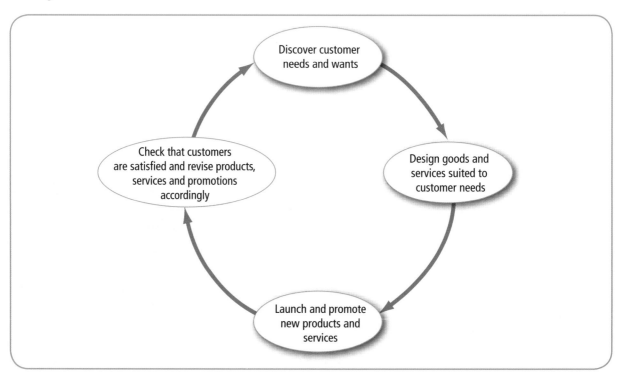

FIGURE 1.6 *The marketing cycle*

customers who will return to them and buy the goods or services again, and even recommend products to friends. Marketing is a cyclical process that starts with customers and ends with customers.

A key function of market research is to audit levels of customer satisfaction. A distinction should be made between customer service and customer care.

There are a number of ways for organisations to monitor and audit levels of customer satisfaction. These include:

* post-sale surveys identifying levels of satisfaction and finding out how sales staff deal with customers

* suggestions boxes to provide an opportunity for customers to make suggestions as to how the buying process could have been improved

* analysing complaint handling.

Forecasting needs

The real benefit of market-research information is determined by how much it improves the marketer's ability to make decisions. Good quality information will enable decisions to be made which satisfy the needs of the target market and also help the organisation to achieve its goals.

The use of market research represents a change from problem-solving by intuition to decision-making based on scientific gathering and analysis of information. The great advantage is that market research systematically provides information upon which managers may base product decisions. For example, many years ago Sir Clive Sinclair invented the C5, a small battery-powered motor vehicle. He saw it as revolutionising how we transport ourselves around. Sadly, his market research was not good. Instead of transforming markets the C5 flopped like a stone. If only he had undertaken market research in order to forecast needs!

Market research by forecasting needs helps not just to reduce business risks. It also helps to create business certainty. Earlier we saw how all of the departments within an organisation work together to meet marketing objectives. With better information it is easier for managers within a business organisation to work together and make decisions that are appropriate for the particular part of the business they manage.

CASE STUDY

DaimlerChrysler (DCS)

DaimlerChrysler have been working with an agency, Maven, to help them to understand their customer needs more fully and guide them in their service provision. Their aim is to improve their customer retention.

The research findings enable DaimlerChrysler to identify key processes and assess where they are performing well and which areas should be the focus for development. The interaction between the dealer and the customer impacts on their business, so it is vital that the needs of both parties are considered.

The research involves identifying the expectations that both customers and dealers have of an ideal finance supplier as well as feedback on the service levels they experienced. The results are used to identify relevant priority areas for improvement, and to set attainment targets in terms of customer satisfaction levels.

The surveys have been designed to cover customers at all stages of their finance contract, from those at the very beginning through to those whose finance contracts have finished, to enable DaimlerChrysler to pinpoint differing needs at various stages of the contract. The research has aided DCS in understanding which types of customers are likely to re-use them and how performance in satisfaction and loyalty could be maximised.

1 Why do DaimlerChrysler need to understand the experience they provide for their customers?
2 How were the results used?

Australian Tourist Commission (ATC)

Established in 1967 to promote Australia as an international tourism destination, the ATC has a clear mission:

'We promote Australia internationally as the world's best tourism experience – for the benefit of all Australians.'

Two of the principle objectives of the ATC are to:

* increase the number of visitors to Australia from overseas
* maximise the benefits to Australia from overseas visitors.

Having conducted an extensive process of market research, the ATC have used this information to provide a range of services to help travellers plan their trip to Australia. The ATC's key activity has been the promotion of 'Brand Australia' – a brand that positions Australia as a colourful, friendly, welcoming, vibrant, free-spirited, informal and optimistic tourist destination. As well as promoting Australia as a desirable travel destination around the world, and emphasising the diversity of holiday opportunities such as snorkelling on the Great Barrier Reef, visiting the National Parks to see a diverse range of wildlife or Uluru (Ayers Rock), finding out about Aboriginal culture and walking and

hiking, the ATC works with a number of partners both within and outside the tourist industry.

It is generally recognised that marketers cannot appeal to all buyers in all markets. Research revealed a real potential for travelling to Australia from the following three market segments:

* backpackers aged 18–24
* independent adventurers aged 25–34
* independent adventurers aged 45–65.

Backpackers are often single students who make their own travel arrangements. Many are on a 'gap year' and travel either on their own or with friends. Backpackers value the experience and see themselves as travellers rather than as tourists. Products that appeal to backpackers tend to have low prices, and might include hostel accommodation, bus passes, sporting activities and Aboriginal experiences in the outback. The use of market research alongside a variety of different experiences and opportunities for these groups has transformed the market to Australia.

1 **Why did the ATC undertake market research?**
2 **How was the market research used by the ATC?**

Planning market research

Setting objectives

Just as marketing needs its own objectives, so does market research and the objectives need to be SMART (see page 3). It is important for marketers to think about:

* the groups they intend to target with research activities
* the costs of the market research
* the techniques used to find out the requirements of potential customers
* the sources of information they intend to use

* the timescales for the completion of the research.

In order to meet these objectives market research should:

1 Identify who are the potential consumers and their requirements.

2 Identify possible sources of information, both **primary** and **secondary**.

3 Decide which method of research to use to collect information.

4 Estimate and set a timescale for the completion of the market research.

Identify who are the potential consumers and their requirements

Market research will assist in identifying potential consumers and their needs by focusing upon each part of the potential market. Research is also made into market trends in order to forecast future customer needs and customer preferences, for example, behaviours, lifestyle and aspirations.

Identify possible sources of information, both primary and secondary

Primary information comes from research which is usually carried out to determine a response from the market to a new product. Secondary information comes from research that has already been conducted for another purchase. For example, BMW may make use of **secondary research** regarding the number of cars purchased by consumers last year, but may conduct **primary research** to discover how consumers feel about their brand and what expectations the market may have of a new BMW. Market research is an expensive business and it is important to ensure that investment in research is well spent.

Decide which method of research to use to collect information

There are a number of different methods that can be used to collect primary and secondary data. The method of research chosen is often dependent upon the cost of conducting the research and the time frame allowed for it. Primary data is often more expensive to obtain but it can be collected by conducting personal interviews face to face or on the phone, by running **focus groups**, and by mailing **questionnaires** to your target audience. Secondary data is often obtained from government statistics, research carried out by specialist agencies and occasionally from news reports and trade journals.

Using appropriate methods is particularly relevant as it may be inappropriate to collect data in a particular way. Not all research is good research, and if the market research has not been well planned or uses the wrong data the results could be biased.

Estimate and set a timescale for the completion of the market research

Market research needs to work hand in hand with product development, operations, human resources and all of the other departmental resources. A timescale for market research should be developed alongside these other important elements, and enough time should be allowed for effective market research. Research may often dictate the way a product is developed or the direction it should take, so it is essential in the development of new products. It should follow other developments across the business in a way that allows appropriate and timely business decisions to be made.

Think it over...

Wembley National Stadium Limited has sold season tickets and corporate boxes worth £200 million for the new national stadium that it is building in London. This means that the project has almost broken even before a ball has been kicked or a concert sung.

Theory into practice

Look at the market for one particular type of product, for example, cars, electricity, confectionery or even beer. Comment upon how organisations within this market behave. What sorts of decisions have some of them recently made? What type of information would they have had available before they made these decisions?

Research into a market

Primary research

Any information that is original and is obtained outside an organisation is referred to as primary data. It is obtained by research conducted by or on behalf of the organisation, is specific to its needs and will involve a range of methods such as observation, discussions, questionnaires and surveys, and testing through pilots and field trials.

Observation

This involves looking at how consumers behave in the shopping environment. Information like this can help marketers to make decisions about packaging or influence the choice of point-of-sale materials designed to attract the attention of shoppers. It may also help to make decisions about where to place particular products in a shop. This is particularly important in the retail trade. The process of putting products in a store in the right place at the right time is known as merchandising.

Experiments

Market researchers may want to identify that changes in one variable are caused by changes in another. For example, they may be able to demonstrate that increased sales (the dependent variable) are the result of changes in the packaging of the product (the independent variable). This will involve changing the packaging of the product and observing the consumer reactions.

Laboratory experiments

Laboratory experiments are artificial experiments, but are useful because the researcher is in complete control of all of the relevant variables. Sometimes, whole mock-up-stores are created

Making on-the-spot decisions in a retail environment

and customers' reactions are observed within them. Such experiments might be used to judge the response to new forms of advertising or changes in the design of either the product or its packaging.

Field experiments

Field experiments test products in real environments, in order to develop an accurate picture of what might happen. These may include:

* in-home placement tests where a sample group is given the products to use in their homes and asked to report back

* store tests where a variety of retail stores are selected to stock the new item, and customer reactions in terms of changes in sales patterns are noted over a period

* test-marketing which involves selecting a specific geographical area and launching a product there with full promotional support. The results are used to predict how sales will

---

CASE STUDY

Costco

Costco, better known for bulk consumer goods, have started test-marketing coffins in its store on the North Side of Chicago. Each of the six models from the Universal Casket Co., in colours including lilac and Neapolitan blue, is priced at $799.99, made of 18-gauge steel, considered medium weight for coffins, and can be delivered within 48 hours.

Shoppers checking out the new coffin kiosk seemed to like the idea that the same store where they buy so many things for this life was branching into the afterlife. Many liked the idea of being able to shop for the coffin long before a loved one's death. Those involved in arranging funerals were not as enthusiastic about discount retailers moving in on their business. Costco's brochure says buyers can cut their overall funeral costs by more than 30 per cent.

1 What is test-marketing?
2 If the test-marketing is successful, what might Costco do next to market their coffins?

go when it is launched generally, and as a result of this the product or promotional plan may be amended prior to the full launch.

Surveys and questionnaires

Many of the market research methods above depend upon the use of a questionnaire as part of a survey. A questionnaire is a systematic list of questions designed to obtain information from people about:

* specific events
* their attitudes
* their values
* their beliefs.

The quality of the questionnaire is linked with the survey. A good questionnaire will result in a smooth interview, giving the interviewer a precise format to follow and ensuring that he or she obtains exactly the information required in a format that is easy for the researcher to analyse later.

Questionnaire design is critical. Although it is easy to make up questions, it is very difficult to produce a good questionnaire – and a badly-designed questionnaire may lead to biased results.

Another problem can be that very few completed forms are returned, or that those returned are only partially completed. In addition, if the questionnaire is being administered by a number of interviewers, there is always the danger that some may misinterpret questions and introduce their own personal bias in a way that prompts certain answers from respondents.

If you were asked to write a questionnaire, where would you start? The starting point would be to think about the focus of your questions. For example, what information do you require and why do you need it? You would also need to think about the target audience that you wish to examine. It would be important to question all of the people who are likely to have relevant opinions or information.

When people give up their own time to answer the questions on a questionnaire, it is useful to tell them who you are and why you are undertaking this research. This is not only polite but will also put the respondent at ease and may facilitate co-operation.

A good questionnaire will:

* ask questions which relate directly to information needs
* not ask too many questions
* not ask leading or intimate questions
* fit questions into a logical sequence
* use the language of the target group
* not use questions that are confusing or ambiguous
* avoid questions relating to sexuality, politics and religion unless they are very relevant.

Sequencing the questions logically is very important. It may be useful to start with a few factual questions that are easy to respond to. Some form of multiple-choice questions may follow these before introducing questions that require the respondent to think about some of the issues being researched. The questionnaire may be closed with 'filter questions' about the background of the respondent, which help to locate them in the sampling frame, i.e. filter questions are used to find out more about the respondent. The answers to these questions might show that it is inappropriate to interview them. The sampling frame is the list of names of respondents before sampling takes place. It is the complete list of everybody within a market.

There is no point including questions that do not relate to the main purposes of the research. The questionnaire should be kept as short as possible. More than 40 questions could put off respondents or cause them to provide hasty replies to questions.

Open and closed questions

The questions in a questionnaire may be 'open' or 'closed'. **Open questions** allow the person answering to give an opinion and may encourage him or her to talk at length. You have to be careful though. Asking questions such as 'What type of music do you listen to?' could lead to such a variety of answers that analysing them would be very difficult. **Closed questions** usually require

Please indicate with a tick which types of music you listen to regularly (tick all that apply):

- ☐ Classical
- ☐ Easy listening
- ☐ Jazz
- ☐ Blues
- ☐ Golden oldies
- ☐ Popular
- ☐ Heavy metal
- ☐ Punk
- ☐ Indie
- ☐ Rap
- ☐ Dance
- ☐ Swing
- ☐ Hip Hop
- ☐ Other (please specify) _ _ _ _ _ _ _ _ _ _ _ _ _ _

FIGURE 1.7 *Extract from a sample questionnaire using closed questions*

an answer picked from a range of options (which may be simply yes/no). Most questionnaires use closed questions, so that they can be answered quickly and a decision has to be made within a range of choices so the answers are easier to analyse (see Figure 1.7).

Rating scales

Sometimes it is necessary to judge the degree of the respondent's feelings on a subject. The best way to do this is to use a rating or response scale.

Likert scales

Likert scales show how strongly the respondent agrees or disagrees with a statement (see Figure 1.8).

Rank order scales

Rank order scale questions ask the respondent to put a number beside various items in order to

These are all considerations when choosing where to buy a new computer. Put them in rank order with 1 by the most important, 2 by the second most important and so on down to 5 against the least important.

Wide choice	2
Helpful sales staff	3
Value for money	1
After-sales service	4
Quick delivery	5

FIGURE 1.9 *Extract from sample questionnaire using a rank order scale*

Put a cross in the box that shows how strongly you agree or disagree with each of the following statements:

	Strongly agree	Agree	Neither agree nor disagree	Disagree	Strongly disagree
The AS course has prepared me well for work		X			
The lecturers at college are well prepared			X		
The lecturers at college are interesting	X				
I was well prepared for my assignments				X	

FIGURE 1.8 *Extract from sample questionnaire using a Likert scale*

put them in some sort of order of preference, as in Figure 1.9.

Intention-to-buy scales

An **intention-to-buy** scale asks respondents to indicate by ticking a box how likely it is that they will buy some items in the future.

If a textbook was available covering this unit / module, I would:

Definitely buy	Probably buy	Not sure	Probably not buy	Definitely not buy
1 ☐	2 ☐	3 ☐	4 ☐	5 ☐

FIGURE 1.10 *Extract from sample questionnaire using intention-to-buy questions*

Semantic differential scales

Semantic differential scales use two words describing the opposite ends of a scale, with a series of points highlighted between them. The respondents are asked to indicate where on the scale their opinion lies. For example:

Place a cross on the scale below to show what feelings you have about Frosty's ice creams:

Frosty's ice creams are:

Good value	| | | | | | |	Poor value
Tasty	| | | | | | |	Tasteless
Well packaged	| | | | | | |	Poorly packaged
Satisfying	| | | | | | |	Unsatisfying

FIGURE 1.11 *Extract from sample questionnaire using semantic differential scales*

Theory into practice

Use the questionnaire below to discuss your feelings about one product which you regularly purchase (Product A):

Total performance of Product A (including product, sales, support, price, etc.):

Dissatisfied ☐ ☐ ☐ ☐ ☐ ☐ ☐ ☐ ☐ ☐ **Very satisfied**

         1   2   3   4   5   6   7   8   9 10

Compared to one year earlier, is Product A's total performance:

☐ Better   ☐ Worse   ☐ Same

Why?

What one thing can _____ do to improve the performance of Product A in meeting your total needs?

1 Explain how the answers you have provided for this brief questionnaire might be used.
2 What information has it provided?
3 Comment upon the structure of the questions.
4 How easy is it to analyse and interpret the information it has provided?

Prompt cards

To help interviewers operate a questionnaire, a prompt card is sometimes used. This means that, if several or all of the questions in the questionnaire have the same range or set of answers, these can be numbered and then the respondent's answers can be recorded as numbers.

Relevant questions

Some questionnaires are designed so that respondents can concentrate on the questions that are relevant, and skip over the questions which do not relate to them (see Figure 1.12).

Question 6   **Do you have a bank account?**

☐ YES

☐ NO

If your answer is **NO**, proceed to question 20

FIGURE 1.12 *Extract from sample questionnaire using relevant questions*

Focus groups

Focus groups are an inexpensive method of obtaining useful qualitative information from consumers. Under the guidance of a chairperson, a group of users of the same product may be invited to provide opinions on its use. Members of a focus group might be members of the public who have opinions on certain products and services. They may be drawn from a certain market segment or from an industry. They are very good at testing customer reactions to new developments or proposals.

A good leader is essential for a focus group. He or she will introduce key topics for discussion, keep order and ensure that every group member has the opportunity to make a contribution. The main benefit of such groups is that new ideas and opinions can be 'bounced off' each group member to refine them and prompt further creative

Focus groups need a good leader

CASE STUDY

Vauxhall

Like other car manufacturers, Vauxhall has to cope with a rapidly changing world. To keep pace it begins planning the next model even as the wraps are coming off a new launch.

This begins with a series of 'clinics' where the reaction to a new shape is tested out on a number of pre-selected motorists. These motorists are recruited by an outside agency from owners of cars in the target group together with a small number positioned above the group (who may be persuaded to trade down) and below the group (who may be persuaded to trade up). They will be people who have no connection with the motor or advertising industries.

Confidentiality is very important at this stage, so the respondents are not told which manufacturer is conducting the clinic. This also avoids any personal prejudices.

1 Why do Vauxhall use focus groups or clinics?
2 What sort of issues are they likely to raise at such groups?
3 Who might be targeted to attend such groups?
4 How is Vauxhall likely to use this information?

thought. A focus group requires a note taker and may also be audio or video-taped.

Secondary research

Secondary marketing information is effectively anything that has previously been published. It can be built from both internal and external sources.

Internal sources of secondary data

Internal data is information already held within the organisation, usually in databases. A database is a large amount of information stored in such a way that it can easily be found, processed and updated. Users may access the database across an organisation.

Information on existing customers will form the core of the database, with sales invoices probably being the most valued source of data. The invoice is created for financial purposes but it contains a considerable amount of customer data that can be made immediately available for others. For example, it might contain information such as:

* **Customer title** — gender, job description, other forms of identification
* **Customer surname** — ethnic coding
* **Customer address** — geographic coding
* **Date of sale** — tracking purchase rates and repurchasing patterns
* **Items ordered** — product category interests
* **Quantities ordered** — heavy / medium / light users
* **Price** — value of customer
* **Terms and conditions** — customer service needs

CASE STUDY

Customer database

An electricity distribution company may set up a customer database by giving each customer a customer reference number and attaching the following information to each entry:

* Tariff type. The price a customer pays for electricity can vary according to whether they are a home or a business, a large or small customer.
* Consumption. The company can then track the amount of electricity a customer uses, and when.
* Method of payment. Some customers prefer prepayment rather than credit, while others prefer to pay monthly rather than quarterly.
* Change of tenancy. The company knows when customers move out of and into a property.
* New buildings. The company knows when and where new buildings that use electricity are being erected, because an electricity supply is applied for.

From such information it is possible to obtain answers to an almost endless list of questions such as:

* What is the size of the market?
* What type of user uses the most / least electricity?
* How do customers prefer to pay?
* What is the average credit period?
* How many new users are coming on-stream?
* How many users is the company losing?
* What is the average consumption per user?
* What is the profitability for each type of customer?
* How does the use of electricity vary during the day?
* Where is the market expanding / contracting?

1 How will answers to these questions improve the way the electricity company manages its business?
2 What other questions might be answered from this type of database?

Tesco loyalty card

Loyalty cards

One way in which organisations in the retail industry keep and analyse data from customers is by the use of loyalty cards. By using loyalty cards, it is possible to match the postcode of the customer with the nature and type of purchases they might make, and then to use this information as a base for making product and merchandising decisions within a store.

External sources of secondary data

External data exists in the form of published materials, collected by somebody else. It can be used to enhance existing knowledge, for example, postcodes may help to group customers geographically. By identifying and labelling certain characteristics of a customer, a company may be able to make assumptions about their needs. Two examples of useful external sources are:

* *Domestic socio-economic data*. Customers are classified according to their house type, the assumption being that a certain lifestyle is associated with that type of house.

* *Industrial classification*. Organisational customers can be classified according to the nature of their activities. Certain types of organisations can then be expected to have predictable demands for services.

External information can complement an organisation's own information by providing direct comparison with competitors, by putting performance within the context of the economy as a whole and by identifying markets offering potential.

Theory into practice

Imagine that you are the owner of a small shop selling sports equipment in your local neighbourhood. What sort of information might give you a better understanding of the purchasing decisions you have to make?

Government statistics

These are principally supplied by the following:

* Office for National Statistics (ONS) www.ons.gov.uk

* Department of Trade and Industry (DTI) www.dti.gov.uk

* Department for Education and Skills (Dfes) www.dfes.gov.uk

* Government Statistical Service (GSS) www.statistics.gov.uk

* Organisation for Economic Development and Co-operation (OECD) www.oecd.org

Some of the key publications include:

* *Monthly Digest of Statistics* – summary information on many economic trends.

* *Regional Trends* – regional profiles, households, labour, living standards, etc.

* *Labour Market Trends* – topical articles, hours worked, sickness, training, vacancies, disputes, earnings and unemployment.

* *Social Trends* – trends in labour markets, incomes, spending by item and by region.

* *Family Spending* – details on who earns and spends what.

* *New Earnings Survey* – earnings listed by industry, area, occupation etc.

* *National Food Survey* – expenditure on and consumption of food by income group and region.

* *Population Trends* – family statistics including births, marriages and deaths, etc., in regions.

* *Annual Abstract of Statistics* – population, social conditions, production, prices, employment.

* *Bank of England Quarterly Bulletin* – articles on financial trends.

* *General Household Survey* – social and socio-economic issues.

* *Consumer Price Index* – changes in prices across the country.

* *Census of Production* – data about production by firms in all industries.

* *Eurostat Publications* – a variety, covering economic, industrial and demographic changes across Europe.

* *Indicators of Industrial Activity* – production, employment and prices across a variety of industries and compared worldwide.

* *Business Monitors* – statistics concerning output in different business sectors. *The Retailing Monitor* is of particular interest, covering what is being bought by region.

Media

Another useful source of information is the media. It is unlikely to provide detailed data but may present a series of stories about key market sectors or larger organisations. Sources normally include:

* *Newspapers* – broadsheets such as *The Times* and *The Financial Times* are authoritative sources. However, the value of local papers and local circumstances should also be taken into account.

* *Magazines and trade journals* – the obvious ones are *The Economist* (www.economist.com) and *The Grocer*.

* *TV and radio* – these include specialist news and current affairs programmes.

* *Teletext* – this provides a variety of current information across many topics.

Business directories

There are many business directories that provide general information about industries and markets. These include Kompass Register (www.Kompass.co.uk), Who Owns Whom and Key British Enterprises.

Trade associations

Trade associations publish information for their members concerning their particular fields. There are associations for almost all trades.

The Internet

The Internet has rapidly become an invaluable research tool providing a rich resource for information from a multitude of sources. As a resource it is predicted to continue to grow rapidly and become much more central to the workings of organisations not just in terms of 'Internet Marketing' but also as a business resource. Try visiting the research agency MORI at www.mori.com.

Many organisations such as Boots (www.boots-plc.com) and Nestlé have their own intranet. Unlike the Internet which is available to all, an **intranet** is a data-sharing facility within an organisation.

Commercial market research companies

There are a number of commercial market research companies offering a range of services including selling data that they acquire from a variety of sources. Mintel (www.mintel.co.uk) is a commercial research organisation which, in return for a fee, provides a monthly journal containing reports on consumer markets such as bread, alcoholic drinks and financial services. Information includes areas such as market size, main competitors, projected growth, market share of main competitors, advertising spend of main competitors and other trends. Mintel also produces in-depth reports on certain markets.

The types of reports produced by agencies include:

1 *Retail Business Market Surveys*. These are published monthly and each carries details of certain industries. It is important for those involved in market research to be able to access those relevant to their particular field. Each copy will carry an index of industries investigated. For example, there will be details on market size, market sectors, price trends, sales abroad, advertising and promotion, consumption, distribution, branding and prospects for the industry.

2 *Key Note Reports* carry even more information with specific information upon each industry.

3 *Retail audits* collect data of retail sales through supermarkets and larger chains and then sell the information to organisations wishing to buy it. These figures enable producers to work out their market shares, the sales of different products and the effects of any recent price change or promotional campaign.

CASE STUDY

Applying to be a market researcher

Market researchers organise the collection of public and business opinion about products, services or organisations. They may also conduct market research interviews and test new questionnaires.

Role

The duties of a market researcher may include the following:

* discussing information with clients
* designing surveys and questionnaires
* organising and managing surveys
* liaising with field workers and their supervisors
* supervising survey staff
* conducting interviews
* undertaking secondary research.

Skills

Market researchers need good research skills and the ability to think logically so that they can design good surveys and questionnaires. They need mathematical and statistical ability and computer skills to analyse and interpret their data. Organisational and time-management skills are also important in this work as well as good written and oral communication skills.

Knowledge

Market researchers should know about questionnaire design, survey methods and marketing techniques. They should also know how to interpret statistics and they need to be aware of different sampling and interview methods. It is important for market researchers to have some knowledge and understanding of the businesses or industries they research.

Personal qualities

Market researchers need to be able to work well under pressure, and juggle many tasks within a project. Accuracy is important, and they should be culturally sensitive when designing questionnaires and managing survey projects. They should be team players, and honesty and the ability to manage tasks and take responsibility are important for this job. Market researchers must also be able to keep information private.

Appearance

As market researchers spend a lot of time dealing with people such as clients, respondents and other professionals outside the organisation, their appearance is important.

1 Using the information from this case study, draft a person specification for a market research post.
2 Look at the above requirements for market researchers. Think about how you might or might not fit the bill for such a post. Draft a letter of application for the post of a market researcher at an organisation you have some knowledge of or interest in.

Interpretation of market research information

Having gathered marketing data for your marketing proposal you need to be able to make sense of it. Information needs to be summarised, classified and presented in a way that aids understanding, interpretation and presentation of results. It is important that marketers have access to information that is clear and provides a basis for decisions to be taken.

Arithmetic mean

One way of summarising information is to use basic statistics through the use of averages. An average is a measure of central tendency that is used to find the number which is representative of a group of numbers, that is, the middle value. Average is also referred to as the arithmetic mean.

To illustrate how the arithmetic mean is calculated, we can use the following information:

15 people were timed assembling an exercise machine and they took, 7, 8, 9, 9, 10, 10, 11, 11, 11, 12, 13, 13, 14, 15 and 16 minutes.

The **arithmetic mean** is calculated by totalling the sum of all the numbers in a group and dividing them by the number in the group. (See box at the bottom of the page).

Median

The **median** is the value of the middle number and is found by arranging the numbers in order and selecting the middle number from the list. In essence it is the value that divides the distribution into two. It is particularly useful when there are

---

The position of the median

$$= \frac{n + 1}{2}$$

where n is the number of values.

In our example:

$$\text{Median} = \frac{15 + 1}{2}$$

(that is the 8th number in the list which is 11)

---

extreme values in a series of numbers that would otherwise distort the arithmetic mean.

Mode

The **mode** is the most frequently occurring item in a list of numbers. In our example, 11 occurs three times and is the mode.

Theory into practice

The following list represents the number of phone calls made to a customer service department within July. Work out the arithmetic mean, median and mode from the data.

Describe how summarising such data could be useful in asking key questions about products and services.

5	6	8	9	9	9	10	11	11	12
12	12	12	16	18	18	19	20	20	20
20	20	22	28	31	33	34	34	35	35
41									

Arithmetic mean	=	Sum of all values / Total number of values

$$= \frac{7+8+9+9+10+10+11+11+11+12+13+13+14+15+16}{15}$$

$$= \frac{169}{15}$$

$$= 11.3$$

Percentages

One series of marketing information that we are constantly faced with is that of **percentages**. Organisations use percentages to describe their sales. We see percentages on literature designed to sell us products. Percentages simply mean an amount out of every 100. 100 per cent is therefore 100 out of 100 which might mean full marks for a test or 100 per cent reliability.

To increase an amount by a specified percentage you need to calculate the percentage and add it to the original figure. For example, to increase £20 by 15 per cent you need to calculate 15 per cent of £20 which is £3. By adding £3 to the original amount you are increasing the amount by 15 per cent.

An alternative way of increasing £20 by 15 per cent is to make the assumption that we now need to know what 115 per cent of £20 is. If we divide 115 by 100, this equals 1.15 and then multiply this by the original figure of £20, it will give you the same answer of £23.

To decrease an amount by a specified percentage simply calculate the percentage and subtract it from the original figure. For example, to decrease £20 by 15 per cent, calculate 15 per cent of £20 which is £3, and reduce the £20 by £3, to make £17.

To find one quantity as a percentage of another involves calculating the percentage one figure is of another and then dividing the first by the second and multiplying by 100.

For example, to calculate what percentage 60 is of 3000: Divide 60 by 3000 which equals 0.02 and then multiply this by 100 which equals 2 per cent.

Theory into practice

You are in the process of re-pricing goods within your store. Work out the following:

1 You want to take 25 per cent off the original price of men's jackets which are usually sold for £80.

2 You want to increase suit prices that sell for £125 by 15 per cent.

Forecasting

If we remind ourselves that the purpose of market research is to collect information that enables us to identify and anticipate customer requirements, we are able to see that the outcome of market research is a prediction of consumer behaviour. A significant amount of expenditure might be risked on the basis of these predictions. For example, organisations make huge investments in new products and new product developments. If they get the market research wrong, this could involve wasting many millions of pounds.

When large-scale risks are taken, then managers are clearly interested in the degree of accuracy of their predictions of customer behaviour. The likelihood that predictions will be accurate is termed **probability**. Complex statistical techniques can be applied to calculating probabilities.

Sales forecasts are usually based upon previous sales results. Many factors can affect sales, for example, competition and consumer trends and their likely effects need to be identified and taken into account within forecasts. One way of dealing with this is by moving average totals (see Figure 1.13).

At the end of December we can see that the total sales for the year is £2,930. By deducting the earliest value in the year (Jan 2004) of 250 and adding the latest value in January 2005 of 240, we can see that the moving average total of sales has dropped from £2,930 to £2,920 because of the impact of a recent value. The moving average therefore takes into account later and more recent values in indicating average sales over a period.

From the figures above it can be seen clearly that sales grew during June, July and August, but levelled off towards the end of the year, reverting to the static sales pattern at the beginning of the year. On this basis, all things being equal, a marketing manager might conclude that the increased advertising during June to August might have resulted in the increased sales growth during the following months which fell back when advertising was reduced to previous levels.

Understanding the needs of customers and anticipating their future needs is vital to success

Year	Jan	Feb	Mar	Apr	May	June	July	Aug	Sept	Oct	Nov	Dec
2004	250	200	160	150	240	310	420	430	280	130	100	260
MAT												2,930
2005	240	210	140	160	260	350	490	570	320	140	100	270
MAT	2,920	2,930	2,910	2,920	2,940	2,980	3,050	3,190	3,230	3,240	3,240	3,250

MAT = Moving average total

FIGURE 1.13 *Moving annual total sales of Fizzy cola 2005*

in today's dynamic markets. Increasingly sophisticated market research systems provide more and more detailed consumer information on which to base forecasts. When assessing that information and making decisions to use expensive resources, marketing managers need to question the validity of the data presented. For example, how reliable is the data? Are they based upon a representative sample size? Is there an element of bias in the results? How strong are the correlations between factors? All these play a part in gauging the probability and the accuracy of the forecasts.

PEST model

One useful way of analysing an organisation's external environment is by grouping external forces neatly into four areas by using a **PEST analysis**. PEST stands for Political, Economic, Social and Technological influences, all of which are external.

Carrying out a PEST analysis involves identifying the key factors external to an organisation which are in a state of flux and are likely to have an influence on the organisation in the coming months and years.

Whereas identifying these factors is relatively easy, assessing their ongoing impact and effect is more difficult. An effective PEST analysis will be based on detailed research using all of the latest journals and publications. For example, if certain taxes are likely to be lowered, how much are they likely to be lowered by? What will be the impact on the sales of each product? If interest rates are expected to go up, how much will they go up? How long will they be raised for? What will be their impact upon sales and costs?

Political, legal and fiscal factors. Business decisions are influenced by political, fiscal (taxation) and legal decisions. For example, although in recent years many people have been encouraged to become self-employed, there has been a feeling by many of these people that they are over-regulated. These influences might include:

* changes in the tax structure
* privatisation
* the influence of unions
* changes in the availability of raw materials
* duties and levies
* regulatory constraints such as labelling, quality, safety.

Economic factors. Though the economic environment is influenced by domestic economic policies, it is also dependent upon world economic trends. Rates of economic growth, inflation, consumption patterns, income distribution and many other economic trends determine the nature of products and services required by consumers, as well as how difficult

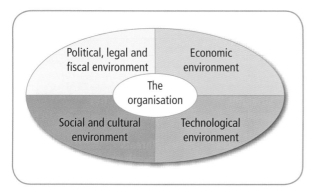

FIGURE 1.14 *PEST analysis*

it becomes to supply them. Influences might include:

* inflation
* unemployment
* energy prices
* price volatility.

Social / cultural factors. To understand the social and cultural environment involves close analysis of society. Demographic changes such as population growth, movements and age distribution will be important, as will changes in cultural values and social trends such as family size and social behaviour. Factors might include:

* consumer lifestyles
* environmental issues
* demographic issues
* education
* immigration/emigration
* religion.

Technological factors. In marketing goods and services, organisations must become aware of new materials as well as developments in manufacturing and business processes. At the same time organisations have to look at the nature of their products and, in particular, their cost-effectiveness as well as their performance in relation to competition. Factors might include:

* new technological processes
* energy-saving techniques
* new materials and substitutes for existing materials
* better equipment
* new product developments.

Forces external to the organisation are rarely stable, and many of these forces can alter quickly and dramatically. It is important to recognise that while some of these forces will be harmful to marketing efforts, others will create new opportunities.

SWOT analysis

A particularly useful approach to examining the relationship between an organisation and its marketing environment is a **SWOT analysis**. A SWOT analysis sets out to focus upon the Strengths, Weaknesses, Opportunities and Threats facing a business or its products at a given moment. It includes both an internal and an external element. The internal element looks at current strengths and weaknesses of the organisation. The external element looks at the opportunities and threats present in the environment in which the organisation operates.

Carrying out a SWOT analysis requires research into an organisation's current and future position. The analysis is used to match an organisation's strengths and weaknesses with the external market forces in the business environment.

As a result of carrying out a SWOT analysis, an organisation should go on to develop policies

Inside the organisation (internal)	Outside the organisation (external)
Strengths (positive)	**Opportunities** (positive)
Weaknesses (negative)	**Threats** (negative)

FIGURE 1.15 *SWOT analysis*

Inside the organisation	The external environment
Strengths +	Opportunities +
Weaknesses −	Threats −

FIGURE 1.16 *The planning balance sheet*

and practices that will enable it to build upon its strengths, minimise its weaknesses, seize its opportunities and take measures that will cancel out or minimise threats. The SWOT is thus sometimes called 'the planning balance sheet' (see Figure 1.16).

A simplified SWOT analysis might show, for example, that a business organisation has the following:

Strengths
* good product
* good relationship with customers
* good management team.

Weaknesses
* operates on a small scale
* regular cash-flow problems
* deals in a limited market.

Opportunities
* new and rapidly growing markets
* changing tastes of consumers
* could diversify into a number of product lines.

Threats
* growing competition from rivals
* recession leading to poor demand in the economy
* development of foreign competitors.

1.2.4 The marketing mix

The marketing mix provides us with a useful way of looking at the marketing of products. Organisations need to create a successful mix of:

* the right product (or service)
* sold in the right place

* at the right price
* using the most suitable form of promotion.

The marketing mix is therefore a series of controllable variables that an organisation can use in order to best meet customer needs and ensure that an organisation is successful in the markets in which it serves.

Product / packaging

The product is the most important element in an organisation's marketing mix. According to Sally Dibb et al (1994):

A product is everything, both favourable and unfavourable, that is received in an exchange.

Brands

Many mass-produced products are almost identical. For example, most washing powders are similar, as are different types of margarine. These goods tend to be produced by two or three large companies who encourage sales by creating a brand that differentiates the products in the minds of consumers.

A **brand** can be a name, a symbol or a design used to identify a specific product and differentiate it from its competitors. Brand names, designs, trademarks, symbols, slogans and even music can be used to distinguish one product from another and allow an organisation to distinguish its products from competing ones.

The business of creating a brand is a particularly important function of marketing. Often people will buy the brand name as much as the product itself. You will see people in supermarkets pick up an item (which they have not seen before) and say, 'this must be a good one because it is made by...'

There are three different types of brands. These are:

1 *Manufacturer brands*. Examples of these include Kellogg's Cornflakes, Nescafé Coffee and Heinz Baked Beans. These manufacturer brands associate the producer with the specific product, and the producer will be heavily involved with the promotion of the product.

2 *Own-label brands*. Examples of these include Tesco, St Michael (Marks & Spencer), Farm Foods (Asda) and Sainsbury's own label. These brands are owned and controlled by retailers.

3 *Generic brands.* Such products are extremely rare in the modern competitive market, and those that exist are usually at the lower end of the market with respect to price and quality. These products have no identifiable name or logo. Examples may include plain T-shirts or bin-liners if they have no branded packaging or labels attached that identify the originator.

Organisations seek to create a portfolio of individual products which support the image of a brand. Well-known brand names will therefore emphasise quality throughout the organisation. A brand which is held in high esteem is worth a lot of money to an organisation. There is a well-known saying in business that, 'an organisation can afford to get rid of its other assets, but not its brand image!'

Product features

Customers do not buy features, they buy what those features can do for them – the problems they solve, the money or the time they save, etc. A product is really a bundle of benefits. A key aspect of marketing is to make sure that products create the benefits that a consumer desires in a particular product and that the product offering is better than those of competitors. Associated with this is the need to make sure that the market fully understands the range of benefits on offer, through strong communications.

When we understand the benefits that customers are looking for in a product, we are best placed to know why they will buy it – and hence focus our marketing accordingly. For example, in buying toothpaste the benefits that customers may be looking for include:

* flavour and product appearance
* brightness of teeth
* decay prevention
* price/value for money
* appealing brand name and confidence in brand.

Knowing that these are the benefits the consumer requires enables the organisation to focus its efforts on creating products that will produce one or more of them, and then promotion can be used to highlight the organisation's ability to create these benefits.

There are often clear and **tangible** features (things you can touch and see) associated with a product. Tangible features might include shape, design, colour, packaging and size.

Intangible features are not so obvious. These include the reputation of an organisation, the brand image, after-sales service, availability of spare parts, service centres and so on.

It is also argued that products provide advantages for customers through three different dimensions:

1 *Generic dimensions*. These are the key benefits of a particular item. For example, shoe polish should clean shoes.

2 *Sensual dimensions*. These have an impact upon the senses. They might include design, colour, taste, smell and texture. The sensual benefits are frequently highlighted by advertisers. This is clearly the case when advertising food and drinks with words such as 'smooth and creamy', 'the amber nectar' and so on.

3 *Extended dimensions*. A wide range of additional benefits are included here. Examples are servicing agreements, credit facilities, guarantees, maintenance contracts and so on.

With any group of products there is a distinct mix of items. They may include:

Product item

A product item is a specific model, brand or size of a product that an organisation sells, for example, a 2kg box of Uncle Ben's Long Grain Rice.

Product line

A product line is a group of closely related product items, with similar characteristics and/or applications, for example a line of Uncle Ben's Rice items, including short grain, long grain and pudding rice.

Product mix

A product mix is all of an organisation's product lines, e.g. including rice, flour, sugar, pickles and other lines. Any product mix can be described according to its width, length, depth and consistency.

Width

Width is the number of different product lines on offer. For example, Coca-Cola produces quite a narrow range of soft drinks including Sprite, Fanta and Coca-Cola. In contrast, a company like Unilever has a wide range of products from Walls ice cream and Birds Eye frozen foods to many different types of soap powders and cleaning agents. Having a narrow range of products enables the consumer to benefit from **economies of large-scale** production whereas breadth enables an organisation to benefit from diversification. Broadening a line to create breadth means extending it beyond its current range.

Length

Length is the total number of items on offer. The decision on the number of lines to offer is very important. Too many lines and you may overstretch yourself, and even start to compete against your own lines. Line stretching involves increasing the product line, either by moving into higher-quality items or moving downmarket. When the car manufacturer Volkswagen bought a 31 per cent share in Skoda in 1991, the leading Skoda model was the downmarket Favorit. Not only were substantial changes made to the Favorit, but in 1995 a new, more upmarket Felicia was added to Skoda's lines with great success. The process of line filling involves filling in gaps in product lines. For example, confectionery manufacturers regularly develop new chocolate bars to fill perceived gaps in their range of products. Line rationalisation involves cutting out lines that are not central to the organisation's major focus of interest, or those that have lost popularity.

Depth

Depth is the number of variants of each brand, for example, the number of different sizes, models or flavours within a product line. Detergent companies like Procter & Gamble or Unilever offer many different sizes of soap powder boxes as well as lots of different kinds of soap powder, all targeted at slightly different groups of customers. It makes sense for a large company to offer a product for all occasions in order to aim for a position of leadership. However, it is important not to cannibalise the sales of your own products. Deepening a product would mean adding more lines within your existing range. Line pruning means cutting the depth of a product line by reducing the number of alternative sizes, models of flavours in the line.

Consistency

Consistency is the closeness of the relationship between each product line.

> **Theory into practice**
>
> Examine the annual report of a well-known public company, for example Cadbury Schweppes. Comment on the width, depth and consistency of their product mix.

Research Machines (RM plc)

Founded in 1973 by Mike Fischer and Mike O'Regan, RM plc is the UK's leading provider of commercial education services and a pioneer in the application of technology to education. The Group's first educational microcomputer was launched in 1977 and schools, colleges and universities have become the main market for RM since then. In recent years RM has expanded its range of products and services to include interactive whole-class teaching services, teacher training, ICT-based needs assessment and school management information systems.

According to RM, *'In the 1990s it became clear that the educational community was looking for more from their suppliers than simple technological expertise. RM rose to the challenge. Looking beyond the* technology, the Group formed long-term partnerships with both educationalists and other learning technology companies. These partnerships allow us to deliver genuine learning productivity. It is a strategy that has worked as our market leadership shows. RM's passion is education and its aim is to explore and exploit the potential of IT to improve educational standards. Today, RM is expanding its relationships with customers further by providing a diverse range of education services.'*

1 **What makes RM different from many other IT organisations?**
2 **In marketing terms describe how it has developed the products it offers.**

Creating the optimum product mix means having the right balance in terms of width, depth, length and consistency An effective product mix should yield a balanced profit contribution from a number of lines – although there will always be some products that are the highest yielders.

Organisations need to decide whether they have the right mix at any one point in time while having an eye on future changes. Key concerns are: Should we stick to the narrow range of lines in which we are successful? What are our current strengths and weaknesses? What are the opportunities and threats of diversifying? How can we avoid competing with ourselves?

Pricing and the techniques of pricing

Price is the only element of the marketing mix that directly generates income – other elements of the marketing mix are costs. The importance of price in the marketing mix varies. In low-cost, non-fashion markets price can be critical (for example, in the sale of white emulsion and gloss paint). In fashion markets, such as clothing, it can be one of the least relevant factors. Certain products are designed to suit a particular segment (e.g. economy family cars), while others perform a specific function regardless of price (e.g. sports cars). For consumers with limited budgets, price is a key-purchasing criterion, while for those to whom 'money is no object' price is less important.

The first pricing task is to create an overall pricing goal for an organisation which is in line with the marketing aims, and then determine objectives for each of the product lines.

Researcher D. Shipley found the following principal pricing objectives of firms:

Pricing objectives	Percentage of firms
Target profit or return on capital employed	67%
Prices fair to firm and customers	13%
Prices similar to those of competitors	8%
Target sales volume	7%
Stable sales volume	5%
Target market share	2%
Stable prices	2%
Other	1%

FIGURE 1.17 *Firms' pricing objectives*

Once pricing objectives have been established, organisations need to establish an appropriate pricing model.

Penetration pricing

Penetration pricing is appropriate when the seller knows that there are many competitors within a market. Penetration pricing enables an organisation to 'penetrate' a market with an artificially low price in order to gain market share away from other competitors. A low price is therefore required to attract consumers to the product. Penetration pricing is normally associated with the launch of a new product for which the market needs to be penetrated (see Figure 1.18).

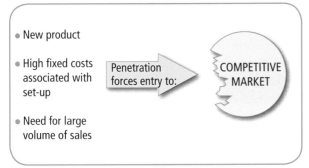

FIGURE 1.18 *An environment appropriate for penetration pricing*

As the price starts low, even though a product will be developing market share, the product may initially make a loss until consumer awareness is increased. For example, a new breakfast cereal or a product being launched in a new overseas market would be launched with a relatively low price, coupled with discounts and special offers. As the product penetrates the market, sales and profitability increase and prices then creep upwards.

Penetration pricing is particularly appropriate for products where economies of scale can be employed to produce large volumes at low unit costs. Penetration pricing is also common when there is a strong possibility of competition from rival pricing.

Skimming

At the launch of a new product, there will frequently be little competition in the market. Consumers will probably have little knowledge of the product. Skimming involves setting a reasonably high initial price in order to yield high initial returns from those consumers willing to buy the new product. Once the first group of customers has been satisfied, the seller can then lower prices in order to make sales to new groups of customers. This process can be continued until a larger section of the total market has been catered for. By operating in this way, the business removes the risk of underpricing the product.

The name 'skimming' comes from the process of skimming the cream from the top of a milk product (see Figure 1.19).

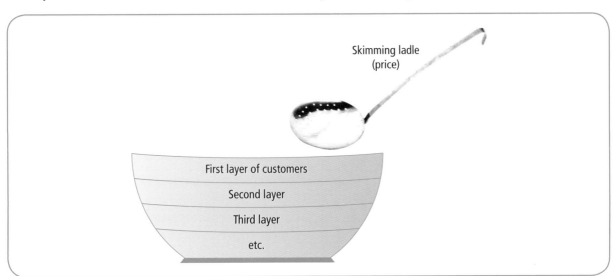

FIGURE 1.19 *Skimming*

Cost-plus pricing

Information about costs is usually easier to piece together than information about other variables such as likely revenue. Firms will often simply add a margin to the unit cost or mark-up each item sold by a certain percentage, for example, fashion items are frequently marked up by between 100 and 200 per cent. The unit cost is the average cost of each item produced. For example, if an organisation produces 800 units at a total cost of £24,000, the unit cost will be £30.

The process of cost-plus pricing can best be illustrated in relation to large organisations where economies of scale can be spread over a considerable range of output. For a large organisation, unit costs will fall rapidly at first as the overheads are spread over a larger output. It is therefore a relatively simple calculation to add a fixed margin (e.g. 20 per cent) to the unit cost. The organisation is able to select an output to produce and to set a price that will be 20 per cent higher than the unit cost of production (see Figure 1.20).

Although cost-plus pricing is very popular, there are many dangers associated with it. If the price is set too high, sales may fall short of expectations and if the price is set too low, then potential revenue is sacrificed. However, the greatest danger of cost-based pricing is that it indicates a production-orientated approach to the market. Emphasis on costs leads to tunnel vision that looks inwards at the company's product rather than outwards at the customers' perception of the product.

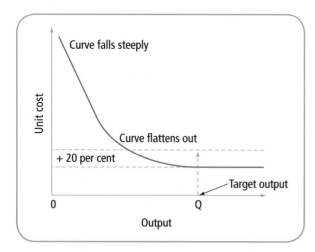

FIGURE 1.20 *Adding a fixed margin to the unit cost*

Value and price

There is a strong link between value and price. Delivery of value is an important ingredient of an exchange. In the longer term, the success of organisations will depend on their ability to provide customers with value for money through the exchange process.

Some customers are value orientated and want to pay low prices for acceptable quality whereas some buyers want high quality and are willing to pay more for it. Many of today's retailers are using emphasis upon 'value' as a form of competition. Instead of focusing simply upon price, they provide customers with a better value package – more for the same price – than other competitors in that segment of the market.

It is therefore important to price according to the nature of customers in the marketplace. On the one hand you may lose customers by charging too high a price where customers feel that they are not getting value for money. On the other hand you may lose custom from charging too low a price as potential customers may feel that the low price indicates lower quality than they are seeking.

Competition-based pricing

In extremely competitive situations, costs have to be treated as a secondary consideration. This is particularly true when competing products are almost identical, customers are well informed and where there are few suppliers.

If a product is faced by direct competition, then it will compete against other very similar products in the marketplace. This will constrain pricing decisions so that price setting will need to be kept closely in line with rivals' actions. An individual organisation might try to insulate itself against price sensitivity by differentiating its products from those of rivals.

In contrast, when a product is faced by indirect competition (i.e. competition with products in different sectors of the market) then there will be more scope to vary the price. For example, a firm might choose a high price to give a product a 'quality' feel. In contrast, it might charge a low price so that consumers see the product as a 'bargain'.

Markets are sometimes classified according to the level of competition that applies. For example,

FIGURE 1.21 *Competition*

an extreme level of competition is termed perfect competition. The other extreme is monopoly where a single firm dominates a market. In the real world, most markets lie between these extremes and involve some level of imperfection.

Where organisations seek to reduce competition and make their products better than their rivals, the development of monopolistic powers enables them to push up prices and make larger profits. The level of competition is a key determinant of price. Where there are many close competitors, there is little scope to charge a price which is above the market price. Organisations in such markets are **price takers**. In a situation where there is no competition, the seller can often charge a relatively high price. In other words they are a **price maker**. However, the seller cannot charge more than the consumer is prepared to pay as consumers can spend their income on alternative products.

Promotion

Promotion includes all of the techniques that an organisation uses to communicate with other individuals and organisations. Organisations are the senders in the communication process and consumers are the receivers. A sender will put information in the form that a receiver can understand. This might involve oral, visual, verbal or written messages to transmit the ideas. This process is called **encoding**. The sender will also choose a particular medium to use to send the message to the receiver (e.g. television, radio, newspapers). If the consumer interprets the message as required, it should have the impact that the seller wished for.

Though the message flows through to the receiver there is no guarantee that the receiver will either receive the full message or understand it. This is because the process may be subject to some form of interference, which affects the flow of

Theory into practice

Categorise the following examples into:

* penetration pricing

* skimming

* cost-plus pricing

* value-based competition

* competition-based pricing.

In each instance explain why you have chosen a particular category.

1 A new book comes onto the market in hardback form at £25, two months later it comes out in paperback at £15, the following year it comes out in a 2nd edition at £10.

2 In order to improve its competitive position in the high street, a major retailer creates a series of sub-brands designed to improve the way in which its customers view its products.

3 A breakfast cereal manufacturer introduces a new type of cereal at a low price in order to attract customers to buy the product.

4 A garden centre sets a margin of 30 per cent on all of its stock.

5 A company launches a revolutionary piece of software.

6 In a fiercely competitive market, a business simply looks at the price charged by others before setting its own price.

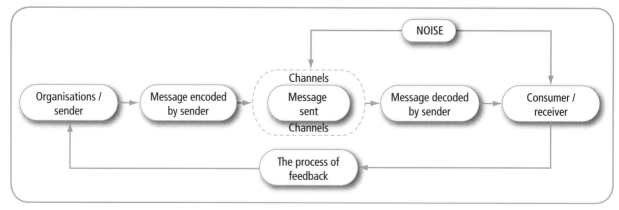

FIGURE 1.22 *The communication process*

information. This is known as noise and may lead to the downfall of the message. It will take the form of any barrier which acts as an impediment to the smooth flow of information and may include linguistic and cultural differences between the sender and the receiver. For example, one leaflet put through your door may be lost amongst a sea of direct mail from other organisations.

To increase the chances of a message getting across, an organisation needs to think carefully about the target audience. For example, it is important to channel the message through the most appropriate media. It might also be necessary to repeat the message several times rather than rely on one transmission.

Once the audience has been identified the communicator also needs to think about the sort

Theory into practice

Competition in the market for personal computers is fierce. Imagine that you work for a small organisation selling machines by mail order and you wish to target 'first-time' purchasers of PCs, particularly the over-60s. Explain what you would do to build your communication planning around the purchasing process.

of response required. If, for example, the final response required through the communication process is purchase, there may be six phases to the buyer-readiness process (see Figure 1.23).

It is important, therefore, that the promotion mix takes into account each of these stages with different types of promotional activities.

Advertising

Advertising is a method of communicating with groups in the marketplace in order to achieve certain objectives. Advertisements are messages sent through the media which are intended to inform or influence the people who receive them (see Figure 1.24).

It can be defined as a paid-for type of marketing communication that is non-personal, but aimed at a specific target audience through a mass media channel.

Advertising messages may be sent through a variety of media forms, such as TV, radio, cinema, posters, billboards, flyers, transport advertising and the press. For more information about advertising look at the World Advertising Research Center website on www.warc.com.

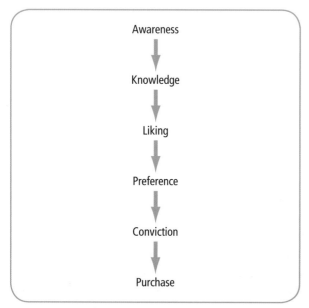

FIGURE 1.23 *Buyer-readiness phases*

Informative	Persuasive (influencing)
'The Shopping Centre is closed on 25 December.'	PRIZES 'Come to the Shopping Centre where you will find bargains galore.' FREE GIFTS SALES PROMOTIONS OFFERS COMPETITIONS

FIGURE 1.24 *Advertisements can inform or influence people*

Advertising must be a directed communication at a targeted market, and should draw attention to the characteristics of a product, which will appeal to the buying motives of potential customers. The ultimate purpose of advertising for organisations is to enhance buyers' responses to its products by channelling their desires and preferences to their products ahead of their competitors.

Within this purpose there may be a range of advertising objectives. For example:

* Promoting goods and services
  - to assist with selling
  - to increase sales
  - to develop awareness of new products or developments to existing products
  - to provide information that may assist with selling decisions
  - to encourage a desire to own a product
  - to generate enquiries.

* Developing the image of the organisation
  - to provide information for a target audience
  - to soften attitudes

  - to assist with public relations activities
  - to change views
  - to provide a better external environment
  - to develop support from a community.

Advertising is often classified under one of three headings:

* *Informative advertising* conveys information and raises consumer awareness of the features and benefits of a product. It is often used in the introductory phase of the **product life-cycle** or after modification.

* *Persuasive advertising* is concerned with creating a desire for the product and stimulating purchase. It is used with established and more mature products.

* *Reinforcement advertising* is concerned with reminding consumers about the product, and is used to reinforce the knowledge held by potential consumers about the benefits to be gained from purchase.

Theory into practice

Compare and contrast two advertising campaigns, where one is clearly trying to promote goods and services and the other is trying to improve an image by developing public support for its activities. Comment upon how their approaches to advertising are a) similar, and b) different.

Advertising plan

The starting point for an advertising campaign is to produce an advertising plan. This will involve allocating a budget to a range of activities designed to meet advertising objectives. There are seven steps in an advertising campaign. These are:

Step 1: Identify the target market.

Step 2: Define advertising objectives.

Step 3: Decide on and create the advertising message.

Step 4: Allocate the budget.

Step 5: Develop the media plan.

Step 6: Execute the campaign.

Step 7: Evaluate the effectiveness of the campaign.

At all stages in the advertising process it is important to assess how effectively advertisements have contributed to the communication process. In order to measure objectives DAGMAR has become a fundamental part of good advertising practice. This stands for: *Defining Advertising Goals for Measured Advertising Results*. In other words, before any advertising campaign is started, an organisation must define its communication objectives so that achievements can be measured both during and after the campaign.

Printed media

Printed media make up by far the largest group of media in the UK. The group includes all newspapers and magazines, both local and national, as well as trade press, periodicals and professional journals. There are about 9,000 regular publications in the UK which can be used by the advertiser. They allow the advertiser to send a message to several million people through the press or to target magazines of special interest such as *Business Education Today*, which allows the advertiser to communicate with people in the teaching profession. As a result, the media allows for accurate targeting and **positioning**. Analysing readership profiles identifies types of customers.

The benefit of printed media is that long or complex messages can be sent and, as the message is durable, may be read repeatedly. If an advertisement appears in a prestige magazine it may take on the prestige of that particular publication.

Broadcast media

Broadcast media includes commercial television and commercial radio. Television is the most powerful medium – reaching 98 per cent of

CASE STUDY

Advertising expenditure

The following table lists the top six advertisers in the UK in 2003 and their allocated advertising expenditure

Rank	Company	Total	TV %	Radio %	Press %	Other %
1	Unilever UK Ltd	205,249,905	60.1	4.5	15.0	20.4
2	Procter & Gamble Ltd	197,895,564	74.6	6.4	13.8	5.2
3	COI Communications	143,698,612	51.2	16.6	24.4	7.9
4	BT Ltd	96,899,977	53.8	6.0	31.6	8.7
5	L'Oreal Golden Ltd	90,375,244	74.0	0.2	21.9	3.9
6	Ford Motor Company Ltd	79,215,351	48.3	6.3	29.0	16.4

Source: Nielsen Media Research

1 What do the allocations of expenditure tell you about the nature and types of advertising undertaken by each of these advertisers?

2 What forms of advertising might fall into the 'other' bracket?

3 Why do you think the six companies have such a large advertising spend?

4 If you were working for one of these companies, how would you evaluate the effectiveness of such a spend?

households – and viewing figures for some programmes can exceed 20 million. Television advertisements are, however, high cost and advertising messages are short-lived.

Direct mail

Direct mail is personally addressed advertising that is delivered through the post. By using direct mail an organisation can establish a direct relationship with its customers or prospective customers. Direct mail has been the third largest medium for over 13 years and now represents 14.3 per cent of all advertising expenditure in the UK. 5,418 million direct mail items were mailed in 2004 and £2,468.63 million was spent by advertisers on this medium in the same year. It is estimated that consumer direct mail generates nearly £27 billion worth of business every year.

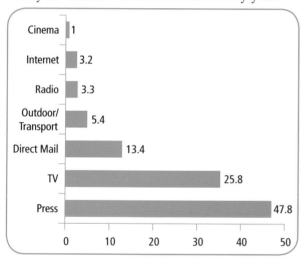

Source: World Advertising Research Center/DMIS

Theory into practice

Over a weekly period collect all of the direct mail entering your home. Try to explain why your family has been the target of such direct mail.

Public relations

The forces in an organisation's external environment are capable of affecting it in a variety of ways. The forces may be social, economic, political, local or environmental and might be represented by a variety of groups such as customers, **shareholders**, employees and special interest groups. Reacting positively to such forces and influences is very important.

Public relations is the planned and sustained effort an organisation makes to establish, develop and build relationships with its many publics (see Figure 1.25).

The purpose of public relations (PR) is therefore to provide an external environment for an organisation in which it is popular and can prosper. Building goodwill in such a way requires behaviour by the organisation which takes into account the attitudes of the many people who come across it and its products.

Whereas many of the other promotional methods are short term, public relations is long term, as it may take a long time for an organisation to improve the way people think about its products and activities. For example, just think about the sort of public relations problems that chemical and oil companies have in a world

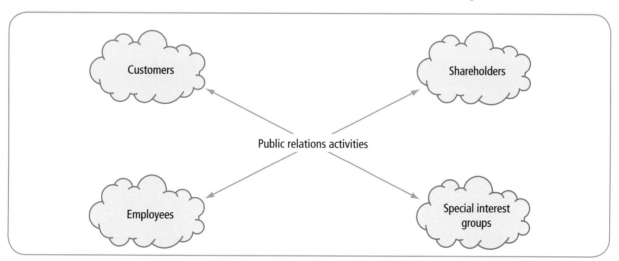

FIGURE 1.25 *Public relations activities*

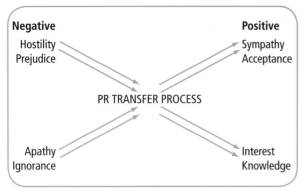

FIGURE 1.26 *The PR transfer process*

where consumers have become increasingly environmentally-conscious.

According to PR guru Frank Jefkins, PR involves a transfer process which helps to convert the negative feelings of an organisation's many publics into positive ones (see Figure 1.26).

There are many different types of public relations activities:

✳ *Charitable donations and community relations* are good for an organisation's image, often provide lots of good publicity and also help to promote and provide for a good cause.

✳ *Hospitality* at top sporting events is a popular method used by organisations to develop their customer relations. For example, there are opportunities to entertain customers at events such as the FA Cup Final, Wimbledon and the Grand National.

✳ *Press releases* covering events affecting the organisation, such as news stories, export achievements, policy changes, technical developments and anything which enhances the organisation's image.

✳ *Visits and open days* are a popular method of inviting people to various events to improve their understanding of what the organisation stands for.

✳ *Sponsorship* of sporting and cultural events is viewed as a useful opportunity to associate an image with a particular type of function. For example, the NatWest Trophy and the Embassy World Snooker Championship.

✳ *Lobbying* of ministers, officials and important people from outside interest groups, so that an accurate portrayal can be made of a problem or a case, may help to influence their views of the organisation.

✳ *Corporate videotapes* have become an increasingly popular way of providing interested parties with a 'view' of an organisation's activities.

CASE STUDY

The Royal Marriage

The marriage of Prince Charles to Camilla Parker-Bowles in Windsor during the spring of 2005, although a great royal occasion, runs in stark contrast to the overwhelming popularity of Princess Diana in his former marriage.

Princess Diana was viewed as the 'people's princess' and was very high profile in her involvement in royal duties, to the extent that she was loved and admired by many. Her tragic death saw a huge outpouring of grief across the nation.

In many ways the marriage to Camilla represents a classic PR problem that has to be dealt with in a variety of ways by Prince Charles. The negative perceptions held by so many, in direct contrast to their feelings about Diana, need to be dealt with sensitively and positively and in a way that transfers such negative images to positive ones. Inevitably, this means that Camilla will have to become involved in a series of public relations activities related to royal duties. As a former mistress to the prince, public relations will be critical in helping the public to identify Camilla with positive virtues.

1 Why is Camilla associated with negative perceptions?
2 How could PR help the public to create positive images of her?

* *Minor product changes*, such as no-testing on animals or environmentally-friendly products may provide considerable PR benefits.

Sales promotions

Sales promotions describes a category of techniques which are used to encourage customers to make a purchase. These activities are effectively short term and may be used:

* to increase sales
* to help with personal selling
* to respond to the actions of competitors
* as an effective alternative to advertising.

The Institute of Sales Promotion defines sales promotion as follows:

> *Sales promotion is the function of marketing which seeks to achieve given objectives by the adding of intrinsic, tangible value to a product or service.*

The essential feature of a sales promotion is that it is a short-term inducement to encourage customers to react quickly, whereas advertising is usually a process that develops the whole product or brand.

As you walk down a town high street or through a shopping mall, you will see many different examples of sales promotions. Such

promotions may serve many different purposes. For example, competitions, vouchers or coupons and trading stamps may be designed to build customer loyalty and perhaps increase the volume purchased by existing customers. Product sampling is often used to introduce new products into the marketplace. Clearance sales of overstocked goods will increase turnover during part of the year in which business might otherwise be slack. Many sales promotions are undertaken in response to the activities of competitors to ensure that an organisation remains competitive. Sales promotions can be divided into two broad areas:

* promotions assisting with the sale of products to the trade
* promotions assisting the trade in selling products to the final consumer.

Selling into the pipeline is an expression used to describe promotions which move products from the manufacturer into the distribution system. Selling out of the pipeline describes promotions which trigger the end-user to make a purchase (see Figure 1.27).

There are many different types of sales promotion:

* *Dealer loaders* are among the inducements to attract orders from retailers and wholesalers. They may include a 'free case' with so many cases bought. For example, thirteen for the price of twelve is known as a 'baker's dozen'.
* *Competitions* may interest dealers and consumers. For dealers they may be linked to sales with attractive prizes for the most successful dealer. Scratch cards, free draws and

FIGURE 1.27 *Selling into and out of the pipeline*

bingo cards are popular promotional methods for consumers.

* *Promotional gifts* such as bottles of spirits, clocks, watches or diaries are considered useful inducements for dealers.

* *Price reductions* and *special offers* are usually popular with consumers. They can, however, prove expensive as many consumers would otherwise have been prepared to pay the full price.

* *Premium offers* may offer extra product for the same price. Coupons which offer money off or money back may also be attractive incentives for consumers. These may appear in magazines, be distributed door to door or appear on the side of a pack.

* *Charity promotions* can be popular with younger consumers, who collect box tops or coupons and send them to a manufacturer, which then makes a donation to charity.

* *Loyalty incentives* are today an increasingly used form of sales promotion. Dealer's loyalty might be rewarded with bigger discounts, competitions and prizes, or they might even have their names published as stockists in advertisements. For consumers, loyalty incentives such as loyalty cards and points may provide 'cash back', free gifts or a variety of other tangible benefits.

Place

The place element within the marketing mix provides the basic structure for customers needs to be satisfied. For example, physical distribution involves getting a product from A to B which is an important part of the place process. In doing so it enables manufacturers and distributors to provide

goods for customers at the right time, in the right place and in the condition required. It may also reduce the time from when a customer first makes an order until the time when that order is delivered.

Physical distribution must balance the need for customer service against the need to minimise costs. To maximise customer service, an organisation may need a lot of stock and warehouse space, efficient staff and rapid transport mechanisms. To minimise costs they need low stock levels, limited storage space, few staff and slower transport. Designing a physical distribution system therefore involves trading off costs against service, or inputs against outputs.

Inputs involve all of the distribution costs such as freight costs, inventory costs, warehousing costs and other service costs. It is important to know exactly what each of these costs is and control the costs in order to minimise waste. This may involve a detailed analysis of labour time, transport time, and other factors spent on each product.

Outputs can primarily be measured in terms of the value of services provided for customers. Distribution can provide a clear competitive benefit in meeting customer needs, for example, by offering a quick and efficient service. Every business must decide how it is going to use distribution and relate this to its competitive advantage. Weaknesses in distribution would clearly need to be compensated for by strengths in other areas of the marketing mix.

The physical distribution system that an organisation selects will largely depend upon the scale of operations and the size of an organisation's market. A business handling a lot of international mail, for example, might locate near a large airport. Key decisions about physical distribution may include the following:

* *Inventory*. A business that wants to maximise customer service will have the highest inventory costs because it needs to hold stock to meet all requests. The key inventory decisions are when and how much to order. The danger of keeping too little in stock is that an organisation could lose custom because of dissatisfaction with the quality of service.

* *Warehousing*. A key decision is where to locate warehouses and how many to have.

* *Load size*. Should units be transported in bulk or broken down into smaller units for delivery? Again, an organisation will have to trade-off customer convenience and the cost of distribution.

* *Communications*. It is important to develop an efficient information processing and invoicing system.

Sales channels

Channels are the networks of intermediaries linking the producer to the market. Direct selling methods do not use an intermediary, but indirect selling methods use one or more channels of distribution through which goods are transferred from the producer to the end user (see Figure 1.28).

Intermediaries such as **wholesalers** stock a range of goods from competing manufacturers to sell on to other organisations such as retailers. Most wholesalers take on the title to the goods

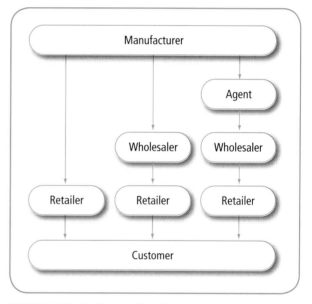

FIGURE 1.28 *Indirect sales channels*

CASE STUDY

Distribution to Sainsbury's stores

Within the M25 area, Sainsbury's has more than 80 branches, each of which requires several deliveries daily. Average traffic speeds in London have fallen to 11 mph over the last decade as traffic densities have increased.

In order to improve their systems of physical distribution, Sainsbury's have consolidated their supplies into fewer, larger loads for final delivery, by using 38-tonne vehicles. This enables goods to be delivered in fewer vehicles, reducing delivery costs, carbon dioxide emissions and congestion. As far as

possible, deliveries are made between 10 p.m. and 6 a.m. to reduce congestion.

'Just-in-time' scheduling reduces time that goods are held in the warehouse. The requirements of branches are relayed via computer, with many product lines on a 24-hour cycle (ordered one day for delivery the following day), while others are ordered once or twice a week for delivery 48 hours later.

1 **What problems might be encountered delivering within the M25 area?**
2 **How could such problems be overcome?**

and so assume many of the risks associated, which include:

* *Breaking bulk.* Manufacturers produce goods in bulk for sale but they might not want to store the goods themselves. They want to be paid as quickly as possible. A number of wholesalers buy the stock from them and generally payment is prompt. The wholesaler then stocks these goods, along with others bought from other manufacturers, ready for purchase by retailers.

* *Storage.* Most retailers have only a limited amount of storage space. The wholesaler can be looked upon as a cupboard for the retailer. Manufacturers are able to unload finished goods on the wholesaler.

* *Packing and labelling.* The wholesaler will in some instances finish off the packaging and labelling of goods, perhaps by putting price tags or brand labels on the goods.

* *Offering advice.* Being in the middle of a chain of distribution, wholesalers have a lot more information at their fingertips than either the retailer or manufacturer. In particular, wholesalers know which goods are selling well. With this in mind they can advise retailers on what to buy and manufacturers on what to produce.

The chain of distribution without the wholesaler would look something like Figure 1.30. Manufacturer 1 has to carry out four journeys to supply retailers 1, 2, 3 and 4, and has to send out four sets of business documents, and handle

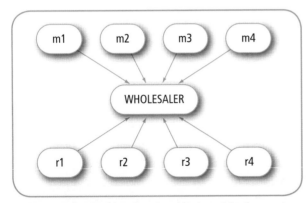

FIGURE 1.29 *The distribution chain with the wholesaler*

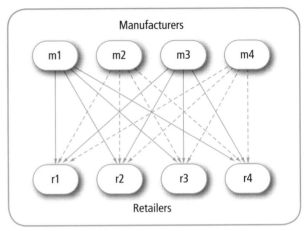

FIGURE 1.30 *The distribution chain without the wholesaler*

four sets of accounts. The same situation applies to each of the manufacturers, so that in total 16 journeys are made and 16 sets of paperwork are required. This is a simplification because, in the real world, thousands of different transactions might be involved!

An intermediary can simplify costs and processes of distribution by cutting down on journeys, fuel and other costs as well as cutting down on paperwork such as invoicing and administration.

By contracting out the process of distribution, a company can concentrate on its core functions.

The French word *retailer* means '*to cut again*'. We have already seen that the wholesaler breaks down bulk supplies from the manufacturer. The retailer then cuts the bulk again to sell individual items to customers. In the modern retailing environment, *the physical environment* for selling to end users has become increasingly complex and in tune with customer focus and needs.

Daewoo, for instance, is distributing cars in the UK without using a traditional local car dealership network. The use of telephone, modem and the Internet as well as fax are also providing the consumer with new ways to view and purchase products. Telemarketing is now being used to sell products such as insurance and pensions, which were previously sold by a one-to-one personal interview. The availability of satellite TV channels has promoted the introduction of home shopping, with the American company QVC launching an English-speaking shopping channel within Europe. Simultaneously, the Internet is increasingly being used for electronic commerce, selling goods to consumers. This new channel of distribution is being investigated by many other organisations such as supermarkets (see e.g. www.tesco.com), who are already involved in the distribution chain. These imaginative approaches to distribution are being viewed as a major new opportunity to meet customer needs within a rapidly changing physical environment.

1.2.5 Presentational skills

One key element of business life is the need, from time to time, to give some form of presentation to others. Just as in the business world, having prepared a marketing proposal, a marketer would then have to present the proposal to a chosen audience. Presentations are useful because they help to:

* provide a basis for discussion and ongoing analysis by a group of colleagues or for an audience

Involving the audience can be the key to a successful presentation

* help to elicit a variety of perspectives from others, and can provide an active forum that fine-tunes and revises a proposal

* develop a key communication skill which is very important within the business world.

It is important to discuss with your tutor beforehand the sort of criteria they are using to analyse your presentation. Remember that the purpose of your presentation is to communicate the key areas of your assessment proposal. Use the guidelines below to help you prepare your presentation:

1   *Do not try to be too ambitious.* In a talk lasting up to 20 minutes you are not going to be able to make more than a small number of key points, summarising various elements of the marketing proposal. If you try to put too much information into the talk, you will end up having to rush through your proposal or find that you are displaying far too much information for your audience to appreciate. It is more important to discuss the key elements of the proposal and to discuss those key elements well, rather than to get through too much.

2   *Show that you understand marketing principles and practices and can use appropriate business terminology.* Remember that the presentation is an assessment of your own **learning**. Marketing has its own terminology, use of language and ways of operating. Try, within your presentation, to show how well

you understand marketing principles and practices by using terms such as 'targeting', 'segmentation', 'placement', 'product life-cycle' and so on. This will help your tutor to appreciate your depth of understanding of how you have planned to meet your marketing objectives.

3 *Use visual aids and other techniques to engage your audience.* There are a variety of visual aids that you may want to use. For example, you may have a film or video clip that you feel complements and supports some of the points you would like to make. Make sure that you know when to use the clip, that the equipment is working and that you describe and contextualise the clip within the talk by discussing it in relation to your proposal. Whereas in the past many presentations used an overhead projector, increasingly most presentations nowadays rely heavily upon you using Microsoft PowerPoint® to prepare and present your talk.

In your PowerPoint presentation, apply a background, company name and logo to the master slide to ensure there is a consistency about the appearance of all the slides. Animations, sound effects and flashy graphics may enhance your presentation but be aware of how many you are using as they can also detract from the talk. Make sure that when using PowerPoint an appropriate size is chosen for the text, which should be at least 32-point. Introduce all pages from the same direction and use only one PowerPoint page for every two to three minutes of the talk. Do not prepare too many PowerPoint slides as you will not have time to get through them.

4 *Structure the talk logically to help the audience to appreciate the points you are making.* It is important to work through the proposal itemising the key areas to be following. As you prepare the talk you may highlight the more important areas for discussion, and have extra materials on hand if your talk is finishing too soon. You may wish to repeat the main parts of the presentation and it is always important to summarise the talk at the end.

5 *Talk clearly and feel confident. This helps the listener to appreciate the main points of the presentation.* It is useful to rehearse and practise the talk several times to make sure that you feel confident with the material as well as to ensure that the timings are appropriate. It also provides you with the opportunity to edit and change different parts of the talk. It is possible to reduce nerves although possibly not eradicate them by:

* making sure that you are confident with the materials and know them well

* focusing upon the materials as you talk, thinking about how to make sure that your audience understands them

* relaxing before the talk. Always take deep breaths and don't speak too quickly

* arriving early and making sure that the room and the materials are prepared and ensuring that the technology works

* providing yourself with water or some other form of drink to consume.

As you conduct your presentation, use a watch or a clock to time yourself. Think about how many minutes to allocate to the various phases of the talk and do not start until everybody is quiet and all attention is focused upon you. Sometimes it is useful just to introduce yourself and explain what you hope to achieve and what you hope the audience will learn from your talk. Explain when you want questions, either in the middle of your talk, after key sections or at the end.

When you speak it is quite acceptable to use postcards as a prompt as they can help you to make sure that your include everything. However, try to make eye-contact with your audience as much as possible and speak clearly and not too quickly. If necessary pause every so often to gather breath. At the end of the talk, sum up all of the points you have made and thank the audience for listening.

Presentation tips

1 Do not talk too quickly.

2 Respect the viewpoints of the questioners.

3 Introduce the talk and sum up the points you make.

4 Try to move logically from one visual aid to the next.

5 Stick to your brief and be careful about improvising on the day.

6 Make eye-contact with your audience.

7 Demonstrate to others that you are enjoying giving the talk.

8 Avoid making the talk unnecessarily complicated.

9 If necessary, provide a handout for your audience.

10 If you are running out of time, do not rush.

11 Make sure that your slides are relevant.

12 Listen carefully when being questioned to make sure that you understand the points being made.

1.2.6 How to judge potential success

Having developed a marketing proposal it is important to audit it. This means that you must try to assess how or whether the marketing proposal would work and what might influence how it would operate. It is essential to evaluate the relative strengths of the market proposal you have developed and then try to think about what would be necessary to fine tune or further develop it. For example, it may be possible to use a SWOT analysis to evaluate the strengths, weakness, opportunities and threats to the proposal.

To evaluate the marketing proposal, you need to consider the following:

❋ whether the marketing objectives are likely to be fulfilled

❋ whether the needs of potential customers are likely to be met

❋ whether the proposal is sustainable over time, both in terms of its potential market position and actions of possible rival competitors

❋ how the marketing proposal fits with the business's current product-portfolio

❋ how the marketing proposal impacts upon the different departments and functional areas of the business.

Are your marketing objectives likely to be fulfilled?

Does the mix have the potential to meet the marketing objectives set within the marketing proposal? How well could an organisation meet the objectives that have been identified? Use the SMART framework to consider how the marketing objectives meet each of the SMART categories. You may want to talk to somebody who either runs a business or is involved with marketing to find out how realistic the proposal is. Try to use reasoned judgements and, if possible, supply some form of evidence about the possible success of your approach.

Are the needs of potential customers likely to be met?

You may want to test out particular elements of your marketing proposal by discussing your marketing mix with potential customers. Collecting evidence is important to support your evaluation. Look to see how other organisations meet similar customer needs and try to judge whether your approach is more appropriate.

Is the proposal sustainable over time?

Will your proposal and plans be able to sustain themselves over a period of time and be successful within a market from one year to another? Try and look at similar products in similar businesses and find out about their successes and failures. What is the failure rate within the markets you intend to serve? What are some of the problems and issues affecting this market and how might that affect or influence your particular proposal?

Does the marketing proposal fit with the business's current product-portfolio?

It is important that the proposal matches the aims and objectives of your company. Are they still the same? If they have evolved, your marketing proposal will need to be modified to reflect the current direction of your company.

How does the marketing proposal impact upon the different departments and functional areas of the business?

You may want to interview people who work within different parts of business organisations. Find out how marketing proposals impact upon their activities and how some of their decisions are affected by marketing proposals.

CASE STUDY

Learning from failure

Is it possible to learn from the mistakes of others? According to a New York marketing agency, it is important to analyse why products fail because then it is possible to understand how to develop marketing proposals that might succeed. The agency argues that the main factor behind most product failures is simply the high number of products appearing on the market, and where there are too many products it is just impossible for products to distinguish themselves.

One very difficult market to compete in is the grocery market. The product might be satisfactory, but if it is put in the wrong packaging or in the wrong place in the supermarket its death is assured. Some of the great marketing disasters have involved the biggest names. Levi's lacked focus upon their customers and let the brand lose its popularity. Burger King went head-to-head to compete with McDonald's instead of identifying their differentiating features. In these instances organisations made decisions about how to market their products in a way that damaged their brand.

1 **What is a marketing failure?**
2 **Why do many products fail?**
3 **Find out more about great marketing failures.**
4 **Evaluate how knowledge of marketing failures helps to reduce some of the problems and issues with your marketing proposal.**

KNOWLEDGE CHECK

1 What is meant by market orientation?

2 Identify the four Ps of the marketing mix.

3 Explain how a finance department helps an organisation to achieve its marketing objectives.

4 Describe the role of 'operations'.

5 What is mass marketing?

6 How does mass marketing differ from niche marketing?

7 Describe what is meant by targeting.

8 What role might a suggestions box have within an organisation?

9 What is a field experiment and how might it be used?

10 Name three attributes of a good questionnaire.

11 How does an open question differ from a closed question?

12 Provide two examples of sales promotions.

13 Why might a market researcher use a prompt card?

14 Explain the purpose of using a wholesaler.

15 What is a moving average and why might a marketer want to use one?

16 Provide two examples of brands.

17 What is a market segment?

18 Provide an example of 'printed media'.

19 What is direct mail?

20 Describe one pricing technique.

Resources

There is a wide range of textbooks to support learning about marketing. Some good sources include:

Needham, D. et al., *Marketing for Higher Awards*, Oxford, Heinemann, 1999

The Advertising Association, *Marketing Pocket Book 2005*, Henley-on-Thames, World Advertising Research Center, 2005

Kotler, P. et al., *Marketing: An Introduction,* Hemel Hempstead, Prentice Hall, 2003

Dibb, S. et al, *Marketing: Concepts and Strategies*, Boston, Houghton Mifflin, 2001

Websites

Some useful websites are listed below. These addresses are current at the time of writing. However, it needs to be recognised that new sites are being launched on the Internet on a regular basis and that older sites may change or disappear.

www.tt100.biz
www.cim.co.uk

www.marketinguk.co.uk
www.dma.org.uk
www.mad.co.uk
www.marketing-society.org.uk
www.brandrepublic.com
www.bitc.org.uk
www.marketingpower.com

TV Choice video

TV Choice (www.tv.choice.com) produces a range of videos related to marketing. Their most topical is called *What is marketing?* This video is a good starting point and shows the impact of TV in the 1950s as well as the consumer boom. It then analyses the classic breakdown of marketing strategies into the four Ps and looks at the promotion of the brand rather than the product and globalisation.

Magazines

Marketing magazine
Marketing Today
Marketing Week

UNIT 2

Recruitment in the workplace

This unit contains eight elements:

2.2.1 Job roles

2.2.2 The recruitment process

2.2.3 The selection process

2.2.4 The induction process

2.2.5 Employee motivation

2.2.6 The legal dimension

2.2.7 Research

2.2.8 How to judge effectiveness

Introduction

It is important to have a good understanding of how businesses acquire one of their key resources – people. Many of you will already be involved in part-time work and a work placement is a beneficial part of the learning process on a vocational course. Studying the processes involved in the recruitment and selection of people to work for a business gives you a better understanding of:

* the various processes that are involved from the business side when recruiting and selecting the workforce

* how you can prepare yourself when applying for jobs and for job interviews.

As you study this unit, you will produce a report with supporting documentation showing how you have set about recruiting and selecting an individual for a particular job role, as well as producing an induction and motivational programme for your chosen job role and successful **applicant**.

Your class peers will adopt the roles of prospective employees applying for your chosen role and will participate in your **selection** process. You will also be expected to assist your class peers in meeting the evidence requirements for this unit by taking on the role of a prospective employee, applying for positions and participating in their recruitment and selection processes for advertised positions. More detailed guidance about the assignment is given at the end of this unit.

Your report will be informed by your research into current human-resource practices used by a range of different businesses and your analysis of the gathered data. Finally, you will make reasoned judgements as you discuss the effectiveness of your chosen approaches to both the recruitment and selection processes and the induction and motivational programmes created for your chosen job role and successful applicant.

2.2.1 Job roles

Before considering the recruitment and selection of individuals to fill new posts, you need to have an understanding of the various job roles and levels of management that can exist in a medium- to large-sized business. These include:

* managers
* supervisors
* IT operatives
* administrators
* customer service operatives.

Manager

A **manager** is someone with responsibility, usually for others, for making decisions and for managing resources. For example, the job description of a marketing manager in a company might state that this person is:

* *accountable* to their marketing director
* *responsible* for staff in the market research function of the company
* *responsible* for planning, organising and delivering market research campaigns

* *responsible* for creating a market research budget and for monitoring that budget each month
* *responsible* for making sure that the company keeps in tune with the changing needs of its customers.

From the example shown above, you can see that management involves responsibility. The level of responsibility depends on the level of management:

* senior managers are responsible for long-term decisions made in a company as well as major resources
* middle managers are responsible for some medium-term decisions and some important resources
* junior managers are responsible for short-term decisions and they have some responsibility for resources.

Supervisor

Supervisors also have an important role to play in an organisation and their responsibilities can be equivalent to those of a junior manager. Supervisors have responsibility for supervising a particular task or group of people.

The following is an extract from an advertisement for a marketing manager in a clothes manufacturing company based in the East Midlands. Read the advertisement and answer the following questions.

BERKELEY BRIDAL WEAR

Marketing Manager

Grantham

Base salary to £25k + benefits
Plus on target bonuses of £10k

An excellent opportunity to join the country's largest independent bridalwear retailer with outlets throughout the UK.

Typically you will be a creative marketing professional with:

- experience of 'high end' clothing or luxury goods
- the ability to develop relationships with leading fashion journalists
- a good knowledge of brand positioning
- experience of internal and external communications
- experience to handle a substantial budget and to manage a team
- experience of marketing websites.

To apply, please send your full CV and covering letter, stating current salary package to recruitment@good.silk.co.uk

1 Do you think the job is classified as a senior, middle or junior management post? Explain why.

2 What evidence is there in the advertisement that the job involves responsibility? List the main areas of responsibility.

Supervisors will often work within fairly tight boundaries. They have responsibility for making sure that:

✳ the right standards are met

✳ time deadlines are met

✳ people or other resources are supervised in an appropriate way.

Just because an employee is not a manager or supervisor does not mean that their work is any less important. Most employees have the potential to become supervisors and managers. Employees have a responsibility to meet legal requirements and the responsibilities of the job set out in a job description. Today many employees are given additional responsibilities because managers recognise that individuals work best when trusted to do fulfilling work.

IT operative

Information technology is very important in modern businesses and most employees need to have some level of IT capability to carry out their work. For example, when you visit a bank the person that serves you over the counter will be using a computer terminal from which they can call up details of your account. Similarly, when you ring up an insurance company to take out a car insurance policy, the person you deal with at the end of the line will be sitting in front of a computer terminal.

Today there is a shortage of IT specialists nationally and as a result the wages of people working with IT are increasing. IT operatives are typically involved with a number of tasks.

Database management

Database management involves creating databases, for example, of customers, or patients in a hospital, by using existing database packages. Usually database management involves creating a number of relevant fields, e.g. creating fields for patients with a certain illness, those seen by a certain doctor, etc. It is then possible to create records for individual customers, patients etc.

Spreadsheet creation

Most businesses process a lot of quantitative information (information that involves numbers) and spreadsheets help organisations to make calculations very quickly. For example, a spreadsheet can be created showing wages paid to particular employees. Deductions can be made from the wage to account for income tax, national insurance and other deductions. IT workers will create a spreadsheet for an organisation or simply enter data into an existing spreadsheet.

Creating presentations

IT specialists may be asked to prepare eye-catching presentations for managers within an organisation. They can then use their expertise with presentation software such as PowerPoint® to create exciting presentations.

Setting up IT systems

IT workers are also expected to trouble shoot and set up IT systems within an organisation. This may involve networking (linking together) various computers or setting up the systems for new computers as well as maintaining them. They will also help out employees who are having problems by troubleshooting for them and maintaining virus checkers and other important software systems.

Administrator

Administrators play an important role in modern organisations by creating a range of paper-based and computer-based systems for other employees in the organisation. All large organisations depend on administrators for dealing with tasks such as enquiries, communicating messages and producing documents for the workforce.

Administrators are very important because they service the work of an organisation, although problems can arise when administrators disturb the functioning of an organisation with administrative work that moves the business away from its central objectives.

Many large firms have a central office that is responsible for controlling key aspects of the firm's paperwork. This department might handle the filing of materials, the company's mail, word-processing and data-handling facilities (such as the creation and maintenance of databases).

Office manager

In many companies, each department will have its own clerical and support staff. However, it is common practice to have an office services manager with the responsibility for co-ordinating office services and for offering expert advice to departmental managers.

The work of the office manager will include the following areas:

* taking responsibility for and organising the training of administrative staff

* advising departments about office layout, office equipment, working practices and staff development

* co-ordinating the supply of office equipment and stationery

* studying and analysing administrative practice within the organisation in order to develop an overall **strategy** for administration

* ensuring the standardisation of administrative work, the layout of documents, letters, etc

* providing and maintain a communications system within a company, including phones, mailing systems, computer hardware and other data-processing facilities

* reporting to, and providing statistics for, the company board about the effectiveness of existing administrative practice.

Customer service operative

Many of you will have direct experience of the work of customer service operatives as a result of your work experience or part-time work. Most organisations depend heavily on their customer service operatives.

For example, the retail store ASDA believes that its success lies in delivering 'legendary customer service'. Every employee is given training in how to deliver 'legendary' customer service which involves developing knowledge about their job and the products that they sell, as well as other skills in dealing with customers on a day-to-day basis.

Customer service employees must know:

* how to do their job efficiently, e.g. serving customers at the till or greeting customers when they enter a store
* about the products they are selling, e.g. where to find them and the various qualities of different products
* how to give priority to customers, what to say to them, how to talk to them and how to make them feel welcome.

2.2.2 The recruitment process

Businesses must plan to make sure that they have the right number of suitable employees for their needs. When a business is looking to recruit a new employee, it needs to be able to define key roles and responsibilities that will be expected in the new post. You need to understand the ways in which businesses set about this task by creating the following recruitment documents:

* person specification
* job description
* job advertisement
* application form.

Qualities in employees

Businesses need to be clear about the sorts of qualities that they are looking for when recruiting employees in order to attract the most suitable applicants. They will need to consider carefully:

* what they expect applicants to already be able to do

* what applicants should already know
* the skills required
* the attitudes required.

Theory into practice

Examine the job advertisement below.

SUPERIOR INDUSTRIES LTD

Admin Assistant

Due to expansion, Superior Industries require an administrative assistant to help in their Customer Service department.

The successful applicant will possess excellent PC literacy and data entry skills and will be responsible for the management of customer orders for the business.

With an excellent telephone manner, you will be reliable and enthusiastic, well-organised, a self-starter and play a pivotal role in the day-to-day running of this busy but friendly department.

For further information and an application form please call Rosamund Manning on 01457 905549

Although this post is not at a high level in the organisation, the company is looking for a number of qualities.

1 What sorts of existing skills is the company looking for?

2 What sorts of personal qualities are expected of the prospective employee?

3 Why might you be tempted to apply for the post?

4 Why might you not be tempted to apply for the post?

Reasons for recruiting staff

There are a number of reasons for recruiting new staff:

1 *The growth of the business*
   One example of a growth area is e-commerce, buying and selling through the Internet, which has led to the recruitment of web page designers and other IT specialists.

2 *Filling vacancies caused by job leavers*
   All businesses have a turnover of staff. For example, supermarket chains like ASDA and Sainsbury's constantly need to recruit checkout staff, car park attendants and other employees. There will be a regular stream of people leaving their jobs, e.g. to go to college or university, who will need to be replaced.

3 *Changing job roles*
   Modern work is constantly changing. Next year's jobs will require different skills from those that are required today. Businesses will therefore constantly create new opportunities and new jobs requiring new people.

4 *Internal promotion*
   Most companies encourage their staff to take on more demanding and better-paid posts within the business. New employees are required to replace those moving up the ladder.

Job analysis

In many companies, when creating new jobs or altering existing ones, it is common practice to carry out a **job analysis** before going on to create a **person specification** and **job description**. Organisations need to attract, recruit and retain the best possible people to fill the posts required and thus help a business to achieve its objectives.

The starting point for many businesses that want to recruit and select new employees to fill a job role is to create a job analysis. A job analysis is a study of the tasks that are required in order to do a particular job. Job analysis is very important in creating a clear job description (see page 63). Job analysis involves carrying out a study of the key components of a particular job.

If a job already exists, such as a business studies teacher in a school, a checkout operative in a supermarket or an apprentice hairdresser in a hairdressing salon, the person doing the job analysis

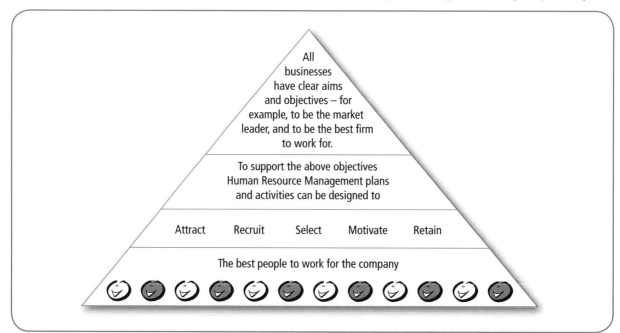

FIGURE 2.1 *How employees contribute to business objectives*

just needs to carry out a study of the tasks involved in carrying out the same or a similar position. This can be done by looking at various documents describing the current job role or by studying the activities carried out by current job-holders. For example, if you were to study the work carried out by a supermarket checkout desk operative for one evening you would have a good idea of what the job involved.

It is more difficult to carry out a job analysis when a new post is being created in a business. One way to carry out the analysis is to study work carried out by an employee in a similar firm. Alternatively, the job analyst may need to interview people to find out what exactly the job will involve, setting out details such as:

✳ the key tasks that the person carrying out the job will be expected to do

✳ the key skills that the job-holder will need to have

✳ the qualifications that the job-holder will need to have

✳ the attitudes and manner that the job-holder will need to have.

Person specification

A person specification should set out clearly what attributes an individual needs to have to do a particular job well. The person specification goes beyond a simple description of the job by highlighting the mental, physical and other attributes required of a job holder. For example, a recent Prison Service advertisement specified the following:

> *At every level your task will call for a lot more than simple efficiency. It takes humanity, flexibility, enthusiasm, total commitment and, of course, a sense of humour.*

A personal specification for police recruits might include physical attributes related to having a particular standard of physical fitness or qualifications including Advanced level or equivalents, etc.

Armed with this sort of specification, those responsible for recruiting and selecting someone to do a particular job have a much clearer idea of the ideal **candidate**. At the same time those applying for a job have a much clearer idea of what is expected of them and whether they have the attributes.

The human resources department may set out, for its own use, a 'person specification', using a layout similar to the one shown in Figure 2.2.

Personal attributes and achievements

A person specification is concerned with identifying those people who have the right qualities to fit the jobs you are offering. For example, personal attributes for a member of the Paratroop Regiment might include physical toughness and alertness. The personal attributes of a teacher may include the ability to work well with others and to find out about the learning

Summary of job			
Attributes	**Essential**	**Desirable**	**How identified**
Physical			
Qualifications			
Experience			
Training			
Special knowledge			
Personal circumstances			
Attitudes			
Practical and intellectual skills			

FIGURE 2.2 *Layout for a person specification*

needs of pupils. The personal attributes of a shop assistant might include punctuality and smartness of appearance.

Personal achievement gives a good indication of the existing abilities of given individuals. For example, someone who has achieved the Duke of Edinburgh Awards shows qualities of enterprise and initiative. Personal achievements can be good indicators of qualities such as the ability to work in a team, to help others, to persevere, etc.

Qualifications

Qualifications are another important part of a person specification. For example, when recruiting a new human resources lecturer it would be essential to appoint someone with formal teaching qualifications and some experience of work at an appropriate level in human resource management.

Qualifications are a good measure of prior learning. This has been simplified in recent years by the development of nationally recognised qualifications such as AS and A2 qualifications.

The idea of a qualification is that it prepares you to do a particular job or activity. In creating person specifications, organisations will therefore need to consider the level of qualification required by a job-holder.

Experience

Someone with experience in carrying out a particular post or who has had particular responsibilities should be able to draw on that experience in new situations. For example, an experienced lecturer has already taught, assessed, administered and carried out a variety of other duties in a college. A new lecturer has not had the same opportunities. However, a new lecturer in a college can bring new ideas or transfer their knowledge from experience of working in an industrial setting.

Employers benefit from recruiting experienced staff as they are able to do a range of tasks. This makes them more flexible workers, which in turn increases the output of the business.

Customers often like to deal with experienced employees. For example, customers will often ask for their car to be serviced by a more experienced mechanic or to have their hair cut by a more experienced stylist.

We talk about the learning curve which results from experience. The implication is that the good learner will learn at a progressively faster rate as they draw on their experience. A person specification should therefore set out the required experience for a job-holder.

Competence

Competence is a word that is widely used today. Competence implies that a person has sufficient knowledge or skill to carry out particular tasks or activities. Most people would rather visit a competent than an incompetent doctor, or be taught by a competent rather than an incompetent teacher. Firms therefore benefit from employing more competent employees who are trusted by customers and are more reliable at producing quality outputs.

Person specifications should set out levels of competence required by a particular job-holder. Hairdressers, for example, need to show competence in a range of performance criteria that make up the elements of hairdressing work. A hairdresser would be foolish to take on a new stylist for dyeing purposes who had not first exhibited competence in mixing and applying hair dye.

Competence is an important aspect of work ability

Theory into practice

List ten situations in which you prefer to deal with more competent and better qualified employees. Are you prepared to pay more for the service provided? In each case explain why you think the organisation will benefit from employing more competent and better qualified employees.

Job descriptions

A job analysis can then be used to create a job description. A job description will describe how a particular employee is to fit into the organisation and will need to set out:

* the title of the job
* to whom the employee is responsible
* for whom the employee is responsible
* a simple description of the role and duties of the employee within the organisation.

A job description could be used as a job indicator for applicants. Alternatively, it could be used as a guideline for an employee and/or line manager as to his or her role and responsibility within the organisation.

Job descriptions can be used by organisations to provide information for use in drafting a situations vacant advertisement and for briefing interviewers.

Job title

One of the most important parts of a job description is the job title. The job title should give a good indication of what the job entails. For example, you may hear people in organisations make statements such as: 'She's supposed to be the Managing Director, let her make the decision,' or 'leave the word-processing of letters to the administrator, that's not your job'.

When looking through job advertisements the first thing that job applicants will look for (apart from the salary) will be the job title.

From time to time job titles will change, often to give a slightly different feel to some jobs or to give the job title a new status, for example, the Principal of a College may become a Chief

Job titles help to make employees feel important

Job descriptions provide useful guidance to employees

Executive, a dustbin man may become a 'disposal services officer' or a petrol pump cashier may become a 'forecourt executive'.

Position within organisation structure

A job description will often establish where an individual stands in a particular organisation's structure. This means it shows who the post-holder is accountable to and who is accountable to him or her.

The position within an organisation will also give a clear idea of responsibilities. Job applicants will be interested in locating the position in order to work out whether their previous experience will be broad enough and to assess the kind of commitment they will be expected to make to the organisation.

Duties and responsibilities

A further important aspect of the job description will be that which sets out the duties and responsibilities of job-holders.

Prior to setting out a job description an organisation may carry out an analysis of the tasks which need to be performed by a job-holder and the skills and qualities required.

If this is done carefully, then organisational planners will have a clear picture of how particular jobs fit in with all the other jobs carried on in an organisation. It also helps job applicants to get a clear picture of what is expected of them, and it helps job-holders to understand the priorities of their work.

Job advertisements

Job advertisements form an important part of the recruitment process. An organisation is able to communicate job vacancies to a selected audience by this means. Most job advertisements are written (or at least checked) by the personnel department, a task involving the same skills as marketing a product. Advertisements must reach those people who have the qualities to fill the vacancy.

Job advertisements take many forms, according to the requirements of the post. Good advertisements include the information shown in Figure 2.3.

Job description	This should highlight the major requirements of the job in a concise format
Organisational activities and market place	There should be a brief description of the environment in which the organisation operates
Location	Applicants need to know the location of the organisation and the location of the job
Salary expectation	Figures are not always necessary, but an indication of the salary level (or a recognised grade) should always be given
Address and contact	This should appear, with a telephone number if appropriate
Qualifications	Certain jobs require a minimum entrance qualification, which should be clearly stated
Experience	This should be made clear as it will have a bearing on the expected salary level for the job
Fringe benefits	The advertiser may wish to mention a company car, health scheme etc.
Organisational identity	This may be in the form of a logo (or simply the name of the organisation)

FIGURE 2.3 *Content of a good job advertisement*

In this unit you are required to recruit and select a candidate for a chosen job role. You can use the table below that we have set out for you to evaluate the effectiveness of the following advertisement for a Director for the New Globe Theatre Company and of other job advertisements that you collect from the national press for a range of jobs.

By evaluating a range of job advertisements you will be best placed to create an effective job advertisement of your own. This work will help you to show evidence of having carried out research and subsequently analysing it.

Does the advertisement give a clear picture of what the job entails?	
Does the advertisement set out clearly where the job is located?	
Do you think the advertisement is focused enough to attract people with the right sorts of qualifications to fill the post?	
What sorts of people do you think are most likely to apply for the post?	
Does the advertisement indicate opportunities for job development and for personal challenges over time?	
Would an applicant know how to apply for the job?	
Would the advertisement in its present form screen out unsuitable applicants?	
What improvements would you make to the advertisement?	

New Globe
Theatre Company

Director

London, Basic £30k + car + bonuses

The New Globe Theatre Company is an established group which will be staging productions in major London theatres. The Director will receive an initial salary of £30,000 but can expect to progress steadily to higher rates as the size of the company increases and the scale of operations expands.

We are looking for someone with extensive experience of theatre production and management who will probably have worked in a similar capacity for at least five years in regional theatre productions.

If you wish to take the opportunity of pioneering this new and exciting venture please forward a letter of application to:

Director of Personnel
The New Globe Theatre Company
1001 The Strand
London WC2 0NG

Telephone 0207 900 1234

The assessment for this unit asks you to produce a report on how you have recruited and selected an individual for a job role. You are also assessed on your research and subsequent analysis. Consult with you tutor on the best way of presenting this information. Make sure it is all kept together in a well-structured portfolio as part of the report that you produce.

A good job advertisement, while providing prospective candidates with helpful information, also helps to deter people who do not have the required qualifications for the job.

Presentation of the advertisement is very important as it gives prospective employees a first impression of the organisation.

Job applications and curriculum vitae

We are now in a position to look at **job applications** and **interviewing**. First examine the two flow charts shown below (Figures 2.4 and 2.5) which show the selection process for a job from the employer's point of view and from the applicant's point of view.

FIGURE 2.4 *Job selection – the employer's point of view*

FIGURE 2.5 *Job selection – the applicant's point of view*

Qualifications and experience

Many jobs require that applicants should have certain qualifications which are necessary to do the job. For examples, doctors need to have completed a degree in medicine and have relevant work experience before they are allowed to practise. The same applies to other professions such as teaching, the law and accountancy, where practitioners are expected to have the relevant qualifications before they can take up jobs. It is not only in the professions where necessary qualifications are required, the same applies to many skilled jobs such as electricians and Information Technology specialists who will typically be expected to have certificates showing that they are qualified to carry out their work.

In addition to qualifications many jobs require previous experience and expertise. For example, when advertising for a job in sales and marketing a company may be seeking to recruit staff who already have experience of doing a similar job.

Sometimes applicants for jobs are expected to demonstrate their skills and expertise by doing tests which measure these skills. For example, an applicant for a teaching job may be expected to carry out a demonstration lesson in front of a class in the school where they are applying for a post.

Letters of application

The following comments relate to how you should go about writing job applications. They are equally relevant in examining what businesses are looking for when they come to choose applicants. All students who are following this course will need at some stage to produce letters of application for jobs and it is important that you get this process right. It is surprising how often there are two students who are almost identical in terms of qualifications, appearance and ability, but one is offered many interviews while the other receives only a few. Usually the difference is in the quality of their letters of application.

A letter should have a clear structure, with a beginning, a middle and an ending. It should state:

* your reasons for applying for the job
* the contribution you can make to the organisation
* how you have developed your capabilities through training and education
* the skills and knowledge you have acquired that would help you to do the job well.

The letter needs to be interesting – you are writing about (selling) yourself. It should contain just enough information to support your application form and CV (see page 71), highlighting the most relevant evidence. You will know that you are writing effective letters if they lead to interviews.

Here are some important rules to remember:

* use good English with accurate spelling – always check in a dictionary if you are unsure of the spelling of a word or use the spell-checker on your computer

Theory into practice

Write a letter of application for the job described below:

* The position: Part-time shelf filler at Strictly Food Supermarket.
* Basic duties: Filling shelves at Strictly Food Supermarket from 6 a.m. to 8 a.m. each morning.
* The company: One of the top ten companies in the UK by turnover and a leading retailer.
* Responsibilities: Shelf fillers are expected to show initiative for displaying goods in ways outlined by supervisors and by training with the company. On completion of training and satisfactory performance you may be required to provide guidance to other trainees.
* Attitudes: New employees are expected to be punctual and co-operative. Good communication skills and willingness to share ideas are desired qualities.
* The training: The initial training will introduce new employees to the values of Strictly Food Supermarket and the nature of the job. Particular attention will be given to teamwork practices and quality presentation of goods.
* Wage: £5.00 per hour rising in increments on the satisfactory completion of training and taking on responsibilities for others.

CASE STUDY

Applying for a job

The following letter was sent by an applicant for the role of trainee accountant with Great Western Trains.

21 Wade Park Avenue
Market Deeping
Peterborough
PE6 8JL

20th February 2005

Great Western Trains Finance Manager,
Room 109
East Side Offices
Bristol
BS3 9HL

Dear Sir/Madam,

I noticed in a national paper that you have a job available for a junior accountant. I am very interested in the post because I see it as presenting a good opportunity for me. I have always been very interested in rail accounts. I am also studing accounts at collage. I understand that on your accountancy training scheme there will be good opportunities for promotion. I am also studying an A2 course in Business (OCR Examinations). This is a very interesting course and I have had good reports from all my tutors on the course. As part of the course I am sing accounts. I have found the accounts to be the most exciting and interesting parts. I am also interested in train spotting.

I am working at the Anglia Co-operative Society. This is a part time post but it involves a lot of responsibility. I have to check the stock and make sure the shelves are well organized. I also have had EPOS training.

I am currently working on my cv and will send it to you next week. Many thanks for your interest in my application.

Yours Sincerly
Charles Lawson

1 What strengths and weaknesses can you spot?
2 If you were to advise Charles Lawson on how he could improve his letter what comments would you make?

High Street Retailers PLC
Application form • Strictly confidential

What job are you applying for? _____   What is your national insurance number? _____

Have you been employed by this organisation before? _____   Give dates of previous employment _____

Surname _____   First name _____

Present address_____   Post code _____

Telephone number _____   Email _____

Date of birth _____   Have you any relatives or connection by marriage already employed by this organisation? _____

Secondary education

Dates From/to	Name and address of current/last school	Examinations taken (subjects/grades/dates)	Examinations to be taken (date, subject, level)
_____	_____	_____	_____
_____	_____	_____	_____

Further education

Dates From/to	Name and address of college	Examinations taken (subjects/grades/dates)	Examinations to be taken (date, subject, level)
_____	_____	_____	_____
_____	_____	_____	_____

Have you been convicted of a criminal offence which is not legally spent? Yes/No

Work History

Please cover at least your last 5 years' employment, leaving no gaps. Include temporary and part-time posts as well as periods of unemployment.

Exact dates	Employer's name and address	Job – Title/position	Pay	Exact reason for leaving
From To	Present employer Address		Basic pay Regular bonus or commission	Is it your own choice Yes/No Current notice period
From To	Previous employer Address		Basic pay Regular bonus or commission	Was it your own choice Yes/No
From To	Previous employer Address		Basic pay Regular bonus or commission	Was it your own choice Yes/No

If you have additional information about yourself which you think would be of interest, please add it here (hobbies, interests, extra qualifications, languages) _____

Please check the information given before signing. To the best of my knowledge the information on this form is complete and correct.

Signature _____   Date _____

Referees

There is no need to complete this at this stage. If an offer of employment is being considered, you may be asked to give details of two people who have known you for at least two years who are aged not less than 18 years who would be willing to provide a personal reference if needed. Do not give the names of employees, your relatives, or your teachers.

Name _____   Address _____   Occupation _____

Name _____   Address _____   Occupation _____

FIGURE 2.6 *An example of an application form*

* use your own words rather than copying those in the advertisement

* do not try to be too clever by using long words

* keep the paragraphs short

* try not to use 'I' too much

* word-process your work

* follow the correct convention of addressing people – either 'Dear Sir/Madam' and ending with 'Yours faithfully' or 'Dear Mr Chanderpaul' and ending with 'Yours sincerely'

* keep a copy of what you have written.

Application forms

Figure 2.6 is an example of an application form for a position in a retail chain. It should give you some ideas about how you can set out your own application form.

Sending a covering letter

Here is some useful advice about how to write a covering letter and its content when you apply for a job that you have seen advertised.

1 *Put yourself in the reader's shoes.* Before you start word-processing your letter, decide on the benefit to the employer of choosing to interview you.

2 *Be clear about what your purpose is.* Always be clear about your purpose, for example, decide whether your purpose is to get a meeting or a job interview.

3 *Make sure that your first sentence grabs the attention of the reader.*

4 *Be short and clear.* Keep the letter to one side of word-processed A4. Try to use short and punchy words.

5 *Use bullet points and tabulation to make key terms stand out.*

6 *End your letter with a clear and positive request for action.* For example, 'I look forward to hearing from you and meeting you to discuss the job offer in the near future.'

7 *Use good quality A4 white paper, with a clear font.* Don't use too much bold, italics or variations in font size.

8 *Write a new letter for every application you make.* The reader needs to see that you have made an individual application for their job.

9 *Check that all the information you have included is correct.*

10 *Make sure that you sign the letter with a neat and clear signature.*

Curriculum Vitae

A **Curriculum Vitae** (usually called a CV) is a summary of your career to date. There are three stages you should follow when setting out your CV:

* assemble all the facts about yourself

* draft the CV

* edit the document several times.

Remember to keep the 4 Ss in mind:

* Simple

* Structured

* Succinct

* Significant.

At the initial stage you are trying to get together as many relevant facts as possible about your career to date. It does not matter if you put down too many to start with – make a list of all your educational, work-based and leisure achievements, as well as training activities and courses you have been on. Make brief notes about each of these as well as about projects and assignments you have been involved in.

Always use a word-processing package with an impressive, yet conservative, font and never lie. Make sure that you are truthful in the way you set out your CV – there is nothing worse than being caught out telling a lie. Divide your CV into the following areas.

Personal profile

Your personal profile includes your name, date of birth, address and telephone number and it is also an opportunity to describe yourself, your aims and objectives and to sell yourself by introducing the positive aspects of your personality.

Keep this section to no more than 10 lines. Remember, this is your chance to make your mark and get yourself noticed by a prospective employer. Any spelling mistakes in this section will be disastrous.

Education and training
As well as your qualifications from school or college, list other achievements and skills such as:

* any first-aid skills
* computer packages you are familiar with or have used
* keyboard skills – can you word-process at a reasonable speed?
* any language skills
* a driving licence, if you have one.

Remember that the key part of the CV is the career history, so the sections that go before should not be too long. For example, when dealing with training, list only the most important and relevant training courses, and then if necessary include some of the others under 'other information'.

Positions of responsibility
List positions of responsibility you have had:

* at school, for example, form captain, prefect, sports captain
* at 6th form/college, for example, 6th form Head, member of Young Enterprise
* elsewhere, for example, Treasurer of local badminton club or any other positions that show your leadership qualities.

If possible try to give examples of a situation where you may have had to make decisions, to build a team or work as a member of a team.

When you set out your responsibilities and achievements, decide whether it is necessary to put some of them under sub-headings.

Interests and activities
Employers do not expect students to put reading as an interest on their CVs as they expect students to read. Do not put down words like socialising that suggest you spend most of your spare time at the pub! Interests may include the following:

* playing an instrument, for example, piano, guitar
* hobbies, such as cookery, amateur dramatics, foreign travel, rock climbing
* an interest in the theatre/cinema
* participation in any sports, such as badminton, scuba diving, swimming, tennis and any medals or awards achieved
* membership of any clubs/societies.

Work experience and references
It is normal practice to start your career history with your most recent job and work backwards in time, because employers are usually more interested in your recent experience.

Briefly include details of any previous part-time or full-time work experience. Describe in more detail any work experience you found particularly interesting or where you were successful.

If some of your experience is of a technical nature, try to present it in a way that can be read easily by the general reader (rather than only by a specialist).

Try to use dynamic words in your CV. Here are some good examples:

Accomplished	Achieved	Conducted
Completed	Created	Decided
Delivered	Developed	Designed
Directed	Established	Expanded
Finished	Generated	Implemented
Improved	Increased	Introduced
Launched	Performed	Pioneered
Planned	Promoted	Redesigned
Reorganised	Set up	Solved
Succeeded	Trained	Widened
Won	Work	Wrote

Curriculum Vitae

Name	Prakesh Patel
Date of birth	1.3.1986
Address	50 Palmerston Road, Reading, RG31 9HL
Telephone	01604 76321
Education and training	Waingels' Copse School Reading, Sept 1998 – July 2004
Qualifications (GCSEs)	Mathematics (B)
	English (B)
	Business Studies (A)
	French (B)
	Geography (B)
	German (A)
	History (B)
	Technology (B)
	All 2004
Interests and activities	Captain of the school football team, house captain and prefect (2002–2004) Venture Scout, Gold Award Duke of Edinburgh. Member of Woodley Chess Club.
Referees	Mr I. Marks Waingels' Copse School Denmark Avenue Woodley Reading RG3 8SL Rev R. Babbage St Jude's Church Street Reading Reading RG4 7QZ

FIGURE 2.7 *An example of a CV*

2.2.3 The selection process

As soon as applications for a particular job role are received, then a business must select the best individuals available. You need to understand that a selection process can be broken down into the following stages:

* shortlisting candidates (you will not be expected to carry out this task)
* writing letters inviting candidates to interview
* preparing interview documentation, such as equal opportunities forms, interview questions, **selection criteria** and interview assessment forms
* designing tasks for interviewees to undertake
* carrying out an interview process
* post-interview taking up references and other security checks
* informing successful/unsuccessful candidates
* gaining the successful applicant's formal acceptance.

Shortlisting procedures

Shortlisting involves drawing up a list of the most suitable applicants from those that have applied for a post with an organisation. Usually a small group of people will be trusted with the task of drawing up this list. Armed with a job description, person specification and other sets of criteria, it is possible to reject candidates who do not meet the required criteria.

Think it over...

It is very important that shortlisting abides by Equal Opportunities legislation. A set of criteria is established usually by using the job description and person specification as a guide.

Theory into practice

Produce an attractively laid-out four-page booklet setting out good practice for recruiting and selecting applicants to fill posts in a specific organisation. You may want to base the work on the organisation in which you have carried out your work experience or had a part-time job. The booklet should consider:

* creating an effective person specification, and job description

* creating a job advertisement

* shortlisting

* interviewing to get the best candidates

* any other areas that you consider relevant.

Once you have developed your material you can use it to evaluate the recruitment and selection processes in different businesses. Using your own experience of being recruited and selected to work in a particular job, evaluate how the process you experienced compares with the good practice guidelines that you have drawn up.

It helps to sort into three piles:

Letters of invitation

Prior to an interview, brief letters are sent out inviting candidates for an interview. These letters set out when and where the interview will take place and any task that the candidate might need to do before the interview. If the advertised job is for an IT specialist, the interviewee might be expected to do an IT-related task to check on their IT skills as well as attending the formal interview.

Preparing interview documentation

It is usual for an interviewer to create forms for use during the interview including a list of questions that the interviewer or panel will ask. Equal Opportunities requirements state that the same questions must be asked of each of the candidates you are interviewing for the job.

A list of criteria judging the effectiveness of each candidate in terms of meeting the required job criteria may also be drawn up.

In preparing to interview other members of your group, the following documentation will be required:

* copies of the interviewees' application forms, curricula vitae, and supporting letters of application.

* copies of the person specification, the job description, and interview assessment schedules showing the criteria which the applicants will be judged against.

It may also be helpful to produce a standardised sheet for the interviewing panel to set out their comments about each of the candidates.

The interview process

Generally speaking, interviewers should try to make the interviewee feel relaxed and comfortable so that the interviewee can show his or her best side. An opening remark might be to ask the interviewee about his or her journey to the

Suitable candidates	Possible candidates	Rejects
Those that meet all or most of the relevant criteria	Those that meet some of the relevant criteria and may show some exciting characteristics that could make them worth interviewing	Those that meet very few of the criteria

Shortlisting – sorting candidates' applications into three piles

A typical job interview

Theory into practice

Create a scoresheet to be used in an interview situation. Relate the requirements to the job specification.

interview on that day: 'Where have you come from?' 'Did you find it easy to get here today?'

When there are several interviewers a starting point might be to introduce the interviewee to each of the panel in turn.

Interview questions

It is important to recognise that the interview is a two-way process and there should be opportunities for both sides to answer questions. Not only is the interviewing panel seeking to find the best candidate for the post, but also the candidate should be seeing if the job is suitable and they want to work for the company. The candidate may ask questions about training, promotion prospects and social facilities.

The interviewee is usually asked a set of predetermined questions. The questions asked should relate to the person specification and job description. The interviewer will have a copy of the candidate's application form and curriculum vitae and will normally make notes to check how each interviewee meets the job requirements. A scoresheet may be used to record these notes (see Figure 2.8). By using a scoresheet it is possible to compare candidates' responses to questions and their behaviour in the interview situation.

Interviewing requires a considerable amount of intelligence and inventiveness. It is also up to the interviewer to try and ask questions that require a detailed response. Follow-on questions are very important here. Some follow-on questions may be planned in advance, while others may need to be developed on the spur of the moment. For example, an interview for the job of a shelf-stacker in a supermarket may proceed as follows:

Interviewer: Have you had experience of shelf-stacking in a supermarket before?

Interviewee: Yes, I worked at Waitrose doing it for three months.

Interviewer: (Follow-on question). Can you tell me exactly what you were responsible for doing in your shelf-stacking job and why you left your previous job?

Post: Junior Retail Manager

Candidate's name: Linda Booth

Requirements	Score 1–5 1 = poor 5 = excellent	Notes
Tidy appearance	3	Untidy hair
Intelligence	5	Answered questions quickly and with good attention to detail
Punctuality	1	Turned up 2 minutes late for interview

FIGURE 2.8 *Part of an interviewer's scoresheet*

Without follow-on questions an interview can pass very quickly with little being found out about the true strengths (and weaknesses) of job applicants.

Interview tests

Many jobs today involve some form of **psychometric** or **aptitude testing** to find out whether individuals have the right sorts of personalities to carry out particular types of work. A psychometric test is a way of assessing an individual's personality, drives and motivations, either by means of a paper and pencil questionnaire or online test.

For example, one of the dimensions the psychometric test might draw out is an individual's willingness or ability to work in a team situation or to handle stress.

A number of organisations place a great deal of emphasis on these tests because they believe they are reliable indicators of the sociability/ personality of individuals, and that they are useful predictors of whether individuals will fit into the organisation.

Aptitude tests are used to find out whether a candidate is suited to carrying out a particular type of work and involve some form of simulation of that type of work. For example, in selecting new pilots a number of airlines will give candidates tests which involve testing their reactions to sudden movements as well as the use of flight simulators to test how quick their reactions are and how they respond to pressure.

Theory into practice

Obtain a psychometric test that is used for selection purposes. Try out the test. What does it claim to show about your personality and disposition? Do you agree?

Using body language

People do not communicate with each other just through words. They also communicate through their **body language**. An interviewer who wants to draw the best out of candidates for a job will use appropriate body language. The interviewer should be seated at the same height as the interviewee with a good frontal or open posture.

The interviewer should not cross his or her arms or make threatening gestures such as pointing a finger or banging a fist down on the table. He or she should smile and use clear eye contact.

Closing the interview

The usual way of closing an interview is that, when the interviewer or interviewing panel have finished their list of questions, they will ask the interviewee if there is anything he or she would like to ask. When this is completed the interviewer will say something like:

> *Thank you very much for coming to the interview, I hope you have a safe journey back. You will be hearing from us by...*

The interviewer will clarify the arrangements through which the interviewee will be informed of arrangements, and explain how any administrative task such as claiming for expenses should be done.

Giving feedback

Often candidates for a post will be given feedback on how they performed in the interview situation. They should be told about their strengths and weaknesses and the reasons why they were or were not chosen for the post. This feedback should be seen as a positive process concerned with the ongoing **development** of the interviewee.

Theory into practice

In groups, carry out mock interviews for a post that you are familiar with from work experience.

Preparing for an interview

There are many ways you can prepare for an interview. You can practise your answers to the questions likely to be asked, possibly with the help of a friend who takes the role of the interviewer.

You may want to try out the clothes that you will wear to the interview beforehand, perhaps by wearing them to some sort of public occasion. There is nothing worse than feeling uncomfortable in the clothes you have chosen for an interview.

Many people like to plan the route they will take to get to the interview, even doing a dummy run beforehand.

Factors	Rating					INTERVIEW ASSESSMENT Remarks
	A	B	C	D	E	
Appearance Personality Manner Health						
Intelligence Understanding of questions						
Skills Special skills Work experience						
Interests Hobbies Sports						
Academic						
Motivation						
Circumstances Mobility Hours Limitations						
OVERALL						

A = Exceptional   B = Above average   C = Satisfactory
D = Below average   E = Unsuitable

FIGURE 2.9 *An interview assessment form*

You may like to prepare yourself by thinking about the kinds of things that interviewers will be looking for in you. Figure 2.9 shows an interview assessment form which gives you some useful indications of the qualities that are looked for in many job-holders.

Interview advice

Showing confidence

It is important to appear confident but not over-confident. You should be confident in your own abilities. One of the most important attributes to have in the interview situation is enthusiasm. An enthusiastic person will tend to radiate confidence whereas candidates who appear timid will be viewed in a poor light, particularly for posts that require some degree of responsibility and initiative.

Body language

At an interview it is important for you to adopt the right body language. Look alert and eager. Look the questioner in the eye, avoid nervous movements, and try not to cross your arms in a defensive position. Try not to threaten the interviewer by pointing your finger or making violent movements. Sit up straight and try to look confident and at ease – not apathetic and too laid back.

Appropriate body language

Answering questions

When you are answering questions, do not give brief one-line answers, but try to expand on your answers so that the interviewer can see you at your best. When you are being interviewed, listen carefully to the questions that you are asked. If you do not understand a question or have not heard it clearly, it may be helpful to say, 'Please could you repeat that question?'

Asking questions

When given the opportunity ask a small number of relevant questions. Don't ask questions that simply involve the repetition of what you have already been told. If you are not sure whether you want the job or not, ask questions that will help you to make an informed choice.

Be clear and concise

Good verbal communication involves asking and answering questions in a clear and concise way.

Think it over...

It is often in the first few minutes of an interview that an interview panel make up their minds about which candidate to appoint. In addition, a recent study reported that the person who is first on the interviewer's list is three times more likely to be hired than the last name on the list. This is often the case because the interviewing panel are usually more alert and interested at the start of a busy interview schedule than at the end of the day.

Theory into practice

Study the following pictures which show three views of one of the people who turned up for an interview for a part-time shelf filler's post – in each case explain why the body language is inappropriate.

DO	DON'T
Find out about the firm before the interview	Be late
Dress smartly but comfortably	Smoke unless invited to
Speak clearly and with confidence	Chew gum or eat sweets
Look at the interviewer when speaking	Answer all questions 'yes', 'no' or 'I don't know'
Be positive about yourself	Be afraid to ask for clarification if anything is unclear
Be ready to ask questions	Say things which are obviously untrue or insincere

FIGURE 2.10 *An interview checklist*

The person who is straightforward, interesting and direct will often sway an interview in a positive way.

The checklist shown above should also be helpful in giving you some useful preparatory advice for interviews.

Interview evaluation

Aspect of performance	Rating				
	Very good	Good	Fair	Weak	Very weak
Eye contact					
Body language					
Appearing confident					
Answering questions					

FIGURE 2.11 *An evaluation form*

After an interview, all interviewers and interviewees should fill in a self-evaluation form which is an opportunity to identify any strengths and weaknesses and improve performance. The types of questions you need to ask are as follows:

* how did you feel about the interview?
* how do you consider the interview went?
* what impression do you think that you gave?
* what do you think of the interviewers'/interviewees':
  * planning and organisation?
  * preparation for the interview?
  * performance at the interview?

Evaluating recruitment and selection processes

Recruitment and selection can be a very costly process for a business. It takes a great deal of time to set up the process which includes drawing up a job description, advertising the position, sifting through applications, checking which applications best meet the criteria set down for the post, interviewing candidates and finally, selecting the best candidate for the post.

There is considerable scope along the way for waste and inefficiency. For example, when a job advertisement attracts 100 applicants there will be a considerable waste of time and resources when reducing the list down to six. If you get your procedures wrong you may eliminate some of the best candidates right from the start and end up with six who are barely satisfactory. If you end up choosing an unsuitable candidate for the job, the company will suffer from having a poorly motivated person, who may make trouble within the organisation before walking out on the job and leaving the company to go through the expense of replacing him or her yet again.

Post-interview procedures

On completion of the interviewing and selection processes, the best candidate for the post will be selected and approached by the chair of the interviewing panel to see if they will be prepared to take up the post. Often this will take place over the telephone as soon as possible after a decision has been made. If the candidate agrees to take up the post and a formal offer has been made then it becomes legally binding on both parties – referred to in law as formal acceptance. In many situations the employer may want to take up the references before the final offer is made.

Once the 'best' candidate has been contacted, then the chair of the panel can contact unsuccessful candidates informing them of the decision. At this time, the unsuccessful parties may ask and be provided with feedback about their performance in the interview and the sorts of areas that they should work on if they want to secure a similar job.

If the person chosen turns down the job offer, then the chair will quickly move on to ask the second 'best' candidate. It is very important to make an offer and have it accepted soon after the interview, because candidates for the post will quickly feel aggrieved if they are not informed about whether their application has been successful or not. The business should not create a bad impression – after all those candidates that it rejects may be customers or may want to work for the firm in the same or another capacity in the future.

2.2.4 The induction process

Induction is the process of introducing new employees to their place of work, job, new surroundings and the people they will be working with. Induction also provides information to help new employees start work and generally 'fit in'.

Once the successful applicant has been selected and offered the post, the human resources department needs to prepare a suitable induction programme for when the new employee starts work. Typical features of an induction programme include:

* an awareness of the workings and objectives of a business
* an awareness of health and safety issues
* requirements when absent, ill or late
* introduction to management and workmates
* identification of any immediate training needs.

It is important to produce an induction programme that meets the needs of the job role and the successful applicant.

The induction process will vary from company to company but it is important that you have an understanding of the sort of induction activities that you will need to design for your assignment for this unit.

To create an induction package you will need to set out:

* the objectives for the induction programme – what are you trying to achieve through it? Perhaps you could set out some outcomes for the induction – in other words what should the inductee know or be able to do at the end of the induction that they did not know or were not able to do at the start?
* a timetable for the induction. Typically this will cover the induction day/s for the new job-holder and any follow-up induction activities.
* an outline of the main induction activities which they will be involved in – e.g. health and safety induction, introduction to the company and its objectives, introduction to key employees in the organisation, team building activities etc.

The workings and objectives of a business

The general purposes of induction are:

* to make the new employee feel welcome and part of a team
* to make sure that they are aware of important issues such as company policies, their rights and entitlements at work, and above all to make sure that they are familiar with health and safety requirements
* to make sure that they can start working productively for the company as soon as possible.

During the induction therefore, new members of the organisation need to:

* find out as much about the organisation as possible, what it is like, what it does, what it is trying to achieve

* find out about where they fit into the organisation, what they will be expected to do and how they will be expected to work

* be motivated and inspired to feel that they have chosen to work for a company that will help them to flourish and develop themselves

* find out about their rights and responsibilities.

Contents of an induction pack

Useful criteria therefore for judging how well you have designed your induction programme is the extent to which – if you were starting work at that company yourself – you would feel that the induction had introduced you to all of the things you need to know and be able to do to start working effectively for the company.

Induction should also consider the initial training needs either on joining a new organisation or on taking on a new function

CASE STUDY

Induction at a financial services company

When Joe started working for a financial services company in Nottingham he had the following induction.

* On the first day, he had a series of talks from important people in the company, including the managing director, the personnel manager and a briefing about health and safety at work from the safety officer. He was given some packs of information and details of how he would be paid, and his various rights in the workplace.

* The second day was spent on team-building exercises with other new recruits at work.

* The rest of the week was spent on IT training.

* The following week Joe worked alongside an experienced employee in the section he was due to work in.

* In the third week Joe started to work independently.

1 What do you think of the structure of Joe's induction programme?

2 How does Joe's induction programme compare with your own work experience or the induction programme you had when you first came to college?

within it. It should also deal with the structure, culture and activities in the organisation. The new recruit will typically be given an induction pack that introduces him or her to the organisation.

Health and safety

Health and safety is the most essential part of any induction programme. Businesses must ensure the health and safety of their employees and the wider public that comes into contact with the business at all times.

Individuals cannot start work until a proper risk assessment has been carried out of the activities that they will be involved in. This is just as true for work experience as for actual full-time work processes.

All places of work must have a written health and safety policy and it is the responsibility of the safety officer and the directors of a company to ensure safe working practices. Failure to produce a safety policy by a company can lead to extensive fines and up to two years' imprisonment for company officials.

In researching health and safety issues you may be able to examine the way in which your school or college inducts new staff, for example, Administrators in health and safety deal with issues related to using computer equipment (to avoid repetitive strain problems) or staff who deal with harmful substances such as spent computer cartridges, fire drills etc.

Health and Safety at Work Act 1974

The main points of the Health and Safety at Work Act are as follows:

It shall be the duty of every employer to ensure, so far as is reasonably practicable, the health, safety and welfare at work of all his or her employees.

The employer has a duty to ensure:

1   The provision and maintenance of plant and systems of work that are, so far as is reasonably practicable, safe and without risks to health.

2   Arrangements for ensuring, so far as is reasonably practicable, safety and absence

of risks to health in connection with the use, handling storage and transport of articles and substances.

3 The provision of such information, instruction, training and supervision as is necessary to ensure, so far as is reasonably practicable, the health and safety at work of his of her employees.

4 Safe means of access to and from work.

The Act also places a responsibility on employees. The employees' duty is to take reasonable care to ensure both their own safety and the safety of others who may be affected by what they do or do not do.

Other Health and Safety Regulations include:

Reporting of Injuries, Diseases and Dangerous Occurrence Regulations

These regulations state that injuries that result from accidents at work where an employee is incapacitated for three or more days must be reported to the authorities within seven days. Injuries involving deaths must be reported immediately.

Control of Substances Hazardous to Health (COSHH) regulations

Employers must carry out assessment of work tasks that are likely to create risks for the health and safety of employees. Employees should then be given the necessary training for dealing with these substances.

European Union Regulations

In addition there are a number of European Union Regulations such as those relating to noise at work. Employees must be given appropriate training e.g. in the use of ear protectors when they are exposed to potentially harmful noise.

Requirements when absent, ill or late

As part of the induction process it is important for trainers to make sure that employees are aware of procedures involved in employees reporting any difficulties which they may be having which may lead to them being absent or late for work.

The human resources department is responsible for planning labour budgets (i.e. making sure that they have enough people available to do the tasks required). Absences can lead to problems for the whole team, and adversely affect production in a company. HR will therefore create procedures.

For example, a well-known retailing organisation requires all employees to report to their supervisor at least one hour in advance of a morning shift that they will be absent. They will then need to produce a written note explaining their absence. If they are absent from work more than twice in any given month they will need to have a meeting with their supervisor to explain the cause of the absence.

Similarly if employees are going to be late they must inform their supervisor when they are likely to arrive so that cover can be provided.

In the case of illness, employees will be asked to provide a note explaining the nature of their illness. Should they be away for more than five days they will require a doctor's certificate, because their absence will affect their entitlement to sickness benefits (from the government).

Immediate training needs

As part of the induction process, new employees may be introduced to new processes or software that they are unfamiliar with. The employer should explain each of these processes to new employees, question them about their experience with the processes or software and listen carefully to their answers to gauge their level of experience. For example, an employee may be familiar with the Microsoft Office software package but may not have had extensive experience with spreadsheets. If this is a requirement of the role, then careful questioning will determine the skill level of the employee and the training required to enable them to do their job. Training may be carried out formally through a course or more informally by a colleague or with training manuals. Identifying immediate training needs and implementing training in a timely manner is important to ensure the new employees are equipped with the skills to properly carry out their duties.

2.2.5 Employee motivation

A business needs to motivate its workforce if it is to retain them and remain competitive. You need to understand some of the methods that are commonly employed. These include:

* financial incentives such as:
    * wages, salaries and bonuses
    * profit sharing
    * share options

* non-financial incentives such as:
    * goal setting
    * perks and status symbols
    * **appraisal**
    * meeting training needs.

Pay and financial incentives

From a management view a payment system should:

* be effective in recruiting the right quantity and quality of labour

* be effective in retaining labour over the required period of time – it is expensive to have to keep advertising for and training new employees

* keep labour costs as low as possible in order to maintain the competitiveness of a business

* help to motivate staff and encourage effort (careful thought needs to be applied to

structuring pay systems in a way that encourages motivation and performance)

* be designed to allow for additional rewards and benefits.

The sum paid for a normal working week is termed a basic wage or salary. Many employees receive other benefits in addition to their basic wage, either in a money or non-money form. The main ways of calculating pay are outlined below. Sometimes elements of these methods are combined.

Flat rate

This is a set rate of weekly or monthly pay, based on a set number of hours. It is easy to calculate and administer but does not provide an incentive to employees to work harder.

Time rate

Under this scheme, workers receive a set rate per hour. Any hours worked above a set number are paid at an 'overtime rate'.

Piece rate

This system is sometimes used in the textile and electronics industries, among others. Payment is made for each item produced that meets given quality standards. The advantage of this is that it encourages effort. However, it is not suitable for jobs that require time and care. Also, many jobs particularly in the service sector produce 'outputs' that are impossible to measure.

Bonus

A bonus is paid as an added encouragement to employees. It can be paid out of additional profits earned by the employer as a result of the employee's effort and hard work or as an incentive to workers at times when they might be inclined to slacken effort, for example at Christmas and summer holiday times.

Commission

Commission is a payment made as a percentage of the sales a salesperson has made.

Output-related payment schemes

Output-related schemes are the most common method used to reward manual workers. Most

CASE STUDY

The best companies to work for

In March, 2005, *The Sunday Times* carried out a survey of the best 100 companies to work for in this country. Aspects of good companies that they identified included:

Holidays	Companies offering a minimum of 25 days' annual leave to all employees – 45 of the top 100 companies.
Maternity	Companies offering at least 10 weeks on full pay during the first period of maternity leave (compared with the statutory minimum of six) – 19 out of the top 100.
Childcare	Companies that provide a workplace crèche or nursery and / or vouchers or cash to contribute towards childcare costs – 47 out of the top 100.
Women	Companies where at least 33% of the senior managers are women – 31 out of the top 100.
Long service	Companies where at least 40% of the staff have worked there for more than five years – 33 out of the top 100.
Pensions	Companies offering a final salary pension scheme, non-contributory scheme or one in which the employer contributes at least double the amount contributed by the employee – 49 out of the top 100.
Health insurance	Companies offering private health insurance for all employees, their spouses and dependants – 16 out of the top 100.
Gym	Companies offering either an on-site gym or subsidised membership of a nearby gym – 70 out of the top 100.
Shares	Companies where employees are offered share options – 33 out of the top 100.
Charitable activities	Companies where at least 10% of staff are known to undertake charitable activities – 30 out of the top 100.

Source: *The Sunday Times*, 6 March 2005

The top 10 large companies using these and other criteria were:

1 Nationwide (financial services)
2 ASDA (supermarkets)
3 KPMG (auditing and tax services)
4 The Carphone Warehouse (mobile telecoms retailer)
5 Mothercare (retailer)
6 Cadbury Schweppes (food and drink manufacturer)
7 Compass Group (catering)
8 Pfizer (pharmaceuticals)
9 Severn Trent Water (utility company)
10 WS Atkins (engineering consultancy)

1 Carry out some research of your own into a medium to large company that a family member or friend works for. Does the company give 25 or more days of holiday a year? Does it provide a workplace crèche or similar facility? What percentage of senior managers are women? What percentage of the staff has worked in the company for five years or more? Does the company provide an on-site gym or subsidise employees' gym membership?

2 What do you see as being the most important ingredients of a 'good company to work for'?

schemes involve an element of time-rates plus a bonus or other incentive. Standards are set in many ways, varying from casual assessment to a detailed work study, based on method study and work measurement (see Key terms above).

A standard allowable time is set according to the two stages. The worker's pay is then determined according to the success of the third stage.

Performance-related pay

In recent years, the emphasis in a number of organisations has shifted towards performance-related pay. Performance is assessed against working objectives and 'company goals'. Scoring systems are then worked out to assess

The police force have adopted performance-related pay

performance against objectives, and these distinguish levels of attainment, e.g. high, medium or low.

Managerial jobs are most affected by performance-related pay. Based on **performance appraisal** techniques, such schemes have been adopted in a wide range of occupations, including the police force, universities, insurance and banking. Evidence indicates that up to three-quarters of all employers are now using some form of performance appraisal to set pay levels.

One way of rewarding performance is to give a bonus if certain targets are met. Another is to give increments as targets are met, with the employee progressing up an incremental ladder each year.

Profit sharing

Profit sharing is an incentive tool which involves giving profit related pay to employees or giving them bonuses based on the profit performance of a business. Using this approach, employees are able to see that the success of the company will also lead to personal rewards for them.

Share options

Employees may be encouraged to take up shares in a company, often as part of a rewards scheme. When employees take up these share options they are then rewarded according to the performance of the business. When the business does well so too does the value of their shares and the dividends they receive as a return to shareholders. Dividends are typically paid twice yearly.

Fringe benefits

In addition to financial rewards, fringe benefits may be provided including:

* pension schemes
* subsidised meals or canteen services
* educational courses
* opportunities for foreign travel
* holiday entitlements
* crèches
* assistance with housing and relocation packages
* discount and company purchase plans (i.e. cheap purchases of company products)
* telephone costs
* discounts on insurance costs
* private healthcare, dental treatment, etc
* time off (sabbatical)
* sports, leisure and social facilities.

Theory into practice

The wages department of a large manufacturing organisation is deciding on the most appropriate payment systems in the following situations. What advice would you give them?

They want to provide a financial reward system for:

* sales people that rewards them according to the number of sales they make

* production line staff that encourages them to be careful in their work

* production line staff that discourages them from slacking off just before the Christmas period.

Non-financial incentives

Some of the fringe benefits listed above, e.g. a crèche on site or a company pension scheme, are non-financial incentives which may improve employee performance and help to create long-term commitment to the company.

Non-financial incentives can also include motivational factors such as goal setting, appraisals, work conditions and internal promotion.

Conditions of work

When you start work, an important motivational factor is the conditions in the workplace, for example the physical environment:

* are you working in a bright, clean and well-lit environment?
* is the temperature suitable for work (not too hot or too cold)?
* is the workplace safe?

The other important aspect is the 'culture' of the organisation. It is important to understand the term culture as it is applied in a business sense because it is such an important ingredient of motivation. We use the term culture to describe the typical way of working in an organisation – sometimes referred to as 'the way we do things around here'. A positive culture is one which encourages people to contribute and makes them feel valued. In contrast, a negative culture is one where people feel that they are not valued and often where they feel they are being criticised. The culture relates to the relationships and typical ways of interacting and doing things in the organisation. Different types of organisations have different cultures:

Favourable cultures	Unfavourable cultures
Warm and welcoming	Unfriendly
Encouraging	Discouraging and based on fear
Welcomes initiative	Have to do what you are told

Theory into practice

Identify one organisation which you have been a part of that had a favourable culture and another that had an unfavourable culture. Make a list of the key differences and discuss these with your class group.

Internal promotion

Promoting people within an organisation (internally) is another good motivating tool, because employees can see that they can develop themselves within the organisation.

Did you know that from the 1970s right through to the 1990s when Liverpool Football Club was so successful, many of its managers were former backroom staff. This encouraged the backroom staff to be loyal to the club with excellent results.

An appraisal in progress

Goal setting

Establishing goals for employees to work towards can be an important motivational factor as the achievement of these goals then creates a sense of achievement and personal fulfilment. Goals can be established for an individual, team or for the whole organisation and achievement may be related to promotion at work.

Perks and status symbols

Perks and status symbols are useful motivational tools in a company. A perk is something extra that you get for doing a particular job. For example, employees of a railway company may get free rail travel for them and their families. A cinema employee may get free cinema tickets.

Status symbols are also important motivators. An obvious status symbol is having a bigger office, or having a sign outside your door with your name on. People often respond very favourably to status symbols because these mark them out as being special.

Appraisal

Most organisations today operate some form of staff appraisal or staff development scheme. Appraisals are a form of goal setting. Appraisals are usually conducted by a line manager or in some cases by someone at the same level in an organisation (peer appraisal). The individual being appraised (the appraisee) and the appraisor will sit down together to establish targets to work to in the coming period. These targets will normally be based on a review of performance in a previous period, and targets for the organisation or team as a whole. Appraisal interviews are carried out on a regular basis and provide an opportunity for the appraisee to communicate his or her needs and requirements. The line manager can also clarify the needs of the organisation.

Appraisal is often related to performance-related pay. Appraisal also provides a good opportunity to establish training and development needs.

Key terms

Training refers to ways of improving the skills and knowledge of individuals so that they can help an organisation to meet its goals.

Development relates to the personal needs of an individual – e.g. to develop new skills, to do more fulfilling work, to take up opportunities for more education and training etc.

Performance appraisal

Key terms

Performance appraisal is a process of evaluating performance systematically and of providing feedback on which performance adjustments can be made. Performance appraisal works on the basis of the following equation:

Desired performance – Actual performance = Need for action.

The major purposes of performance appraisal are to:

* define the specific job criteria against which performance will be measured

* measure past job performance accurately

* justify the rewards given to individuals and/or groups, thereby discriminating between high and low performance

* define the experiences that an individual employee will need for his or her ongoing

development. These development experiences should improve job performance and prepare the employee for future responsibilities.

Stages of staff appraisal

Common stages of staff appraisal are as follows:

1 The line manager meets with the job-holder to discuss what is expected. The agreed expectations may be expressed in terms of targets, performance standards or required job behaviours – attributes, skills and attitudes.

2 The outcome of the meeting is recorded and usually signed by both parties.

3 The job-holder performs the job for a period of six months or a year.

4 At the end of the period, the job-holder and line manager or team leader meet again to review and discuss progress made. They draw up new action plans to deal with identified problems and agree targets and standards for the next period.

Think it over...

The process of 360° appraisal involves appraising an individual from above by a line manager, from the sides by work colleagues at the same level in an organisation and from below by people that the individual supervises or is in charge of.

Meeting training needs

Mentoring

Mentoring and coaching are seen by many organisations as essential ways of motivating employees so that they feel valued and cared for in their work.

Mentoring involves a trainee being 'paired' with a more experienced employee. The trainee carries out the job but uses the 'mentor' to discuss problems that may occur and how best to solve them.

This approach is used in many lines of work. For example, it is common practice for trainee teachers to work with a mentor who is responsible for their early training and development. The student teacher will watch the mentor teach before starting his or her own teaching. The mentor will then give ongoing guidance to the student teacher on how best to improve his or her performance. If the student teacher has any problems or difficulties he or she can talk to the mentor for advice.

Coaching

Coaching involves providing individuals with personal coaches in the workplace. The person who is going to take on the coaching role will need to develop coaching skills and will also need to have the time slots for the coaching to take place. The coach and the individual being coached will need to identify development opportunities that they can work on together – ways of tackling jobs, ways of improving performance, etc. The coach will provide continuous feedback on performance and how this is progressing.

Of course, coaching does not just benefit the person being coached; it also aids the coach's own personal development. It is particularly important in a coaching system that:

* the coach wants to coach the person and has the necessary coaching skills

* the person being coached wants to be coached and has the necessary listening and learning skills

* sufficient time is given to the coaching process

* the organisation places sufficient value on the coaching process.

Some of the best sports people in this country have improved their skills and abilities by working closely with a coach they respect.

A coach can be invaluable to a sports person

Having your training needs met in an organisation is also an important motivator. People who do not have their training needs met are not fully able to develop themselves and may be held back in seeking the promotion they would like. Intelligent organisations therefore carry out a **Training needs analysis** to find out the training needs of their employees so that these needs can be met.

Motivational theories

As we have seen, motivating people at work can be achieved through a combination of financial and non-financial rewards. Motivational theorists such as Maslow, Herzberg and McGregor show that true motivation can rarely be achieved through financial packages alone. They show that non-financial motivators are essential – such as creating an exciting work environment, and providing opportunities for individuals to develop themselves and to enjoy contributing to decision-making in the workplace.

Maslow

Maslow identified a hierarchy of needs split into five broad categories. He suggested that it is possible to develop a hierarchical picture of needs, split into the following:

Basic needs are for reasonable standards of food, shelter and clothing and those other items that are considered the norm to meet the needs of the body and for physical survival. This base level of need will be attained at work from receiving a basic wage packet that helps the employee to survive, for example by receiving the minimum wage.

Security needs are also concerned with physical survival. In the workplace, these needs could include safety, security of employment, adequate rest periods, pension, health schemes and protection from unfair treatment.

Group needs are concerned with an individual's need for love and affection (within a group). In groups there are always some people who are strong enough and happy to keep apart. However, the majority of people want to feel that they belong to a group. In small and medium-sized organisations (up to 200 people) it is relatively easy to give each member of the group a feeling of belonging. However, in large organisations individuals can lose their group identify, becoming just another number, a face in the crowd. Managers therefore need to think about how they can organise their people into teams so as to meet group needs.

Self-esteem needs are based on an individual's desire for self-respect and the respect of others. Employees have a need to be recognised as individuals of some importance, to receive praise for their work and to have their efforts noticed and rewarded.

Maslow placed *self-fulfilment* at the top of the hierarchy of needs. Self-fulfilment is concerned with full personal development and individual creativity. In order to meet this need, it is important for individuals to be able to use their talents and abilities fully.

Maslow argued that individuals firstly have to have their lower-level needs met, but if they are not to experience frustration it is also important for their higher-level needs to be met. Frustrated employees are likely either to develop a 'couldn't care less approach' or to become antagonistic to working life. If employees are to become committed to work these higher-level needs must be met.

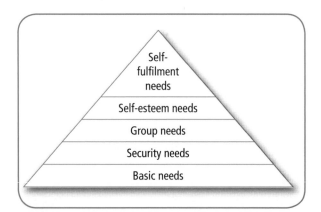

FIGURE 2.12 *Maslow's hierarchy of needs*

Think it over...

The Chinese philosopher Confucius said that 'The person that finds a job they like never does a day's work in their life.'

Which of Maslow's needs do you think the following scenarios are looking to satisfy at work? How might managers go about seeking to meet these needs?

1 Simon is working part time in a supermarket to save up enough money to go back to university with. He is prepared to work long hours, providing his total pay is good. He is not interested in taking on responsibilities, but wants to work in a safe environment.

2 Pritesh is a graphic designer who recently graduated from art college. Ideally he would like to do something which allows him to express his artistic talent. He feels that his current job working in an advertising agency does not allow him to express himself. He works in a junior role in the company copying work that has been created by senior designers.

3 Gillian has recently been promoted to the post of supervisor in the food processing plant where she works. This has meant a rise in salary enabling her to take out a mortgage to buy a house and put down a deposit on a new car. The supervisor post gives her the status she desires and she likes her working environment and the relationship she has with colleagues.

Herzberg

Herzberg carried out research on 200 engineers to find out what motivated them at work. He made a distinction between things that *move* people, which he referred to as KITA (kick in the ass), and factors that *motivate* people.

He argued that if he kicked his dog, this would get the dog to move (out of fear), but it would not motivate the animal. When we are motivated we do something because we want to do it. In other words it provides an intrinsic (internal) reward.

Herzberg identified nine factors which he referred to as 'dissatisfiers' and when these factors reached a certain level they would cause employee absenteeism, poor levels of output, resistance to change, obstruction, and other negative actions.

The '*dissatisfiers*' are:

* dominating or unpredictable company policy and administration
* low pay
* poor working conditions
* confrontational relationships between different levels in the organisation
* unfriendly relationships within the chain of command
* unfair management and supervision
* unfair treatment of employees
* feelings of inadequacy
* impossibility for development of the individual.

By reducing these dissatisfiers you can reduce negative feelings but they are not the real motivating drives.

In contrast, Herzberg identified five motivating factors which relate to the content of jobs. He called these '*satisfiers*'.

They are:

* recognition of effort and performance
* the nature of the job itself – does it provide the employees with appropriate challenges?
* sense of achievement
* assumption of responsibility
* opportunity for promotion.

Herzberg suggested that jobs could be given more meaning if they included elements of responsibility and a more creative use of individuals' ability, as well as opportunities to achieve.

From your own experience of working life, identify situations in which you felt highly motivated. How did these motivating factors relate to Herzberg's satisfiers?

Douglas McGregor

McGregor divided managers into two main types – theory X and theory Y.

Theory X managers tend to have the view that:

* the average person naturally dislikes work and so will avoid it when possible so management needs to encourage high levels of production by incentive schemes to encourage effort

* because people naturally dislike work, people need to be pushed, threatened and driven to get things done

* the average person likes to be told what to do and to avoid responsibility, they have little ambition, and therefore require 'managing'.

Theory Y managers have a contrasting view and believe in trusting employees to take on responsibilities. Theory Y managers have the view that:

* work is a natural activity which people can enjoy and it is up to the manager to create the right conditions in which work is enjoyable

* external control is not the only way to manage people as employees who identify with the organisation's objectives will be motivated to work hard

* the most significant reward that will motivate people is self-fulfilment (see Maslow) so managers need to identify opportunities for employees to fulfil themselves while working to meet company objectives

* the average human being learns, when given the opportunity, to accept and to seek responsibility

* many people can contribute to a business's objectives when given the chance

* people's potential is rarely achieved in the workplace.

McGregor saw the potential to make organisations far more effective by unleashing the people who work for them.

Rosabeth Moss Kanter

Moss Kanter

Rosabeth Moss Kanter argues that we can **empower** people by giving them greater responsibility in the organisation. Empowerment involves passing power and responsibility down in the organisation, so that good ideas can bubble up to the surface from below. Empowered individuals enable an organisation to be more successful by coming up with lots of good ideas. In turn, empowered people are motivated people.

Theory into practice

Study one organisation to find out about how it motivates its people. This can be done by:

1 Using your own work experience.

2 Interviewing a human resources manager.

3 Looking at the human resources section of a company website.

Think it over…

Employees at Rank Xerox are allowed to reward each other. Under a scheme called you deserve an X today any employee can give an X certificate to another employee. The X certificate is worth up to 50 dollars and is given for 'excellent support, excellent attendance, extra work or excellent co-operation'.

2.2.6 The legal dimension

There are a number of legal and ethical requirements which businesses must meet when obtaining employees to work for them. These laws seek to prevent **discrimination** in areas such as the recruitment and selection of staff. The European Union Equal Treatment Directive now makes it unlawful to discriminate on grounds of sexual orientation and religion or other belief. By 2006, age discrimination will also be unlawful.

The Sex Discrimination Act (1975 and 1986)

These acts were introduced to encourage equal treatment of people and respect for people in the workplace. The Sex Discrimination Act 1975 sets out rights for both men and women. This act was amended in 1986 to make it unlawful to discriminate on grounds of sex in employment, education, advertising or when providing goods, facilities, services and premises.

Unlawful discrimination means giving less favourable treatment to someone because of their sex or because they are married or single, and can be either direct or indirect. *Direct sex discrimination* means being treated less favourably than a person of the opposite sex would be treated in similar circumstances, for example, a policy to appoint only men to management levels. Direct marriage discrimination means being treated less favourably than an unmarried person of the same sex.

Indirect sex discrimination means being unable to comply with a requirement which, on the face of it, applies equally to both men and women, but which in practice can be met by a much smaller proportion of one sex. For example, an organisation may be indirectly discriminating against women if access to certain jobs is restricted to particular grades which in practice are held only by men.

Individuals have the right of access to civil courts and employment tribunals for legal remedies for unlawful discrimination under the Sex Discrimination Act.

Race Relations Act (1976 and 2000)

The Race Relations Act (1976 and 2000) makes it unlawful to discriminate against a person, directly or indirectly, in the field of employment, training and related matters on the basis of race, colour or national origin.

Direct discrimination means treating a person, on racial grounds, less favourably than other people are treated or would be treated in the same or similar circumstances. Segregating a person from others on racial grounds constitutes less favourable treatment.

Indirect discrimination consists of applying a provision, requirement or practice which, although applied equally to persons of all racial groups, is such that a considerably smaller proportion of a particular racial group can comply with it. Examples are:

✱ a rule about clothing or uniforms which disproportionately disadvantages a racial group and cannot be justified

✱ an employer who requires higher language standards than are needed for safe and effective performance of the job.

Disability Discrimination Act (1995 and 2004)

The Disability Discrimination Act (1995 and 2004) applies to people who are defined as disabled:

A disabled person is someone who has a physical or mental impairment, which has an effect on his or her ability to carry out normal day-to-day activities. That effect must be:

✱ *substantial (that is more than minor or trivial)*

✱ *long-term (that is, has lasted or is likely to last for at least 12 months or for the rest of the life of the person affected)*

✱ *adverse.*

Employers must cater for the needs of disabled employees by providing access to buildings as well as free movement around buildings and by providing training and development opportunities where appropriate. Employers

Which of the following would be inappropriate questions for an interviewer to ask in an interview from an equal opportunities angle?

'Mrs Young, I see you are married. Do you intend to start a family soon?'

'What will happen when your children are ill or on school holidays? Who will look after them?'

'Your hair is very long, Mr Lang. If offered the job are you prepared to have it cut?'

'Mr Benjamin, as you are 55 do you think it's worth us employing you?'

'Miss Kiali, as a woman do you think you are capable of doing the job?

'Do you think your disability will affect your performance in the job?'

'How do you feel about working with people from a different ethnic background from yourself?'

'As a man, Mr Lazerus, you will be working in a department consisting mainly of women. Are you easily distracted?'

'Miss Gladstone, don't you think your skirt is rather short?'

must not discriminate against the disabled by limiting recruitment and selection opportunities in situations where disability does not impair an individual's ability to carry out work satisfactorily.

Ethics

In addition to the bare essentials of legal requirements outlined above, organisations need to consider the ethical side of their recruitment and selection policies. **Ethics** is about doing the right thing consistently rather than compromising sometimes. What this means in effect is that good employers will go beyond the letter of the law to provide excellent opportunities for all their employees.

2.2.7 Research

There are two main kinds of research: primary and secondary. You need to do both primary

and secondary research in order to produce an appropriate report for your unit assessment.

Primary research

Primary research involves finding out information by carrying out your own research rather than using someone else's existing research information.

The sorts of primary research that you will carry out will include the following:

* face-to-face discussions
* questionnaires
* interviews.

Face-to-face discussions

Face-to-face discussions are a direct way of finding out relevant information. For the purposes of your unit assessment, you should hold a discussion with a person from a human resource department. Discuss the following areas:

* a description of typical recruitment, selection, induction and motivation procedures
* typical paperwork which is used to support these processes (ask for examples)
* the importance of relevant legislation in determining how these processes should be carried out.

Discussing these processes first hand will give you a good insight into the running of this department. Important things to find out are:

* how is job analysis, specification and description carried out?
* what are the essential ingredients of a good job advertisement?
* what sort of criteria are used in the selection process?
* how can equal opportunities be assured in these processes?
* what sorts of characteristics is the company looking for in successful applicants?
* what are the key processes that you can learn from in order to inform your own work on recruitment and selection as well as induction and motivation?

Recruitment

How many new employees do you need to recruit each year?

Which of the following media do you use for advertising jobs?
- word of mouth
- job centres
- local newspapers
- national newspapers
- company websites
- specialist magazines and journals
- other (please state)

What are the main items that go into a job advertisement that you place in a newspaper e.g. title of job, location of job etc.?

Selection

Which of the following are most important in setting out criteria for selecting new employees?
- job description
- job analysis
- person specification
- job advertisement
- other (please state)

In the selection process are all candidates given the same set of questions to answer, or does this vary with the person being interviewed?

What other steps do you take to ensure equal opportunities in the selection process?

Induction

How long is the typical initial period / course for new employees?

What are the main ingredients of your initial induction course for new employees? Please list up to eight main ingredients.

What steps do you take to evaluate the effectiveness of your induction programmes?

Motivation

Does your company place more emphasis on financial or non-financial rewards to motivate employees? Please explain. Who is involved in the appraisal process for your employees? How often does appraisal take place?

FIGURE 2.13 *Example questions to ask a human resources department*

Questionnaires

Well-constructed questionnaires are an important way to find out information first hand. Working in a group, you may want to create a questionnaire to be used on a human resource department of one or more local companies:

* break down the questionnaire into relevant headings, e.g. recruitment, selection, induction and motivation

* create questions which are unambiguous and clear

* try to create questions that don't take too long to answer

* make sure that the answers to the questions are helpful to you in writing up your assignment report.

The table opposite gives examples of questions which could be included in your questionnaire.

The exemplar questions shown are only illustrative and you will probably be able to improve on them. You should note that some of the questions are closed while others are more open ended. For open-ended questions you should leave an appropriate amount of space for the person answering the questions.

The interview process

In carrying out the assignment for this piece of work, one of the most important pieces of primary research is the actual interview process. Your tutor will either allow you to choose a job role (manager, supervisor, IT specialist, customer-service worker or administrator) or will assign you one of these roles that you have to prepare documentation for a selection interview.

Preparing the paper work for the interview (job descriptions, advertisements, interview assessment checklists etc), and then conducting the interview will provide you with a lot of useful primary information and evidence to put in your report as follows:

* the paperwork that you created (e.g. job specifications, job descriptions, advertisements, application forms etc)

* A description of the process of recruitment, and selection. Set out in detail:
  * how the interviews were constructed
  * what happened in the interviews
  * what you were looking for in the successful candidate
  * why a particular candidate was chosen.
* A description of the induction and motivational activities that you have designed for the successful job applicant.

Secondary research

Carrying out secondary research involves using existing published sources. You can gather a lot of secondary research information that will be helpful in your assignment from the human resource departments of existing local companies. It always pays to have contacts, and perhaps your teacher can arrange for a group of students to interview someone from a local company (human resource manager) who will be willing to provide you with the relevant documentation.

Examples of material you might like to gather include:

Job advertisements used in the local business which are similar to those you are researching for your project e.g. manager, supervisor, IT specialist, administrator or customer-service employee.
A job analysis for one of these posts
A job specification
A job description
A job application form
A list of questions typically used at interviews
A set of criteria for selecting successful candidates
Any supplementary material setting out job selection procedures
Copies of induction materials used by the company
A programme for an induction activity
Details of financial rewards offered by the company
Details of non-financial rewards offered by the company

FIGURE 2.14 *Example documents and details worth collecting*

2.2.8 How to judge effectiveness

An important part of any report is an evaluation of the effectiveness of processes, procedures and actions that have been taken. You will therefore need to evaluate the effectiveness of the recruitment, selection, induction and motivational activities that you have prepared.

The assignment for this module asks you to assist in the recruitment and selection of an individual for a particular job role. You need to produce a report and supporting documentation of how you do this including a range of documents that you produce for the recruitment and selection process.

The tables in Figure 2.15 and Figure 2.16 will help you to evaluate the effectiveness of various documents that you produce for this purpose. By evaluating documents that are produced by organisations that you research during the module, and draft documents that you and classmates produce, you will be best placed to create effective documents to support your assignment work.

The issues that you need to consider include the following areas:

* Was the human-resource documentation fit for the purpose and likely to produce the desired end result?
* Did your procedures fit the legal framework within which human-resource activity is expected to take place?
* Was your research wide-ranging enough to inform the development and construction of your report? You were asked to carry out a range of both primary and secondary research to help you carry out your report. To what extent have you researched widely? Use the table in Figure 2.16 to record your results.
* Are there are any aspects of your chosen approaches that you would change if the activity were repeated or a different job role were chosen?

Was the job advertisement that you created attractive and informative? Perhaps you can create a short evaluation sheet to see what the people who applied for the job thought of the advertisement.	
Was the job description clear? Was it useful to job applicants in helping them to choose whether to apply for the job?	
Was the person specification clear? Did it cover the requirements of the job? How useful was it in enabling you to create a set of appropriate questions to ask at the interview?	
Was the job application form well structured? Was there enough room / space for the candidates to fill in the appropriate sections? Were there any important omissions that could have helped in choosing the best candidates to interview?	
Were there clear criteria for selecting the best candidates from the interview process?	
If you set tasks for the interviewees to do on the day, were they appropriate?	
How effectively was the interviewing carried out? Consider issues such as time given to each candidate, opportunity for candidates to ask questions, whether each candidate was given a fair opportunity to present their strengths and what they could offer the business etc.	
How effective were the materials provided for the induction activities for the selected candidate?	
How effective was the motivational package?	

FIGURE 2.15 *Evaluating the documents and activities you created*

Primary Research	
Have you carried out effective face-to-face discussions with a speaker from a human resources department? Did you make clear and relevant notes on these discussions?	
Have you constructed effective questionnaires for the human resources department of a local business? Have you used the results of the questionnaire to provide useful information for your report?	
Have you interviewed the group members who applied for the job role that was assigned to your group? Have you also found out what these group members thought about the quality of the paperwork provided, the interviewing process, and the equal opportunities aspects?	
Secondary Research	
Have you made good use of information available from an existing business such as human resource documentation?	

FIGURE 2.16 *Evaluating your research*

KNOWLEDGE CHECK

1 Explain how the responsibilities of a manager's role might differ from those of a supervisor. Give at least five examples to illustrate your answer.

2 Describe five major features that you would expect to find in a job description. What purposes are job descriptions likely to be used for?

3 How might a well-constructed person specification help with the recruitment process?

4 What suggestions would you make to someone filling in a job application which would help them to secure an interview for a post as a trainee market researcher?

5 What do you see as being the essential characteristics of a powerful CV (curriculum vitae)?

6 How does the creation of a shortlist help an organisation to select the best candidates for a particular interview?

7 Outline what you consider to be the most important aspects of positive body language that can be employed by an interviewer in the selection process.

8 What is a psychometric test? What is it used for?

9 Ramesh Pancholi is starting work in the Information Technology support department of a major retailing organisation. Describe five aspects of an induction programme for Ramesh which you regard to be essential. In each case describe the outcomes that you would expect Ramesh to achieve from that aspect of induction.

10 How might being attached to a coach help Ramesh to quickly build up appropriate skills required in the organisation? How will good coaching improve motivation?

11 Who or what is a mentor? What are the advantages to a) an employee, and b) an organisation from operating a mentoring scheme?

12 Describe a payment method that you think would motivate employees carrying out routine production work. Contrast this with a payment scheme that you feel would be a more effective motivator for a different type of worker.

13 How can payment schemes be complemented with non-financial incentives to increase motivation at work?

14 What do you understand by the term 'performance-related pay'? What do you see as being the benefits and drawbacks of operating such a scheme?

15 If you were going to introduce an appraisal scheme to a business or organisation that you are familiar with, what would be the key ingredients of the scheme? Justify your selection of different ingredients.

16 Give examples to show how individuals have basic needs, security needs, group needs, self-esteem needs, and self-fulfilment needs. Show how these needs could be met in a particular work setting.

17 Why do you think that Herzberg argued that what he termed 'dissatisfiers' could cause employee absenteeism, poor levels of output and other negative aspects of work behaviour? What did he see as the way of truly motivating employees?

18 How could you persuade candidates who are being interviewed for a particular post that your organisation will provide them with the sort of fulfilling work activities that will help to motivate them in the longer period?

19 Do you think that it is useful to distinguish between 'Theory X' and 'Theory Y' managers? How might an understanding of the differences help management training programmes?

20 Cite examples of legislation to combat discrimination which have benefited minority groups in the workforce. Explain how specific bits of legislation have benefited particular groups.

Resources

There is a wide range of textbooks aimed at Advanced Level Business candidates. The list below provides some useful examples which are appropriate for use at this level.

Textbooks

Arnold, J., *Managing Careers in the 21st century*, Pearson Books, London, 2003

Corfield, R., *Preparing Your Own CV*, The Times, London, 2003

Dransfield, R. et al, *Business for the BTEC National Award*, Heinemann, Oxford, 2004

Dransfield, R., *Human Resource Management*, Heinemann, Oxford, 2002

Foot, M. and Hook, C., *Introducing Human Resource Management*, Longman, London, 2002

Jay, R., *The Successful Candidate: How to be the Person They Want to Employ*, Financial Times, London, 2004

Pettinger, R., *Mastering Employee Development*, Palgrave Master Series, Palgrave, Basingstoke, 2002

Yale, M., *The Ultimate CV Book*, Kogan Page, London, 2003

Websites

Some useful websites are listed below. These addresses are current at the time of writing. However, it needs to be recognised that new sites are being launched on the Internet on a regular basis and that older sites may change or disappear.

www.tt100.biz
www.bized.ac.uk
www.tutor2u.net
www.ft.com
www.aloa.co.uk

Journals and periodicals

Local and national newspapers, particularly the jobs advertisement pages and specialist pull-out sections on recruitment in particular sectors.

Videos

TV Choice provides a range of useful videos on recruitment, selection and motivation issues. For further details look at www.tvchoice.com

Other resources

If you or your tutor are able to undertake the following activities and collect the suggested resources, they will be helpful when following this unit:

* visits, work experience and part-time employment, providing opportunities for interviews and for collecting human resource documentation and data

* a talk by a human resource manager about the recruitment, selection, induction, and motivational programmes employed by his or her organisation

* briefings on current legislation produced by trades unions, employer organisations, and other interested parties

* case studies based on the recruitment and selection process

* role play activities, especially relating to recruitment, appraisal and induction for a particular job role.

UNIT 3

Understanding the business environment

This unit contains ten elements:

3.2.1   Business ownership

3.2.2   Sources of finance

3.2.3   Budgeting and budgetary control

3.2.4   Break-even analysis

3.2.5   Cash-flow forecasts and statements

3.2.6   Importance of accurate record-keeping and technology

3.2.7   Analysis of the current market position

3.2.8   Economic conditions and market conditions

3.2.9   Ethical, legal, social, political and environmental factors

3.2.10 Stakeholders

Introduction

Business decision-making is shaped by a range of factors that are internal to a business, such as the way that it is financed and the cash available to it, and external factors, such as changes in competition in the market place. This unit helps you to start to develop an understanding of these important internal and external factors.

The internal part of this unit involves examining factors which are inside a business that influence decision-making. As well as looking at financial

Well-known organisations are influenced by internal and external factors

factors you will also be expected to consider other internal factors such as the type of business ownership, internal stakeholders and the impact of technology on decision-making.

The external element requires an understanding of economic, social, legal, environmental, political and technological issues and external stakeholders who make up the broader business world in which any business operates. An important aspect of studying these external themes is that they need to be understood in theory and also in the context of the business within the case study pre-released before your examination.

How you will be assessed

This unit is assessed through a pre-released case study followed by an external assessment.

Throughout this unit there are a number of activities to reinforce your learning.

There are ten main aspects to consider:

* business ownership
* sources of finance
* budgeting and budgetary control
* break-even analysis
* cash-flow forecasts
* importance of accurate record-keeping and technology
* analysis of the current market position
* economic conditions and market conditions
* ethical, legal, social, political and environmental factors
* stakeholders.

3.2.1 Business ownership

Sole trader

The **sole trader** is the most common form of business ownership and is found in a wide range of activities, such as window cleaning, web page design, plumbing or electrical work. It is a business which is owned by one person although this business might employ several people.

No complicated paperwork is required to set up a sole trader business. Decisions can be made quickly, and close contact can be kept with customers and employees. All profits go to the sole trader, who also has the satisfaction of building up his or her own business.

However, there are disadvantages. As a sole trader you have to make all the decisions yourself, you may have to work long hours, you have to provide all the finance yourself and you do not have limited liability. This means that if the business does not do well and builds up a range of debts, the sole trader is personally liable for all of these debts which could mean selling personal assets in order to pay for them, such as a house, car and other personal possessions.

CASE STUDY

The creation of Pout cosmetics

Emily Cohen

When an afternoon of shopping for cosmetics in London failed to inspire her, Emily Cohen, the founder of Pout, started to think about setting up her own cosmetics business (although at the time she had no previous experience of running such an enterprise). Cohen felt that the existing make-up service offered by department stores was intimidating.

At the time (1999) Cohen had noticed a new trend for 'nail bars' was starting to develop in London after crossing over from the United States. It made her think that it would be possible to create a new non-intimidating make-up business in Britain. Her research at department stores showed that all the leading make-up brands such as Lancôme, Stila and Laura Mercier were international – she wanted to create a British brand.

Cohen wanted to create a new concept in which women of all ages would feel happy to play and experiment with lotions, tonics, creams and cosmetics. She saw potential in a beauty parlour where women could get make-up done, have eyebrows plucked or false eyelash extensions applied. Working with a friend and business partner, Chantal Laren, she developed a business plan and with a third partner, Anna Singh, they put in £50,000 each to set up the business. They remortgaged their homes to raise an additional £50,000, and an investor put £500,000 into the business.

This gave them £700,000 of capital to set up a flagship store. The following year they raised a further £1m of capital by selling 20% of Pout. The following year they raised an extra £1.5m from a small number of shareholders.

Pout's flagship store in Convent Garden was launched in June 2001. In the next three and a half years Pout opened up 95 outlets worldwide including boutiques in leading stores such as Harvey Nichols in Britain.

The concept of the brand is to make a woman feel sexy, whether she lives in America, Australia, Britain or Japan. In 2004, Pout's sales were £4.2m and are expected to reach £7.5m in 2005.

The Pout case study illustrates how a great business idea can be turned into a successful business. Of course, one of the most important decisions is to decide on the most appropriate type of business ownership.

1 **What was Emily's idea? Where did her idea come from and how did it evolve?**
2 **Discuss the challenges she faced in setting up the business and turning her idea into a reality.**

Key terms

Limited liability – if a business with limited liability goes **bankrupt** because it is unable to meet its debts, the owners will not be liable (responsible by law) to lose their possessions to pay the money that is owed. The maximum sum that they could lose is the sum that they have put into the business. Note that sole traders do not have limited liability.

Theory into practice

Looking at the case study of Pout cosmetics on this page, what would have been the advantages and disadvantages to Emily Cohen of setting up the business as a sole trader? Where does the balance of advantage / disadvantage lie?

	Initial capital	Area of expertise
Emily Cohen	£50,000	An expert in public relations
Chantal Laren	£50,000	12 years' experience in film production
Anna Singh	£50,000	A fashion retail background
Cohen + Laren remortgage their homes	£50,000	
Investor	£500,000	

Sources of capital for Pout

Partnership

An ordinary partnership can have between two and twenty partners. Professional partnerships may have more, for example, some modern accountancy partnerships are very large.

People in business partnerships can share skills and the workload, and it may be easier to raise the capital needed. For example, the partners that set up Pout had a range of expertise and were able to put up the initial capital using their own capital and by remortgaging their homes.

In a similar way, a group of vets is able to pool knowledge about different diseases and groups of animals, and two or three vets working together may be able to operate a 24-hour service. When one of the vets is ill or goes on holiday, the business can cope.

Partnerships are usually set up by writing out a deed of partnership which is witnessed by a solicitor. This sets out important details, such as how much each partner should put into the business, how the profits and losses will be shared, and the responsibilities of each partner.

Partnerships are particularly common in professional services, such as doctors, solicitors and accountants. A small business such as a corner shop may take the form of a husband and wife partnership.

The disadvantages of partnerships are that people may want to sever ties, ordinary partnerships do not have limited liability and partnerships can rarely borrow or raise large sums of capital. Business decisions may be more difficult to make (and slower) because of the need to consult all the partners, and there may be disagreements about how things should be

done. A further disadvantage is that profits will be shared.

Today, limited partnerships are allowed in large partnerships of accountants and solicitors so that individuals are protected against the liabilities of others in their business.

Companies

A **company** is set up to run a business. It has to be registered before it can start to operate, but once all the paperwork is completed and approved the company becomes recognised as a legal body.

The owners of a company are its shareholders. However, other individuals and businesses do not deal with the shareholders – they deal with the company. Shareholders put funds into the company by buying shares. New shares are often sold in face values of £1 per share but this is not always the case. Some shareholders will only have a few hundred pounds' worth of shares, whereas others may have thousands of pounds' worth. Directors are appointed to represent the interests of shareholders.

There are two types of company – private companies and public companies.

Private limited company

Private companies tend to be smaller than public ones and are often family businesses. There must be at least two shareholders but there is no maximum number. Shares in private companies cannot be traded on the Stock Exchange, and often shares can only be bought with the permission of the Board of Directors.

The **Board of Directors** is a committee set up to protect the interests of shareholders. The members of the board choose the managing director, who is responsible for the day-to-day running of the business. The rules of the business set out when shareholders' meetings will take place and the rights of shareholders.

Private companies may find it possible to raise more cash (by selling shares) than unlimited liability businesses. The shareholders can also have the protection of limited liability. The main disadvantages, compared with unlimited liability businesses, are that they have to share out profits among shareholders and they cannot make decisions quickly. They also cost more to set up, and accounting charges are likely to be higher. The real issue with private companies is that they cannot sell more shares to the general public by advertising them. This means that although they are limited companies they are not able to use the Stock Exchange to raise investment funds by selling stocks and shares, which is always likely to limit their size.

Public limited company

A public company has its shares bought and sold on the Stock Exchange. Companies can go to the expense of a 'full quotation' on the Stock Exchange.

The London Stock Exchange

The main advantage of selling shares through the Stock Exchange is that large amounts of capital can be raised very quickly. One disadvantage is that the original shareholders can lose control of a business if large quantities of shares are purchased as part of a 'takeover bid'. It is also costly to have shares quoted on the Stock Exchange.

In order to create a public company the directors must apply to the Stock Exchange Council, which will carefully check the accounts. A business wanting to 'go public' will then arrange for one of the merchant banks to handle the paperwork.

Being a public limited company gives a business access to huge sums of capital enabling it to expand and dominate its market. Examples of public limited companies are:

* top football clubs such as Tottenham Hotspur and Manchester United
* top retailers such as Tesco and Sainsbury's
* large high street banks such as Halifax.

Theory into practice

What would be the advantages and disadvantages to Pout of becoming a public limited company?

Co-operatives

Co-operatives are an alternative form of business organisation. The basic idea behind a co-operative is that people join together to make decisions, work and share profits. There are many different types of co-operative, the three most common are discussed below.

Producer co-operatives

Producer co-operatives are usually registered as companies 'limited by guarantee', which means that each member undertakes to fund any losses up to a certain amount. There are many types, for example a workers' co-operative is one that employs all or most of its members. In a workers' co-operative members:

CASE STUDY
Scenario

The growth of 'Exotic Fashions'

In 1986, Jenny Parsons set up her own dress shop selling her own designer dresses in a small shop in Nottingham. Over the years the shop gained in popularity and Jenny found that her dresses were being ordered by customers from all over the UK and even by other European customers.

As Jenny was designing the dresses and selling them herself this created a lot of work pressure. Of course, she was able to pay her own staff to make the dresses to her patterns which they did initially from a small workshop over the shop, but as orders built up Jenny hired a small factory unit on an industrial estate on the outskirts of Nottingham.

Jenny realised that she was overstretching herself but was fortunate in 1995 to meet Sylvia Burns who had just graduated from the London School of Fashion. Sylvia had recently come into an inheritance and was looking to branch out into business for herself. As part of a research project she had met Jenny, and she realised that they shared a common interest, had similar styles and a common flair for fashion. They decided to set up in partnership. With their combined capital they bought outright a new factory in Nottingham and a large shop in central London. The London site was to become the focus for retailing operations.

Within months they had a backlog of orders from all over Europe and they realised that they would need to expand again. They decided to set up a private company in which they would be the major shareholders. However, they also needed extra share capital from a few wealthy individuals. They felt that the provision of limited liability would be a valuable protection. They were now dealing with some major buyers and if one failed to pay up they could end up with serious cash-flow problems. In addition, putting Ltd after the company name gave it extra status. They began trading as Exotic Fashions Ltd.

However, expansion seemed to demand further expansion. They had a chain of shops in ten major cities in the UK but there seemed to be a never-ending demand for their products. This time they decided to go public and sell shares on the Stock Exchange. They produced a prospectus for potential share buyers and on 15 August 2004 they went public. They sold £1 million of shares at £1 each. They could have sold over twice this number and on the day of issue share prices rocketed from £1.00 to £1.97.

1 Describe each of the forms of business ownership that Exotic Fashions has been through since 1986.
2 Why has it been necessary for Exotic Fashions to change its form of organisation?
3 What problems might Exotic Fashions have encountered when it changed from being a sole trader into a partnership?
4 What are the advantages of being a private company rather than a partnership?
5 What type of organisation is Exotic Fashions today? How would this be reflected in its name?
6 What are the disadvantages of having its current form of organisation?

* share responsibility for the success or failure of the business
* work together
* take decisions together
* share the profits.

Other examples of producer co-operatives are groups to grow tomatoes, to make furniture or to organise child-minding.

The main problem that co-operatives face is finance as they can find it difficult to raise the capital from banks and other bodies because they are not groups that primarily seek to make a profit. However, some co-operatives in recent years have raised finance by selling shares.

Marketing co-operatives

Marketing co-operatives are most frequently found in farming areas. The farmers set up a marketing board to be responsible for, among other things, grading, packing, distribution, advertising and selling their products.

Retail co-operatives

Retail co-operatives buy items for resale. A co-operative seeks to reward loyal customers and the community to which they belong rather than to make profit for a small group of shareholders.

The emphasis in a co-operative retailing society is on fair dealing. Co-ops in this country buy a greater percentage of products through fair trade than any other retailing organisation. For example, they pay a fair price to growers of cocoa (the raw material in chocolate manufacture) in countries of origin such as the Ivory Coast, in Africa. Co-ops also believe in paying fair wages to employees and getting involved in community activities such as giving money to local charities.

Theory into practice

Look at the following website: www.co-opunion. coop. Use the website address to make a list of the advantages of marketing co-operatives.

Not-for-profit or charity

The voluntary sector consists of organisations whose main aim is to provide a service rather than to make a profit. Many of these are charities, and they may use the services of volunteer staff, but most of their staff are employed on a professional basis.

In recent times new government legislation has been introduced to tighten up the rules about charities. The main aim of a charity should be to serve the wider community. Under new legislation, the objects of a charity which are recognised as being lawful are:

* the prevention and relief of poverty
* the advancement of education
* the advancement of religion
* the advancement of health
* social and community advancement
* the advancement of culture, arts and heritage
* the advancement of amateur sport
* the promotion of human rights, conflict resolution and reconciliation
* the advancement of environmental protection and improvement
* other purposes beneficial to the community.

An example of a charity is Childline, the free 24-hour helpline for children and young people in the UK. Children and young people can call the helpline on 0800 1111 about any problem, at any time – day or night.

Theory into practice

Find out about a charity. You may use literature delivered at home to help you or investigate using the World Wide Web. Identify the objectives for the charity and describe briefly how it operates.

Franchise

In the USA, about one half of all retail sales are made through firms operating under the franchise system. It is a form of business organisation that has become increasingly popular in the UK.

Franchising is the 'hiring out' or licensing of the use of 'good ideas and business systems to other companies'. A franchise grants permission to sell a product and trade under a certain name in a particular area. If I have a good idea, I can sell you a licence to trade and carry out a business using my idea in your area. The person taking out the franchise puts down a sum of money as capital and is issued with equipment by the franchising company. The firm selling the franchise is called the franchisor and a person paying for the franchise is called the franchisee. The franchisee usually has the sole right of operating in a particular area.

Examples of this type of trading include Pizza Hut, Dyno-Rod (in the plumbing business), Body Shop and Prontaprint. Recent franchises include Energie Fitness Clubs, Wiltshire Farm Foods, Green Clean and Contours Express. There are now numerous franchise opportunities in the health and fitness sector.

Where materials are an important part of the business, such as hamburgers or confectionery,

A well-known franchise opportunity

the franchisee must buy an agreed percentage of supplies from the franchisor, who makes a profit on these supplies as well as ensuring the quality of the final product. The franchisor also takes a percentage of the profits of the business, without having to risk capital or become involved in the day-to-day management.

CASE STUDY

The Countrywide Estate Agents Group

The Countrywide Estate Agents Group that includes Bairstow Eves and Mann & Co is in the process of setting up estate agency franchises. The Group feels that franchising will help it to increase its share of the estate agency market and franchising will also help it to distribute its products and services through a larger number of agency outlets.

The Group is offering franchises of its own brands, either to established businesses or on a start-up basis, to infill the existing owned network and extend network coverage. The lead brand being franchised in this way is Bairstow Eves as this is the Group's biggest brand with over 300 outlets across the UK.

The Bairstow Eves brand will provide the franchisee with the advantages of:

* the strength of a national network of agents
* independent ownership
* franchisees being able to run and operate their own business within the franchise package
* other benefits such as centralised work referrals, purchasing and supply systems, marketing materials, training and other activities.

1 Why do The Countrywide Estate Agents Group want to use franchises to expand their business?
2 What are the benefits for the franchisee?

The franchisee benefits from trading under a well-known name and enjoys a local monopoly. Training is usually arranged by the franchisor. The franchisee is his or her own boss and takes most of the profits.

Business decisions and objectives

The type of decisions a business makes is shaped by the objectives of the business. For example, there are substantial differences between the decisions made by 'not-for-profit' organisations like charities and voluntary organisations and those made by 'for-profit' organisations such as sole traders, partnerships and companies.

Decisions made by 'not-for-profit' organisations involve seeking to achieve wider social objectives such as to provide famine relief (Oxfam) or confidential support for children (Childline). Decisions prioritise the needy and socially disadvantaged.

By contrast, in 'for-profit' organisations, decisions favour the interests of shareholders – although customers and other groups are also highly important. Because of the relatively small scale of sole trader organisations and partnerships their objectives and decisions may also be relatively limited, e.g. focusing on decisions to provide products in relatively local areas. In contrast, the objectives and decisions made by a company (particularly a public company) can be far more ambitious because, with access to more funds, they are able to set their sights on 'being the market leader' or 'developing a major presence in international markets'.

Decisions that co-operatives make will be influenced by their members who may balance not-for-profit with profit-based objectives. As we shall see in the next section, for whatever type of organisations we study, the accessibility and amount of finance available will constrain objectives and thus the decisions that the organisation is able to make.

3.2.2 Sources of finance

Another important managerial responsibility is obtaining finance for a business or part of a business. Each year, individual managers will need to bid for funds. This involves putting

Theory into practice

Think of three examples of managers bidding for funds in an organisation.

forward a case for levels of funding that are appropriate to the activities that need to be carried out. For example:

✳ a course manager in a school or college will need funds to manage a course

✳ a production manager in a factory will need to bid for funds to buy new machinery, equipment, and to purchase stocks of raw materials.

Internal sources of finance

It is usual to think of finance coming from outside the business organisation, but it is possible to raise money from within the business. For example, one of the most frequent sources of finance is from retained profits. Most organisations only allocate a portion of their profits each year to their shareholders, and hold back some profits either to form reserves or to reinvest in the business. Initially, profits are subject to corporation tax, payable to the Inland Revenue. Corporation tax is a tax upon the profits of a business, taxed as a percentage of the final or net profits of a business. Then a proportion of what is left is distributed to shareholders as **dividends**. Finally, profits can be ploughed back into expansion.

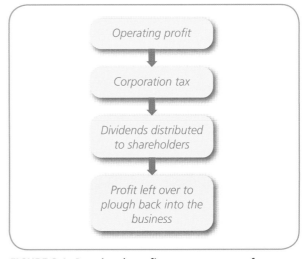

FIGURE 3.1 *Retained profits are a source of internal finance*

Another way of raising finance within the business organisation is to take money from working capital. **Working capital** is the 'liquid' capital required to run the business, comprising the short-term funds such as the money in the bank, money owed to the business by debtors and stocks less short-term debts such as money owed to suppliers or **creditors**. If the business reduces its stocks and calls in money owed to it from its **debtors**, it can, by having more liquid cash around, use such liquidity for investment, possibly in fixed assets such as machinery. Many organisations try to manage their short-term finances in a way that enables them to use these finances to benefit the business.

It is possible to raise finance within the business by selling off some of the fixed assets of the business. For example, it may be possible to sell off some property in order to raise finance. In recent years some organisations have injected finance into their activities, by selling off their property and then leasing it back. Sale and lease-back involves a firm selling its freehold property to an investment company and then leasing it back over a long period of time. This releases funds for other purposes.

At an organisation-wide level financial managers will have responsibility for securing funds for the business to enable it to operate well.

External sources of finance

Organisations have available to them a number of sources of external finance such as:

* individuals
* organisations providing venture capital
* banks and other financial institutions
* suppliers
* government.

In deciding what types of finance to draw on, financial managers need to consider:

* the length of time for which they need the finance
* the cost of raising the finance in one way rather than another.

Owner's capital

Owner's capital is raised from individual owners of a business such as partners or shareholders. This type of capital is raised when starting up a new business venture or when expanding a business.

When issuing shares, careful consideration needs to be given to the need to pay a dividend (share of the profit) to shareholders. The amount of dividend paid is decided on by the Board of Directors of the organisation. One advantage of raising finance from shareholders is that the organisation is not legally obliged to pay a set return each year (as for example, it has to do with loans). However, if the company keeps asking shareholders for more funds they will lose confidence in the company.

Venture capital

Venture capital companies such as 3i provide finance in return for an equity (ordinary) shareholding in the company and an element of control. This is a quick and relatively cheap way for a new business to raise capital but it may not want to lose some control to the venture capitalist.

Borrowing

The charge made for borrowing money from the bank and other financial institutions is termed interest.

Bank loans

Bank loans are taken out for a fixed period, and repayments are made either in instalments or in full at the end of the term. Banks generally provide funds on a short-to-medium term basis, with relatively few loans over more than ten years' duration. As well as the interest payment there may be an arrangement fee.

Debentures

Debentures are certificates issued by companies acknowledging their debt. The debt is paid at a fixed rate of interest and the certificate sets out the terms of repayment at the end of the period of debt. Debentures can usually be traded on the Stock Exchange.

Bank overdrafts

Bank overdrafts are the most frequently used form of short-term bank finance and they are used to ease cash-flow problems. Arrangements are made between the customer and the bank to include an agreed limit on an account beyond which the customer will not draw. Interest is calculated on the level of the overdraft on a daily basis. Often a bank will make a special charge for arranging an overdraft. A bank can take away the customer's right to use an overdraft if they think the position is being abused.

Hire purchase

Hire purchase (HP) allows a business to use an asset, for example, a photocopier or computer, without having to find the money immediately. A finance house buys the asset from the supplier and retains ownership of it during the period of the hire-purchase agreement. The business pays a deposit and then further payments to the finance house, as set out in the agreement. At the end of the HP agreement, ownership of the asset is passed to the business. The repayments made by the business are in excess of the cash price of the item. The difference is the finance charge to the finance house.

Leasing

Leasing an asset provides similar benefits to hire purchase, in that a leasing agreement with a finance house (lessor) allows the business (lessee) to use an asset without having to buy it outright. However, leasing does not give an automatic right to eventual ownership of the asset. It is a very popular form of finance for company vehicles, office equipment and factory machinery.

The lessee benefits from not having to put up large sums of capital to be able to use the asset and they can exchange the asset for a more modern version when technology changes. The lessor is also usually responsible for the maintenance of the item.

Mortgages

A commercial mortgage is a loan secured on land and buildings and can either be used to finance the purchase of the property or to provide security for a loan applied to some other purpose. It is a long-term financing arrangement typically from 10 to 30 years. Repayments are made including a considerable interest rate.

Suppliers

Suppliers are a valuable source of finance for many businesses. Many businesses buy raw materials and finished goods from suppliers. Typically they will buy these goods on credit and only pay for them later (for example 30 days later). The business is thus effectively receiving finance for the period they are given credit for. Just as the business may give credit to its own customers, the firm may be able to negotiate credit terms with its suppliers. Credit terms are typically 30 days from date of supply or the end of the month following a delivery, i.e. 30 to 60 days. This essentially means that for a period of time a business has the use of goods and services 'free', which is essentially a form of short-term borrowing until they are paid for.

Factoring

A debtor is an individual or business that owes you money – for example, because you have supplied them with goods which they have not paid for yet.

When a business is owed money by its debtors but has to wait for them to pay and requires cash urgently it can sell off part or all of this debt for collection by a third party – a factoring company. The factoring company will buy the debts of the business and provide immediate cash for their urgent needs.

Government loans

Businesses can acquire loans and grants from the government for various purposes depending on circumstances. These grants and loans may come from European Union sources, UK national government or from local government. National Lottery funds can be obtained in some circumstances. Typical purposes might be funds for helping with government schemes such as Modern Apprenticeships and job creation schemes. Other grants may be for building development, and machinery purchase particularly in areas of economic decline.

CASE STUDY

The Countryside Stewardship Scheme

The ancient craft of dry stone walling is thriving in 21st-century England, thanks in part to the Countryside Stewardship Scheme. The Countryside Stewardship Scheme offers payments to farmers and land managers to improve the natural beauty and diversity of the countryside under ten-year agreements. Payments range from £20 to £555 per hectare depending on the type of land management agreed.

The scheme has helped to protect an important countryside feature and provide a better habitat for valuable wildlife as well as a better habitat for plants. Areas under Stewardship have seen a marked increase in previously declining bird species, including the stone curlew, cirl bunting, bittern and lapwing. Around 13,500 miles of grass margins have been established, almost 9,000 miles of hedgerows have been restored or planted and over 800 miles of permissive footpaths have been provided for the enjoyment of the public. At the same time it has helped to maintain and promote a valuable countryside skill.

1 **What was the purpose of the Countryside Stewardship Scheme?**
2 **How has it influenced the actions of farmers?**

Theory into practice

You are the financial manager of an organisation that is opening a petrol station on a new city by-pass. Match the organisation's financial needs with the possible sources of finance available:

Needs:	Possible sources of finance:
✳ Land and buildings: £500,000	✳ Hire purchase or leasing
✳ Shopfittings: £50,000	✳ Bank loan for two years
✳ Petrol pumps: £100,000	✳ Commercial mortgage
✳ Stocks of petrol and retail items: £75,000	✳ Bank overdraft
✳ Computer terminal: £6,000	✳ Trade credit
✳ First few weeks wages: £8,000	✳ Owners capital: £100,000

Theory into practice

Imagine you are a financial manager in the following organisations. What type of finance would you use in each case?

1 A school wishes to replace its existing photocopier with a more elaborate version which they want to pay for over a period of time.

2 The Queen's Medical Centre in Nottingham wishes to build a new hospital wing on vacant land close to its existing site.

3 Prakesh Patel needs a new computer system costing £7,500 for his business. Identify two ways of financing the purchase and state the circumstances in which either would be most appropriate.

4 A medium-sized company wants to expand its factory building. The cost will be £1m. Identify two ways of financing the expansion and state the circumstance in which either would be more appropriate.

5 A small firm is temporarily having problems with its cash flow. Identify two ways of financing any shortfall it might currently have in its cash requirements and state the circumstances in which either would be more appropriate.

Short-term vs long-term sources of finance

Organisations may need long-term, medium-term or short-term finance for the following reasons:

* Long-term finance — e.g. to purchase other businesses, or buildings

* Medium-term finance — e.g. to update machinery, equipment and fittings, motor vehicles

* Short-term finance — e.g. to buy new stocks, to pay wages etc

An organisation needs to match the sort of finance they require to the time period they require it for. For example, in the short term they may simply want to pay wages or buy new stocks. In order to do this they will probably raise money within the organisation, perhaps from their debtors, so as to have more cash to pay outstanding debts, pay wages and make other pressing payments.

Alternatively, they may consider some form of factoring.

An organisation might need medium-term finance to buy machinery. A suitable form of finance for this might be a loan of some description. Finally, for longer-term finance such as buying a building they may seek to take out a mortgage or possibly increase their shareholding. It would be inappropriate and possibly damaging for a business to use the wrong source of finance for the wrong purpose. For example, taking out a long-term loan to meet debts in the short-term would simply push up the costs of the business because they would have to make interest payments on the borrowing), even if it did provide them with cash in the short period.

Type of ownership and business decisions

Different forms of finance are used by different types of organisations, and some businesses may find it difficult to raise finance, whereas for others,

Long-term finance is required for property ownership

it might be much more straightforward. Sole traders, for example, cannot issue shares and are likely to have more difficulty raising finance than long-established large companies, with untarnished reputations and a good market position.

Whereas a large public limited business may simply issue more shares, a sole trader, as a much smaller business, has fewer options. They may want to change their ownership structure by becoming a partnership, but that might not be a good option for them, and so they would have to think carefully about whether they approach a bank, attempt to factor some of their debts or go and discuss their situation with an enterprise agency.

3.2.3 Budgeting and budgetary control

Budgets help businesses to plan, set targets and control expenditure. To understand how budgets are used you need to know what they are, how they work and their particular purposes. You will need to be able to identify and interpret variance and explain the benefits of budgeting to businesses.

Financial planning involves defining objectives and then developing ways to achieve them. To be able to do this, a financial manager must have a realistic understanding of what is happening and what is likely to happen within the organisation, for example, when is money going to come in, what is it needed for and would it be possible to use some of it for expansion and development? In the 'money-go-round' (see Figure 3.2), capital and sales revenue come into a business, but is there enough left over, after paying all the costs, for expansion and development?

Looking into their future helps all organisations to plan their activities so that what they anticipate and want to happen can actually happen. This process of financial planning is known as budgeting. It is considered to be a system of **responsibility accounting** because it puts a duty on budgeted areas to perform in a way that has been outlined for them, and its success will depend upon the quality of information provided. Businesses that do not budget may not be pleased when they view their

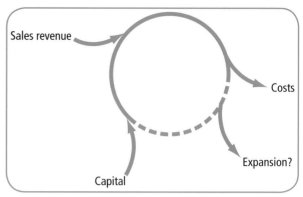

FIGURE 3.2 *The money-go-round*

final accounts. Budgeting helps the financial manager to develop an understanding of how the business is likely to perform in the future.

We all budget to a greater or lesser extent. Our short-term budget may relate to how we are going to get through the coming week and do all the things we want to do. Our slightly longer-term budget may involve being able to afford Christmas presents in two months' time. Our longest-term budget could involve the planning necessary to afford the car tax, MOT and motor insurance, which all fall due in ten months from now, or planning when we can afford in the longer term to replace the car.

CASE STUDY
Managing student finances

One of the big problems for most students today is how to manage their finances effectively. The need to spread their income and student loan across all of their financial responsibilities calls upon students to be both sensible and resourceful. Students have many different financial commitments and yet for many of them, it is the first time away from home, in a different environment and in a situation where they have to manage money for the first time. Some of the consequences of not managing their money can be quite serious.

1 Why is it important for students to budget?
2 What practical steps could they take to budget?

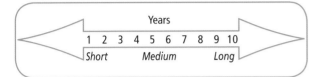

FIGURE 3.3 *Budgetary periods*

A budget is a financial plan developed for the future. Many businesses appoint a budget controller whose sole task is to co-ordinate budgetary activities. A short-term budget would be for up to one year, a medium-term budget would be for anything from one year to five years, and a budget for a longer period than this would be a long-term budget (see Figure 3.3).

Wherever budgeting takes place, it is important to draw upon the collective experience of people throughout the business. A budgeting team might consist of representatives from various areas of activity. The team will consider the objectives of the budgeting process, obtain and provide relevant information, make decisions, prepare budgets and then use these budgets to help to control the business.

Budgeting provides a valuable benchmark against which to measure and judge the actual performance of key areas of business activity. There are many benefits of budgeting:

* It helps to predict what the organisation thinks will happen. Given the experience within the organisation, budgets help to show what is likely to take place in the future.

* Budgets create opportunities to appraise alternative courses of action. Information created for budgeting purposes forms the basis of decisions that have to be taken. The research necessary for budgeting will look at alternative ways of achieving the organisation's objectives.

* Budgets set targets. If communicated to people throughout the organisation, the budgets will help them to work towards the targets that have been set.

* They help to monitor and control performance. This can be done by studying actual results, comparing these to budgeted results and then finding out why differences (known as **variances**) may have occurred. Sometimes variances are bad, while at other times they may be good. Whatever the causes of the variances, they are a useful starting point for dealing with issues within the business.

* Budgets are fundamental to the process of **business planning**. They provide a series of quantitative guidelines that can be used for co-ordination and then followed in order to achieve the organisation's business objectives.

* They can be used as a source of **motivation**. As part of the consultation process, budgets help to keep people involved. They also help to ensure that the aims and objectives of the individual are the same as those of the organisation.

* Budgets are a form of communication. They enable employees from across the organisation to be aware of performance expectations with regard to their individual work area.

Budgeting may also have some useful spin-offs. Every year the business is reviewed and this gives members of the various departments a better understanding of the working of the organisation as a whole. In fact, by participating in the budgetary process they feel their experience is contributing to policy decisions.

It also increases co-operation between departments and lowers departmental barriers. In this way, members of one department can become aware of the difficulties facing another department.

By being involved in the budgetary process, non-accountants also appreciate the importance of costs.

In reality, budgeting may take place in almost all parts of an organisation. Budgeting should also be viewed as something that is going on all the time and as a source of useful information and guidance for managers.

The process of budget setting

The process of setting budgets has to be seen within the context of the longer-term objectives and strategies at the highest level of management of any organisation. The administration of the budgeting process will usually be the responsibility of the accounts department. Many organisations set up a budget committee to oversee the process.

The budgetary process is usually governed by a formal budget timetable. This helps to link the budget in with all other aspects of business planning (see Figure 3.4).

Spreadsheets are an effective 'what-if' tool that are often used to help within the budgeting process.

Setting up a system of 'responsibility accounting' such as budgeting involves breaking down an organisation into a series of 'control centres'. Each individual manager then has the responsibility for managing the budget relating to his or her particular control centre.

Budgetary reports, therefore, reflect the assigned responsibility at each level of the organisation. As all organisations have a structure of control, it is important the budgetary system fits around this. The reports should be designed to reflect the different levels within the organisation and the responsibilities of each of the managers concerned.

If the budgeting process reflects the different levels of control, managers will be kept informed not just of their own performance but also of that of other budget holders for whom they are responsible. They will also know that managers above them will be assessing their performance. This system can be reviewed regularly at meetings attended by all the individual managers concerned.

Budget timetable for year 1 April 2004 to 31 March 2005

Date	Narrative	Responsibility
1 Sept	Board of directors to review long-term objectives and strategies and specify short-term goals for the year	Directors
22 Sept	Budget guidelines and standard forms issued to line managers	Accounts
6 Oct	Actual results for year are issued to line management so that comparisons can be made with current budget and last year's actual results	Accounts
20 Oct	Budget submissions are made to the management accountant	Line management
27 Oct	First draft of the master budget is issued	Accounts
3 Nov	First draft of the budget is reviewed for results and consistency – line managers to justify their submissions	MD and individual directors
8 Nov	New assumptions and guidelines issued to line management	Accounts
12 Nov	Budgets revised and resubmitted	Line management
22 Nov	Second draft of master budget issued	Accounts
29 Nov	Final review of the draft budget	MD and Financial director
1 Dec	Final amendments	Accounts
10 Dec	Submission to the board for their approval	Financial director

FIGURE 3.4 *A budget timetable*

Theory into practice

Find out more about the budgeting process within your school or college. For example, how are budgets set, what processes take place and who are the budget holders? What happens if budget holders overspend?

Budget plan

Working from one year to another assumes that changes can be predicted and that the business is working in a linear way, which does not always realistically reflect business activity. Parts of the business may expand more quickly than others and this can be limited by the system of historic budgeting (see page 119). The result is that historic budgeting can carry over mistakes from one year to another. However, even though it does mechanise the budgeting process, it is quickly applied and does not require extensive consultation with budget heads.

Zero budgeting (see page 119) needs to be justified and this helps to minimise expenditure. It allows the person supervising the budgetary system to spring clean the budgets every year and start from scratch so that budget heads have to justify all new items of expenditure. This provides everybody with a good understanding of changes within the business but can be time consuming and difficult for those who find some of these justifications complex.

The overall budget, as a plan, will have real value only if the performance levels set through the budget are realistic. Budgets based upon ideal conditions are unlikely to be met and will result in departments failing to meet their targets. For example, the sales department may fail to achieve their sales budget, which may result in goods remaining unsold. Budgets can be motivating only if they are pitched at a realistic level.

There are two approaches to budget setting. The top-down approach involves senior managers specifying what the best performance indicators are for the business across all departments and budgeted areas. The bottom-up approach builds up the organisational budget on the basis of the submissions of individual line managers and supervisors, based upon their own views of their requirements. In practice most organisations use a mixture of both methods (see Figure 3.5).

Budget setting should be based upon realistic predictions of future sales and costs. Many organisations base future predictions solely on past figures, with adjustments for forecast growth and inflation rates. Although the main advantage of this approach is that budgets are based upon actual data, future conditions may not mirror past ones.

One of the dangers of budgeting is that, if actual results are dramatically different from the budgeting ones, the process could lose its credibility as a means of control. Following a budget too rigidly may also restrict a business's activities. For example, if the budget for entertainment has been exceeded and subsequent visiting customers are not treated with the usual hospitality, orders may be lost. On the other hand, if managers realise that towards the end of the year a department has underspent, they may decide to go on a spending spree.

Budgeting is a routine annual event for many different types of organisations. The process may start in the middle of the financial year, with a revision of the current year's budget and with first drafts of the budget for the coming year. Some organisations plan further ahead with an outline plan for three to five years.

Variance analysis

An essential feature of the budgetary control system is the feedback of actual results. The process of measuring the difference between budgeted (intended) and actual outcomes is known as variance analysis. Wherever actual differs from budgeted performance a variance takes place. Variance analysis makes it possible to detect problems. Reasons can be sought for variances and speedy action can be taken to improve performance.

Variances are recorded as being either adverse (A) or favourable (F), depending upon whether actual expenditure is more or less than budget. For example, if actual expenditure is less than budgeted expenditure, the variance would be favourable; i.e. actual expenditure

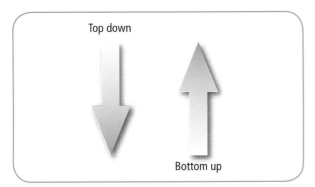

FIGURE 3.5 *Approaches to budget setting*

Theory into practice

If the wages of a business over a half year are £15,000 and the budgeted amount for wages was £12,000, is this an adverse or favourable situation? What decisions might managers take based upon this situation?

could be £10,000 and if this is less than budgeted expenditure of £12,000, then there is a favourable variance. On the other hand, if actual expenditure is more than budgeted expenditure, the variance is adverse; i.e. if actual expenditure was £25,000 and budgeted was £15,000, then there would be a £10,000 adverse variance.

Variances may arise for a number of reasons. These include:

* *Random deviations* which are uncontrollable. As we saw above, these are outside the control of individual managers.

* *An incorrectly-set budget*. This may require further research and management action.

* *Failure to meet an agreed budget*. This would be because a manager has failed to meet the appropriate figures and deadlines.

CASE STUDY

Scenario

Wayne's Workout Warehouse produces high quality sportswear and equipment. The shop has recently expanded and has introduced two new lines: trampolines and compact multi-gyms. Look at the sales budget below.

	Nov	Dec	Jan	Feb	Mar	Apr
Trampoline	£1,140	£2,185	£1,615	£760	£1,045	£1,235
Compact multi-gym	£1,575	£3,500	£2,625	£875	£1,750	£2,100
Total	£2,715	£5,685	£4,240	£1,635	£2,795	£3,335

1 Where could the sales manager get information on which to base these expected sales revenues?

2 Trampolines are sold at a price of £95 each. How many does the firm plan to sell in December and January? Would reducing the price of the trampoline automatically cut the firm's sales revenue?

3 Compact multi-gyms are £175 each. What would the firm's planned revenue be in April if they sell all their Compact multi-gyms at £185 each?

4 Assume the cost of producing each trampoline is £70. How many trampolines would Wayne need to sell in a month to earn a profit of £500 on this product?

Theory into practice

Calculate the variances and complete your own table stating in the 'comment' column whether the variance is favourable or adverse.

January budget

	Budget	Actual	Variance	Comment
Sales revenue	150	180		
Less material costs	(75)	(90)		
Less labour	(15)	(21)		
Gross profit	60	69		
Less overheads	(20)	(22)		
Net profit	40	47		

CASE STUDY

Scenario

Tupps Curtains is a business based in the East Midlands. They manufacture curtains and blinds for domestic use. Their main fabric supplier is a small, local, family-run firm which they have been dealing with for many years. This supplier has decided to retire and sell the premises. The management team has reviewed their budget for December and has held a management meeting to discuss any variances in the budget. Their findings were that:

- sales have dropped by 15 per cent compared to what was predicted in the budget
- labour costs have increased by 5 per cent
- material costs have fallen by 20 per cent.

You are hired as a consultant to analyse the findings at a budget meeting.

1 Explain why the variances have occurred.

2 What suggestions would you make to avoid further adverse variances?

3 Explain the importance of variance analysis.

Historic budgeting

Historic budgeting occurs where the year's targets for costs and revenues are based upon last year's budget. For example, it should be possible to forecast next year's costs and revenues by looking backwards at previous costs and revenues and analysing how they have changed from year to year.

Zero budgeting

Zero budgeting is where the budget is initially set at zero and then each department has to justify their spending and negotiate funds for the oncoming year. This is an important way for departments to calculate and then negotiate their spending based upon where they expect to be over the next accounting period. It helps managers to plan ahead and gives them the freedom not to base their spending upon previous years, but to seek and then justify other avenues in which their areas are developing.

Budgeting contexts

There are many different forms of budget ranging from those for sales and production, through to raw materials budgets, labour budgets, overhead budgets, capital budgets and cash budgets. The reason for this is that almost every activity within a business organisation can be budgeted for. Budgets are simple to prepare using appropriate information. They do not involve extensive analysis, but they do involve logically putting the right information in an appropriate format.

Sales budget

The purpose of the sales budget is to forecast sales and sales **turnover** for a forecast period. An example of a sales budget is shown below in Figure 3.6, where an organisation intends to sell 1,000 units per month for the next six months (January–June) at a selling price of £50.

Theory into practice

Construct a sales budget for a six-month period. For January to March sales are likely to be 1,000 units per month and for April to June 1,500 units. The selling price is to be £85 per unit.

	Jan	Feb	Mar	Apr	May	Jun	Total
Forecast sales	1,000	1,000	1,000	1,000	1,000	1,000	6,000
Selling price	£50	£50	£50	£50	£50	£50	£50
Sales turnover	£50,000	£50,000	£50,000	£50,000	£50,000	£50,000	£300,000

FIGURE 3.6 *Example of a sales budget*

Direct labour budget

A direct labour budget might be as follows:

An organisation intends to make 9,000 cabinets over a year. It takes 3 labour hours to make a cabinet and the wage rate per hour is £10. The direct labour budget would be:

Forecast production units	9,000
Direct labour hours per cabinet	3
Total direct labour hours	27,000
Wage rate per hour	£10
Total wages	£270,000

The direct labour budget would, therefore, have forecast the cost of labour over the period of a year.

Capital budget

A capital budget might be as follows:

A forecast for a business shows that over six months £50,000 is needed for a CNC machine, £20,000 for two motor vans, £5,500 for a new building extension, £40,000 for improving the production line and £9,500 for installing a new air-conditioning system.

The capital budget (see Figure 3.7) quickly provides an indication that £125,000 is needed for capital purchases for the six months and then itemises the amounts required month by month.

Potential problems with the budgetary process

Budgetary and control systems vary from one organisation to another. They are found both in the private sector and the public sector, and in all sorts of organisations from the very small to the very large. Given the different aims of organisations, budgetary systems reflect the context in which they are put to use. There are, however, certain problems associated with budgeting processes that have to be recognised.

First, reliance upon budgeting and its processes is no substitute for good management. Budgeting should simply be viewed as one tool among many for managers to use. If forecasting is poor or inadequate allowances are made, the process may create unnecessary pressure upon managers to perform in a particular way. This may be stressful and cause antagonism and resentment within the organisation.

The creation of rigid financial plans that are 'cast in stone' may cause inertia in certain parts of a business and reduce its ability to adapt to change. Budgets may also not reflect the realities of the business environment and act simply as a straitjacket upon the performance of managers and decision-makers. It has also been argued that delays and time lags can make it difficult to compare budgeted and actual results.

3.2.4 Break-even analysis

Before looking at **break-even analysis** we need a basic understanding of costs. One method of classifying costs is according to changes in output. This identifies costs as either fixed or variable.

Fixed costs

Fixed costs are costs that do not increase as total output increases. For example, if an organisation

	Jan	Feb	Mar	Apr	May	Jun	Total
CNC machine				£50,000			£50,000
Motor vans	£20,000						£20,000
Building extension			£5,500				£5,500
Production line			£40,000				£40,000
Air-conditioning						£9,500	£9,500
Total	£20,000	–	£45,500	£50,000	–	£9,500	£125,000

FIGURE 3.7 *Example of a capital budget*

has the capacity needed it might increase its production from 25,000 units to 30,000 units. However, its fixed costs such as rent, rates, heating and lighting will be the same, since they also had to be paid when the organisation was producing 25,000 units.

Variable costs

In contrast, **variable costs** are those costs that increase as total output increases because more inputs need to be employed in order to increase outputs. For example, if you produce more items you need more raw materials.

Marginal costing

Marginal costing is a commonly employed technique that uses costs to forecast profits from the production and sales levels expected in future periods. The benefit of marginal costing over other costing methods is that it overcomes the problem of allocating fixed costs – only variable costs are allocated as we shall see.

> **Key terms**
>
> **Contribution** = Selling price per unit less variable costs per unit.

Marginal costing is particularly useful for making short-term decisions – for example, helping to set the selling price of a product, or deciding whether or not to accept an order. It might also help an organisation to decide whether to buy in a component or whether to produce it themselves.

The difference between an item's selling price and the variable costs needed to produce that item is known as **contribution**. By producing and selling enough units to produce a total contribution that is in excess of fixed costs, an organisation will make a profit.

For example, Penzance Toys Ltd manufactures plastic train sets for young children. They anticipate that next year they will sell 8,000 units at £12 per unit. Their variable costs are £5 per unit and their fixed costs are £9,000. From the above formula we can deduce that the contribution is £12 minus £5, which is £7 per unit. Therefore, for each unit made, £7 will go towards paying the fixed costs as shown in the figures and the table below.

	(£)
Sales revenue (8,000 × £12)	96,000
Less: Marginal costs (8,000 × £5)	40,000
Total contribution	56,000
Less: Fixed costs	9,000
Net profit	47,000

Units of production	Fixed costs (£)	Variable costs (£)	Total costs (£)	Revenue (£)	Profit / loss (£)
1,000	9,000	5,000	14,000	12,000	(2,000)
2,000	9,000	10,000	19,000	24,000	5,000
3,000	9,000	15,000	24,000	36,000	12,000
4,000	9,000	20,000	29,000	48,000	19,000
5,000	9,000	25,000	34,000	60,000	26,000
6,000	9,000	30,000	39,000	72,000	33,000
7,000	9,000	35,000	44,000	84,000	40,000
8,000	9,000	40,000	49,000	96,000	47,000
9,000	9,000	45,000	54,000	108,000	54,000
10,000	9,000	50,000	59,000	120,000	61,000

Break-even point

The concept of break-even is a development from the principles of marginal costing. **Breaking even** is the unique point at which an organisation neither makes profit or loss. If sales go beyond the break-even point, profits are made, and if they are below the break-even point, losses are made. In marginal costing terms, it is the point at which the contribution equals the fixed costs.

To calculate the break-even point there are two stages:

1   Calculate the unit contribution (selling price less variable cost per unit)

2   Divide the fixed costs by the unit contribution:

$$\text{Break-even point} = \frac{\text{Fixed costs}}{\text{Unit contribution}}$$

For example, in Penzance Toys Ltd the contribution per unit is £7 and the fixed costs are £9,000. The break-even point would therefore be:

$$\frac{9,000}{7} = 1,286 \text{ units (to nearest unit)}$$

Sales value at break-even point

The **sales value** at the break-even point can be calculated by multiplying the number of units by the selling price per unit. For Penzance Toys this would be:

$1,286 \times £12 = £15,432$

Penzance Toys has covered their costs (fixed and variable) and broken even with a sales value of £15,432. Anything sold in excess of this will provide them with profits.

Profit target

If an organisation has a profit target or selected operating point to aim at, break-even analysis can be used to calculate the number of units that need to be sold and the value of sales required to achieve that target.

For example, if Penzance Toys wanted to achieve a target of £15,000 profit. By adding this £15,000 to the fixed costs and dividing by the contribution, the number of units can be found that need to be sold to meet this target:

$$\frac{£9,000 + £15,000}{7} = 3,429 \text{ units (to nearest unit)}$$

Margin of safety

The difference between the break-even point and the selected level of activity designed to achieve the profit target is known as the **margin of safety**.

Break-even charts

A break-even chart can be used to show changes in the relationship between costs, production volumes and various levels of sales activity. The following procedure should be followed to construct a break-even chart:

* label the horizontal axis for units of production and sales

* label the vertical axis to represent the values of sales and costs

* plot fixed costs – fixed costs will remain the same over all levels of production, so plot this as a straight line parallel to the horizontal axis

* plot the total costs (variable and fixed costs) – this will be a line rising from where the fixed cost line touches the vertical axis and is plotted by calculating the total costs at two or three random levels of production

* sales are then plotted by taking two or three random levels of turnover – the line will rise from the intersection of the two axes.

The break-even point will be where the total cost line and the sales line intersect. The area to the left of the break-even point between the sales and total cost lines will represent losses and the area to the right of the break-even point between these lines will represent profit.

For example, Eddie Bowen plans to set up a small restaurant. In doing so he knows he will immediately incur annual fixed costs of £10,000. He is concerned about how many meals he will have to sell to break even. Extensive market research indicates a typical customer will pay £8 for a meal, and Eddie knows that variable costs (such as cooking ingredients and the costs of serving customers) will amount to about £3. Eddie has set himself a profit target of £14,000 for the first year of operation. Eddie needs to work out the number of meals he has to sell and find out his margin of safety.

Eddie's *unit contribution* is:

£8 – £3 (selling price – variable cost)
= £5 per meal

His *break-even* point in units will be:

£10,000 (Fixed costs) divided by £5 unit contribution = 2,000 meals

The *sales value* of the meals will be:

2,000 meals × £8 (Selling price) = £16,000

His *profit target* will be achieved by:

$$\frac{£10,000 \text{ (Fixed costs)} + £14,000 \text{ (Profit Target)}}{£5 \text{ (Unit contribution)}} = 4,800 \text{ meals}$$

The *margin of safety* will be the difference between the selected level of activity and the break-even point. It will be between 4,800 meals with a turnover of £38,400 and 2,000 meals with a turnover of £16,000.

The three random levels of variable costs and sales chosen for the purpose of plotting the break-even chart are at 1,000 meals, 3,000 meals and 5,000 meals. They are:

	1,000 meals	3,000 meals	5,000 meals
Variable costs (£3 per meal)	£3,000	£9,000	£15,000
Fixed costs	£10,000	£10,000	£10,000
Total costs	£13,000	£19,000	£25,000
Sales	£8,000	£24,000	£40,000

We can now plot the break-even chart (see Figure 3.8) which shows graphically the break-even point of 2,000 meals with a sales revenue of £16,000. The margin of safety can be seen on the chart if we identify the selected level of profit (at 4,800 meals) and the targeted turnover (of £38,400), and compare this point with the break-even point.

The break-even chart is a simple visual tool enabling managers to anticipate the effects of changes in production and sales upon the profitability of an organisation's activities. It emphasises the importance of earning revenue and is particularly helpful for those who are unused to interpreting accounting information.

The break-even chart can be used to explore changes in a number of key variables. These may include:

* *Sales volume and value.* By looking at the chart it is possible to predict the effects of changes in sales trends. For example, a sudden fall in sales may lead to a loss and a sudden increase may improve profitability.

* *Profits or losses at a given level of production.* The break-even chart enables a business to monitor levels of production. By doing this, important decisions can be made if changes take place.

* *Prices.* It is possible to use the break-even chart to analyse different business scenarios. For example, given market research information, what would happen if the price was reduced by £2?

* *Costs.* The effects of any sudden change in costs can be plotted on the break-even chart.

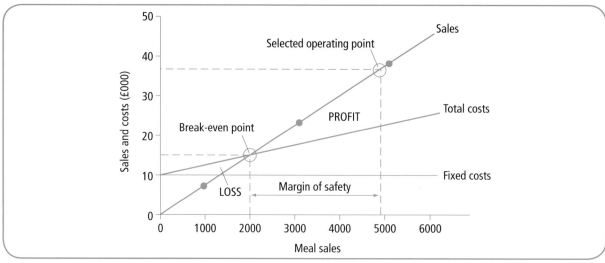

FIGURE 3.8 *Eddie Bowen's break-even chart*

Scenario

Saul Brinestone had a visit from an aged relative who wanted advice. For many years she has run a small hotel in a market town in the Thames Valley. After careful consideration she has decided to 'call it a day' and retire, but she is keen to see the business continue and wishes to retain her ownership in it.

Saul is interested in a proposition she has put forward, which involves running the hotel on her behalf. The hotel has been allowed to deteriorate over the years and, in Saul's opinion, it is obvious that extensive refurbishment is necessary before he could realistically consider her proposal. The hotel is, however, in a prime spot, was extensively used little more than ten years ago, and Saul feels that, with hard work, it has the potential to become successful again.

He has arranged a number of quotations to be made for the building work. The most favourable received is for £180,000, which involves extensive interior redecoration and refurbishment as well as completely reorganising the reception and kitchen areas.

Saul's intention is that the finance for the building work should come from a five-year bank loan with a fixed annual interest rate of 10%, payable each calendar month and based upon the original sum. The loan principal would be paid back in five equal annual

instalments. He has estimated the following fixed and variable costs:

Fixed	– Annual loan repayment	£36,000
	– Annual interest on loan	£18,000
	– Business rate and water rates	£7,000 per annum
	– Insurance	£4,500 per annum
	– Electricity	£1,300 per quarter
	– Staff salaries	£37,000 per annum.

Variable

These include direct labour (such as cleaners and bar staff), as well as the cost of food, bar stocks, etc. After careful research Saul has estimated these to be £2,000 for each 100 customers who visit the hotel.

Saul has organised for a local agency to conduct an extensive market research survey and feels confident that the hotel will attract about 100 customers per week, who will each spend on average (including accommodation, food and drinks) about £70 in the hotel.

1 Work out the break-even point for the hotel in both numbers of customers and value.
2 Work out the numbers of customers required to make a gross profit of £35,000.
3 Draw a break-even chart showing the break-even point, the profit target and the margin of safety.
4 What other information might Saul require before deciding to go ahead with the project?

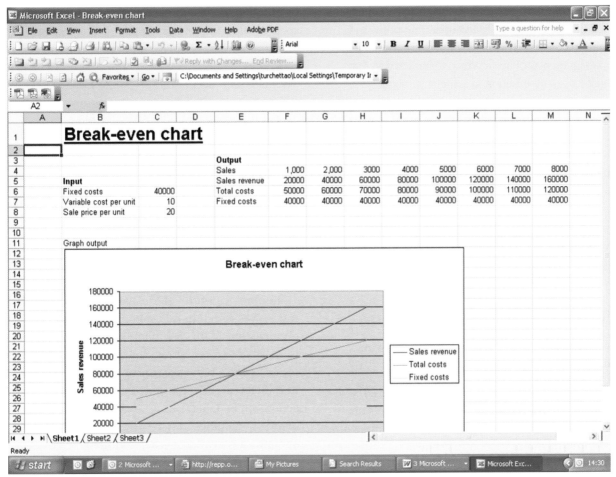

FIGURE 3.9 *An example of a break-even chart using a spreadsheet package*

CASE STUDY

Scenario

Theme Holidays Ltd are a private company that specialise in overseas theme park holidays for adults and children. Half the packages are based upon Disneyland Parks, while the other half are based upon theme park destinations in the USA.

Theme Holidays are currently reviewing their profitability for 2005. They anticipate fixed overheads will be £450,000 for the year. With the Disneyland Paris packages, a quarter of the variable costs will go on travel costs, at an average of £30 per package. They anticipate selling packages at an average of £160 per holiday in 2005.

The American holidays are sold at an average price of £650 per holiday. Travel costs of £200 for the American holidays comprise half the variable costs of the holiday.

Market research has revealed that, during 2005, Theme Holidays expects to sell 400 holidays.

1 Work out the contribution for both the European and American holidays.
2 Calculate the company's profit for the year before tax and interest.
3 Market research also revealed that, if Theme Holidays reduced their prices by 10%, they could sell 300 more holidays per year. Calculate how this would affect profitability and advise accordingly.
4 Theme Holidays are aware of the size of their fixed overheads. How would a 10% reduction in fixed overheads through cost-cutting measures affect both of the above?

Any of these changes may affect an organisation's ability to achieve its selected operating point and margin of safety. The break-even chart is a useful management tool upon which to base action that enables an organisation to achieve its plans.

Entering figures into a spreadsheet can also be used for break-even analysis. The great benefit of doing this is that spreadsheets such as Excel are linked to charting tools and the spreadsheet can be used as a basis for producing a break-even chart shown in Figure 3.9. In the example the fixed costs are £40,000, variable cost per unit £10 and sales price per unit £20. Output is then calculated at various levels from 1,000 units to 8,000 units. These are then highlighted and an appropriate line chart is chosen, such as the one on page 125.

Break-even analysis limitations

Break-even analysis does have the following limitations:

* it can be argued that, in real situations, fixed costs actually vary with different levels of activity, and so a stepped fixed-cost line would provide a more accurate guide

* many organisations fail to break even because of a limiting factor restricting their ability to do so (e.g. a shortage of space, labour or orders)

* the variable cost and sales lines are unlikely to be linear (i.e. straight) as discounts, special contracts and overtime payments mean the cost curve is more likely to be curved

* break-even charts depict short-term relationships, and forecasts are therefore unrealistic when the proposals cover a number of years

* break-even analysis is (like all other methods) dependent upon the accuracy of forecasts made about costs and revenues – changes in the market and in the cost of raw materials could affect the success of this technique.

3.2.5 Cash-flow forecasts and statements

Whereas profit is a surplus from trading activities, cash is a liquid asset that enables an organisation to buy the goods and services it requires in order to add value to them, trade and make profits. It is therefore possible for an organisation to be profitable while, at the same time, creditors have not been paid and liquid resources have not been properly accounted for.

On the other hand, an organisation must look carefully to see that its use of cash is to its best advantage. For example, if it holds too much cash in the bank, it might be sacrificing the potential to earn greater income.

An organisation must therefore ensure it has sufficient cash to carry out its plans and that the cash coming in is sufficient to cover the cash going out. At the same time it must take into account any cash surpluses it might have in the bank.

Looking carefully at the availability of liquid funds is essential to the smooth running of any organisation. With cash planning or budgeting it is possible to forecast the flows into and out of an organisation's bank account so that any surpluses or deficits can be highlighted and any necessary action can be taken promptly. For example, overdraft facilities may be arranged in good time so funds are available when required.

The **cash-flow forecast** is an extremely important tool within an organisation and has a number of clear purposes as follows:

* The forecast can be used to highlight the timing consequences of different expenditures, ensuring that facilities, such as an overdraft, can be set up to pay bills.

* It is is an essential document for the compilation of the business plan. It will help to show whether the organisation is capable of achieving the objectives it sets. This is very important if the business applies for finance, where the lender will almost certainly want to know about the ability of the applicant to keep on top of the cash flow and meet the proposed payment schedules.

* It will help to boost the lender's confidence and the owner's confidence. By looking into the future it will provide them with the reassurance they require that their plans are going according to schedule.

It will also help with the monitoring of performance. The cash-flow forecast sets benchmarks against which the business is expected to perform. If the organisation actually performs differently from these benchmarks, the cash-flow forecast may have highlighted an area for investigation. As we have seen, investigating differences between forecast figures and actual figures is known as variance analysis.

To prepare a cash-flow forecast you need to know what receipts and payments are likely to take place in the future and exactly when they will occur. It is important to know the length of the lead-time between incurring an expense and paying for it, as well as the time lag between making a sale and collecting the money from debtors. The art of successful forecasting is being able to calculate receipts and expenditures accurately.

When working though a cash-flow forecast, it is important to look carefully at the timing of every entry.

Most business transactions take place on credit and most payments are made weeks or months after the documentation has been sent (see Figure 3.10). For example, goods are often paid for three months afer a sale. This means that in April the cash for sales in January will be received.

Example 1

C. Moon Ltd has £500 in the bank on 1 January. The owner, Christine Moon, anticipates that her receipts over the next six months are likely to be:

Jan	Feb	March	April	May	June
£2,300	£1,400	£5,300	£6,100	£4,700	£1,400

She has also worked out what her payments are likely to be over the next six months:

Jan	Feb	March	April	May	June
£1,400	£4,100	£5,600	£5,000	£3,100	£900

Christine Moon is concerned about whether she needs an overdraft facility and, if so, when she is likely to use it. She constructs the following cash-flow forecast:

	Jan	Feb	Mar	Apr	May	Jun
Balance	£500	£1,400	(£1,300)	(£1,600)	(£500)	£1,100
Receipts	£2,300	£1,400	£5,300	£6,100	4,700	£1,400
	£2,800	£2,800	£4,000	£4,500	4,200	£2,500
Payments	£1,400	£4,100	£5,600	£5,000	3,100	£900
	£1,400	(£1,300)	(£1,600)	(£500)	1,100	£1,600

The forecast shows that C. Moon Ltd needs to set up an overdraft facility between the months of February and April.

Example 2

A cash-flow forecast for the six months ended 31 December 2005 can be drafted from the following information:

1 Cash balance 1 July 2005: £4,500

2 Sales are £15 per unit and cash is received three months after the sale. For the period in question, the sale of units is:

2005

Mar	April	May	June	Jul	Aug	Sept	Oct
60	60	75	90	55	140	130	150

2006

Nov	Dec	Jan	Feb
150	160	170	150

3 Production in units

2005

Mar	Apr	May	June	Jul	Aug	Sept	Oct
40	50	80	70	80	130	130	150

2006

Nov	Dec	Jan	Feb
145	160	170	160

4 Raw materials cost £4 per unit and these are paid for two months *before* being used in production.

5 Wages are £5 per unit and this is paid for in the same month as the unit is produced.

6 Running costs are £4 per unit. 50% of the cost is paid for in the month of production, while the other 50% is paid for in the month after production.

7 Sundry expenses of £50 are paid monthly.

Receipts from sales			£
July	60	(April) x 15 =	900
August	75	(May) x 15 =	1,125
September	90	(June) x 15 =	1,350
October	55	(July) x 15 =	825
November	140	(Aug) x 15 =	2,100
December	130	(Sept) x 15 =	1,950

Payments per month
July

Raw materials	130	(Sept) x 4 =	520
Wages	80	(July) x 5 =	400
Running costs	80	(July) x 2 =	160
	70	(June) x 2 =	140
Sundry expenses		=	50
			£1,270

August

Raw materials	150	(Oct) x 4 =	600
Wages	130	(Aug) x 5 =	650
Running costs	130	(Aug) x 2 =	260
	80	(July) x 2 =	160
Sundry expenses		=	50
			£1,720

September

Raw materials	145	(Nov) x 4 =	580
Wages	130	(Sept) x 5 =	650
Running costs	130	(Sept) x 2 =	260
	130	(Aug) x 2 =	260
Sundry expenses		=	50
			£1,800

October

Raw materials	160	(Dec) x 4 =	640
Wages	150	(Oct) x 5 =	750
Running costs	150	(Oct) x 2 =	300
	130	(Sept) x 2 =	260
Sundry expenses		=	50
			£2,000

November

Raw materials	170	(Jan) x 4 =	680
Wages	145	(Nov) x 5 =	725
Running costs	145	(Nov) x 2 =	290
	150	(Oct) x 2 =	300
Sundry expenses		=	50
			£2,045

December

Raw materials	160	(Feb) x 4 =	640
Wages	160	(Dec) x 5 =	800
Running costs	160	(Dec) x 2 =	320
	145	(Nov) x 2 =	290
Sundry expenses		=	50
			£2,100

These can now be transposed into a cash-flow chart as shown below:

	July	Aug	Sept	Oct	Nov	Dec
Receipts						
Sales	900	1,125	1,350	825	2,100	1,950
Total receipts	900	1,125	1,350	825	2,100	1,950
Payments						
Raw materials	520	600	580	640	680	640
Direct labour	400	650	650	750	725	800
Variable expenses	300	420	520	560	590	610
Fixed expenses	50	50	50	50	50	50
Total payments	1,270	1,720	1,800	2,000	2,045	2,100
Receipts – payments	(370)	(595)	(450)	(1,175)	55	(150)
Balance b/f	4,500	4,130	3,535	3,085	1,910	1,965
Balance c/f	4,130	3,535	3,085	1,910	1,965	1,815

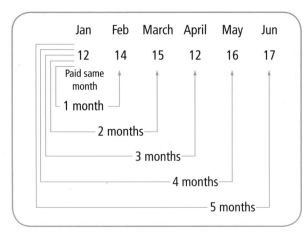

FIGURE 3.10 *Payments made on credit*

3.2.6 Importance of accurate record keeping and technology

Look at the financial pages of any newspaper and you will see the extent to which external confidence in the management of a large business is determined by its financial performance. Shareholders and other external stakeholders keenly await information on financial performance in the business. If you are working for the business, your work will contribute to this financial performance and you may have a role in recording the financial transactions of the business. Even the smallest transaction will be audited so that the final accounts accurately represent what the business has been doing during the year. Public confidence in a business and the confidence of all employees will rely upon good accounts.

Monitoring business performance

Accounting is concerned with identifying, measuring, recording and reporting information relating to the activities of an organisation. Accounting information may be used both within and outside an organisation. It involves providing important data that may form the basis for decisions.

We can break each of the accounting activities down into the following:

* *Identifying*. This involves capturing all the financial data within a business related to how it is performing. For example, this would include all information about the sales of goods to customers, data about the payment of expenses (such as wages and rent) and also information about the purchase of any stock, as well as data about the purchase of new vehicles and machinery.

* *Measuring*. Money, in the form of pounds and pence, is used as the form of measurement of economic transactions. In the future, the form of measurement might change to become euros. For accounting purposes, instead of saying a business sold 10 cars in a week which can be meaningless if you do not know the value of the cars, it may be useful to specify the value of the cars. For example, 10 cars valued at £15,000 would mean a turnover during the week of £150,000.

* *Recording*. Accounting data and information must be recorded into either handwritten accounting books or into a suitable computer package, such as a specialised accounting package or a spreadsheet.

* *Communicating*. The reporting of financial information may take a variety of different forms. For example, although some financial information may be required and extracted from the accounts weekly, such as sales totals, there are standard financial statements (such as profit and loss accounts and **balance sheets**) that have a set format for reporting the activities of organisations.

It is important that, throughout this accounting process, the accounting information is:

* reliable – free from errors and bias

* comparable – accounting information should be comparable with information from other organisations

* relevant – accounting information should relate to many of the decisions that have to be made about the business

* understandable – information should be capable of being understood by those at whom it is targeted.

Decision-making

In a fast changing business environment both managers and employees need information that will help them with decision-making. Accounting information provides help with knowing what to order and the requirements within the business for the next few months. At a more senior level, managers may be concerned with profitability and some of the wider decisions that need to be taken within the business organisation.

Credit control

As we have seen most products or services transacted by business organisations are done on credit. Credit control involves managing the credit transactions within a business organisation. Financial information will help a credit controller to understand who the business owes money to and the period over which it has been owed. Depending upon that and what is considered to be a reasonable credit period, bills will be settled. Similarly, it helps the organisation to know who owes them money and over what period so that phone calls or some other form of contact can be made in order to bring some money in.

Financial position

Every business has to meet internal and external reporting requirements to show its financial health and to meet legal and other requirements. The following stakeholders of a business need financial information about the performance of the business:

* internal users – groups within the organisation, such as managers
* external users – groups outside the organisation, such as shareholders and creditors.

Every business environment is competitive and some will inevitably perform better than others. Where a business does well, there are many rewards and benefits for individuals and organisations affected by its actions. However, if a business has a bad year or does not do well, there can be a range of consequences for individuals and organisations that may be affected by its poor performance.

CASE STUDY

Not all businesses are profitable

There are around 460 loss-making companies listed on the London Stock Exchange and some of these are fairly well-known companies. So, is it advisable to buy shares in organisations that make losses? Many new businesses are loss-makers from the moment they start and never seem to make money. Some organisations make losses because a sudden change in their business environment causes them to make losses. For example, the events of 11 September 2001 suddenly hit the aviation industry. For companies like Sabena this was the final nail in their coffin.

Some businesses make losses over a considerable time as it is difficult to generate revenues to cover expenses. For example, with new high-tech companies or drug companies it may take years to generate revenues.

Despite their lack of profits, many investors like loss-makers, mainly because there is always a chance of a turnaround, and the shares may be cheap.

1 Why do we assume that all businesses will be profitable?
2 Is it possible to identify a sector in which few businesses are profitable?
3 Why might an investor wish to buy shares in unprofitable companies?

Meeting legal requirements

Businesses also need to keep accounts in order to meet a range of legal requirements from Companies Acts and other legislation. In addtion, they also need to provide information for the tax authorities such as the Inland Revenue and Customs & Excise.

Financial and management accounting

The process of accounting can be divided into two broad areas:

* financial accounting
* management accounting.

Financial accounting

Financial accounting is concerned with the recording of financial transactions and the preparation of financial reports to communicate past financial performance.

Subject to accounting regulations, financial accounting:

* provides reports/statements that follow a standard approach
* provides a broad overview of the whole business using totals
* provides information to a particular date
* produces general statements and reports
* quantifies information in monetary terms and values.

Management accounting

Management accounting involves looking to the future using a knowledge of past performance where relevant, to aid the management of the business.

In management accounting, reports are only for internal use so no restrictions are necessary. This sector of accounting:

* provides extracted information which relates to parts of the organisation where it is used to help with a particular decision

* will look at future performance as well as at past perfomance
* produces reports with a specific decision in mind
* may include non-financial information such as stocks.

Profitability and liquidity (solvency)

Managing a business organisation requires those within it to keep accurate and up-to-date records, so that decisions can be made about a range of issues that involve profitability and liquidity. The records help the organisation to pay bills upon time and meet the requirements of their creditors; they are also used to assess their tax liabilities. Such records are then used to assess whether a business is profitable, so that managers can make key decisions that help it to make the most of opportunities that arise.

Profitability

Following the financial reports in any newspaper will reveal that one of the key newsworthy areas constantly emphasised by the press is that of profits. For example, 'Eurostar' might be 'rocked by profit warnings' or 'Somerfield to retreat to the high street'. Profits are a key indicator when judging business performance. It is the first point of reference for many organisational stakeholders.

It is all very well saying that sales have risen, productivity is soaring and the organisation is growing. However, shareholders and providers of capital will always ask the question: 'But, have you been making a profit?'

Think it over...

In 2004, the net rate of return upon the capital invested for UK private businesses was 13.6 per cent. For manufacturing companies it was at 7.6 per cent, but for service companies it was 17 per cent.

Liquidity / solvency

The words '**liquidity**' or '**solvency**' mean 'to be able to meet financial obligations'. A business becomes 'technically **insolvent**' when it has sufficient assets to meet all its financial obligations, but insufficient time to convert these assets into cash. It is 'legally insolvent' if it is in a situation of permanent cash shortage.

A number of users of accounting information will want to check regularly on the solvency of business organisations. For example, owners and shareholders will want to know their money is 'safe'. In this respect they will want to look at the distribution of assets and liabilities a company has. In other words, they will want to know what a business owns and what a business owes. For example, the company may have money coming in at 'some time in the future'. However, unless it has money coming in now, tomorrow and the next day, it may face cash-flow problems that make it 'technically insolvent'.

Lenders of money to organisations want to know their loans will be repaid and that interest will be paid at regular intervals. Employees and other stakeholders in organisations will want the security of knowing the organisation is solvent.

Managers will want to know the extent of solvency so that they can restructure assets and liabilities into an appropriate form. For example, they will want to manage their assets in a way that enables them to pay bills as and when they arrive in the organisation, without being too liquid and having too much cash not doing anything. Solvency is a base-line for ongoing business operations.

When auditors carry out a periodic audit of an organisation's accounts, one of the key areas they need to emphasise is how solvent the organisation is.

Use of modern technology

The success of business organisations depends on the efficient and accurate production of goods or services and on the rapid and accurate processing and distribution of information. In today's business environment this process is almost totally dependent upon new technology. This is because:

* the scale of many large organisations makes it impossible for every meeting to be conducted face-to-face

* many organisations are geographically spread out and require communication links between interrelated plants and offices

* modern business decision-making frequently requires up-to-date information from a variety of sources

* competition between business organisations is more fierce

* the pace of industrial development has increased so organisations must be quicker in responding to factors such as technological change, market forces and competition from rivals.

Technology is now an ongoing issue for many organisations. Technology has been associated with having the knowledge and competence necessary to ensure that organisations compete successfully within their chosen market sectors.

Advantages of using ICT

Technology provides a range of benefits such as:

* increased productivity – with new machinery and equipment producing goods or providing services at lower cost

* although introducing technology can be expensive, over a longer period the costs of technology can be recovered through improved efficiency

* the ability to compete more efficiently – technology provides a range of updated and more efficient processes, for example, technology may help a production line to run more quickly

* speed and accuracy of operations – technology not only enables things to work more quickly but may improve the way in which customer needs are met with better accuracy and few problems and mistakes

* the need for fewer staff and reductions in operational costs – in many circumstances technology takes staff away from mundane and boring jobs, and reduces costs, where the technology takes over the tasks

* technology allows staff to do more and increases the variety of tasks they undertake, enabling both the staff and the organisation to become more flexible

* better presentation of materials – the finish of materials as well as the quality can be improved through technology

* improved forms of communication – information and communication technologies have transformed the way in which people share thoughts and ideas

* a more modern feel about an organisation – technology and its uses often say a lot about an organisation and have the potential to improve how others perceive it.

Technology can have a huge influence upon staff performance and productivity and dramatically increase the efficiency of different members of staff. Although it may push up costs it can dramatically improve quality and provide a

A typical modern office

different feel about perceptions of an organisation and its brands.

Disadvantages of ICT

The disadvantages of using modern technology in an organisation are as follows:

* the need to constantly invest in new technologies in order to retain their market position

* staff have to adapt and gain experience of different technologies and this means that they need to be trained and the costs of such training can be high

* if technology improves efficiency, this could lead to redundancies as organisations are able to operate with fewer staff

* staff must work in a way that maximises the investment in such technologies

* over-dependence upon a system may lead to a range of serious issues if the system fails

* there is a constant security risk – somebody could enter the system and manage to obtain access to data.

Theory into practice

List the different ways you communicate with friends in a typical day. How many of these different forms of communication such as MSN Messenger and the telephone are dependent upon technologies? Describe how such technologies are transforming the ways in which individuals communicate.

Replacement of technology takes place all of the time as does the need to update and redevelop software. In response to this staff have to be constantly trained to meet new technological requirements.

Software applications

Over the last ten years the modern office workplace has changed dramatically. Paper may still be around in many of these offices, but it is usual for almost every employee to have access to a computer terminal and the expectation is that, where employees use computers, they have the capability to use the many different software applications relevant for their particular jobs. For example, when using computers individuals may be required to use a range of applications such as databases, spreadsheets, word-processing packages, the use of the Internet, e-mail, and so on.

Spreadsheets

A **spreadsheet** is a table of numbers which can be organised and altered on a computer according to preset formulae. Spreadsheets are particularly useful for forecasting and financial modelling as they show the effects of financial decisions without the need to repeat the calculations manually. An organisation can make a forecast of all the money coming in and going out over a twelve-month period, and a spreadsheet is able to alter the inputs to calculate the effect, for example, of lowering a heating bill by a certain amount each month. The computer will automatically recalculate the columns to change the heating figures, total cost figures and cash flows for each month. In this way a manager, accountant or other user of a spreadsheet can quickly carry out business calculations such as introducing and finding out the effect of minor changes of variables.

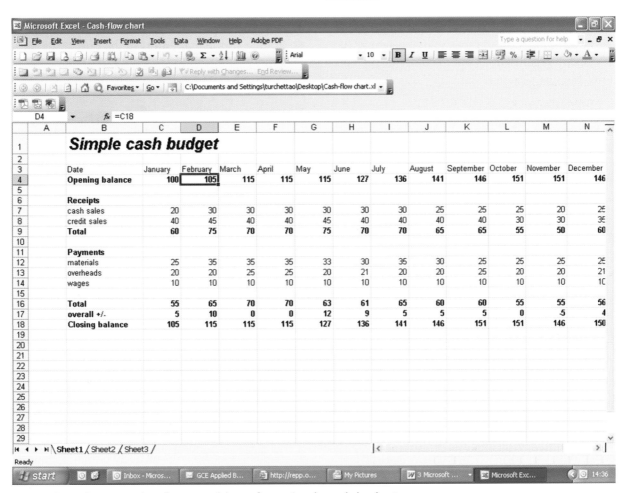

FIGURE 3.11 *An example of a spreadsheet for a simple cash budget*

One of the benefits of using a spreadsheet is that, having developed and entered the formulas, it is possible to change figures and predict different outcomes.

The example shown on page 135 is of a spreadsheet. The receipts simply involved totalling two boxes to produce total receipts which in this instance involved the sum of C7+C8. The total for payments involved totalling materials, **overheads** and wages which came out at C12+C13+C14. Overall +/− was C9-C16 and the closing balance was C4+C9−C16. The closing balance has to become the opening balance for the next period and so C18, the closing balance on the first column, is the same as D4, now shown to =C18. Calculations can be extended across the page.

Spreadsheets that forecast either cash or profits are relatively simple to construct and easy to change. By simply changing the opening balance at the beginning of the spreadsheet all of the other calculations instantly change. The widespread use of computers by all types of organisations has seen many organisations opt to computerise their book-keeping systems.

Accounts packages

There are a number of advantages of using computerised accounting packages:

* computers help to improve the control of funds coming into and going out of an organisation and make this control more effective

* they improve accuracy, particularly where large amounts of data are entering into accounts (i.e. they take away much of the tedium of data entry into double-entry accounts)

* accounting data is, by its very nature, arithmetical, which is well suited to being recorded and maintained by computer

* computerised book-keeping systems can supply reports and account balances much more quickly (such as trial balance, stock valuation, payroll analysis, VAT return, etc.)

* many reports can be produced quickly and easily in a way that would not be possible in a manual system because of time and cost, for example, it would be easy to go through the sales ledger to find out all the customers who have not paid their debts and send them reminders to do so

* they help to provide managers with a readily accessible view of how the business organisation is functioning.

Computer programs for financial accounts usually follow the same system of ledger division into general and personal. In doing so the system provides an element of continuity with past practices. Commercially available accounting software is usually described as an '**integrated accounts package**', covering a range of accounting activities. For example, an accounting package would:

* update customer accounts in the sales ledger

* update supplier accounts in the purchases ledger

* record bank receipts and payments

* print out invoices

* make payments to suppliers and for expenses

* adjust records automatically.

Many packages offer more than just the control of each of the ledgers. Some may also provide for payroll, stock control production planning, electronic data interchange (EDI) and financial planning. These can be integrated with the rest of the accounting system.

An integrated accounting system means that, when a business transaction takes place and is input into the computer, it is recorded into a range of accounting records at the same time. For example, if a sales invoice is generated for a customer:

* the customer's account will be adjusted with the invoice total

* the sales account will increase and VAT will be applied

* stock records will change.

Databases

A **database** is an organised collection of information and data. By having data organised in such a way, it is possible to have easy access to huge volumes of information. Databases enable:

* an organisation to store information only once and access information from several files

* files to be linked together so that it is possible to update a whole range of files at the same time

* rapid access to information

* files to be accessed and manipulated quickly with little likelihood of data becoming lost.

The main problem with databases is that if a computer breaks down, it may be difficult to access information. Another problem might be unauthorised access to records, although data can be protected with passwords. Training in the use of databases can be costly.

Theory into practice

Use a range of tabulated information which you collect from a range of sources. It might simply be market research information, or information about the hobbies of members of your class. Put the data into a spreadsheet and then graphically present it in at least two forms together with appropriate labels.

3.2.7 Analysis of the current market position

Businesses operate in competitive markets. In making decisions about their position in the market, businesses need to be aware of the actions of competitors.

SWOT analysis

Organisations keep a very close eye on each other by carrying out a SWOT analysis (see page 32) which involves assessing:

* the internal strengths of the company (S)
* the internal weaknesses of the company (W)

* the external opportunities (O)
* the external threats. (T)

The SWOT analysis is also sometimes referred to as a WOTS-up analysis. We use the term WOTS-up because it is a way of finding out any problems that an organisation might be having which can be put right. It is easy to remember because people often say 'What's Up?' – meaning 'What is the problem?' In this book however, we will use the expression SWOT because you will need to carry out a SWOT as part of your assessment. It is a very useful tool in helping the business to achieve its marketing objectives.

Marketing objectives are the end purposes which the business hopes to achieve through marketing activities. Examples of marketing objectives might be:

* to become the market leader in a particular market

* to increase market share

* to become more customer focused.

Carrying out a SWOT analysis helps the business to focus its activities on these marketing objectives. For example, to become the market leader it helps to be able to:

* identify strengths relative to competitors, and then to build on these strengths

* identify internal weaknesses and to seek to reduce and eliminate these weaknesses. For example, an internal weakness might be that the company is not market focused enough. Addressing this weakness might involve employing more people who understand about marketing and market research.

* identify opportunities – such as new products and new markets that are developing

* identify threats – such as the development of a new product coming onto the market produced by a rival – helps a business to respond appropriately.

CASE STUDY
Shell and BP

In February 2005, Shell and BP both announced record profits for British companies. They operate in the same sector – oil and gas exploration, refining and sale and have similar but slightly different approaches.

BP's strategy has been to invest heavily in oil and gas exploration, seeking new fields to exploit. They have been very successful, but the problem is that oil and gas are finite resources – the discovery of new fields is limited. Increasingly, to exploit new fields exploration has had to take place in remote areas of the globe and pipelines have to cross politically sensitive areas.

Shell has pursued a strategy of exploration but not to the same extent as BP. Instead, Shell has focused a lot of investment in the development of so called 'future fuels' which are seen as the ones that will replace hydrocarbons. For example, future fuels include the development of a hydrogen fuel for the hydrogen car (service stations for hydrogen fuel have already opened up in Iceland and Japan). Other future fuels are based on bio-fuels, such as burning plant matter, and wind farming.

These two companies keep a very close eye on each other by carrying out SWOT analyses. We can set out a simple SWOT analysis for BP to compare its position with Shell in the following way:

Strengths – a very profitable company with exploration taking place across the world. Oil and gas drilling, refining and distribution taking place on a global scale. One of the best-known names in oil and gas in the world.	**Weaknesses** – oil and gas are finite resources. The company may be over relying on the future of hydrocarbons.
Opportunities – possibilities to develop new pipelines in areas of the world that are opening up such as China and Eastern Europe. As oil and gas become increasingly scarce their prices will rise.	**Threats** – global warming may lead to government actions to ban hydrocarbon fuels. Threats of wars and military action may threaten BP facilities across the globe. Competitors may develop future fuels.

Set out a SWOT analysis for Shell to compare its position with BP.

Theory into practice

Carry out a SWOT analysis for an organisation that you are familiar with, e.g. one where you are carrying out work experience, one that you have researched on the Internet or in the newspaper, or even your local college or school. Show what needs to be done about the internal strengths and weaknesses of the organisation. Explain how the organisation should respond to market opportunities and threats in order to achieve its marketing objectives.

CASE STUDY
Tesco supermarket

The supermarket industry in this country is very competitive – but one store stands head and shoulders above the rest in terms of its success in recent years. In January 2005 the market share of the main firms in the industry stood as follows:

Food retailer	% share of the market
Tesco	29
ASDA	17
Sainsbury's	16
Morrisons and Safeway	13

Source: Euromonitor International

Tesco takes almost one in three pounds spent in Britain's grocery stores. It has almost 2,000 stores across the UK and stocks a range of items from music downloads to household mortgages. Tesco has been very successful in clothing lines (such as Florence and Fred) and its cut-price electrical stores have been very successful.

There are some indications of unrest with the success of Tesco, particularly coming from environmental pressure groups and local residents who fear the effect that the arrival of Tesco will have on local shopping choice. As Tesco is making record profits, many people feel that we are becoming too dependent on the store and that it is limiting our choice.

Set out a SWOT analysis for Tesco using the information provided in this case study and the Internet (try www.tesco.com to start).

Of course, because Tesco operates in a highly competitive market environment the nature of this environment may have changed – for example, with the development of increased competition from rivals like Sainsbury's and ASDA.

CASE STUDY
Time for a change for Smarties

The maker of Smarties announced in February 2005 that it was replacing the sweet's tube-shape packet after almost 70 years. Nestlé Rowntree will be replacing the cylindrical design known to generations of children with a long, hexagonal pack. The plastic disc on the top of the tube will also be replaced in favour of a cardboard flip-top lid.

The confectionery giant said the revamp was needed to ensure the brand remained 'fresh and interesting' to youngsters. The so-called Hexatube packet will be sold in stores from the summer of 2005.

Nestlé Rowntree carried out extensive market research which showed that young people have so many different influences that they want to keep the products that they buy contemporary. Nestlé Rowntree realised the importance of keeping the packaging and the brand fresh and interesting for consumers.

1 How would a SWOT analysis have helped Nestlé Rowntree to decide to make the change?
2 What was the significance of market research in driving the change?
3 What marketing tools has Nestlé Rowntree used in making the change?

PEST and SLEPT analysis

Another type of analysis that most businesses carry out in order to analyse their market position is the PEST or **SLEPT analysis**.

These analyses are used to examine the environment in which the business operates. They are employed because modern businesses operate in very turbulent environments in which it is essential to understand the changes that are taking place.

Theory into practice

Set out a SLEPT analysis to outline ways in which a particular product or group of products can be made more sensitive to market conditions as a result of a SLEPT analysis. For your table, use the same headings shown in the case study on page 141.

PEST analysis	
P – Political factors	Political factors include such things as a change in government. For example, the election of a Conservative government might lead to the lowering of some business taxes.
E – Economic factors	These are changes in the wider economy such as changes in general economic activity. For example, is the economy growing leading to lots of spending in the shops which would encourage businesses to invest more? Other important economic factors include changes in the interest rates (the price of borrowing money), the price of the £ in exchange with other currencies, the level of unemployment etc.
S – Social factors	Changes in social trends are very important for business. They include such things as changes in the age structure of the population, for example, there are more elderly people than in the past. Other factors include changes in tastes and buying patterns, for example, as people live busier lives they purchase more ready-made meals rather than cooking their own.
T – Changes in technology	New technologies regularly come on stream, making old ways of doing things old-fashioned. Successful businesses are ones that adapt and apply new technologies.

FIGURE 3.12 *PEST analysis*

SLEPT analysis	
S – Social	Changes in social trends.
L – Legal	Changes in the law – businesses must keep abreast of changes in the law e.g. changes in environmental legislation requiring tougher pollution controls, changes in equal opportunities laws requiring better facilities for disabled workers etc.
E – Economic	Changes in economic variables.
P – Political	Political changes.
T – Technology	Changes in technology.

FIGURE 3.13 *SLEPT analysis*

CASE STUDY

Carrying out a SLEPT analysis

The following SLEPT analysis was carried out for a well-known chocolate bar which had been marketed as being 'supersize'.

1 What would be the purpose of this SLEPT analysis?
2 Use an example from below to show how the SLEPT might have influenced some management decisions.

SLEPT factor	Description	Implication for company
S – Social	Increasingly consumers are becoming aware of the importance of healthy eating. Some are turning away from products with lots of calories – although many are still eating highly-calorific chocolate bars.	Company may need to produce smaller size products – although perhaps it should continue to cater for those seeking a supersize bar. The company should seek ways of reducing fat and sugar content in chocolate bars.
L – Legal	Government legislation requires food manufacturers to specify the content of food products including calorific content. Government is also looking at how food products are advertised – particularly to children.	Essential to comply with legal requirements.
E – Economic	Rising living standards mean that increasing numbers of people are able to afford treats such as chocolate products.	Economic trends indicate that people across the globe are increasingly able to afford to buy chocolate products.
P – Political	The UK (Labour) government has placed a strong emphasis on healthy eating, bringing the attention of the public to the importance of a healthy diet. The government has created a Healthy Schools programme encouraging teachers to make pupils aware of the importance of diet and exercise, and making sure that schools focus on providing healthy products for pupils.	It is important for companies to comply with government requirements. There is a danger that companies that produce unhealthy products and promote unhealthy practices will be 'named and shamed'. Therefore an important requirement for companies to focus on is producing 'healthier' chocolate bars e.g. with less sugar and fat content.
T – Technology	New technologies provide sophisticated ways of mixing and making existing products as well as producing appropriate packaging.	Food technology can be combined with an understanding of healthy eating issues to change the make-up of chocolate bars to make them 'healthier'. Packaging can be altered to alert consumers to the need for a balanced diet.

Linking SWOT and SLEPT analysis

You should be able to see that the SWOT and the SLEPT analyses are closely related.

The SLEPT analysis examines changes in the external environment. It therefore primarily relates to the opportunities and threats facing a business.

Whereas these SLEPT factors primarily relate to opportunities and threats (i.e. external factors in

	Opportunity	Threat
S – Social factors	e.g. changes in tastes and hence demand in favour of our product.	Changes in the population structure that have an adverse effect on demand for our product.
L – Legal factors	A change in the law that our company is already prepared for e.g. we have in place all the necessary environmental controls.	A new law that our company is not ready for.
E – Economic factors	Rising living standards, falls in interest rates etc.	e.g. a downturn in the economy.
P – Political factors	e.g. government policies that favour business.	e.g. a government that taxes businesses more heavily.
T – Technological factors	e.g. new technologies that our business can adapt quicker than competitors.	e.g. new technologies which our rivals have adapted more quickly than us.

How a SLEPT analysis helps us to understand our business's environment

a SWOT analysis) we also need to look at internal strengths and weaknesses.

Strengths primarily relate to having the right type of resources to do well in the market. These resources include:

* having managers who can make change happen and who understand the market.

* having good human resources – people who are flexible and are equipped to satisfy the market, for example, through interacting well with customers (customer service).

* having a good financial resource base, for example, from making healthy profits.

* having an excellent marketing department that understands what customers require.

In addition, organisations which have adopted the most suitable technologies will flourish.

Weaknesses stem from having inappropriate resources to satisfy customers and from being weak compared with rivals.

When you are analysing the current market position of a business you should make links between external and internal issues. For example, any economic data such as high interest rates (an external issue) needs to be linked to the effect on loan capital of the business (an internal issue). A firm with a lot of borrowing will be adversely hit by a rise in interest rates. The threat (rising interest rates) combines with the weakness (too much borrowing) to create a double problem for the business.

In a similar way, changes in social trends (an external issue) e.g. consumers wanting to spend more money on lifestyle goods will combine with the success of a firm having excellent market research and marketing (an internal issue).

Theory into practice

Give examples of the way in which:

1 A change in technology (external issue) will combine favourably with a company being a technology leader (an internal strength).

2 A change in the law (external issue) will combine with a firm having strong management (an internal strength).

3 A change in the actions of competitors (an external issue) will combine with a firm having excellent and highly motivated employees (an internal strength).

3.2.8 Economic conditions and market conditions

There are a number of external influences that affect businesses and these factors can have a real impact on day-to-day business decision-making.

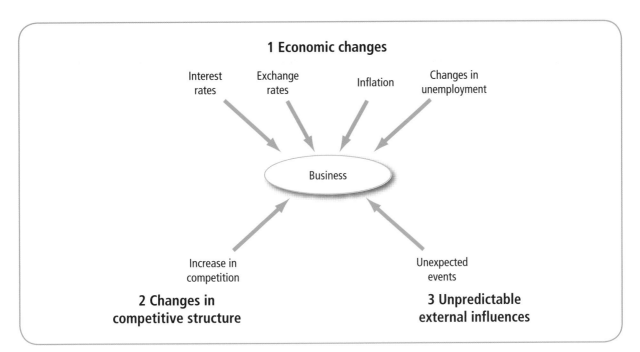

FIGURE 3.14 *External influences on organisations*

These influences relate to:

* changes in economic indicators such as interest rates (the price of borrowing money)

* changes in the competitive structure of the market the organisation operates in, for example, the arrival of new competitors make the market more competitive

* unpredictable changes such as the influence of 11 September 2001 when a terrorist attack on the heart of New York's central business district led to a sudden loss of confidence in the world economic system.

Changes in economic indicators

Organisations are affected by conditions in the local and wider economy:

* when the economy is booming this leads to a general increase in demand for products and also an increase in business costs

* when the economy is depressed this leads to a general slump in demand for products and costs fall.

Important economic changes that affect organisations are shown above.

Inflation

Inflation is a sustained increase in the general price level which leads to a fall in the value of money.

The rate of inflation is measured by the annual percentage change in the level of consumer prices. The British government tries to keep inflation within a target level of 2 per cent. The average increase in prices is measured using a measuring tool known as the Consumer Price Index (CPI). The Consumer Price Index is a monthly indication of the average price changes to a particular 'basket' of consumer goods and is used as a general indicator of price inflation. The CPI therefore shows how average prices are changing over time. This is an important measure. For example, it shows how prices are changing in comparison with incomes (a measure of how well-off households are).

Inflation is a problem for business because it adds to business costs. One of the most common reasons for inflation is increases in the price of essential raw materials and goods. For example, oil prices are much higher than they were 20 years ago and are likely to rise in the future as oil reserves run out. As oil is an essential fuel that goes into producing so many goods this is

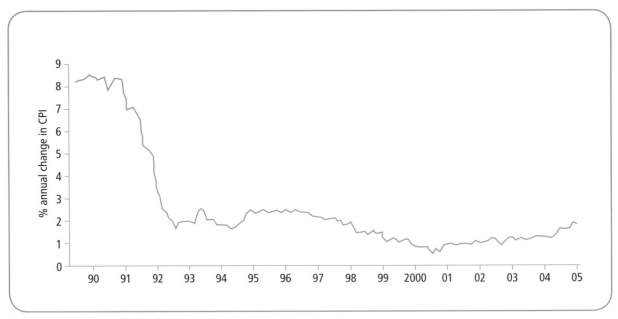

Source: Central Statistical Office Monthly Report

FIGURE 3.15 *Consumer price inflation in the UK*

likely to have an inflationary impact. There are also some other factors that have brought prices down such as the widespread use of computer-based technology in so many different goods and services. As computers have become more efficient prices have fallen.

The chart in Figure 3.15 shows that consumer price inflation in the UK has been at quite a low level over the last 10 years.

Theory into practice

Explain how inflation might affect:

* a motor car manufacturer
* a taxi firm
* a large insurance company.

Think it over...

In the chronic German inflation of 1926 the value of money fell so quickly that when one day a man took a wheelbarrow full of money to buy food at his local shops, a thief tipped out the money in the street and stole the wheelbarrow.

Interest rates

Interest rates are closely related to inflation. In this country interest rates are set by the Bank of England's Monetary Policy Committee. When inflation starts to rise the Monetary Policy Committee (MPC) may raise interest rates to discourage people from borrowing money. This is to dampen down the demand for goods and services in the economy. If there is too much demand this pushes up prices (leading to inflation) which can be harmful to business.

However, when the MPC raises interest rates this can have an adverse effect on businesses that have borrowed money. This is because they have to pay more in interest on the sums they borrowed than before. If they have borrowed a lot of money this can raise their costs substantially and lower their profits.

The Monetary Policy Committee seeks to set interest rates that help the government to achieve its target of keeping inflation at the 2 per cent target level.

Exchange rates

The exchange rate measures the external value of a currency, for example, the pound sterling in terms of how much of another currency it can buy – such as how many euros you can buy with £1.

| Raise interest rates. | Raises business costs. Helps to lower demand inflation. | Can lead to a reduction in business profits (some businesses go bust). |
| Lower interest rates. | Lowers business costs. Helps to raise demand inflation. | Can help to raise business profits. |

FIGURE 3.16 *Effect of a change in interest rates*

The daily value of the pound is determined in the foreign exchange markets (FOREX) where billions of pounds of currencies are traded every hour. The value is determined by the demand and supply. If lots of people want to buy pounds, for example, to be able to buy British goods, then this will raise the value of the pound.

The problem is that the pound is used in a fairly small market place – the UK is a market of only 60 million people. It is a nuisance for businesses to have to buy foreign currency to buy goods from overseas, or vice versa because often there is a charge for making the transaction. This is why many large British businesses would like to join the euro zone. The euro zone is made up of all those countries that use the common currency of the euro including the Netherlands, Germany, France, Italy and Spain.

In recent times the pound has fallen in value against the euro. This means that when we want to buy goods from the euro zone we have to give increasing numbers of pounds to purchase the same quantities of goods and services than we did before the fall of the pound.

When the sterling exchange rate is high, it is cheaper to import raw materials, components and machinery and equipment. Of course, this is good news for businesses that rely on imported components or who are willing to purchase high-tech machinery and equipment from abroad.

A strong exchange rate, however, has the beneficial effect of keeping inflation down because British suppliers now face more intense competition from cheaper imports and will look to cut their costs accordingly.

Theory into practice

What do you think are the advantages and disadvantages of having a weak (falling value) pound? Set out your findings in a table.

Unemployment

The level of unemployment in a local area is important for an organisation as they may need to compete for the scarce resource of labour.

The official way to count the numbers unemployed is to record those who are registered as able, available and willing to work but who cannot find work despite actively searching for a job.

In recent years there has been a fall in those measured as being unemployed.

There are two main ways of counting the unemployed:

1 The Claimant Count covers those people who are eligible to claim the Job Seeker's Allowance.

2 The Labour Force Survey covers those who have looked for work in the past month and are able to start work in the next two weeks. Typically the Labour Force Survey measure is higher than the claimant count method by about 400,000.

Theory into practice

In recent years there has been a fall in those measured as being unemployed as shown by the following table.

Year	Labour Force Survey %	Claimant Count %
1995	8.8	7.6
2000	5.6	3.6
2003	5.2	3.1
2004		

Find out the unemployment figures for 2004 and enter them into the above table.

The level of unemployment is very important to business particularly in:

* *Determining costs.* The lower the level of unemployment, the higher the level of wages is likely to be. This is because labour is scarce relative to demand and employers are likely to have to compete for labour by offering higher wages and better opportunities.

* *Determining the investment required in the labour force.* When unemployment is low employers will need to invest more in training, developing and motivating their existing employees in order to keep them.

Changes in the competitive structure of the market

Businesses are continually aware of the competitiveness of the markets in which they operate. For example, if we look at supermarkets in this country, there is a clear competitive structure:

Tesco	The market leader with £1 out of every £3 of grocery sales.
Sainsbury's and ASDA	Are some way behind Tesco but are continually seeking to gain a bigger market share.
Morrisons	In fourth position and has recently taken over Safeway.
Other smaller supermarket chains	Each fighting for remaining sales – often taking a different position in the market, e.g. low-cost / limited range of items such as ALDI and NETTO.

In banking, the main competition is between:

* HSBC
* Halifax
* Barclays
* Lloyds TSB
* NatWest.

In markets like banking and supermarket retailing there are considerable advantages to being large. For example, a giant bank like Halifax is well placed to compete with smaller banks by offering better rates of interest to new customers. Supermarket chains like Tesco are able to buy millions of units from suppliers in any one order and therefore drive down costs.

Most markets where there are considerable **economies of scale** to be had are dominated by a small number of firms.

Large firms are able to:
* invest in the best assets
* spend more than their rivals on advertising and marketing
* get the best terms from suppliers
* invest heavily in market research to find out what customers want.

Of course, the competitive position is always changing – new firms enter the market, and new technologies and other opportunities present themselves for the development of competition.

For example, the development of the Internet as a way of buying goods online has threatened businesses such as:

* wine merchants
* book sellers
* travel agents.

However, in some ways the development of new technologies and other cost cutting developments can also reduce competition:

* although there is now intense competition between the major supermarket chains, they face reduced competition from small grocers and retail shops many of which have had to close down because they can't compete on costs
* many door-to-door milk rounds have closed down because small sellers can't compete with supermarket prices.

Theory into practice

Identify examples of situations where:

* competition has increased in an industry
* competition has been reduced in an industry.

Explain how these changes impact on the decisions that businesses make about their own future development in these industries.

Theory into practice

Your old TV is doomed which is great news for electrical retailers. By 2012 we will all need digital TV equipment because the analogue signal will have been switched off. Explain how this is likely to affect competition in the market for TV equipment. What objectives might firms have in order to win a leading position in this market?

Unpredictable external influences

Although businesses can think ahead and anticipate many changes in the market such as possible changes in interest rates and the arrival of new competitors, there are some occurrences which are too unpredictable to be anticipated.

One such occurrence was when terrorists attacked the heart of New York's business district

11 September 2001 – the terrorist attack led to a collapse of business confidence worldwide

CASE STUDY

Marks & Spencer

In March 2005, Marks & Spencer decided to take on its high street rivals by slashing the price of key items in its springwear collection. The high street giant confirmed that it had begun introducing new cheaper products in line with a strategy outlined by the company. M&S saw the price cutting as part of a way of creating lower entry price points into the market.

M&S embarked on the strategy in February, bringing down the prices of basic items such as T-shirts, jeans and trousers, and this was seen as part of a plan to refocus on the customer – giving the customer greater quality and value.

Overall, the costs cut M&S prices by 24% with clear implications for profit margins. At Christmas 2004 M&S was forced to make deep cuts to get rid of excess stock.

1 To what extent do you think the cuts at M&S were dictated by changing market conditions?
2 What will be the knock-on effect of M&S's strategy on rivals?
3 What do you think will be the likely outcome of M&S's strategy of moving to lower entry price points?

in September 2001. When this event happened there was panic in the world's stock markets and the value of many investments plummeted overnight, leading to a loss of confidence. For example, there was a dramatic fall in airline traffic and tourism during the ensuing year. This had a knock-on effect as other businesses also suffered leading to rising unemployment and a lot of businesses went bankrupt.

A similar catastrophe was the South East Asian crisis in the 1990s when there was a sudden loss of confidence in banking systems in countries like South Korea. This had a massive impact on business confidence across the globe.

Coping with changing economic and market conditions

Businesses need to create plans to deal with changes in the economic and market conditions. Important areas of planning include:

* *Managing finance*. Businesses shouldn't borrow too much externally because if market conditions take a downturn, then they may not be able to pay the high interest rates on borrowed money.

* *Keeping costs under control*. Businesses that allow their costs to rise too much when things are going well will struggle when profit margins fall. For example, Manchester United always keep their wage costs at under 50 per cent of their turnover.

* *Investing in market research and marketing activities*. Businesses that find out what customers want today and tomorrow will stay ahead of the competition.

* *Trying to become the market leader*. The market leader produces on a larger scale than rivals and therefore has lower costs.

* *Always being aware of current interest rates and exchange rates* means that businesses can make plans for any unfavourable changes.

* *Finding out what your competitors are doing*. Businesses should anticipate their strategies to keep one step ahead.

* *Always being prepared for unforeseen events*. Businesses must have a contingency plan to fall back upon.

* *Keeping employees informed* about what is going on in the business, in the economy and in the market will enable employees to help the business to be successful.

3.2.9 Ethical, legal, social, political and environmental factors

To stay competitive, modern businesses cannot solely focus their plans and activities on making a profit. They have to take on board what is referred to as a Triple bottom line. This term refers to the profit that appears on the bottom of a profit and loss account. The Triple bottom line refers to not only being successful in the economic (profit based) bottom line, but also in looking after society (a social bottom line) and the environment (an environmental bottom line).

Think it over...

Sir Terry Leahy, Chief Executive of Tesco, believes that each of the three parts of the bottom line are mutually supportive. He describes this as a win-win situation. In his 2004 statement in the Tesco Corporate Social Responsibility report he said that: 'Corporate responsibility is a win-win for Tesco and for the communities we serve. Because we have served more customers over the past year, we have grown as a business and have created 16,000 new jobs in the UK, many in deprived areas. Our regeneration and award-winning training schemes have created rewarding and fulfilling careers in retail for many people including staff who were previously long-term unemployed. We have given £8m in computer equipment for schools, and have raised £2.5m for Barnardo's, our charity of the year.'

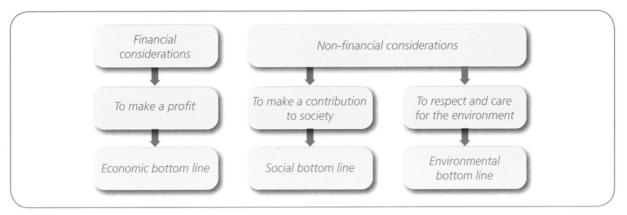

FIGURE 3.17 *The Triple bottom line*

Laws and ethics

Laws

Many of the activities that businesses carry out are constrained by laws. Laws are created in two main ways:

1 By Act of Parliament. New laws have to be passed by Parliament and then they become legally enforceable. In addition to UK national laws, many activities are controlled by European Union created laws. Some laws that affect business are created by local councils.

2 Other laws have been created by custom and practice over long periods of time. These are referred to as common law.

The sorts of laws that businesses are constrained by include:

* employment law governing issues such as contracts of employment, minimum wage legislation (the minimum wage is now set at over £5 an hour), rights to maternity leave, paternity leave, sick leave and other benefits

* Health and Safety at Work legislation governing an employer's and employees' responsibilities for health and safety practices

* equal opportunities and discrimination at work legislation

* laws governing the way in which businesses offer credit terms, control interest rate payments and the conditions of loans

* laws about company formation, limited liability, and the running of companies

* data protection legislation governing the sorts of information which companies must make publicly available and the types of information that data holders cannot put into the public domain

* laws about contracts that businesses can make with others etc.

* laws about the limitation of wastes that businesses create and the control of pollution.

* many other laws that affect business dealings with external parties and dealings that take place within a business.

Businesses must comply with legislation. Failure to comply with legislation can lead to penalties such as warnings, fines and even prison sentences for directors and others that break the law.

CASE STUDY
Smoking bans
In March 2005, it was widely reported that more than 30 cities and town in England were considering local bans on smoking in public places following the government's refusal to implement national rules. Some were expected to follow the example of Liverpool and the Greater London Authority which started preliminary steps to enable them to implement a ban in 2006.

Ethics

Ethics are moral principles or rules of conduct generally accepted by most members of society. Most organisations today believe it is necessary to take a stance that shows the public they operate in an ethical manner. Emphasis on the interest of the consumer is a key aspect of many organisations. Some ethics are reinforced through the legal system and provide a compulsory constraint on business activities, while others are the result of social pressure to conform to a particular standard.

Potential areas of concern for organisations include product ethics, where issues such as genetically modified foodstuffs or contaminated food may seriously and quickly affect short-term demand. For example, complaints about the marketing of various baby milk products in developing countries in the 1980s resulted in widespread criticism and boycotts of powdered milk manufacturers. The fact these practices ended 20 years ago is not fully appreciated by many members of the public and shows that bad business practice takes a long time to forget.

Another area of concern relates to business practice, where restrictive practices and poor treatment of employees have been highlighted in the media, and businesses have faced criticism from the public. The trading policies of companies who buy cheap imports from overseas organisations involved in 'sweat-shop labour', or who trade with businesses employing young children in unacceptable conditions, have also faced critical scrutiny from both the media and the public. For example, in the early 1990s Nike was found to be using some factories in South East Asia to produce Nike products, where child labour was being employed, for example, to stitch footballs. Since this time Nike has been able to put this right, and makes sure that as far as possible child labour is not employed in the factories where it gives contracts to produce Nike branded products.

Differences between legal and ethical responsibility

The law provides the baseline for sound business decision-making. Good businesses comply with every aspect of the law. However, 'better' businesses go further than just complying with the law. They also seek to do the right thing because they believe that this is the way to conduct business. In other words they take a moral/ethical stance.

CASE STUDY

Bad business practice

In 2004 the respected charity Christian Aid produced a report 'Behind the mask: the real face of corporate social responsibility'. The report focused on case studies of British American Tobacco and Coca-Cola highlighting some of the bad practices of these companies. The report argued that legislation is required to control the activities of business, because business on its own does not effectively regulate itself.

British American Tobacco stresses the importance of upholding high standards of health and safety among those working for them and claims to provide local farmers with the necessary training and protective clothing. However, contract farmers in Kenya and Brazil claim this does not happen and report chronic ill health related to tobacco cultivation.

Coca-Cola emphasises 'using natural resources responsibly'. Yet a wholly owned subsidiary in India is accused of depleting village wells in an area where water is notoriously scarce and has been told by an Indian court to stop drawing ground water.

1 Should we allow businesses to regulate their own activities or do we need laws to keep businesses doing the right things?
2 What other pressures can be put on business to do the right thing?
3 How might a business benefit from taking an ethical approach?
4 What other recent examples can you think of which reflect bad business practice? What have been the financial implications for the businesses concerned?

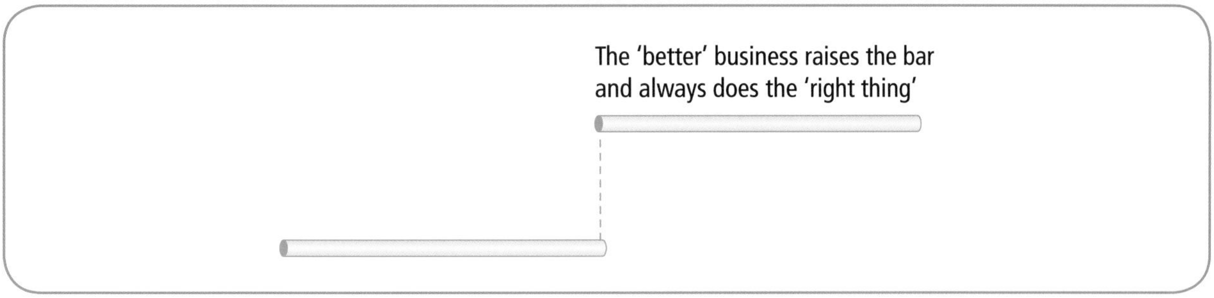

The 'better' business raises the bar and always does the 'right thing'

FIGURE 3.18 *A 'good' business complies with every aspect of the law*

CASE STUDY

Tesco's business ethics policy

Here is an extract from Tesco's business ethics policy:

> Tesco is committed to conducting business in an ethical and socially responsible manner. This relates to all aspects of our business, treating employees, customers, suppliers and shareholders in a fair and honest manner and ensuring that there are constant and open channels of communication.
>
> Tesco has a Code of Ethics for its staff, which includes a policy on the receipt of gifts and a

grievance procedure that covers employment issues. In 2003, Tesco launched a confidential telephone help line, Protector Line, for any employee who wishes to raise concerns relating to alleged criminal offences, failure to comply with legal obligations, miscarriages of justice, health and safety, damage to the environment and concealment of any of these issues.

1 Why has Tesco got an ethics policy?
2 Provide an example of who benefits from such a policy. Describe why they might benefit.

CASE STUDY

Banks cheating customers

A report produced by savings account provider ING Direct in March 2005 showed that many banks are taking advantage of loyal customers. Existing customers are losing out to new customers because banks are failing to offer them the best rates.

Savers and borrowers who stick with their bank are likely to suffer huge financial penalties because they are not offered the competitive deals designed to attract new customers. The big banks make a good part of their profits by penalising those customers they consider 'captive'.

The ING Direct survey found that 60 per cent of customers wanted financial services companies to stop short-term, headline-grabbing deals – commonly found on credit cards, mortgages and savings accounts – and

instead offer products with competitive rates available to all.

The ING survey showed that 40 per cent of individual customers who had left a financial institution in the past year did so because of the way the bank treated its loyal customers.

1 What do you think of banks' policies of rewarding new customers at the expense of existing ones?
2 Do you think that this is good or bad business practice?
3 Is it legal? Is it ethical?
4 Why might it be bad business practice in the longer term?
5 How should banks treat new and existing customers if they want to act in an ethical way?

Changing social trends

Over time many changes take place in society which are relevant to business including changes in population, in tastes and buying patterns and in employment patterns. An example of a change in employment patterns includes the growing numbers of women in the workplace which has led to an increased demand for convenience food. Other important social changes are shifts in values and culture, education and health, and distribution of income.

Social trends typically relate to such factors as:

* changes in values and attitudes over time which influence buying patterns, for example, people becoming more environmentally aware or health conscious

* changes in population structures which affect demand patterns, for example, the growth in the number of elderly people and those living in cities rather than rural areas.

The importance of environmental responsibility

In recent years, environmental issues have been highlighted by accidents at chemicals plants or at sea with oil tankers. These accidents can damage the image of the organisation concerned as well as wildlife and the environment.

With many companies' environmental performance becoming central to their competitiveness and survival, a range of new tools for environmental management have been developed. These include environmental impact assessments, which assess the likely impact of major projects and environmental audits or eco-audits, which involve carrying out an audit of current activities to measure their environmental impact. Alternatively, by looking at the environmental impact of a product through its life-cycle, from the sourcing of raw materials to the final disposal of waste products, a product life-cycle analysis can be established.

Taking a cost-benefit approach

A cost-benefit approach is often used by businesses in weighing up the advantages of particular actions.

* Costs include all the financial, social and environmental costs of taking a particular action. These costs will be measured in money terms.

* Benefits include all the financial, social and environmental benefits of taking a particular action. These benefits are measured in money terms.

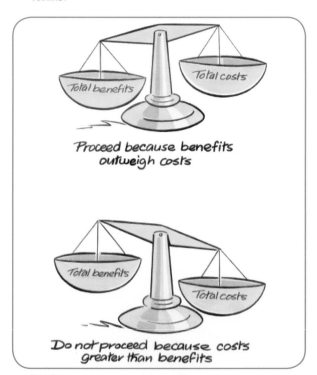

Weighing up costs and benefits

Total benefits – Total costs = Net benefit

In taking a particular action, organisations need to see that the total benefits outweigh the total costs. For example, if a supermarket decides to replace some of its non-organic fruit and vegetables with organic ones then the benefits and costs would include:

✳ *Economic benefits*. More customers for the shop who spend more on other goods which leads to greater profits.

✳ *Social benefits*. Leads to healthier society, better incomes for organic farmers and a better reputation in society for the supermarket.

✳ *Environmental benefits*. Less pollution as pesticides and chemicals are not used which can damage land, water and air systems.

✳ *Economic costs*. Might lose some customers who prefer non-organic produce. Organic products are more expensive to buy from farmers and therefore prices charged have to be higher.

✳ *Social costs*. Some non-organic farmers may suffer and have to close down their farms.

✳ *Environmental costs*. Few.

More and more businesses are realising the importance of corporate social responsibility because it helps a company to project a strong image. People trust some companies more than others. Companies with a good triple bottom line such as Tesco and Boots are much more highly thought of than companies who don't place much emphasis on corporate social responsibility.

Theory into practice

Can you think of examples of situations in which a businesses reputation has been threatened by the following:

✳ mis-selling products to the wider public

✳ failure to maintain appropriate standards of product safety.

✳ a business causing harm to the environment.

Theory into practice

Identify recent actions taken by companies that you are familiar with or are in the news which involve a corporate social responsibility dimension. For each action identify what you perceive to be the benefits and the costs. Estimate whether the benefits will outweigh the costs.

Think it over...

The term corporate social responsibility has been defined as an organisation taking responsibility for society which goes beyond the legal minimum requirement.

3.2.10 Stakeholders

Stakeholders are a number of different groups of individuals who have a stake in the decision-making process of a business:

✳ owners

✳ employees

✳ suppliers

✳ pressure groups

✳ creditors

✳ government

✳ society

✳ local community.

In the past businesses typically placed most emphasis on meeting the needs of its owners (shareholders). The emphasis was therefore on creating profit, and so decisions involving profit maximisation where given priority. However, today businesses are more aware of the need to create a successful triple bottom line. Businesses will create policies and plans covering a wide range of corporate social responsibility areas. For example, Boots have policies about:

✳ looking after disabled employees and customers

✳ Animal Rights – not testing new products on animals

* giving fair deals to suppliers
* making sure that all their supplies are created in ethical conditions e.g. no exploitation of child labour
* the environment, waste minimisation and pollution control.

Meeting the needs of all stakeholders

Business leaders at Shell coined the phrase 'earning a licence to operate' from stakeholders. It is all very well complying with the law to keep on the right side of government. However, the 'better' business recognises the needs of all of its stakeholder groupings and sets out to serve them. Businesses need to balance the needs of the various stakeholder groupings.

Meeting the needs of customers	Finding out what they want through market and customer satisfaction research, and then serving the needs of customers.
Creditors	Paying up on time and in a friendly spirit.
Employees	Paying them good wages, offering opportunities for promotion and personal development. Giving them a company to work for that they can be proud of.
Government	Paying the right amount of taxes on time and backing government initiatives such as those in relation to the environment.
Communities	Creating attractive jobs, providing clean and attractive premises, getting involved in community activities, giving money, time and skilled personnel to help with community projects.
Other stakeholder groups	Meeting the needs and requirements of these groups

Meeting stakeholder requirements

Shareholders

The **shareholders** have invested funds in a business. They receive two benefits from the firm doing well: the shares may rise in value if the firm is successful and also dividends that they receive will increase if profits improve. Conversely, they could lose all of the value of their investment should the business fail. Shareholders will vote at the AGM in support of or against decisions taken by directors. Shareholders can therefore have a direct impact on business decision making:

* they can vote to elect directors with ideas similar to their own
* the can vote off directors they disapprove of
* the can vote not to accept a company report
* they can threaten to sell their shares if they are not happy with company policy and direction.

No Board of Directors can ignore the wishes of major shareholders and shareholder groupings.

Directors

Directors are chosen by the shareholders to represent their interests. Their jobs will depend upon the success of the firm, as may the level of their remuneration. This may vary according to bonuses related to the financial success of the firm. Directors often hold positions of authority and make senior decisions across the whole of an organisation.

Directors therefore are key decision makers. They shape the policies and plans of the organisation. They create guidelines for managers to implement in making day-to-day decisions.

Employees

Employees' jobs also depend on the success of the firm, but the nature of the work that they are required to do may change according to its success. A firm in a competitive environment may experience regular change and the nature of work and the levels of responsibility that workers may be required to undertake may change. Firms that are struggling may 'release' some staff which would mean remaining staff may then have to take on more responsibility than they would choose. A solid firm, however, provides the employees with job security which lends security to their personal lives.

Employees are important stakeholders with a range of potential sanctions such as industrial action. They are also, of course, internal customers. Such power might influence senior managers who might be cautious about making decisions that would affect morale and influence the actions of the workforce. Most modern organisations involve a considerable amount of empowerment. Empowerment means passing the responsibility for decision making to lower levels within the organisation. This means that ground-level employees have considerable decision-making powers – e.g. how to deal with a consumer complaint, what to do if faults are occurring in production etc.

In large decentralised organisations many important decisions will be taken a long way away from the Head Office, or from the central directors of the organisation.

Customers

If a company works in a competitive market, customers may benefit through lower prices, but too much competition could leave them looking for a new company to buy from. If customers are unhappy with a business organisation, they may not buy its products. Customers therefore should be seen as key decision makers in determining what a company produces, where it sells those products, and how it presents those products.

We can see the power that consumers have in decision making by taking the example of modern university courses. Students decide what they want to study by choosing from different degree programmes – those that are unpopular may have to close down. They decide how they want to study e.g. at a university campus or by distance learning. They decide whether the course is good enough for them – by staying on the course or leaving if they are not satisfied. They also voice their opinions about the quality of the teaching and the resources they are provided with – even about the times of their lectures.

Suppliers

Companies that supply goods or services to a firm will want the firm to do well so that they have regular customers. Such suppliers may take sanctions against late payments by the organisation.

Suppliers provide terms of payment for the organisation. If the organisation does not work in their interests, they may change the terms. The Rover Group had to stop trading when suppliers started to refuse to offer them credit in April 2005. Where suppliers are very large compared to the buyer, suppliers are in a much better position to dictate terms. For example, a company like Coca-Cola which supplies in huge quantities can often dictate how its goods will be displayed, how they will be promoted, and other aspects of the marketing mix. However, when buyers are also very large – e.g. massive supermarket chains such as Tesco and ASDA there is greater equality in decision making.

Creditors

Creditors are people or organisations that are owed money by a business, for example, bankers who have lent the business money. They would like to see the firm succeed so that they get their money back and make a profit from the deal. If the company fails, the bank could be left with a bad debt, but if it is successful the relationship could be mutually profitable.

Creditors have considerable influence within the workplace. If a creditor suffers from late payment, they have a variety of sanctions at their disposal that might influence business decisions. For example, creditors may go to the courts to demand repayment, or request that the business that owes them money be placed into receivership. (An official receiver is then appointed to sell off the goods, machinery and equipment of that firm.)

Creditors are in good position to influence decisions made by a business. For example, when a bank lends a business money it may insist that it carries out certain actions or behaves in certain ways.

Government

Every firm pays corporation tax from profits and most raise VAT through sales, so all firms are of some interest to the government. Some firms are more significant, however. The government would not like to see a company that is a major employer in a town struggling. If it should fail that would leave the government with a substantial problem in terms of the number of newly-unemployed people.

Government also influences business through creating laws which a business must comply with. Decisions made by government (e.g. to create tighter environmental regulations) directly affect a business. Businesses spend a lot of time and money seeking to make sure that they comply with government rules and regulations.

Pressure groups

Pressure groups are collections of individuals who are organised into a group to create pressure on organisations to make a specific change in policy, plans or activities or a general change in the way in which organisations operate. Examples include Friends of the Earth or specific organisations such as a rail users protest group. Many pressure groups are highly organised to influence decision-making processes in an organisation. Actions of pressure groups range from buying shares in a company (so that they can have a voice at the AGM – **Annual General Meeting**) to direct action protests, such as unfurling a banner at the top of Nelson's Column in Trafalgar Square.

Pressure group activities

Pressure groups are designed specifically to influence decision making. Some of them are highly organised to campaign on specific issues such as the environment. They will identify businesses with a poor record on environmental issues and then concentrate on forcing businesses to change the way they operate e.g. through high profile campaigns in the press etc.

Society

Society would like to see businesses trading in a responsible manner so that danger to the public is minimised along with damage to the environment. If the firm is struggling, cost cutting may compromise these objectives. Pressure groups may be formed to put pressure on the firm to conform. In the 21st century most firms have become aware of the need to make sure that they have policies for Corporate Social Responsibility (CSR) which is all about building good relationships with society at large.

Local community

There are many local businesses that will depend on the success of another business. A number of businesses will spring up to service the needs of a large local company and to provide for the needs of the people who work there. Newsagents, public houses, restaurants and sandwich shops will all rely on the business continuing to succeed. If it fails, they may go down with it.

UNIT ASSESSMENT

Expanding a business

Julie set up a sandwich making business called Healthy Appetites two years ago, in partnership with her brother Simon. The initial finance for the business came from a loan from their parents, and a bank loan. This enabled them to buy the equipment, and to take out a rolling lease on a High Street premise.

In addition to offering sandwiches, cakes, tea, coffee and other refreshments to customers six days a week, they also launched a van delivery service to local firms. Key issues in setting up and running the business have been those of complying with Health and Safety, and Food Safety laws. These are 'hot' issues for any business involved in providing food to the general public, and it is a costly business to create the systems and maintain them to guarantee the required standards of safety.

Healthy Appetites focuses on providing 'healthy' options eating, for example, by using wholemeal bread, salad fillings and minimising the use of fats, sugar and salt in food products offered. Julie and Simon both enjoy a healthy lifestyle and are passionate about providing good quality food. Their approach has found favour with customers. Two gyms and a health club have recently set up in town, and many of their customers are healthy livers who like to keep fit.

They were able to borrow money from the banks in 2002 when interest rates were very low (the UK base rate was under 4%).

The business has been very successful and has built up a regular clientele, both for the High Street premises and for the delivery service. The business is situated in the small market town (population 30,000) of Littleham. In recent years the town has been growing as more businesses have been setting up there.

However, Simon is due to go to University in September, and so will be pulling out of the business. This leaves Julie with some difficult decisions to make. One option would be to bring in another partner, a friend called Helen who she went to school with. Helen has no experience of working in the food business, but has good Information Technology skills and is currently studying for a book-keeping and accountancy qualification. Another alternative would be to set up a private limited company. She could then convert the loan she has had from her parents into shares in the business, and perhaps bring in one or two family friends as shareholders. A third option might be to go it alone as a sole trader, taking a further bank loan. The business is in need of a fresh injection of cash, because the existing delivery van is now unreliable. Making reliable deliveries to factories and offices in the town is very important, because failure to deliver could lead to a loss of orders. A new van will cost £20,000.

The business has only just started to break even. It took Simon and Julie longer than they expected to break even because the initial costs of setting up were higher than expected. Now that the break-even point has been reached it is important to start making profits in order to repay some of the start-up loans.

A number of factors are likely to influence the potential to make profits in the future. One of these is that unemployment has been falling steadily in Littleham and the surrounding villages.

The following figures for unemployment have been calculated using the Labour Force Survey method of calculation:

Unemployment in Littleham (LFS method of calculation)

Year	Numbers
1995	2,470
2000	1,633
2005	1,200

Another issue that Julie is concerned about is the development of competition. Since she started up, some of the major retailers in the town, including Boots, have also added a sandwich service to their existing services. There is also talk of a well-known 'coffee shop' multiple setting up on the High Street in a vacant premise not far from Healthy Appetites.

In order to make her decision Julie has set out a cash-flow forecast to cover the 12 months starting from January 2006. (assuming she purchases the van)

	Jan	Feb	Mar	Apr	May	Jun	Jul	Aug	Sep	Oct	Nov	Dec
Income												
Sales	9500	10000	10000	11000	11000	12000	12000	12000	12000	12000	12000	12000
Loan	20000											
Total income	29500	10000	10000	11000	11000	12000	12000	12000	12000	12000	12000	12000
Expenditure												
Materials	2200	3300	3800	3800	3800	3800	3800	3800	3800	3800	3800	3800
Labour	2000	2800	3200	3200	3200	3200	3200	3200	3200	3200	3200	3200
Fixtures and fittings	5000						5000					
Rent	2000	2000	2000	2000	2000	2000	2000	2000	2000	2000	2000	2000
Insurance	50	50	50	50	50	50	50	50	50	50	50	50
Electricity	30	30	30	30	30	30	30	30	30	30	30	30
Water	25	25	25	25	25	25	25	25	25	25	25	25
Advertising	100	100	100	100	100	100	100	100	100	100	100	100
Bank Loan Repayments	500	500	500	500	500	500	500	500	500	500	500	500

	Jan	Feb	Mar	Apr	May	Jun	Jul	Aug	Sep	Oct	Nov	Dec
Total expenditure	11905	8805	9705	9705	9705	9705	9705	9705	9705	9705	9705	9705
Net cash flow	17595	1195	295	1295	1295	2295	2295	2295	2295	2295	2295	2295
Opening balance	2000	19595	20790	21085	22380	23675	25970	28265	30560	32855	35150	37445
Closing balance	19595	20790	21085	22380	23675	25970	28265	30560	32855	35150	37445	39740

Here is some additional information that was available to Julie about changing economic circumstances in early 2005 when Julie was making her decision.

Monetary Policy Committee decisions on interest rates

Month	Change in interest rate	New interest rate
Feb 2005	0	4.75%
Jan 2005	0	4.75%
Dec 2004	0	4.75%
November 2004	0	4.75%
October 2004	0	4.75%
September 2004	0	4.75%
August 2004	+0.25%	4.75%
July 2004	+0.25%	4.5%
June 2004	+0.25%	4.25%
May 2004	+02.5%	4.0%

Labour market statistics showed that in February 2005 employment continued at record levels but the number of unemployed was also growing. 28.52 million people were in work in October to December (2004) according to the Labour Force Survey. This was up by 90,000 over the last three months and up by 296,000 over 2004.

At the same time there was clear evidence of earnings growth in the economy.

Banks offering better deals for new customers

Many High Street banks are offering exciting packages to new account holders. What this means is that if you are an existing business, with good growth prospects it is possible to switch from your existing bank to a new bank and gain a number of perks which are there to attract you. Such perks include deferral of interest repayments on loans for up to six months and a special low rate of interest on certain types of loans. Banks also are offering free business advice to new business customers.

In the questions, figures in brackets show available marks.

1   Identify and describe two advantages to Julie of setting up her business, Healthy Appetites, as a private limited company.

Advantage 1 _____

_____ (1)

Description _____

_____ (1)

Advantage 2 _____

_____ (1)

Description _____

_____ (1)

2   What would be the potential problems of setting up as a partnership with her old
    school friend?

    _____

    _____

    _____

    _____ (2)

3   Julie's bank manager has said that he would be prepared to give her a loan to buy the
    vehicle she requires.
    a   Explain what is meant by a loan   (2)
    b   What might be the dangers to the business if Julie takes out a loan?   (2)
    c   Explain one other method of financing the vehicle that would involve less risk to the business.
        Evaluate why it would be less risky.   (3)

4   Complete the SWOT Grid for Healthy Eating at the time Julie took over control of the business
    after the partnership with Simon terminated.

SWOT analysis for Healthy Appetites

Strengths	Weaknesses
1	1
2.	2
Opportunities	**Threats**
1	1
2	2

(10)

5   Complete the SLEPT grid for Healthy Appetites

Social	
1	2
Legal	
1	2
Economic	
1	2
Political	
1	2
Technological	
1	2

(10)

6   In setting up Healthy Appetites, Julie and Simon were very concerned to make sure that they provide people with Health Foods. They are very aware of new government concern and legislation to make sure that food producers put less salt and fat into foodstuffs and take the issue of obesity seriously. Julie is very aware of nutritional issues and has studied all the legal requirements about what goes into food produce. She believes strongly that the business should operate in an ethical way.
  a   Explain what is meant by the term business ethics.   (2)
  b   What is the difference between ethical and legal requirements.   (2)
  c   Analyse why the issue of ethical responsibility is important to Julie and her business.   (2)
  d   Evaluate one of the costs to Healthy Appetites if the business failed to adopt an ethical
      approach.   (2)
  e   Assess the implications of the government passing stricter laws on food safety and food
      contents for the food manufacturing industry as a whole.   (8)

7   Quality of written communication is assessed in this question.

    A major constraint on the future success of Healthy Appetites is the level of competition in the sector of the ready-made food market that Julie is operating in. New competitors are entering the market.

Advise Julie on whether she should continue to grow her business by purchasing a new van and by expanding the range of food and drinks that she offers in her store:

You should make reference to the following factors:

* the nature of the competition and market conditions

* economic trends (12)

8 When Julie and Simon first set up they identified the following information that was relevant to their business.

> Average selling price per item sold by Healthy Appetites £1.40
>
> Average variable cost per item 60p
>
> Fixed Costs £54,100

a Define the term 'break-even point' (3)
b Explain the formula for working out the break-even point using contribution. (2)
c Calculate the break-even point for Healthy Appetites using the information above.

> Show your working
>
> Break-even point =

(2)

d Explain the impact on the break-even point if the cost of materials used by Healthy Appetites proved to be lower than expected. (2)
e Evaluate the likely impact on the break-even point of a fall in interest rates (2)
f What is meant by the term 'margin of safety'? Why might Simon and Julie want to calculate the margin of safety for a given level of sales? (3)

9 In planning out the first year of the business Julie and Simon created a budget.

a Explain what is meant by a budget (2)

b Who are budgets typically produced for? Give three examples. (3)

c Critically analyse one way in which creating the budget would have given Simon and Julie greater control of their business. (4)

10 Examine the following figures for Healthy Appetites at the end of year one. Calculate the variances between the actual figures and the budgeted figures.

	Budget	Actual	Variance
Income			
Sales	135500	140000	
Loan	20000	20000	
Total income	155500	160000	
Expenditure			
Materials	43500	41000	
Labour	36800	37000	

	Budget	Actual	Variance
Fixtures and fittings	10000	10000	
Rent	24000	26500	
Insurance	600	700	
Electricity	360	370	
Water	300	320	
Advertising	12000	15000	
Bank loan repayments	6000	6000	
Total expenditure	133560	136890	

(7)

11 Identify one variance which you think would cause concern to Healthy Appetites and explain one management action that could be taken to try and correct this variance. (4)

12 Discuss how using computer accounting packages would help Simon and Julie to manage the budgetary control of their business effectively. Explain the costs and benefits of using this type of technology. (5)

Total available marks: (100)

Resources

There is a wide range of textbooks aimed at Advanced Level Business candidates. Some good up-to-date sources include:

Dransfield, R. et al., *BTEC National Business*, Heinemann, Oxford, 2004
Marcouse et al., *Business Studies*, Hodder and Stoughton, Tonbridge, 2004
Dransfield, R. and Dransfield, D., *Economics Made Easy*, Nelson Thornes, Cheltenham, 2003

For the more financial elements of this unit:

Dransfield, R. and Coles, M. *Accounts Made Easy*, Nelson, Thornes, Cheltenham, 2002
Dransfield, R., *Financial Information Made Easy*, Nelson Thornes, Cheltenham, 2002

Websites

Some useful websites are listed below. These addresses are current at the time of writing. However, it needs to be recognised that new sites are being launched on the Internet on a regular basis and that older sites may change or disappear.

www.tt100.biz
www.tutor2u.net
www.ft.com
www.uk.finance.yahoo.com
www.aloa.co.uk

BIZ / ed – business education on the Internet

This is a free information service on the Internet which provides a range of notes and worksheets. This includes:

* key economic statistics
* company information
* case studies
* outline assignments and study skills
* curriculum updates.

Its address is www.bized.ac.uk

Videos

TV choice (www.tv.choice.com) produces a range of useful business videos including *The Balance Sheet*, and *The Profit and Loss Account*.

UNIT 4

The impact of customer service

This unit contains seven elements:

4.2.1 Definition of a customer

4.2.2 Definition of customer service and its importance to any business

4.2.3 Customer needs and their potential power

4.2.4 How businesses gather information on customer needs and the issues surrounding the storage of this information

4.2.5 Impact that legal and ethical issues can have on the provision of customer service

4.2.6 Implications for maintaining a high level of customer service on staff and senior management

4.2.7 Assessing the quality and effectiveness of customer service

Introduction

Customers are the most important people for any organisation. They are simply the natural resource upon which the success of any organisation depends. When thinking about the importance of customers it is useful to remember the following points:

* repeat business is at the backbone of selling as it helps to provide security and certainty

* organisations are dependent upon their customers – if they do not develop customer loyalty and satisfaction, they could lose their customers

* without customers, organisations would simply not exist
* the purpose of the organisation is to fulfil the needs of customers
* customers make it possible to achieve everything the business aims for.

How you will be assessed

Throughout this unit there are a number of activities to reinforce your learning. The unit is assessed through a pre-released case study followed by an external assessment. At the end of the unit there is a sample assessment which you can use to practise your examination techniques.

There are seven main aspects to consider:

* definition of a customer
* definition of customer service and its importance to any business organisation
* customer needs and their potential power
* how organisations gather information on customer needs and the issues surrounding the storing of this information
* impact that legal and ethical issues can have on the provision of customer service
* implications for maintaining a high level of customer service on staff and senior management
* assessing the quality and effectiveness of customer service.

4.2.1 Definition of a customer

It is easy to forget that just about every moment of the day you are a customer. If you do not sleep well it could be the fault of a bed that has been purchased. The toothpaste, shampoo and soap you use in the morning reflect the purchases made either by you or members of your family. If they do not perform in the way you would like, then you may buy other brands. Similarly your breakfast items have all been purchased and if you catch a bus to school or work, you are once again a customer.

As a frequent customer you will be faced with many different decisions every day and these decisions will be influenced by a number of factors. For example, if the person in the newspaper shop is not friendly in the mornings or is rude and abrupt, you may use a different shop.

Similarly, if the bus is not cleaned properly or is always crowded, you may decide to make alternative travel arrangements.

Peter Drucker wrote, 'There is only one valid definition of a business purpose – to create a customer.' It has been estimated that it costs five times as much to attract a new customer as it does to retain an old one. Therefore, an organisation will gain more value from working on retaining existing customers than looking for new customers (*The Essential Drucker*, 2003).

Internal and external customers

Organisations have both **internal** and **external customers** (see Figure 4.1). The quality of customer service provided outside the organisation is dependent upon how well employees within the organisation treat each other. For example, if an employee makes an enquiry to personnel or writes out a requisition

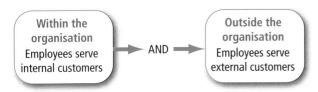

FIGURE 4.1 *Organisations have internal and external customers*

for some stationery, he or she should expect to be treated with the same respect as a customer outside the organisation. This approach helps to encourage the teamwork and customer care which leads towards total quality management.

Many UK companies try to explain the concept of the internal and external customer by referring to the link which starts with the needs of external customers and then includes all of the people involved in bringing together resources to satisfy such needs. Everyone has a role in satisfying customers. This process helps to emphasise that all employees within an organisation are part of a quality chain which is improved with better teamwork, training, employee and communications procedures.

Internal customers

Internal customers within an organisation include all colleagues, ranging from support roles such as delivering post within the organisation to jobs at the top level of the organisation. For example, if a senior manager is dictatorial and treats his or her subordinates badly, which creates a stressful situation for them, they may pass on this stress to other colleagues. The internal customer may also include contracted staff such as electricians.

External customers

External customers may include individuals from different organisations working in business-to-business markets (**B2B**) as well as individual customers. Business-to-business customers may include overseas clients whose culture and background needs to be observed. Customers in international markets may reflect different purchasing habits and trade according to different rules and procedures which may be difficult to understand. It is

important that their cultural differences are taken into account as well as linguistic differences and different types of legal systems.

It is also important to respect the other factors that might affect or influence customer behaviour, for example their age might reflect the sort of services they associate with the product. By taking these factors into account, it is possible to match the products or services on offer with their individual motivations. Knowing why consumers behave in the way they do helps businesses to make the right decisions to meet consumer needs – for example, how to make a product more user friendly.

Adapting to different types of customers

A key element in meeting the needs of different customers is to understand what customer group they belong to and how their behaviour might be influenced by being part of a certain group.

It is possible to break customers down into different segments, each of which will have their own characteristics:

Individuals

Individuals may have different requirements and needs. For a business to be successful there must be some attempt to understand and respond to the needs of individuals, in order to maintain their custom. For example, elderly customers may want particular services, such as a chair within a shop or may find it difficult to understand certain product characteristics. Equally, young customers may have particular characteristics and may want their needs met in a particular way, such as through different technologies.

Groups

Groups, such as clubs and societies, need to be catered for and may have specialist requirements. For example, groups may expect special discounts for sporting products that could be passed on to their members. Similarly, groups may want to put on an exhibition, or may want to hire products for certain events.

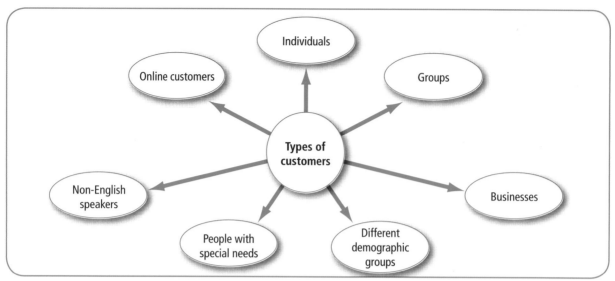

FIGURE 4.2 *Types of customers*

Businesses

Businesses may be particularly important customers. Selling to businesses is usually called business to business (B2B) and may involve personal selling. The needs of customers within business markets are complex. Often products or services have to be customised for clients, such as giving a significant discount, or the products may have to be specially designed for the customer. Businesses may be very large buyers, and so will expect to be dealt with in a particular way. For example, they may expect discount and credit arrangements.

Online customers

Online customers are increasingly important for many businesses with the development of ecommerce. This is a growing and evolving market-place. Amazon has had an impact upon the book market and grocery shopping on the Internet is really beginning to show signs of growth.

Different demographic groups

One important factor in understanding buyers' needs so that appropriate customer service can be provided is **demographic** characteristics. These may include age, sex, race and stage in our family life-cycle. Every customer will have particular demographic characteristics. It is important that organisations understand the demographics of their market so that they can meet the requirements of their customers in an appropriate way.

Non-English speakers

Non-English speakers are increasingly important in the more diverse and multicultural environment in which we live and they may have specialist requirements. The non-English speaker market may also include selling products or providing services overseas. With greater internationalisation of trade and even though English is considered to be a business language, individuals within organisations need to improve their language skills in order to provide better customer service. Dealing with these customers and in overseas markets there may be particular ways in which business is undertaken.

People with special needs

People with special needs also must be catered for, for example by providing wheelchair access or specialist facilities that enable individuals to shop in an environment that suits their needs. There is a huge number of special needs to be catered for in a modern and inclusive business environment, from facilities for the partially sighted to catering for individuals with learning difficulties. Organisations today have to be inclusive, and it is important that they take into account the difficulties that customers might face within the trading environment.

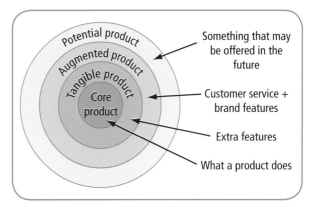

FIGURE 4.4 *The product concept*

4.2.2. Definition of customer service and its importance to any business

Having created customers, the next step is to satisfy them: '**customer satisfaction**' has become the watchword of business in the early twenty-first century. A key reason for this change is oversupply which has led to customers being more demanding. They want what is available in the market-place to meet their demands.

Customer service involves finding out what customers want and developing suitable service procedures to satisfy their needs in a way that exceeds their expectations. The starting point in providing appropriate customer service is to identify potential customers and their expectations by listening to their views. For example, organisations need to find out:

* what customers want

* how important this is for them

* why they need to have it

* how to provide it in the best possible way.

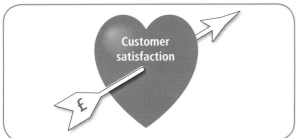

FIGURE 4.3 *Customer satisfaction is at the heart of the selling process*

Customer service has become increasingly important in a rapidly changing market-place. In marketing terms, it is useful to think of customer service as part of the total product concept (see Figure 4.4). At a very basic level, the core product is what a product does. For example, a lawn-mower is expected to cut grass. If that is all mowers did, they would all be nearly identical, but differentiation then begins to take place. In the tangible product, additional features provide an organisation with competitive advantage, for example the lawn-mower cuts the grass and collects the clippings. In the augmented product, customer service or a brand image is provided. The mower may be attractively designed, have a distinctive brand label and have free servicing for five years. This layer is fundamental in influencing consumer choices and for many organisations has become the basis upon which they compete. Finally, the potential product covers aspects that may become part of the product offer for the future, for example there may be a number of additional parts that could be bought for the lawnmower, particularly as technology evolves.

According to Sarah Cook in her book *Customer Care* (4th edition, 2002), customer relationships can be depicted in terms of a loyalty ladder (see Figure 4.5). The willingness of individual customers to ascend the loyalty ladder will depend upon how they are treated when doing business with the organisation. Well-targeted sales methods and efficient personal service will help to convert one-off purchasers to occasional users, then to regular customers and advocates.

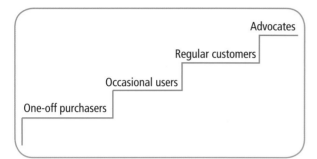

FIGURE 4.5 *The loyalty ladder*

Theory into practice

On the basis of your own experiences, provide two examples of:

✳ good customer service

✳ poor customer service.

In each instance, explain how these affected your repeat-purchasing patterns.

Advocates are very important as these are the people who recommend goods and services from one organisation to all of their friends and colleagues. For example, a person who does not enjoy travelling by train but has to do so, would never become an advocate. However, somebody living on a bus route, with clean vehicles running every 15 minutes to their destination of choice might become an advocate.

In developing suitable ways of meeting the needs of their customers, organisations have to balance their own objectives against the needs of customers (see Figure 4.6). To be able to do this, they need to understand how customers view their organisation as well as what their customers want from their organisation.

Roderick M. McNealy, in his book *Making Satisfaction Happen* (1994), refers to the 'Making Customer Satisfaction Happen' model (see Figure 4.7). This, he claims, is a continuous circular process that provides an equation for satisfying customer needs that can then be used as part of an organisation's strategic approach to business.

In her influential 1992 book, *The Popcorn Report*, the American guru Faith Popcorn charts the rise of consumer bonding or relationship marketing. The principles that she identifies are encapsulated in the following sentence:

'We do need to build relationships with our consumers, to create a dialogue, expose them to our corporate values, establish a bond based on something more deep-seated than product quality, brand image, or even simply meeting consumer needs.'

The American writers Don Peppers and Martha Rogers (*Customer Relationship Management*, 2000) urge organisations to form secure relationships with individual customers, and they provide a range of examples of ways in which even mass marketers can strike up relationships. This involves gathering as much information as possible about individual customers and then developing the organisation to meet individual needs. They refer to this as customer segmentation.

For example, Peppers and Rogers give the following example of gift order catalogues to highlight their point:

✳ the customer may order gifts for friends and relatives many months in advance

✳ the supplier then schedules the delivery of gifts on the right days

✳ the customer would be charged for each gift two days before delivery

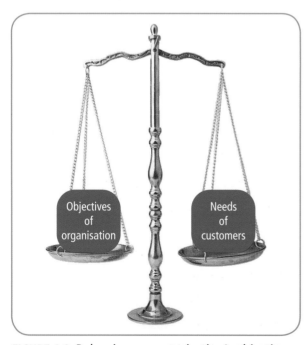

FIGURE 4.6 *Balancing an organisation's objectives against the needs of customers*

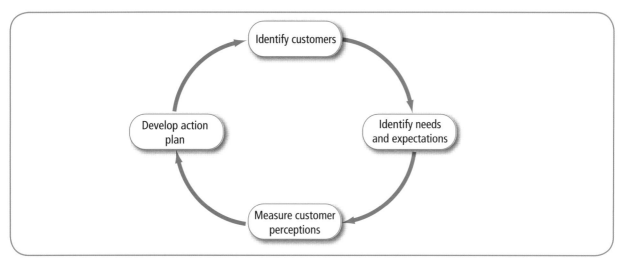

FIGURE 4.7 *Making Customer Satisfaction Happen model*

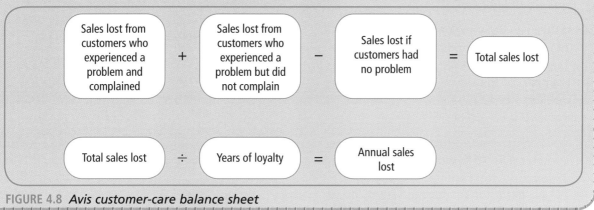
✳ the customer would receive a reminder postcard ten days before each gift is sent

✳ when the annual catalogue is sent to the customer, they would receive a reminder form of last year's gifts and addresses.

Although the authors acknowledge that the product must remain important, they identify the change in focus from high-quality products towards high-quality relationships.

Customer service involves many aspects:

✳ presenting an image of the business
✳ providing information
✳ giving advice
✳ taking and relaying messages
✳ keeping records
✳ providing assistance
✳ dealing with problems
✳ handling complaints
✳ providing after-sales service.

Virgin Mobile have won the Best Customer Service award from *Mobile Choice* magazine for each of the past three years. An independent study by JD Power and Associates in May 2004 ranked Virgin Mobile as the number one pre-pay mobile telephone service for customer satisfaction in the UK.

A growing market within the UK in recent years has been that of leisure centres particularly in the private sector. Names such as Roco, David Lloyd and Holmes Place are becoming established brands. Put yourself in the position of a marketing assistant at one of these leisure centres and describe some of the tangible steps you would take to ensure that as many members as possible renewed their membership.

CASE STUDY
United Airlines

A market-orientated airline

Customer service is increasingly important within a changing market-place and particularly important for airlines as service is at the heart of the choice made by customers as well as a key base upon which airlines compete. United Airlines has:

* developed a route structure spanning five continents and offering the most non-stop flights from the Pacific Rim to the US
* set standards for comfort and safety of its fleet and with an average plane age of just eight years old, has one of the youngest fleets of aircraft in the industry
* developed the Star Alliance Network bringing together 14 carriers who offer services to over 700 airports in more than 120 countries
* further developed and invested in its airport lounges

* created the Red Carpet Club providing members with access to over 40 facilities worldwide
* offered First- and Business-class customers the use of an arrivals suite with the opportunity to shower, enjoy a continental breakfast and make use of business services
* installed large-screen electronic display systems as well as gate readers and baggage scanners to improve the tracking of luggage
* received the highest ranking among airlines for their effective use of the Internet.

At the heart of United's operations in this difficult business environment is market orientation. United Airlines' Chief Executive believes that although the leasing of aeroplanes and manpower may be reduced, marketing activities should not be cut. For United Airlines this means that marketing helps to sustain, maintain and in the medium- to longer-term, develop customers' perceptions and thoughts about the business by developing a series of brand values that keep the brand of United Airlines moving forward.

1 How important is it for United Airlines to be market focused?
2 Discuss how their procedures influence transactions with First- and Business-class customers.

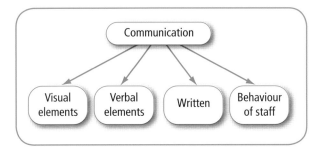

FIGURE 4.9 *Processes of communication*

Presenting an image of the business

Communication

A basis of customer service is to present an appropriate image of an organisation. This involves communication. It is very difficult for service to happen at all without any form of communication and it is this process of communication that provides the basis for people to evaluate what an organisation and its people represent.

For example, the visual elements come into play the moment a customer looks at anything associated with another organisation. At a very basic level it might simply include how the building that the organisation operates from looks, but may include the appearance of staff, advertisements, any printed materials or anything that might influence how the customer perceives the organisation.

Verbal elements of customer service are also important. It is important that staff have good interpersonal skills and know how to deal with customers in an appropriate way. Training is clearly important in helping to equip staff to deal with customers. The verbal element may also include meetings or any form of discussion with either internal or external customers.

There are many different forms of written communication. Letters and emails are an important communication medium for providing good customer service as are newsletters or customer-focused magazines. Again they help to form an appropriate impression for the organisation, based upon how they are presented.

It is easy to forget that behaviour is an important and vital part of the customer service process. Although the degree of training may depend upon the priorities of a business organisation, it is generally accepted that training in service quality is not just about developing a customer care philosophy but about providing employees with the specific skills and attitude of mind to deal with customer service issues in a retailing workplace.

It must be remembered that any form of training aids an employee's personal and professional development as part of his or her career. Once training has taken place, an organisation needs to record each employee's training achievements and use this as a basis for ongoing training and development.

Appearance

The appearance of staff is particularly important in creating the right first impressions of an organisation. If staff are scruffily dressed or are unclean, it will similarly communicate such values about the organisation itself. Clearly, the appearance of staff will depend upon the sort of organisation that the customer enters. Many people associate appearance with the values that an organisation represents. They might associate smart appearance with efficiency and professionalism. For example:

* most schools expect their male teachers to wear ties

* in most banks, staff are usually smartly dressed in dark uniforms

* in a butchery department of a large supermarket, it would be expected that staff would need to wear suitable white coats, which would also be regularly cleaned and meet health and hygiene regulations

* on a railway station, staff are expected to wear uniforms which help them to be recognised and able to provide suitable customer service.

Theory into practice

Discuss whether you are influenced by uniforms worn by others. What does the wearing of a uniform signify?

Uniforms can help to represent a series of values

Providing information

One important element of customer service is in being able to provide accurate and reliable information. For example if you were told that a train will leave the station at 11.35 am but when you arrive there is no 11.35 train, then you would not be very happy. Similarly, if you are told that as part of a service you are going to receive something, then it is frustrating to later find out that you are not entitled to it.

Accurate and reliable information informs customer expectations and creates a certainty that gives customers confidence in what they receive. It is part of the service they expect. On the other hand, inaccurate information confuses their expectations, and makes the customer less certain or confident in the organisation.

Giving advice

In a customer-focused environment, customers want to deal with individuals who know what they are doing and can be trusted to provide reliable and accurate information and advice. At the heart of all customer service training is the provision of **product knowledge** in order to provide staff with the ability to deal with any queries or issues that arise.

Taking and relaying messages

Although in some circumstances it may not be easy to provide answers to a query straight away, customer issues should be dealt with promptly. It may be necessary to refer a query to another member of staff or somebody with a particular expertise.

Keeping records

It is important to keep customer records to monitor complaints and customer compliments. Feedback from customers helps to provide an important form of market research data and enables the organisation to monitor customer service levels. However, the monitoring of complaints can be a little misleading as usually only a few customers complain formally. However it may be possible to take feedback from staff who are in customer-facing positions who deal with customers every day and are able to provide a more accurate picture of customer feedback.

The purpose of monitoring customer complaints is to ensure that issues have been dealt with fairly and resolved in an appropriate way. By monitoring customer feedback, it may be possible to take measures that deal with causes of customer dissatisfaction.

Providing assistance

Prompt service and helpfulness is also important when dealing with customers. We can probably all think of situations when we have had to wait in queues to return goods to a shop or been angered by employees who seem to have their own agenda and have ignored or not listened to the customer.

When dealing with customers, staff should not:

* turn away from the customer
* leave the customer without any form of explanation
* be rude to the customer
* talk to other staff and ignore the customer
* imply that the customer is wrong and stupid
* criticise the customer or attempt to argue with them
* treat the customer dismissively
* fail to believe the customer or treat them seriously
* make the customer feel guilty
* shout at the customer
* tell the customer that they are wasting their time
* leave the customer dissatisfied.

These points may sound a bit like stating the obvious, but they are very important. Providing customer service is not easy. It requires the right approach based upon meeting customer expectations and it is imperative that those involved in customer service have the right personal qualities.

Dealing with problems

A key function of customer service is to resolve problems and deal with customer-related issues. Even if a customer might not be happy with a service or a product on one or two occasions, if the complaint is handled well it is possible to sustain a positive relationship with the customer. An important reason for sustaining customer relationships is that existing relationships create new business opportunities and, as it is more expensive to create new relationships than sustain old ones, existing customers have to be treated well.

Handling complaints

There is nothing worse than customers having their complaints passed around from person to person and department to department. This creates a bad impression of the organisation, wastes time and may cause a lot of personal anguish. An efficient customer complaints procedure may help to retain business that might otherwise be lost if the complaint is handled inefficiently.

An organisation has a responsibility to its many different stakeholders and, through its actions, it will attempt to balance its responsibilities in a variety of different ways. For example, on the one hand it has to take into consideration the needs of its managers and shareholders but on the other it has to take into account the needs of their customers, members of the wider community and employees.

Providing after-sales service

Customer service does not just happen. It is a process that has to be built and developed across the relationships that an organisation has with the customer. It means creating expectations before the transaction takes place, building customer service into the transaction process and then dealing with post-transactional support.

Pre-transaction → Transaction → Post-transaction

Emphasis upon customer service will change from one product to another. For example, before a transaction it is important to understand the motives of customers so that it is possible to

CASE STUDY
Profit before help from O_2

A recent example the author of this chapter faced was when his mobile phone, a relatively new one, went wrong. Complaints were made to O_2's customer service facility but these calls were charged for and the author spent a considerable time on the phone before the calls were answered, usually 15 minutes or more on a premium line. More than 10 calls were made to O_2. O_2 failed to repair the phone or even recognise that the author had purchased it from them even though he faxed the appropriate records to them. Over the period during which they failed to repair the phone he was charged the line rental and yet was not receiving any service. It took nearly four months before the contract could be cancelled at considerable expense and inconvenience to the author who now refuses to carry any form of mobile phone as a matter

of principle. It was clear that in this instance O_2 put their own needs before their customers, were not interested in dealing with the customer service issue, and used the problems that the customer had as another way of earning revenue. Even though the author sent emails to O_2 they remained unanswered. The situation was one of frustration and involved the author contacting his local trading standards department as well as looking for other ways to bring pressure on O_2. When a 'negotiator' from O_2 eventually apologised it was too late.

1 In what way was O_2's service biased towards themselves rather than the needs of their customers?
2 How should O_2 deal with problems their customers have?

respond to their precise needs. Knowledge of competitors and their products enables an organisation to create expectations that help to show how their products are differentiated to those of their competitors. During the transaction it is important that customer service helps to relate the product or service to the needs of the customer. There may be many queries during the transaction that will need to be dealt with. It is also important to use this time as an opportunity to deal with any misunderstandings, making sure that the product or service relates to customer expectations. It is always important to use customer service to follow up a sale. Promises that might have been made during the transaction need to be met. If the product or service involves a guarantee by a certain date, then the date must be held. It is also important to contact individuals to check that they are happy with the product and service and then use this feedback for future customer service transactions.

Developing a high standard of customer service

Within an increasing number of industries, the provision of customer service is there to give organisations a competitive edge. In other words the quality of service provides the base upon which they compete. In the past many of these organisations would have competed on the basis of different product features or price, but as competition has developed customer service has become the key differentiator. So what has using customer service as a base for competitive activity provided for the customer?

High-quality products and services

In order to compete on the basis of customer service, organisations have had to provide high-quality products and services. The customer care element associated with these products and services is, as we have seen, an important part of the product itself as it not only adds value to the product but also adds value in a way that makes the product more competitive. For example, the product and accompanying services will provide a higher level of satisfaction designed to make the customer more of an advocate for the future.

Fostering customer loyalty

An organisation that can develop repeat and frequent business with its customers will have a more established market position. Some customers may only use an organisation's products once, while others will make multiple and repeat purchases. The ways in which customers will be treated will determine whether or not they decide to continue to do business with a particular organisation. By providing efficient and high value services, customers are much more likely to remain loyal and to become advocates.

The notion of adding value to products and services in order to foster customer loyalty is an important one. Adding value is simply the taking of something of lower value and constantly increasing its attractiveness for customers. A manufacturer of clothes, for example, might take raw materials and produce an item of clothing that has more value to the customer, therefore commanding a higher price than the original cloth. For example, developing a brand image helps to add value to products in a way that makes customers more loyal as long as that brand image conveys positive values. Anything that further adds value to the finished item is clearly beneficial to the organisation because of the loyalty it fosters.

The customer care and marketing processes can identify such opportunities for adding value. For example, it might be aimed at identifying how customer services could be improved. It might even provide evidence of how much more customers would be willing to pay for additional features. It would not be unreasonable to set targets for the amount of new or repeat business that the programme should attract.

> **Think it over...**
>
> If you have a Boots Advantage Card, every time you spend £1 at Boots you get 4 points. Every point is worth a penny, so if you save up 1,000 points you will have £10 to spend.

Schemes that add value and encourage customer loyalty include:

* Loyalty cards – these use a form of points system to foster repeat purchase. For example, Boots Advantage Card and Tesco Clubcard points create cash opportunities that can be reclaimed using the card.

* Discounts – these are a good way of retaining regular customers by providing them with tangible advantages. It is possible to provide some form of 'club' identity which enables members to get special discounts, in the same way that members of Co-operative societies are granted special privileges. For example, members of an air-softing club, which is a slightly more sophisticated form of paint balling, might get special privileges and treatment both from the air-softing venue and also from retailers who have an arrangement that provides discounts for club members.

* Mailshots, leaflets and other publicity materials – these may be used to inform regular customers about events and special deals. For example, Nottinghamshire Cricket Club regularly inform Notts members about events within the club as well as about offers within the club shop.

Increasing sales levels

The general public will have an overall impression of the level of service they expect an organisation to provide, and this will take some changing if it is wrong. People's preconceptions affect the way they interpret what happens, so if a customer approaches expecting poor service he or she will interpret everything that happens in a negative way in order to reinforce that opinion. However, if customers approach expecting high-quality service, an organisation will have to perform very badly in order to change that opinion. Changing **customer perceptions** of existing organisations may take time and long-held opinions are difficult to dislodge. It took Tesco many years to shake off their original image as a low-cost, low-quality supermarket, but it is now the most profitable UK supermarket with a reputation for high quality and good customer service.

Key terms

Customer perceptions – the general public will have an overall impression of the level of service they expect an organisation to provide.

Total Quality Management (TQM) is a philosophy that shapes relationships between suppliers and customers. Three principles guide the relationship:

1 The customer is an important stakeholder in a business – quality should be judged by the customer and all products and services contribute value to the customer and lead to customer satisfaction.

2 The most productive relationships are the ones where all parties benefit from an activity – there are no winners or losers, but rather everybody wins.

3 The underpinning basis of any relationship is trust.

Within the context of sales this means that a salesperson must be constantly gathering information on customer needs, informing management of their requirements and contributing to the design of the company's products and the services that support the sale of the product. Within the wider marketing context, total quality marketing involves energising and engaging everybody within an organisation with the needs of the customer so that they can each appreciate the value of the contribution they make towards customer satisfaction.

Encouraging a motivated and efficient workforce

Doing something well and having customers who are satisfied with the products and services they have been provided with is good for the morale of employees. They know that they are working for an organisation that is highly regarded and that they are contributing to how well the needs of their customers are served. Customer service has the added benefit of impacting upon the internal customer, by helping to set standards that enable employees to feel proud and motivated about the roles that they undertake.

Failing to meet the needs of customers

The market-place is littered with organisations that have at one stage of another failed to meet the needs of their customers, usually because of poor customer service. For a short time, customers might put up with poor customer service and accept the limitations of an organisation. but as other organisations come into the market and offer more they will be happy to take their business elsewhere. Failing to meet the needs of customers is a significant reason for customers switching their purchases to other organisations.

4.2.3 Customer needs and their potential power

In a modern market-place, organisations cannot afford to compete simply on the basis of price, or minor product modifications. Service differentiation helps organisations to achieve their business strategies better than many of their competitors. According to Sarah Cook in *Customer Care* (4th edition, 2002), 'Surveys suggest that service driven companies can charge up to 9 per cent more for the products and services they provide. They grow twice as fast as the average company and have the potential to gain up to 6 per cent market share.'

Organisations are finding it more and more difficult to demonstrate product superiority or even product differentiation over competitors.

FIGURE 4.10 *The movement towards customer care*

Customer service is an area that offers almost endless opportunities for developing product superiority. The ideal relationship is one where the customer feels that he or she is receiving the desired quality and good customer care.

Customer care programmes are designed to improve the experience for customers and to encourage them to become loyal to an organisation. The findings from such programmes should help an organisation to build changes into their procedures that enable them to meet customer needs more effectively. There are a number of specific customer needs that include:

* safety and security
* clear and accurate information
* impartiality and objectivity
* special needs
* expecting consumers' rights to be upheld.

Theory into practice

To what products or services are you loyal? Explain why you are loyal to those products and services?

Think it over...

According to the insurance industry, customer service is a significant differentiating factor in this service-orientated market-place. Research within the industry has indicated that firms that provide first-class customer service are more successful at retaining and attracting loyal, profitable customers.

Safety and security

In any situation in which customers come into an organisation, safety and security are important. For example, if someone visits a factory showroom they would not expect to be exposed to any serious mechanical hazards. Some organisations provide special health and safety codes of practice or requirements for visitors. For example, an organisation providing cave visits would have to ensure that visitors were supervised, kept to particular routes and wore hard hats.

Organisations may have a **code of practice** or procedures that cover any of the following influences upon customers:

* safety and valuables – they may have to be put in a safe place

* bomb threats – there may be specific procedures

* fire – there will be procedures and regulations alongside a drill and practice dates

* control of hazardous substances – there may be particular concern about their influence in certain environments

* behaviour of customers/guests – particularly in the hotel industry, where unpleasant behaviour could disturb or damage the experiences and comfort of others

* security – in the interests of others, there could be certain specified security arrangements.

In order to ensure that the working environment is safe for customers, staff have to be trained to ensure that they can carry out procedures to deal with such hazards.

Theory into practice

Think of a recent trip you have been on or a visit you have made. Discuss the various safety and security measures that contributed to the success or otherwise of the occasion.

Clear and accurate information

Information may refer to products or purchasing procedures and may influence the final decision that a consumer makes. In particular, consumers may wish for advice that helps them weigh up a range of alternatives.

Impartiality and objectivity

The nature and type of information that customers may want depends upon the sort of environment in which staff work. However, in providing information it is important that it is:

* *Accurate* – a key source of irritation may occur if the customer is told one thing and then finds out that what they have been told is wrong or inaccurate. This could be a source of a later complaint or difficulty with a particular customer.

* *Impersonal* – providing the customer with the staff member's own tastes, preferences and interests is usually not appropriate. It is important to be impartial and try to analyse what the needs of the customer are in order to satisfy them.

* *Objective* – information should be unbiased and should include everything that a customer needs to know if they are purchasing a product. This means that no information must be hidden and the customer must be helped impartially to make comparisons with the products on offer from one organisation with those from another.

Special needs

Different groups of customers may have different needs. How many stores can you think of that provide the following:

* wheelchair access

* access for mothers with young children in buggies

* free delivery outside the boundaries of a local town

* credit facilities

* flexible opening hours

* specialist products for all types of consumers

* a customer helpline

* ordering facilities?

Expecting consumer rights to be upheld

We would all ideally want to work in an environment where organisations always have consumers at the heart of their focus and provide good customer service based upon charters and codes of practice. In reality, relationships between organisations and their customers are not always good, and in some circumstances there needs to be some form of framework around which organisations can deliver their own customer service. This framework is provided by legislation both within the UK and the European Union. This framework ensures that consumers have rights that can be supported by the legal and judicial system. For example, consumers expect not to be misled, but told the truth. They also expect that the places they visit are safe and will not adversely affect their health.

CASE STUDY

Competing on the basis of customer service

In 1988 Travis & Arnold and Sandell Perkins, two building merchant **public companies**, merged to create Travis Perkins. Sandell Perkins had origins stretching back to 1797. The business originally traded as joiners and carpenters but then moved to selling and trading in hardwoods before becoming a public company in 1986. Travis & Arnold was founded in 1899 by Ernest Travis in London, before moving to Northampton where it sold timber and other wood products before **diversifying** into other building materials. Today the Travis Perkins Group is one of the largest buildings materials distribution businesses. Travis Perkins uses customer service at the centre of its staff development programme to develop a culture that provides a foundation for growth.

At the heart of Travis Perkins culture is the simple lesson that the quality of service is more important than price. When people buy materials from Travis Perkins they want to pick up the right materials quickly so that they can get on with their projects – the Travis Perkins **vision** is to 'deliver a professional, high quality service that keeps ahead of the competitors in our customers' eyes'. To achieve this vision and to turn this commitment towards customer service into practical actions, Travis Perkins have invested heavily in a process of training, development and performance monitoring.

It was not so long ago that the UK Government published what became known as the Competitiveness White Paper, 'Our Competitive Future: Building the Knowledge Driven Economy.' The paper emphasised that in a modern and changing world employees are the assets of the future that help organisations to develop 'a culture in the workplace that allows knowledge, creativity and commitment of the workforce to be fully exploited'. For Travis Perkins, the products and the locations do not in themselves meet customer needs, it is their employees and their understanding of how to help customers solve problems and deal with issues that makes the organisation distinct and provides a base of care so important for their continued competitiveness.

1 From the case study above, what seem to be the business objectives of Travis Perkins?
2 How might an organisation in the buildings materials industry exceed customer expectations?
3 Explain how customer service would help Travis Perkins to compete more effectively than other organisations within their industry. Provide examples to support your argument.

Quality

Consumers know what they mean by desired quality and the marketer needs to find this out and translate the concept into required goods and services. Desired quality does not necessarily mean the most expensive – it means the solution that best meets a customer's need. For example, in Japan a chain of 'capsule hotels' has been set up for business people in major cities. Each room is only just large enough for a person to lie down and watch TV. However, they are popular because they are 'fit for purpose' in that they meet the needs of busy business people. In contrast, other people prefer to hire a spacious penthouse suite in a large hotel. The job of marketing is to identify how different market segments perceive quality and then to deliver a marketing mix that provides it.

Negative aspects of customer service

It could be argued that an organisation might go the other way and become too customer focused at the expense of the needs of the organisation. It is possible to offer customers too much and this could affect the profitability of the business. Hoover's famous sales promotion in which they offered customers free flights to the USA certainly helped to move products, but at the same time it caused the company a lot of financial problems.

CASE STUDY

How not to provide customer care!

This particular episode is based on the experience of a customer who was disappointed with the customer service provided by a major UK hardware chainstore.

'I had already selected my items and needed batteries. I went to the counter that sells batteries and waited for the staff member to finish a telephone call before serving me. However, putting down the telephone, he came out from behind the counter – completely ignoring me – and simply started chatting to another staff member and began to walk away.

'I then called after him asking him if I was invisible. He told me that he had been dealing with a customer. I told him that he had finished his telephone call and that he had walked past me around the counter. He then told me that the counter wasn't open for sales service.

'I replied that he could have told me that, as I wanted batteries and that was the only place they were stocked in the store. Besides, the counter had a sales till as well.

'He then had the cheek to say that he didn't know that I had wanted to be served. I informed him that I was standing by the counter with a credit card in my hand and an arm full of products. Being a sales staff member, he would have had enough hints. I then proceeded to place my items down (worth around £40.00 in total) and told him not to bother serving me as he had obviously ignored me in the beginning and was coming up with various lies as to why he hadn't served me.

'He then had the audacity to tell me that I was out of order and was angry for nothing.'

1 Why was the customer service provided in this instance poor?
2 How should the assistant have dealt with the issue?
3 Discuss how this might influence the customer's actions when shopping for hardware goods again.

Working in pairs, create a scenario in which you would deal with the following:

'Waiter, I have a fly in my soup.'

'The jacket I bought does not fit.'

'My flight time is 11.00 am. Nobody told me I had to turn up 1 hour beforehand.'

'I have just waited 35 minutes to be served and you are telling me that I am at the wrong counter.'

'But when I phoned up you said that you had the item I wanted in stock and were going to hold one back for me.'

The power of the consumer

Consumer power cannot be underestimated and there are consumer groups that adopt policies towards certain products. A well-known and powerful consumer group is the Consumers' Association, which produces the magazine *Which?* The group is funded by subscriptions from members who buy the magazine. The Association uses its funds to test a wide variety of products on which it then produces reports in its monthly magazine. It also produces books on consumer-related matters.

Which? – *the magazine of the Consumers' Association*

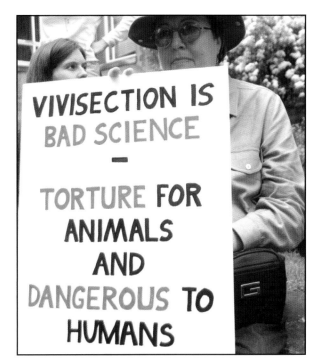

Consumer power influences decisions

The influence of the Consumers' Association goes beyond the publication of *Which?* because its reports are frequently reported in the national press. Consumer programmes also get a fair amount of time on national television, the most famous being *Watchdog*. Typical media coverage involves the investigation of complaints and the comparison of goods and services.

In some circumstances, consumers organise themselves into groups to stop buying certain products. For example, Animal Rights campaigners encourage their members and others not to buy products that have been tested on animals and this has influenced the policies of industries such as the cosmetics industry. Many organisations who do not want adverse publicity avoid events or actions that might influence their goods or services.

McDonald's provides a good example of a business that has suffered from adverse publicity in recent years. Typical criticisms of McDonald's are that:

* the company pays low wages and provides little career opportunity, indeed the word 'McJob' has entered the English language to represent poorly paid jobs with poor terms and conditions

* the company produces products that are not healthy. Concerns have been raised that a diet of McDonald's meals encourages the development of obesity, particularly in the young, who are seen as a junk-food generation

* take-away meals contribute to waste and that some of the packaging is poorly designed with little understanding of environmental considerations.

In France, there has been considerable criticism of McDonaldisation which is seen as representing the breakdown of traditional values and a process of Americanisation. In one famous incident the anti-globalisation protestor José Bové and a group of French farmers dismantled a McDonald's outlet and towed it away on their tractors.

Of course McDonald's could respond to this consumer pressure by doing nothing. If they did the media and protestors would have a field day, and the company would suffer from declining popularity, sales and profits.

Theory into practice

Describe how McDonald's should try to respond to such adverse publicity.

The company has had to respond to this external pressure – the power of the consumer. They have therefore taken a number of steps to restore their image as a value for money quick service restaurant chain.

Some of these actions include:

* Making sure that the company now pays wages which are above the industry average and creating career opportunities for new employees. For example, McDonald's is proud that most of its restaurant managers started as crew members.

* Changing the packaging used so that it uses less paper and card, and not using materials which create greenhouse gases. McDonald's also takes responsibility for making sure that the area within a square mile of a restaurant is regularly cleared up – not just of McDonald's related litter, but of all litter.

* Changing their menu to offer salads and other healthier alternatives. Recipes have been altered to reduce fat, salt and sugar content. Of course, people can still buy a Big Mac and Fries but that is a choice which they make as a consumer.

McDonald's provides a good example of an organisation which is having to respond to consumer pressure, and if they are sensible they will continue to listen to the consumer's voice – through market research and by reading the press and protest literature.

There are many reasons why consumers put pressure upon business organisations to change their activities including:

* recycling policies
* provision of organic foods
* better labelling.

Recycling policies

One of the real costs of business activities is pollution. Industries cause water pollution, air pollution, dereliction, traffic congestion, noise and so on. To minimise the effects of all of these damaging activities, consumer pressure might encourage organisations to recycle more waste. For example, most organisations today recycle paper as a matter of course. In 2003, recycled paper and board provided about 66% of the source materials for the 6.7 million tonnes of paper manufactured in the UK. A further 7.7 million tonnes were imported.

Provision of organic foods

Many consumers question the products we consume and the potential damage of food additives as well as synthetic ingredients. The medical profession has pointed out the dangerous side-effects of additives, particularly with regard to hyperactivity in children.

Theory into practice

Describe why supermarkets today stock organic products.

Most supermarkets now stock organic goods

Better labelling

Consumer pressure has led to considerable changes to labels on a range of products. Specific nutritional information that appears on labels includes:

* energy
* protein
* carbohydrate
* starch
* sugars
* saturated fat
* monounsaturated and polyunsaturated fat
* sodium.

Food labelling is strictly governed by law and must not mislead the consumer. A food can't claim to be 'reduced calorie' unless it is much lower in calories than the usual version. However, you should be aware of certain claims, e.g. something which is '90 per cent fat free' is still 10 per cent fat.

Theory into practice

Obtain various items of food packaging. Identify how the products have been labelled. What aspects of the labelling do you find informative and are there any aspects that are confusing?

4.2.4 How businesses gather information on customer needs and the issues surrounding the storage of this information

In a business environment that has become increasingly more difficult, the quality of service today differentiates organisations from one another. Organisations have realised that if they want to achieve their marketing objectives and meet the needs of their shareholders, they first have to meet the needs and requirements of their customers which means gathering information about their shoppers. This may take a variety of forms including:

* mystery shoppers
* informal comments
* suggestion boxes
* questionnaires
* freephone numbers
* focus groups / consumer panels
* general observation.

Mystery shoppers

Mystery shoppers are a useful way of adding to customer feedback. A mystery shopper involves somebody working for the organisation acting as a customer to find out how customers are treated. Although employees see mystery shoppers as spies, it is a useful way of finding out about customer service from the perspective of the customer.

Informal comments

It is possible to obtain data from customers informally. Customers constantly provide informal comments to shop assistants or those working in customer service, many of which are really helpful. For example, people working with customers face-to-face will know exactly how they feel, particularly if there are any service changes, and will be able to provide feedback to their managers.

Suggestions box

Another way of collecting customer feedback might be through providing a **suggestions box** so that customers can provide their thoughts and ideas about a particular good or service. For example, recently Asda in West Bridgford in Nottingham put ticket machines in for customers in the car parks, enforcing customers to pay £1 for a ticket which could be reclaimed from purchases. So many customers complained using the in-store suggestions box that shortly after the introduction of the scheme it was withdrawn.

Theory into practice

On a suggestions slip, produce a series of comments indicating how the quality of service could be improved within your school / college environment.

Questionnaires

Organisations might choose to include **post-sale surveys** as part of their customer care programme to help identify the levels of customer satisfaction experienced by customers who have recently purchased items. These may be sent home to purchasers shortly after purchase, although some retailers might hand them out before a customer leaves a store. Other organisations may conduct a telephone survey. A typical post-transaction survey might cover the following:

How did the sales staff deal with the customer as he or she made the buying decisions. This might include:

* where the product or service was bought

* whether the literature was suitable and informative
* staff telephone manner
* whether the customer was offered a demonstration of the product
* the appearance of staff
* the quality and clarity of the explanations given by sales staff
* how well the sales staff understood the customer's requirements.

Delivery details might include:

* was the product available from stock or was there a delay before delivery
* was the customer informed of any guarantees
* was the customer told how to access after-sales service
* was the product in good condition when received
* was delivery on time and as agreed
* was the delivery time acceptable to the customer?

The retail outlet, which might include:

* whether the location of the outlet was convenient
* the quality of the parking facilities
* the convenience of the opening hours
* the appearance of the outlet – tidiness and cleanliness.

The customer's overall level of satisfaction, probably rated on a scale.

Recommendations – whether the customer would be prepared to recommend the product or company to friends.

Suggestions opportunities – an opportunity for the customer to make suggestions as to how the buying process could have been improved.

Of course, post-transaction there is no guarantee that customers will complete a questionnaire, but it is possible to improve the completion rate by making it straightforward to use.

Theory into practice

Consider the last major purchase you made. Design a series of questions that could be included in a post-sale survey for that purchase. Swap questions with a fellow student and examine each other's questions critically. How easy are they to answer and analyse? Will they reveal the information required?

TDC web-based questions

Look at the customer service questionnaire below, used by TDC, a distributor of electrical components:

The TDC Catalogue

	Very well done	Good	Could do better
Quality	○	○	○
Layout	○	○	○
Range of Products	○	○	○
Information Content	○	○	○
Overall Satisfaction	○	○	○

What if anything were you disappointed with?

SALES – How would you rate our Sales Team

	Very well done	Good	Could do better
Friendliness	○	○	○
Product Knowledge	○	○	○
Technical Support	○	○	○
*Follow-ups	○	○	○
Overall Satisfaction	○	○	○

What if anything were you disappointed with?

Look at the questions above.

1 If you were a TDC customer, how easy would it be to fill in the above questionnaire?
2 What sort of information would this questionnaire provide and how might it be used?

Freephone numbers

Setting up a *freephone enquiry line* is a popular way of gaining feedback from customers. This is a good way of encouraging customers to provide useful data adding to an organisation's understanding of customer perspectives.

Theory into practice

Look for a freephone number in the general press or linked to product information. Describe the purposes of the freephone number.

Focus groups / consumer panels

Another way of collecting data could be through *consumer panels, focus groups* or through any other form of *consumer group*. This is a powerful technique that encourages direct consumer feedback. Customers will meet in small groups, perhaps of between 8 and 10, to discuss a series of issues and questions related to an organisation's products and services. For example, they could discuss their views on particular products and any issues such as areas of improvement and ideas for new products and services.

Product feedback from a focus group

Customer Comments

Some pubs and restaurants ask customers to fill in questionnaires to say what they think of the food, the quality of the service and the general atmosphere of the place. A questionnaire might look something like the following:

Welcome to Ploughman Pubs

Please take a few minutes to answer the following questions. Your views are important to us, and we will take note of your comments.

1. How often do you eat out?

☐ Once a week or more   ☐ Once a fortnight

☐ Once a month   ☐ Once every 2–3 months   ☐ Less often

2. Have you eaten here before?

☐ Once   ☐ Every week   ☐ Every 1–2 months

☐ Less often   ☐ Never

3. Would you come here again?

☐ Yes   ☐ No

If not why not?

4. Using the scale of 1 to 10, where 10 is excellent and 1 is poor, please rate the following by circling the appropriate number

Quality of the food	1 2 3 4 5 6 7 8 9 10
Value for money	1 2 3 4 5 6 7 8 9 10
Service	1 2 3 4 5 6 7 8 9 10
Surroundings	1 2 3 4 5 6 7 8 9 10
Toilets	1 2 3 4 5 6 7 8 9 10
Overall experience	1 2 3 4 5 6 7 8 9 10

5. Please add any other comments or suggestions that you would like to make:

1 What is the purpose of a questionnaire like this one?
2 How might this information be used?

Third party surveys

It may also be possible to get an agency to undertake some *third party surveys* where they monitor customer satisfaction not only of the business paying for the survey but also of all of the competitors.

Internal customer surveys

It is also important to remember the views of the internal customers. *Internal customer surveys* are important for monitoring how well the organisation is geared to meeting the expectations of internal customers. Service quality programmes are important to show how changing practices are influencing the expectations of employees as customers.

Quality circles

Another way of collecting information within an organisation would be through the use of **quality circles**. These provide a valuable opportunity for employees to meet together and think of how they can improve the ways in which they work and how they meet both internal and external customer needs. They are, in essence, a form of internal consulation.

General observation

It is also possible to observe the actions of customers and from these observations to generalise about their needs.

Negative feedback

Very few organisations encourage complaints even though they provide valuable information for planning. It takes brave managers to implement a system that encourages negative feedback, but it can help to provide an accurate picture of an organisation's activities. The proportion of people feeling disgruntled is usually only small, and so complaints usually only represent a small number of people who feel dissatisfied. Making it easier to complain can provide more accurate analysis of how an organisation is faring. This may be undertaken by:

* providing forms for customers to complete and post back using a Freepost address – sometimes customers may be prepared to write down their feelings, even if they lack the courage to complain face-to-face

* providing telephone numbers where customer care assistants will assist with complaints

* providing an email address to which customers could address their concerns

* randomly writing to customers to obtain their views

* making customer follow-up calls – telephoning buyers of large items a few days after purchase to check their satisfaction with what they have bought. Car retailers often adopt this practice. Sales assistants will ring recent purchasers within a month to check satisfaction levels and follow up any problems that have been identified.

If complaints are collected they can then be monitored and analysed, and this will provide a rich source of data about the organisation and its activities. By looking at such data consistent problems can then be addressed. Complaints are a good source of data about customers and provide an opportunity to benchmark the quality of service provided by their organisation against those of competitors. The word 'benchmark' means setting standards of service or best practice against which comparisons can be made. For example, it may be possible to buy goods from competitors and see how their service features compare to the organisation's own goods or services. If their service is higher, then this is something to aim for.

Analysing customer care should be constantly undertaken to examine the current situation of an organisation. It should examine customer-care methods and careful and regular monitoring of the process will reveal where additional effort and training is required.

A scheme run by BT involved telephoning customers who had either called directory enquiries or used BT repair or installation services. After a number of years they realised that this system prevented them from talking to a large section of

Telewest wins Broadband award at Call Centre Association's Excellence Awards

For many people, broadband is changing the way in which they live. There are many decisions to be made about which broadband supplier to use and customer service has become a key differentiator in what is becoming a crowded market. Telewest recently won the Best in Sector (IT, telecoms and utilities) award at the Call Centre Association's Excellence Awards.

Anne Marie Forsyth, chief executive officer of the CCA, said: 'We would like to congratulate Telewest Broadband on their success. Their achievement highlights our members' dedication to providing better standards of service, as well as their support of the CCA.

'We were overwhelmed by the quality and quantity of entries for these awards, which are a reflection of commitment to high standards of professionalism. Both the judges and myself were impressed with the exceptional standard of entries and every single submission was of a commendable quality.'

Telewest has undertaken several major initiatives used to develop their customer care initiatives. These include a focus on resolving customers' issues at first point of contact, a service excellence development programme for employees, customer feedback channels and online guides to topical issues.

1 Why is customer service important in the market for broadband services?
2 Discuss and comment upon the initiatives undertaken by Telewest.

their customers who did not fall into either of these categories. They have since employed a system of contacting a random sample of customers and using a wider variety of sampling techniques than simply using pre-coded telephone numbers. This example indicates a problem in the way in which many customer care programmes are designed – they are event driven, often measuring what the organisation thinks the customer wants, rather than the customer's actual needs.

It is now commonly accepted that the best starting point for such programmes is to engage in qualitative research aimed at ascertaining exactly what the customer wants from the organisation. The Post Office ran a customer care scheme monitoring how quickly letters travelled from the collection box to await delivery after sorting. The scheme seemed to indicate that customers should be happy as targets were being met, but what it failed to recognise was that customers judged the standard of service on the time from collection box to delivery – and this was not always what it should have been. The Post Office had failed to check initially exactly what their customers were looking for; this should always be the first step in monitoring customer feedback.

Storage of information

When storing data about customers, organisations have to take into account the following:

* accuracy
* safety
* quality
* ethics.

Accuracy

Although listening to customers is a vital element in customer care, both within and outside the organisation, it is important to think about the reliability and accuracy of data that is collected. Organisations have to make decisions about where and when to capture data, and clearly the reliability and accuracy of data will depend upon the methods of collection and the particular group that the data is collected from. Making sure that data is accurate is essential, particular as decisions may be taken upon the basis of it. Data may age quickly and so it needs to be kept up to date in order to remain accurate.

Safety

It is essential that data is kept safely and cannot be taken and used by others for fraudulent purposes. Credit card information and other financial information on customers may have value and so needs to be stored so that it cannot be accessed for wrong purposes. Data may also be of value for competitors.

Theory into practice

Make a list of the different sort of data that an organisation might hold about its customers. Describe in each instance how the data could be kept safe.

Quality

Data needs to be stored so that it can be used in an appropriate way. Data quality is fundamental to its use. Poor quality data will lead to poor quality of decision taking. Data quality needs to be monitored and its quality must be checked, revised and evaluated for.

Ethics

Ethical considerations about the use of data are a key element in data handling. It is unethical to use some data, particularly if it is attached to customer details. Data use should take into account how customers might respond to its use for customer service reasons. Access to such data should also be controlled.

4.2.5 Impact that legal and ethical issues can have on the provision of customer service

In order to meet the requirements of customers organisations will not only have to deal with legislation that governs their activities, but may also have their own internal policies.

Internal policies

A service charter or code of practice emphasises an organisation's commitment to its customers and will attempt to show how any issues can be resolved. Such statements reinforce an organisation's commitment to customer service in a way that can be communicated to customers and also emphasise to employees the importance of good customer service. It is important, however that if an organisation makes such a commitment and publishes this in a charter or code of practice, the promises are met.

The customer charter will underpin the organisation's commitment to its customers. For example, the charter might set out response times for dealing with customer complaints or for replying to emails or faxes.

Theory into practice

Produce what you think would be a useful code of practice for your college or school that could be followed and acted upon by lecturers and students. Identify a range of commitments that your school and tutors could give to you as a school customer. How might the code of practice influence the quality of service you receive?

Legislation

Within the context of customer service, the following areas of legislation must be met:

Sale and Supply of Goods Act 1979 / 94

The purpose of **The Sale and Supply of Goods Act** is to ensure that sellers provide goods that are of 'merchantable quality' – that is, they must not be damaged or broken. Goods sold must be fit for the purpose intended. If you bought a pair of shoes and they fell apart within a week, they would not have been fit for the purposes for which they were sold – serving as footwear. Under this law you can ask for replacements if goods do not meet the specified requirements and the seller must have a replacement procedure available for the customer.

This important piece of legislation is at the centre of the customer-seller relationship. The customer can expect goods to work and be fit for

CASE STUDY

The Football Association customer charter

The Football Association has a customer charter which focuses upon the following areas:

* staff conduct and response time
* stakeholder consultation on customer issues
* ticketing
* loyalty and membership schemes
* merchandising.

According to the FA 'Every professional club in the country now has a "Customer Charter", as do the FA Premier League and Football League.

'A hierarchy of complaint handling has been established to ensure that complaints about customer issues are handled initially at the correct level with the Independent Football Commission as the final stage in the complaints hierarchy.'

1 **Identify some of the issues that might arise under each of the headings within their customer charter.**
2 **What is the FA telling customers through its customer charter?**
3 **How should the FA deal with clubs that do not adhere to the charter?**

CASE STUDY

Vodafone Ireland

Look at Vodafone's code of practice below:

'Our aim is to resolve your enquiry on initial contact with Vodafone. Where we cannot resolve your enquiry we will let you know, within three hours of your initial contact, the estimated time of resolution. We will keep you informed of progress and notify you of the resolution.

'We commit to providing a high level of service under the following enquiry categories within the maximum time to resolve the enquiry where the solution is within our control. All your enquiries will be uniquely recorded so that we will always know the status of any particular enquiry. In extreme circumstances and where it is beyond our control e.g. if a third party is involved, if we lack complete information or in the case of adverse weather conditions, we will keep you informed of progress and respond to your enquiry as soon as possible. In the instance of a billing error, Vodafone will reimburse the affected account as soon as we become aware of the discrepancy. We will notify you by text message once your rebate has been applied.

'In exceptional cases where we are unable to respond or acknowledge your query within the times specified below, Vodafone have established a Customer Guarantee Scheme to compensate for that delay. Where it is brought to our attention that, in relation to your query, we have failed to meet the response time outlined in the table below, we will apply a credit to your account*.

Enquiries by letter

Enquiries sent to Vodafone by letter or fax will be responded to by letter within three working days. Where we cannot resolve your query in this timeframe, we will send an acknowledgement of your query by letter and follow up with a telephone call in line with our Code of Practice.

Enquiries by email

For enquiries sent to us by email, we will automatically confirm on receipt and aim to respond with a resolution within 24 hours. Where we cannot resolve your enquiry in this time, we will resolve it in line with our Code of Practice.'

* A credit offered for this purpose is given as a gesture of goodwill only and does not imply an acceptance of liability, breach of contract or otherwise on the part of Vodafone.

1 **What is the purpose of this code of practice?**
2 **How would it influence the actions of employees within Vodafone Ireland?**

what they are intended and this legislation provides the customer with some important rights against what they expect from the seller.

Supply of Goods and Services Act 1982

The Supply of Goods and Services Act focuses upon services rather than goods and requires traders to provide services to a proper standard of workmanship. For example, if a definite completion date or a price for work has not been fixed, then the work must be completed within a reasonable time and for a reasonable charge. Another part of this Act is that any material used or goods supplied in providing the service must be of satisfactory quality.

Many of us may have heard about building 'cowboys' who misquote jobs and do not provide customers with value for money. This Act ensures that services provide customers with value and are undertaken in a way that benefits customers.

Trade Descriptions Act 1968

The Trade Descriptions Act attempts to ensure that the description given of the goods forms part of the contract the buyer makes with the seller. This Act makes it a criminal offence for a trader to describe goods falsely. One type of case frequently prosecuted under this Act is the turning back of odometers on used cars to make them appear as if they have covered fewer miles than they really have. The main objective of the Trade Descriptions Act is quite straightforward – descriptions of goods and services must be accurate. Articles described as 'waterproof' or 'shrinkproof' must be exactly that. Those involved in customer service have to ensure that they provide accurate descriptions of goods and do not describe goods falsely.

Describing goods falsely clearly deceives customers. This legislation ensures that organisations think carefully about how they advertise, promote and describe their products or services.

Consumer Protection Act 1987

It is important that the consumer is protected against anything that may cause them physical harm. Toys are a particular product that need to be tested against the possibility of causing damage to children. The Consumer Protection Act established a right of redress for death or injury caused by using defective consumer goods. This right now lies against any supplier (including the manufacturer, or importer), rather than simply the person from whom the goods were purchased. The Act also requires that all goods for domestic use must be reasonably safe. In a customer service environment it is important to ensure that goods are safe and are not used in a way that might lead to some form of injury for the consumer.

Consumer Credit Act 1974

The Consumer Credit Act requires most businesses that offer goods or services on credit or lend money to consumers to be licensed by the **Office of Fair Trading**. The Act also tries to ensure that credit agreements do not confuse customers and so requires certain credit and hire purchase agreements to be set out in a particular way and to contain certain information. Credit deals involve a lot of quantitative information that consumers may not understand. The figures may be meaningless or be used to confuse consumers. Providing confusing information is not only illegal, it could seriously damage the organisation's reputation and so it is important that there are rigid guidelines about how such information is represented.

Key terms

Office of Fair Trading – a government body set up to look after the interests of consumers and traders.

Weights and Measures Act 1985

The **Weights and Measures Act** ensures that consumers receive the actual quantity of a product they believe they are buying. For example, prepackaged items must have a declaration of the quantity contained within the pack. If a customer is buying a pint of beer, they will expect to get a pint of beer. It is an offence to give 'short measure'. Providing short measure in a customer service context does not help sales of a product as many customers may feel that they have not got their money's worth and may change to a competitor's product.

Data Protection Act 1984 / 98

Under the Data Protection Act it is a criminal offence to hold personal data, such as data about customers, without registering under the Act. The Act emphasises a number of principles, for example data held for any purpose should be adequate, relevant and not excessive in relation to that purpose. This ensures that customer data is not used unfairly against them.

Disability Discrimination Act 1995 / 2004

The Disability Discrimination Act provides disabled people with rights in the area of employment, as well as access to goods, facilities and services or buying and renting land or property. For example, it is now unlawful to discriminate against somebody on the grounds of disability and since 1999 service providers have had to make adjustments to the services they provide so that disabled users can access them. For example, this might include wheelchair access. To provide good customer service, an organisation must take into account the needs of all types of customer that may use their premises.

Health and Safety at Work Act 1974

The basis of British health and safety law is the Health and Safety at Work Act. The Act sets out a series of general duties which employers have towards their employees as well as the duties they have to members of the public, many of whom may be customers, and the duties that employees have to themselves and to each other. The law emphasises the importance of good management and the need for employers to take sensible precautions to avoid risks. Having a disorganised and unsafe working and trading environment says a lot about a business and may lead to lost custom. When a customer enters premises, they do not expect to be put into hazardous situations.

Non-compliance

It is important to remember that these pieces of legislation, in one way or another, impact upon a range of customer service issues affecting either or both the internal and external customers of an organisation. Failure to comply with such legislation could lead to:

* legal action by employees or customers who feel that their rights have in some way been harmed, for example, receiving short measure or having been sold goods that are not of merchantable quality, may lead to a claim through the courts system

* an investigation by the Competition Commission which conducts inquiries into breaches of regulations by organisations

> ### Think it over...
>
> The UK has an Institute of Customer Service.
>
> The Institute of Customer Service (ICS) is the not-for-profit, independent professional body for customer service dedicated to helping organisations and individuals in all sectors to raise their service standards and performance. They have a diverse organisational membership drawn from across the private and public sectors. Members share good practice and leading edge thinking, for example through the Institute's Breakthrough Research programme. A key aim is to raise the performance and recognise the professionalism of individuals working in all areas of customer service.

* adverse publicity that could impact upon the image of an organisation and affect both its sales and profitability.

Local authorities and trading standard departments

Local authorities and trading standards departments investigate a range of issues such as misleading offers or prices, inaccurate weights and measures, and consumer credit.

Environmental health departments

Environmental health departments enforce legislation covering health aspects of food, for example, unfit food or unhygienic storage and the preparation and serving of food.

British Code of Advertising Practice

Advertisers, agencies and the media whose representatives make up the Code of Advertising Practice Committee support the British Code of Advertising Practice. This code sets out rules which those in the advertising industry agree to follow. It also indicates to those outside advertising that there are regulations designed to ensure advertisements can be trusted.

Chartered Institute of Marketing

The Chartered Institute of Marketing has its own code of practice to which members are required to adhere. The code refers to professional standards of behaviour in securing and developing business, and demands honesty and integrity of conduct.

British Standards Institution

Voluntary subscriptions and government grants finance the British Standards Institution (BSI). Its primary concern is with setting up standards that are acceptable to both manufacturers and consumers. Goods of a certain standard are allowed to bear the BSI Kitemark, showing consumers the product has passed the appropriate tests.

Professional and trade associations

Professional and trade associations promote the interests of their members as well as the development of a particular product or service area. In order to protect consumers, their members will often set up funds to safeguard consumers' money. For example, the Association of British Travel Agents (ABTA) will refund money to holiday-makers should a member company fail.

Corporate image

Another area of concern relates to organisations where restrictive practices and poor treatment of employees have been highlighted in the media and businesses have faced criticism from the public.

The trading policies of companies who buy cheap imports from overseas organisations involved in 'sweat-shop labour' or who trade with businesses employing young children in unacceptable conditions have also faced critical scrutiny from both the media and the public.

Think it over...

With many companies' environmental performance becoming central to their competitiveness and survival, a range of new tools for environmental management have been developed. These include environmental impact assessments, which assess the likely impact of major projects, and environmental audits or eco-audits, which involve carrying out an audit of current activities to measure their environmental impact. Alternatively, by looking at the environmental impact of a product through its life-cycle, from the sourcing of raw materials to the final disposal of waste products, a product-life-cycle analysis can be established.

Theory into practice

Over the period of a month, look at various types of advertisements by surveying magazines and periodicals. Make a list of advertisements (if any) you feel are not totally 'legal, decent, honest and truthful'. Explain why in each instance.

Key terms

Pressure groups – these may be set up to fight a specific issue, such as the closure of a plant or the increased traffic on a road as a result of a local business.

CASE STUDY

Eating GM convenience foods

Green pressure groups have dubbed genetically modified products 'Frankenfoods', arguing they are unsafe and that their development is ecologically unsound. During their early introduction into the UK, genetically modified foods faced little resistance. However, increasing knowledge about such foods has resulted in offensives being mounted by some consumer and green pressure groups against companies such as Unilever, who became one of the first manufacturers to put their weight behind genetically modified foods when they launched their Beanfeast brand.

With the European Union about to rule upon whether these products should be specially labelled, Unilever have accepted consumer concerns. Their food labels inform customers about the presence of genetically modified foods. They have also undertaken a campaign to tell customers more about genetic modification.

1 **What are the arguments for informing consumers about specific details of the products they are consuming?**
2 **Is it possible to change negative perceptions of GM foods into positive ones?**
3 **Can you think of another instance where food labelling should be changed?**

Theory into practice

Set up your own consumer group to monitor the standards of products and services you regularly use. For example, you might set up a consumer group that monitors whether the cost of visiting your local football Premiership side is worth the money. You might set one up to look at the social facilities for young people in your district or perhaps a group that provides feedback to your course leader on the quality of your course.

In recent years environmental issues have been highlighted by accidents at chemical plants or at sea with oil tankers. Such accidents can not only damage wildlife and the environment but also the image of the organisation concerned.

Organisations face many potential dangers with regard to ethics and public opinion, and no organisation is capable of satisfying all stakeholders but, by becoming good corporate citizens and being socially responsible, they can generate considerable goodwill. This strategy can be developed as a marketing advantage.

The idea of organisations working in and for the community is not new. Companies like Boots and Marks & Spencer have long advocated and contributed to community programmes, with involvement in areas as diverse as health care projects, education and training, arts and sport.

Legal action

In the sort of competitive environment in which UK businesses exist, failing to comply with EU and UK legislation should not be an option. Although it is sometimes difficult to work within a regulated environment, organisations that do not are likely to have their name tarnished if they

CASE STUDY

Scenario

Summer Sun Holidays

A number of customers from Summer Sun Holidays were recently moved from the location they chose in a catalogue to some different apartments. Many people were disappointed with the accommodation they were allocated, which was dark and dismal. Summer Sun Holidays apologised for the suffering caused and provided refunds, but they soon went into liquidation.

1 **Is it possible for a business to be successful if it treats customers badly?**
2 **Look at each of the different forms of consumer legislation. To what extent do they provide genuine protection for consumers?**

contravene any of the consumer and customer-focused legislation identified within this section.

Consumers want to have confidence in the organisations supplying them with goods and services and if such organisations abuse the law this will influence their perceptions as well as the decisions and choices they make about the products or services they buy.

By failing to comply with regulations, not only do organisations put themselves in a situation where litigious customers could take action against them, they are also in a position where such actions and subsequent publicity could seriously harm their competitive advantage.

4.2.6 Implications for maintaining a high level of customer service on staff and senior management

Staff at different levels within an organisation will have different priorities for customer service. Senior managers will be concerned with looking at customer service in terms of the planning process. For the quality of service and customer care to be considered at the heart of the activities of an organisation, it is important for senior management to try to establish a way of orientating the business around the notion of service quality. One way in which this can be done is to create a 'mission statement' or 'vision' as a long-term overview emphasising the direction in which the business is orientated. Some organisations talk about mission statements while others emphasise their vision.

Mission statements

A mission sets out the long-term purpose of an organisation and helps to emphasise why the organisation is there. Some examples of mission statements include:

'To provide our customers with a range of finest quality ready meals, through commitment to innovation, service and value, in a mutually profitable relationship.'

'Our main goal is to provide a professional yet personal service to our clients with service and customer care as our primary objective.'

'Our mission is to enjoy exceeding our clients' expectations.'

'To deliver quality IT solutions on time and to budget whilst ensuring the highest level of customer satisfaction and service is delivered by our staff.'

'We will provide quality logistic and support services that meet the real needs of all our customers.'

One of the purposes of a mission is to co-ordinate the needs and expectations of all stakeholders. Some stakeholders, for example, shareholders, may have a limited objective such as profits. This may be in direct contrast to final customers who may want value or employees who may want promotion and professional opportunities. As a result there are several sides with the potential for conflict. One of the purposes of having a mission is to try to bring the different stakeholders together and unify them within the context of a mission or vision. For example, the company could emphasise how important it is to provide good quality customer service on one hand, but to do so profitably so that it can afford to invest more in producing higher value services and goods.

Priorities for the workforce and staff

Developing a service culture will always present a challenge for an organisation. Every member of staff at every level within an organisation is involved in one way or another with customer service. For example, if a senior manager treats an employee badly they are clearly not respecting that employee as an internal customer.

A service culture will be of little value to an organisation if it does not take into account the views, interests and feelings of the internal customer within the organisation. For example, a manager within an organisation will have little respect if they keep emphasising the role of customer service and the need to listen to customers but, at the same time, fail to listen to the views of staff when they have complaints or issues that they wish to discuss.

Middle and lower management

Within the workplace and in order to provide good service to other employees, the priorities for managers should be to:

* encourage dialogue and communication
* be good listeners
* foster trust and confidence
* solve problems and welcome feedback
* look for new ideas
* be prepared to delegate responsibility
* be honest with staff.

To ensure that internal procedures take on processes of quality, managers might set up some form of internal complaints procedure which, like an external complaints procedure, provides individuals with a series of guarantees that problems and issues are dealt with in a responsive and responsible way.

Workforce

At the lower level the priorities for members of the workforce might be to:

* develop good team working skills
* respond quickly to queries made by managers
* be supportive to other members of the workforce
* keep up to date with paperwork
* attend meetings.

Senior managers

At the very highest level, senior managers will be concerned with planning how to implement customer service provision. This may involve taking feedback from staff who deal with customers and thinking about how the provision of customer service might help the organisation to compete more effectively in the market-place. For example, if an organisation provides better customer service than its closest competitors this

might provide it with a competitive advantage that differentiates it from its competitors and enables it to compete more effectively.

Training and development

The main priority for middle and lower managers may be to develop forms of training and development for staff that enable them to meet the customer service policies that have been set by senior managers. The first step in assessing the training requirements for customer service is to look at how well employees are already trained in customer service, and then look at what they need to meet the new customer service strategy.

A **training needs analysis** may be carried out by the personnel department or by someone from outside the organisation. This may take place after a discussion and after interviewing a few members of staff. The needs analysis should identify the dimensions required for a new customer service strategy. It will create a picture of current skills and attitudes towards customer service and identify areas that need to be developed in the future.

Any training in customer service will prioritise the areas that require training and development most and then determine the methods required to meet these needs. There are a number of different training methods, ranging from role plays to formal lectures. In developing the most appropriate, it is important to recognise that different employees will have different learning styles. Clearly, developing skills and understanding involves high levels of employee involvement, while telling and showing will require little participation from employees.

It is argued that most training in customer service is simply common sense. The training may help those who have developed bad habits to get back on track and also improve the attitudes of staff. A typical programme will be unique to a particular organisation and relate to its specific needs in the area of customer service. Training may also occur at a range of levels, to include:

* senior managers
* line managers

* supervisors

* other employees.

A typical workshop for employees might include the following:

1 An explanation of why an organisation is undertaking a customer service strategy.

2 A definition of service quality and customer care, with clear examples.

3 An assessment of current performance.

4 The setting of customer service standards.

5 A customer service action plan to meet such standards.

6 A description of how the process of customer service will continue.

Contributing to the customer service target

Front-line staff are often the people who have the greatest exposure to external customers. From the moment a customer enters the building they will have expectations about how they feel they should be dealt with and their thoughts will be influenced by the standard of service that they receive. It is important that staff:

* are well trained in customer care procedures and know how to deal with customers and the issues that arise from dealing with customers

* have a range of good interpersonal skills that enable them to handle people and situations

* understand the organisation they are working for as well as its procedures and policies

* have a good understanding of the products and services on offer from their organisation

* are experienced in dealing with customer complaints

* know how to manage what might be potentially stressful situations

* are able to make decisions and contact the right people in response to complaints from customers

On the customer service front line

* are able to defuse stressful situations and deal with difficult customers

* do not get stressed themselves

* are empowered to provide customers with appropriate and informed feedback

* are able to make apologies to customers where required.

Many organisations now work within flatter structures in order that they can respond more closely to changing customer service requirements. For many of these organisations the operation of teams has become an important customer service tool. In a customer service environment, a team is a group of people who work together and who have clear, agreed and shared objectives, coupled with an effective communication system. Where teams are successful they may contribute to improved customer service and higher levels of customer satisfaction.

Theory into practice

Discuss how members of a customer service team might learn from each other.

Addressing customer service

Within the organisation many customer service issues may affect internal customers. Such issues may arise from human resource management, the use of computer systems, communication procedures, teamwork problems, marketing issues and so on. Improving customer service procedures within the organisation involves a total focus upon how the organisation and its people operate.

Outside the organisation issues might not simply focus upon customer contact with the organisation. For example, issues that might involve changes could include sales and promotions, the value customers receive from doing business with the organisation, customer support procedures, the image of the organisation and customer and supplier relationships.

In order to change procedures and become more customer focused, organisations have to be flexible and often this flexibility will include a level of teamwork. Some organisations will even restructure in order to be more flexible and more responsive to change based upon the evolving needs of their customers. By cutting layers of management, they often feel that they are then in a position to make frequent changes to fine-tune their activities in a way that creates a better customer response.

An organisation may have a department dedicated to dealing with customer service. The role of that department would be to co-ordinate customer service arrangements across the organisation and also ensure that employees are sufficiently well trained in customer service. More specifically a customer service department may have individuals who are trained to deal with customer queries or complaints. Centralising the role of customer service in this way does enable the organisation to deal with customer service in a consistent way.

The alternative to a customer service department is to allow each part of the organisation to deal with customer service issues that relate to their activities.

Handling complaints

However customer service is addressed, every organisation should have some form of complaints procedure which outlines how complaints should be dealt with.

Handling complaints is not always easy and can be stressful, particularly when there are aggressive customers. When handling complaints it is important for the person involved in customer service:

* not to be upset by the complainant
* not to take any comments made personally
* to try not to work against the interests of the organisation
* to try and deal with the customer in a constructive way
* to provide the customer with accurate information
* to ask the customer how they would like the situation to be rectified
* to follow through the complaint and use the procedures within the organisation to try and rectify the problem.

Theory into practice

Describe some of the customer service situations that you have been faced with. Discuss how organisations could improve service or products if they listened to your views.

Customer influence

Although all organisations have a different approach to customer service, there are a number of issues that need to be addressed because they influence how customers make judgements about business organisations.

Premises

It is easy for customers to make value judgements based upon how premises look or how they are arranged. A key objective for an organisation is to use its physical resources in a way that helps to meet the overall business objectives of the organisation.

Layout

Layout is particularly important. In order to provide and improve customer service many organisations have changed their methods of dealing with customers in recent years to make their premises more focused upon meeting customer needs. For example, banks aim to increase throughput of

Many banks have dedicated assistants for particular services

customers through the various methods they use for automating transactions within the banking hall. Some banks have dedicated assistants for particular types of services such as for foreign exchange, mortgage advice and so on.

Tidiness

Tidiness is another factor that may influence the quality of the customer service being provided. From the moment the customer enters the premises they will be making judgements about the organisation and people that they are to do business with. If the premises are badly decorated and untidy, they may question whether this is the sort of business organisation with which they wish to do business. We can probably all think of examples of untidy or scruffy organisations and we might link our perceptions of their premises with their levels of efficiency.

Accessible

Premises must also be accessible. If it is difficult to locate the premises or they are located in an area that may be inconvenient for a customer to visit,

then this may influence the choices that customers make. For example, to provide good customer service a sandwich bar would have to be located in a city centre, whereas an envelope manufacturer would be located in the suburbs where accessibility to good transport links would be paramount.

Demographic data will help to provide information about the best location for customer-focused organisations. Some business organisations undertake a pedestrian or traffic count in order to choose a good location. Visibility and signage may also create appropriate impressions of an organisation and may be important so that customers know that the business is there. Another factor associated with premises and their accessibility is access to parking and other facilities for customers.

Stock

There can be few things that frustrate a customer more than for an organisation to offer various resources within its catalogues and then for the customer to turn up to find that it does not have such items in stock. Stocks are a resource that flow into and out of a business organisation. It is the stock inventory system and how that is managed that ensures that balances of goods are kept in order to meet customer requirements over a period of time.

Written communications

Written communications serve to provide an image of an organisation. In many instances, written communications are the main methods for communicating and keeping in contact with both internal and external customers. For example, a mail order business would keep in touch with their customers through the catalogues they supply and all of the follow-up documentation they provide.

Internal communication is communication that takes place within an organisation while external communication takes place between the organisation and the outside world. Both internal and external communications change from time to time, particularly in recent years where digitisation and developments in information and communications technology have transformed the ways in which groups of employees (internal customers) and external customers communicate.

It is important that the same standard of care is taken with all forms of written communication as it is a very important form of customer service. For example, a customer may be impressed by the staff they meet from an organisation, but their values may be challenged if they feel that the written communications are poor and convey a bad image.

Verbal communications

When dealing with customers on a face-to-face basis employees will use a combination of both verbal and non-verbal communications.

Verbal communications involve speaking in a way that is acceptable to customers. Although many people have regional accents, these are not generally considered to be a strong barrier to communication as long as the person speaks clearly and is aware that elements of their accent might be difficult to understand. The voice is a powerful medium and there may be a range of circumstances in which the tone of the voice as well as the emphasis and expression help to communicate particular items of information.

Non-verbal communications

Face-to-face communication skills accompany a variety of other very personal qualities that are necessary for customer service activities. For example, how an employee looks and their personal hygiene will reflect upon the organisation as well as their general attitude and behaviour in a situation when they have to deal with customers.

Non-verbal communications involve communications based upon body language. Body language is a visual form of communication that may convey a host of information about you and may be interpreted in a variety of different ways by customers. It is important that when working in a customer service environment individuals are careful about how they represent themselves through their body language. For example, a range of studies has shown that around 7 per cent of a message is verbally transmitted, while almost 93 per cent of the message comes from non-verbal cues. This shows that body language is an extremely important part of customer service. Body language is said to be the oldest language of all. For example, if we said to someone 'have a nice day' and then sneered at them or made some very negative signs, the 'nice day' message would have been nullified. Body language may involve facial and bodily expressions and foot movements. It involves the way we use our bodies to send messages to somebody else.

It is argued that body language helps individuals to develop effective powers of persuasion and make better presentations. By using body language to spot agendas in conversation it enables individuals to reduce conflict.

Body language can be of two different kinds: open body language and closed body language. Open body language is welcoming and outgoing, showing the customer that the employee is interested in what they have to say and is positive about the transactional relationship they are going through. On the other hand, closed body language implies that the customer service operative is negative about the transaction and is disinterested.

Theory into practice

Comment upon your reaction to each of the following situations:

* a receptionist uses bad language in front of you

* a shop assistant refuses to listen to you and simply wants to sell you a particular item

* a customer service assistant at an airport fails to point out vital pieces of information to you.

4.2.7 Assessing the quality and effectiveness of customer service

Organisations may use a number of specific criteria against which to assess the quality and effectiveness of customer service.

Price / value for money

Services have to be at the right price and this price must represent value for money for customers. It is important to get the balance right so that customers become advocates. This means that they feel that they have got value from the service, will advertise the service to others and come back to make repeat purchases.

Customer retention

This is a key area for so many organisations as it costs a lot more to get new customers than it does to retain existing ones. Gyms and sports clubs spend a lot of time developing relationships with customers in order to meet their needs so that they take out repeat subscriptions.

Reliability

Services have to be reliable and consistent so that the customer knows exactly what is on offer. Setting customer service standards such as response times is particularly important in informing the customer that he or she is being attended to.

Staffing levels

Levels of staffing will determine the quality of service on offer. Sometimes it is difficult to balance the number of staff against peak-period demand but, despite this, an organisation has to make every attempt to meet the needs of its customers.

Cleanliness / hygiene

Customers develop an image from what they see and if an organisation's premises are unclean then it could influence repeat business.

Provision for individual / special needs

Organisations need to know the specific needs of their customers and be flexible in their approach to meeting them.

Customer service improvements

Developing customer service techniques that meet customer service requirements is not always easy. There are a number of factors that could influence whether or not a customer is satisfied by the level of customer service they have encountered. For example, their expectations may differ from what is being offered by the organisation or there may be some form of IT problem that causes systems to fail so that customers are not satisfied.

An organisation that can develop repeat and frequent business with its customers will have a more established market position. Some customers may only use an organisation's products once, while others will make multiple and repeat purchases. The ways in which customers will be treated will determine whether or not they decide to continue to do business with a particular organisation. This is why customer service is so important. To meet these expectations organisations need to find out what the issues are with their customer and seek to make improvements which match the customer service requirements of their customers. For example, this might include:

* *Adding value to services* – The notion of adding value to products and services in order to foster customer loyalty is an important one. Adding value is simply the taking of something of lower value and constantly increasing its attractiveness for customers. The customer care and marketing processes can identify such opportunities for adding value. For example, it might be aimed at identifying how customer services could be improved. It would not be unreasonable to set targets for the amount of new or repeat business that could be attracted by increasing the services an organisation provides for customers.

* *Customer surveys* – Finding out how customers would like service to be improved by interviewing them or asking them to fill in a questionnaire. This direct approach enables the organisation to find out exactly what customers require.

* *After-sales service* – There are all sorts of ways of providing support to customers after they have bought an item or received a service. Obvious examples are servicing arrangements for cars, washing machines, televisions etc. The customer is thus able to see that the seller cares about them rather than just forgetting about them when they walk out of the door with their purchase. For example, when purchasing a new car you may be entitled to a free service after six months and a year, or on completing a certain number of miles. The servicing arrangement helps the seller to create a long-term relationship with the customer.

* *Providing a customer helpline* – This is particularly important with technical equipment such as broadband Internet connections and complicated machinery. Faced with problems the customer is able to ring a number and speak to an expert who will advise them on how to deal with problems – a trouble-shooting process.

* *Setting customer service standards* – Organisations may have a range of standards designed to meet customer expectations and these may appear in their code of practice. From time to time, in order to improve customer service, it may be possible to set higher and more rigorous standards designed to meet with changing expectations.

* *Training* – Customer service is not something that just exists. To provide customer service effectively staff need to be adequately trained. Therefore, if an organisation wishes to make service improvements, they need to train their staff to make such improvements.

* *Pricing strategies* – Customer service needs to be seen to match all of the other elements of the marketing mix. It may be possible to use a range of pricing strategies to segment the market-place alongside different levels of service. For example, there are a variety of different ticketing strategies available on the railways allowing the customer to choose the level and type of service they require.

* *Provision for special groups and needs* – By knowing customers and their requirements it may be possible to identify service strategies for special groups. Wheelchair facilities, for example, are particularly important within a service market-place as well as access for guide dogs.

Think it over…

Mercedes offer customers the opportunity to collect their new car from their factory in Germany for a low and subsidised price.

Theory into practice

Working in a team of five or six people, develop a customer service strategy for your school or college, using the guidelines for improving customer service techniques shown above.

Evaluating customer service

Evaluating customer service techniques may involve:

* getting feedback from customers to see if an organisation is meeting its customer service standards or the organisation's code of practice. For example, if phone calls are not being answered within a particular period of time or if queries are not being dealt with in a particular way, there is some tangible evidence of what the issues are and this evidence can be used to improve customer service standards.

* finding out how well training is addressing any weaknesses in customer service. It is important to match the training directly to the requirements of customers and make sure that it meets their needs.

* looking at particular techniques or areas of the marketing mix and evaluating the extent to which they provide for customer needs. For example, to what extent are loyalty cards working and providing customers with an augmented or extended product that

encourages them to come back for repeat business? Similarly, are prices perceived by customers as providing value for money?

* finding out how well customer service is meeting specific needs, such as for wheelchair access.

KNOWLEDGE CHECK

1 Set out a brief definition of:
   a) a customer
   b) a consumer
   What is the difference?

2 Which are more important – internal or external customers? Explain your answer.

3 Why is customer service so important to the modern business?

4 Give examples of aspects of 'appearance' that a bank might want to convey to its customers.

5 Give examples of situations in which the quality of information provided by an organisation is an important part of customer service.

6 What is Total Quality Management? Why is TQM important in providing customer service?

7 Give examples of ways in which pre-transactional, transactional, and post-transactional support are important elements of providing after-sales service for a specific product.

8 How does brand image help to create loyal customers? Give examples to illustrate your answer.

9 Give examples of ways in which organisations can provide customer service through catering for customers with special needs.

10 What is the role of the Consumers' Association in helping to give more power to consumers?

11 Explain how 'mystery shoppers' help to increase levels of customer service in retail organisations.

12 What is a 'focus group'? How does this help to provide feedback to an organisation?

13 What is a 'service charter' or 'code of practice'? How do they help organisations to be more consumer focused?

14 Give a brief summary of the Trade Descriptions Act.

15 Explain how the Data Protection Act empowers consumers.

16 What is the role of the British Standards Institution in raising standards of customer service?

17 Give examples of organisations that might refer to customer service in their mission statements? Why do these organisations give such a high priority to customer service?

18 Outline two major approaches to developing the customer service skills of employees in a DIY store.

19 Explain key procedures that staff would need to follow in handling a customer complaint – for example, in relation to having to queue too long at a supermarket checkout.

20 Outline four ways of improving customer service for a budget airline.

In order to achieve this unit you will be required to sit an external examination based on a pre-released case study. You could use the paper below to practise your examination techniques. The questions in this sample paper are based on the following scenario. The marks for each question are shown in brackets.

Look at the following Customer Complaint Procedure:

ASSESSMENT SCENARIO

Customer Complaint Procedure

The complaint will be fully investigated by the firm and a full response will be provided. If the complaint is ongoing you will be provided with reports at regular intervals.

Procedures

1 Complaint (whether received by telephone call, meeting, letter) is recorded and documented on customer's file within 1 working day.

2 Acknowledgement letter issued to complainant within 14 days of receipt of complaint.

3 The complaint is investigated with immediate effect. Should there be a delay with the investigation, the Complaint Officer will update the complainant of progress of the investigation at intervals of not more than 2 months.

4 When the complaint has been finalised, the complainant will be notified in writing of the outcome within 7 days of the completion of the investigation. If applicable, terms of any offer of settlement will be issued to the complainant.

5 Customer (complainant) file is updated and maintained in an orderly fashion.

6 All correspondence in relation to customer complaint will be retained on file for a period of 6 years from the date of last correspondence.

---

1 Comment upon the reason for the customer complaint procedures. (4)

2 Explain how an internal customer would differ from an external customer. (6)

3 Describe two reasons why customer service is important to all organisations. (4)

4 Explain the purpose of the customer complaint procedure. (4)

5 Discuss how the customer complaint procedure would be used by
   a) managers
   b) administrative staff. (6)

6 What is an online customer? Why might their needs differ from those of other types of customer? (6)

7 Using your knowledge of a customer service experience that you have recently encountered, describe four elements of that experience that provided you with good customer service. (8)

8 Describe three aims / objectives that an organisation might have for customer service. (6)

9 Identify two special needs that a customer might have. (4)

10 Name two consumer organisations. (4)

11 Identify and discuss four Acts of Parliament that affect the consumer. (12)

12 Identify four ways in which an organisation collects information from its customers. (8)

13 Evaluate how information collected from customers might be used. (4)

14 Evaluate the role that a customer charter might have in improving standards within an organisation. (12)

15 Discuss and evaluate strategies that could used by an organisation to retain customers. (12)

(100 marks)

Resources

The Institute of Customer Service, 2 Castle Court, St Peter's Street, Colchester, Essex C01 1EW provide a number of publications that support the delivery of this unit, including:

*Coaching – Knock Your Socks Off Service (Code 1676)

*Customer Service for Dummies (Code 1519)

*Telephone Tactics (Code 1675)

*The Big Book of Customer Games (Code 1677)

*The Customer Service Handbook (Code 1678)

*The Nordstrom Way (Code 1681)

Textbooks

Bee, F. and Bee, R., *Customer Care*, Chartered Institute of Personnel and Development, 2002

Blanchard, K. and Bowles, S., *Raving Fans*, Harper Collins, 2003

Boden, A., *Handling Complaints Pocket Book*, Management Pocket Books, 2001

Clutterbuck, D., *Making Customers Count*, Management Books, 2000

Newby, T. and McMahon, S., *The Customer Service Pocket Book*, Management Pocket Books, second edition, 2003

Websites

Two websites are listed below. These addresses are correct at the time of writing. However, it needs to be recognised that new sites are being launched on the Internet on a regular basis and that older sites may change or disappear.

www.dataprotection.gov.uk (Office of the Data Protection Registrar)

www.instituteofcustomerservice.com (Institute of Customer Service)

Many organisations provide information about customer service on their website. Using a search engine type in the name of a selected organisation and customer service.

Videos

The following videos are available from TV Choice Ltd, PO Box 597, Bromley, Kent BR2 OYB.

A Guide to Consumer Rights – Three lively scenarios illustrate customer's rights and explain the laws which apply.

Coaching in Customer Care – How do you coach people in customer care? Three case studies illustrate the problems.

Keeping the Customer Satisfied – A travel firm sets out to improve its approach to customer care.

Who Wins – Customer Care is also available from BBC for Business.

Magazines, journals and publications

There is a wide range of magazines and journals available to support the delivery of customer service across a broad range of sectors, for example *Business Studies Review* available from Peacock Press, Scout Bottom Farm, Mytholmroyd, Hebden Bridge.

Company data, publications and promotional literature

There is a wide range of printed material available from organisations at little or no cost. Learners will find such materials useful in explaining customer service and how it is supported by a range of products and services in different organisations.

UNIT 5

ICT provision in business

This unit contains seven elements:

5.2.1 How ICT is used by businesses

5.2.2 Forms ICT provision can take

5.2.3 Benefits/drawbacks of introducing ICT provision

5.2.4 Contingency planning

5.2.5 Research

5.2.6 Presentational skills

5.2.7 How to judge viability

Introduction

ICT in business involves carrying out the following activities with information:

* processing – the processing activities of an information system are what it does and the software is the programme that makes these functions possible. For example, hotel chains will have an information system for processing customer orders using specific software.

* storing – keeping documents and spreadsheets in files which are stored onto a hard drive, a website, a floppy disc, CD or some other form of storage device

FIGURE 5.1 *Setting out your ICT proposal*

* displaying – setting out finished documents so that they can be used to illustrate business trends, presented as posters or other forms of text and visual display

* communicating – sending text messages, emails, making PowerPoint® presentations, etc.

This unit will give you an insight into the impact that ICT can have on a business and its implications for both business and the people responsible for using ICT.

As you study this unit you will explore ICT provision in a business through an investigation into either:

* a business that is about to start up and so needs its ICT provision to be introduced, or
* a business that is looking to improve and update its current, limited ICT provision.

You need to produce an ICT proposal showing how you would introduce, or update, the ICT provision in your chosen business. This proposal will be presented in the form of an oral presentation to your peers, your teacher or a speaker from a local business where there is established ICT provision.

The material in your ICT proposal will be derived from your research into your chosen business, and the subsequent analysis of the gathered data.

You also need to show evidence of reasoned judgements as you discuss the viability of your ICT proposal for your chosen business.

A summary of how you should set out your ICT proposal is shown in Figure 5.1.

There are a number of activities throughout this unit to reinforce your learning.

5.2.1 How ICT is used by businesses

From the outset it is important to understand where the term ICT comes from. Until fairly recently the term IT or Information Technology referred to activities related to computers and computing. However, in recent times the distinction between modern forms of communication and IT have become blurred. For example, you can now access the **Internet** over your mobile phone. The convergence between IT and telecommunications technologies has led to the development of the new term ICT to refer to a range of modern technologies. Business has seized the opportunities provided by ICT to develop ecommerce (electronic commerce), trading over the Internet, and now m-commerce (using mobile phones as a business tool).

ICT is used by businesses in a number of different ways. For example:

* communicating between individuals, departments and customers, both internal and external to the business

* storing and retrieving information

* providing access to international markets by establishing a presence on the Internet

* ensuring access to market information by researching via the Internet.

Communicating between individuals, departments and customers, both internal and external to the business

ICT is the backbone of modern business communications. ICT has transformed the way in which communication can take place between:

* members of the same organisation
* a company and its customers
* a company and the wider public (public relations)

  a company and its suppliers
* a company and its shareholders
* a company and others.

Forms of communication

There are many ways of communicating information within an organisation. Some of the most important are:

* *Email* – This has become the most frequently used method of communication within an organisation. A business internal email system should make it easy for members of an organisation to access the email addresses of colleagues.

* *Electronic data interchange (EDI)* – This is used within an organisation to place orders electronically without having to fill in the paperwork. It is used within a company that has discrete departments or business units that trade with each other but is more frequently used for external communication.

* *Websites* – **Websites** are used both for internal and external communications. A company Intranet enabling internal electronic communication has replaced many more traditional forms of communications such as company meetings and notice boards.

* *Portable devices*– These devices, such as mobile phones, laptops and **personal digital assistants** (PDAs), are widely used in business, for example, sales people can communicate orders to their companies through such means.

* *Video conferencing* – Enables face-to-face links between members of an organisation who may be at a considerable geographical distance. This helps to reduce the time and expense of travel and enables instant communication.

Communication within a company

ICT has a range of communications applications within a company. Companies will typically have a network system. A network is the means of internal and external communication.

A network consists of end-user devices which give access to the network. These are known as client devices or workstations. The other part of the network are the servers which provide the network services (such as file sharing, email etc). Both the workstations and the servers will typically be computers. Servers will be sophisticated high-capacity computers, whereas the workstations can be much simpler devices such as desktop computers, personal digital assistants (PDAs) and, increasingly, mobile phones.

Many people use computers as part of their work

In most organisations, employees have access to shared information systems. The communications benefits are:

* ease of sharing information – for example, a new company policy can be communicated to every member of a company through an internal website

* ease of finding information – rather than each individual having to keep individual files and records they can quickly access information that is available to all members of the organisation such as addresses, phone numbers, details of how to carry out procedures etc.

* time saved – well-organised company files save employees a lot of time and trouble.

Communicating with customers

ICT provides a range of useful tools for communicating with customers and has led to the development of what is termed **ecommerce** (electronic commerce). At the heart of company communications is a well-organised customer-focused website. An effective website has become a must for almost all businesses that are selling items directly to customers. Websites need to be designed so that:

* customers want to visit the site

* will make repeat visits and

* find the site exciting each time they visit.

CASE STUDY
Communications within a supermarket

Bar coding has enabled instant capture and communication of sales data in retail outlets

The development of bar codes was one of the main breakthroughs in enabling sophisticated modern communication systems in supermarkets and other retail stores. Bar codes are read by a laser scanner in a fraction of a second. When a bar code is passed over the scanner the product number is read and the description of the goods and the price is obtained from the computer. The sale is recorded automatically making possible the creation of an itemised customer receipt. At the same time a record is created of the sale in the company stock control and accounts system.

This instant communication process enables:

* sales staff to automatically communicate sales they have made with a high degree of accuracy
* stock controllers in a retail outlet to have a detailed knowledge of stocking positions and sales information
* buyers in a retail outlet to know what items are selling well (or badly) to adjust their buying activities
* accounts staff in an organisation to have an up-to-the minute knowledge of sales and profit performance
* senior managers to have at their fingertips information about how the business is performing.

In order to run this system a modern supermarket chain like ASDA or Tesco will have some of the most sophisticated servers (mainframe computers) available, situated in centralised computer centres.

1 Which are the client devices and which the server devices in the communications network described above?
2 How does an organisation like Tesco benefit from operating such a sophisticated communications system?
3 How are customers able to benefit from the supermarket's sophisticated internal communication system?

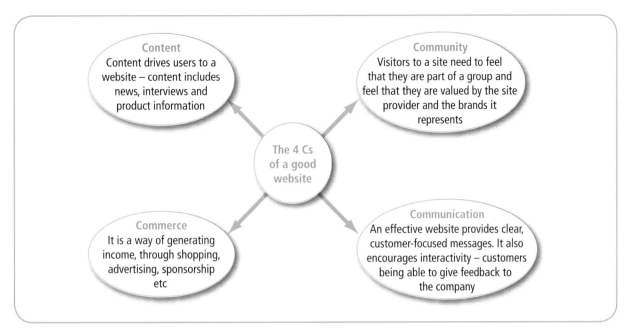

FIGURE 5.2 *Components of an effective website for ecommerce*

There are four attributes that make a website effective for ecommerce. These are shown in Figure 5.2.

Ecommerce makes it possible for businesses to communicate to customers by advertising and creating an online shop window. Customers are then able to communicate their orders to etraders, and receive online information about the processing of their order and to check when it will be delivered. Ecommerce is a very useful market-research tool because it provides the seller with details of the buyer, such as their address, buying preferences etc.

Other aspects of customer communications using ICT include:

* **electronic data interchange** whereby customers can place their orders online

* customer profiling, for example, businesses use computers to analyse the data collected from loyalty cards to build up a picture of their customers and their individual buying preferences in order to make ongoing offers to them

* a range of customer communications, such as ordering by using mobile phones and new low-cost businesses offering telephone banking and telephone insurance

* providing improved customer service, such as a well-organised company website. For example, a supplier of machinery can provide online details about the correct methods of installing and maintaining the machinery.

Businesses can be classified according to whether they are:

* *B2C (business to consumers)* – a business that sells directly to consumers, such as Top Shop (clothes), Shell service stations (petrol, oil, food, newspaper, etc), multiplex cinemas or high street banks

* *B2B (business to business)* – a business that sells primarily to other businesses, such as Cummins, who provide engines for vehicle and marine vessel manufacture, Pittards, who sell leather to football-boot and golfing-glove manufacturers, and so on.

Some B2C businesses find little need for epromotion, eadvertising or eselling. Examples might be a local independent hairdresser, bakery or greengrocer. They may prefer to concentrate on more traditional methods such as word of mouth, local newspaper advertising and using their own shop front to present themselves to their public.

However, today there are very few businesses that ignore the Internet completely. Ecommerce involves buying and selling through the medium of the Internet. Even when a business does not create a website for selling it is likely to access the Internet for buying activities because epurchasing is such a convenient way of browsing for good deals. For example, a hairdresser is likely to be able to cut purchasing costs for shampoos, cutting equipment and other materials through online purchasing.

Communicating with the wider public, shareholders and suppliers

ICT also improves communications with a range of other groups, and a well-managed website provides an excellent public relations (PR) tool for a business for the following reasons:

* members of the public wishing to find out more information about a company often seek information about that company by accessing its website

* companies communicate with their shareholders through their websites where an online company report can be accessed

* companies are able to communicate with suppliers using electronic data interchange which speeds up the ordering process as well as web-based communications.

Storing and retrieving information

One of the main strengths of ICT is that it provides the ability to store and then to retrieve information rapidly. For example, the title of this book is kept in records by the book publisher on a promotional website enabling anyone to carry out an Internet search to find out more about the book by entering the name of the book and the authors.

Theory into practice

When you are creating an ICT proposal you need to identify all the different ways in which an organisation needs to communicate, both internally and externally, and then suggest ways of developing and / or improving a system for creating such communications.

A useful chart for identifying the different communication processes is set out below. Copy the table and give examples of the different types of communication that your chosen organisation needs to carry out for each of their functional areas on a day-to-day basis, then suggest appropriate means of communication using ICT. Add additional rows for other departments.

	Internal communication	Means of communication	External communication	Means of communication
Marketing				
Accounts				
Human resources				

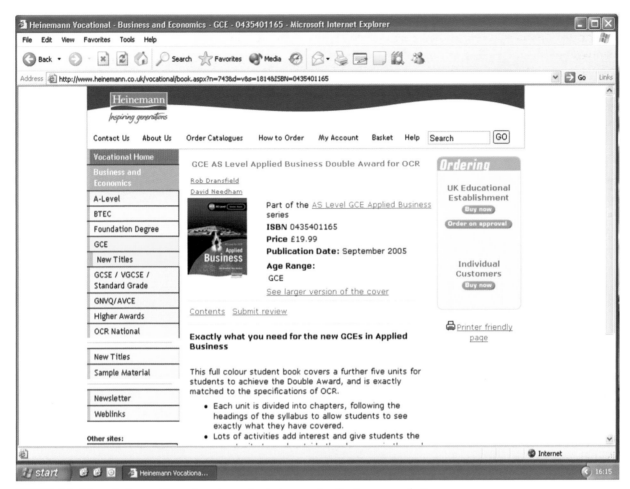

FIGURE 5.3 *More information about products is easy to find on a website*

Every information system relies on data. A high-street bank, for example, needs to store hundreds of thousands of names, account numbers, balances and individual transactions securely. An air traffic control centre needs to store aeroplane codes, flight paths, arrival and departure times, heights, speeds, directions, weather information and much more. All this data needs to be not only correct, but available for complex calculations and interrogation.

A database administrator is responsible for the usage, accuracy, efficiency, security, maintenance, administration and development of an organisation's computerised **database**, and provides support for some or all departments depending on the size of the organisation.

Databases

Databases are used in business to store collections of data records for accounts, stock management, personnel records, and other record keeping. Databases can be cross-referenced to each other so that information may be collected and manipulated from various data sources.

Data warehouses

Today, large companies have developed 'data warehouses' which are systems for storing, retrieving and managing huge quantities of data. A data warehouse needs to be organised so that the data is structured, for example distinguishing between transactions that were recorded last year and those that were recorded yesterday. Data warehouse software therefore involves metadata, i.e. information about data, such as the source of the data and when it was last updated.

Retrieval systems

Simple retrieval systems can be used to locate specific data. For example, a search to find the

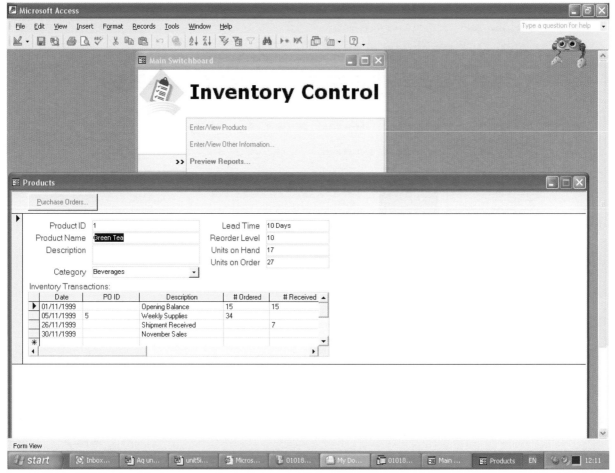

FIGURE 5.4 *An example of a database for stock inventory*

phone number of a member of an organisation can be found by entering the surname and first name of the person. In the same way, banks can search for details of recent account payments, withdrawals and balances.

In addition to these simple retrieval operations, large organisations can make sense of the raw data available to them by organising it into meaningful patterns. This is referred to as data mining. Data mining is the process of analysing the data in a database using tools that search for trends and anomalies (unusual patterns). For example, a data-mining tool might spot an unusual pattern in a customer's spending which suggests that some form of credit card fraud is taking place.

Since the development of loyalty or reward cards it has been possible for retailers to identify opportunities for cross selling. For example, if the data-mining software indicates that 90 per cent of customers who buy a certain type of butter also buy wholemeal bread then it may be possible to locate these items close together in a supermarket or use some other form of cross-selling technique.

Data mining is particularly useful in analysing visitors to websites, for example, to see which types of visitors are most likely to make purchases etc.

Providing access to international markets by establishing a presence on the Internet

An online presence means that a website is accessible for **browsing** and **surfing** by potentially millions of people. For example, in 2004 the top five global brand searches on the Internet (through Google search engines) were:

* Ferrari

* Sony

* BMW

* Disney

* Ryanair.

Theory into practice

Carry out an Internet search to examine the sites of the five companies listed above. What aspects of these sites do you think help to make them so popular?

A product-related website can:

* educate consumers about new or existing products and their use

* provide information, for example, about new product developments, different product specifications, what to do if things go wrong with a product and so on

* provide recreational activities such as games, competitions and fun activities

* offer commercial benefits such as enabling consumers to buy through the medium of the Internet, and sellers to sell their products and services.

Theory into practice

If you look at the website for Nokia you will find details of a phone that combines the worlds of information technology and communications, providing a range of state-of-the-art facilities such as email, web browsing, widescreen viewing and even a mobile fax.

1 Why is it important for Nokia to have a website?

2 Study Nokia's website and then explain how having the website enables Nokia to access international markets.

Ensuring access to market information by researching via the Internet

The World Wide Web is the most sophisticated research tool that has ever been invented. It was first developed as a means of sharing academic research between universities. The World Wide Web consists of web pages that are accessed on the Internet and are connected through clickable 'hypertext links'.

Today, it serves as a very useful information tool for businesses, in particular in giving access to marketing information.

A number of market research organisations such as **Mintel** provide detailed market research information on the Internet which is available for a subscription. Companies that want regular market research information can subscribe to these online services. They can then carry out their own research using this secondary source to give them up-to-the-minute facts and figures about consumer expenditure on different categories of goods, changes in buying patterns and so on.

Additional useful market-research information can be accessed from government statistics and databases.

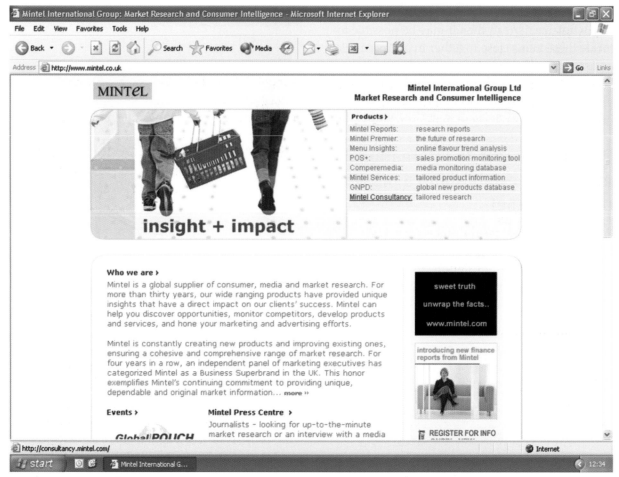

FIGURE 5.5 *A page from Mintel's website*

How business departments benefit from ICT provision

A key focus of your ICT proposal needs to show how your chosen business's different departments would benefit from some sort of ICT provision. Having already learnt about departments in Unit 1: Creating a Marketing Proposal, you need to understand how ICT could be used by these different departments on a day-to-day basis. Examples include:

* finance using **spreadsheets** to monitor levels of sales and expenditure

* marketing using artistic packages to promote a particular product or service

* human resources using databases to keep records on the workforce.

Using ICT in the finance department

Spreadsheets provide a very powerful tool in finance and accounts. The spreadsheet presents the user with a worksheet made up of rows and columns. Columns are named letters of the alphabet and rows are numbered. The box where a row and a column meet is called a cell and the cell reference or address is made up of its column letter and row number.

You can enter the following into a spreadsheet:

* text, for example for column headings

* numbers (often referred to as values)

* formulae – the real strength of the spreadsheet lies in the ability to input formulae, for example a formula can be used to automatically deduct costs from the value of sales to give profit figures.

Spreadsheets can be used widely to help in increasing the speed and accuracy of work in business, for example:

* marketing – in analysing quantitative data collected in market research

* finance – in calculating repayments on loans, calculating profit etc

* for human resources to calculate pay, tax and national insurance deductions.

ICT in marketing and sales

Marketing and sales can create exciting publicity materials using artistic packages to promote a particular product or service. Graphics packages will also be useful in other parts of the organisation, such as in public relations when providing promotional materials about the company.

ICT in human resources

Databases are particularly useful in human resource management, including:

* employee records, such as recruitment records/staff absences/illnesses

* planning labour hours budgets – planning who will work when

* records relating to pay/tax/national insurance etc.

Theory into practice

Identify ways in which databases might be used by other departments.

5.2.2 Forms ICT provision can take

Computers have today become so much of a part of our lives that we almost take them for granted. In the same way that the television 40 years ago had a profound impact upon how families socialised, learnt about the world, kept up to date with world events and entertained themselves, the computer is another generation of technology that is transforming our interactions and influencing many of the things that we do. Computers can be found in the workplace, in schools and in all public and private institutions. In fact, some form of computer or terminal can be seen just about everywhere we go.

There are two parts to all computer systems, known as the hardware and the software. As well as having hardware and software, many of the functions of the computer today involve linking the hardware and the software to networks.

In the past there were few choices of types of personal computer. However, nowadays many individuals buy, adapt and add to their hardware as they constantly develop their personal computer for their own very specific needs. For some, the need to upgrade and constantly look at their requirements for their machine is to match their machine with software requirements but for many others it has become a hobby and an interest, with computers playing an increasing role in their lives.

ICT products are increasingly portable

Hardware

Hardware is all of the tangible elements or parts of a computer system – anything that you can touch or handle. It is essentially the physical components of the computer and is the group name given to all of the devices and pieces that make up a computer.

To run a computer you need certain elements of hardware that enable the user to input to the system and output from the system. The hardware at the heart of the system will comprise a central processing unit alongside memory and auxiliary storage. We shall look at each of these elements of hardware in detail.

The physical elements of a microcomputer

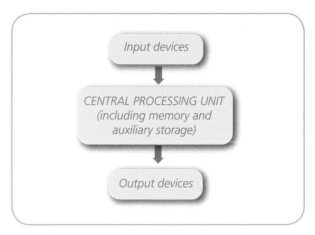

FIGURE 5.6 *A basic computer system*

The central processing unit

The central processing unit is sometimes called the CPU. This unit:

* controls the transmission of data from input devices to memory

* processes the data in the memory

* controls the transmission of data from the main memory to output devices.

The CPU will have a microprocessor of integrated circuits or 'chips', will be around 1.25 cm square and will hold millions of micro-components such as transistors and resistors all held on a main circuit board. Microprocessors or chips are also used to control devices such as washing machines and microwave ovens.

Memory

All of the instructions and data within the computer are held within the main memory, which is divided into millions of storage units called bytes. Each byte can hold one character or one part of an instruction by a piece of computer software. The total number of bytes in the main memory is referred to as the computer's memory size.

Memory sizes vary from kilobytes to megabytes, then gigabytes and terabytes. A letter takes up around 50 kilobytes of space, a CD holds 750 megabytes and a hard disk around 40 gigabytes. A megabyte is 1,000 times larger than a kilobyte and a gigabyte is 1,000 times larger than a megabyte, and so on.

Other than the main memory there are two other kinds of memory within a computer known as RAM and ROM. Random Access Memory (RAM) is used for storing programs which are running when the PC is switched on and the data is being processed. This type of memory loses all of its contents as soon as the machine is switched off.

Read Only Memory (ROM) has its contents permanently etched in the memory chip. It is used to hold programs such as the bootstrap loader, which is the program which runs as soon as the computer that loads the operating system into the memory is switched on.

All PCs also come with an in-built hard disk. The capacity of this is measured in gigabytes. For example, the capacity of a hard drive may be 30 GB.

Computers are digital and so use the binary system for representing data of all kinds such as numbers, characters, sound, and pictures. The reason for this is that digits such as 1 and 0 are represented by a series of electrical circuits that can either be switched on or switched off.

An ergonomic keyboard

Theory into practice

Look in the press and find some advertisements for PCs. Discuss the specifications and prices with other members of your teaching group.

Input devices

There are a number of different ways of inputting data into a computer.

Keyboards

Perhaps the most well-known way of capturing data is to use a keyboard. Almost all computers have a keyboard, and keyboards are suitable for a wide range of applications from keying into a word processor through to entering data into a database or spreadsheet. The great advantage is that as a key is pressed the operator or user can see the impact of pressing that key on the monitor.

However, keyboards do have their weaknesses. They can be slow to enter data, and they are limited by how fast or how competent the user's keyboard skills are. It is possible for the operator to copy data wrongly from the source although spellcheckers can find and amend spelling errors.

Another issue is repetitive strain injury (RSI). This can affect people who use keyboards all of the time because of the strain the keyboard puts on their arms and wrists. RSI can make it difficult for people to carry out even simple household tasks. As a result, a number of organisations have built and developed ergonomic keyboards to try to prevent injuries from RSI.

Touch-screen keyboards – With a touch-screen keyboard the user simply interacts with the monitor screen by touching the character or command required.

Concept keyboards – These are specially designed keyboards where the keys represent data rather than characters. These have been developed to help groups of individuals with physical disabilities, and they are also used in restaurants where the keys represent choices for meals.

Mouse and other pointing devices

A standard mouse has two buttons (on a Mac one button). An arrow or curser will appear on the screen and the user can then move this about, clicking the left button to place it elsewhere. The mouse can be used to drag and highlight items. For example, double-clicking on a word will highlight the word and clicking three times will highlight the paragraph.

There are a variety of other different pointing devices that can be used for data entry.

* *Joysticks* can be used for games and may improve the enjoyment of playing.

* *Trackerballs* or *touch sensitive pads* are more usually associated with laptops, enabling the user to manipulate around the laptop screen. Their shape is like an upside-down mouse that allows the user to point and select items on screen by rotating the ball with the fingertips.

* *Lightpens* are light-sensitive pen-shaped devices that enable the user to draw onto a screen and are more commonly associated with interactive whiteboards. An interactive whiteboard links a computer with a projector so that a PC screen can be created upon a whiteboard at the front of a class or training room. The pens enable the trainer or teacher to interact directly with the whiteboard.

* *Graphics tablet / pads* are flat surface devices that use a pen or stylus to draw on a table pad for projection onto the monitor screen.

Rollerball or trackerball

FIGURE 5.7 *A lottery ticket*

Automatic data capture

Increasingly there are opportunities for data capture which involve data being transferred to a computer without any form of conversion. There are various sorts of automatic data capture such as:

* *optical mark reading* in which pencil marks are made in certain grids or boxes and the data is sent to the computer. For example, many examination papers for multiple choice tests are read like this as are lottery tickets.

* *optical character recognition* (OCR) involves using scanners to read typed or even hand-written documents and then software can be used to edit the text and export it to a word processor or data file.

* *magnetic ink character recognition* (MICR) is a way to read numbers on a document printed in magnetic ink such as those on the bottom of a cheque. This not only prevents fraud but makes processing much quicker.

* *magnetic strip recognition* – A magnetic strip on a plastic card may contain information about

the holder of the card. The card is swiped through a machine which then reads the information. Cards with magnetic strips are found in libraries, on buses, on security devices for entry to buildings as well as across a whole host of other applications.

* *bar codes* – These are used in a variety of settings where data needs to be scanned. We probably think about them more frequently when shopping in a supermarket where the scanning machine reads the data on the bar code including the description and price. The bar code reader will be linked to the stock system so that new products can automatically be re-ordered.

* *voice data entry* – It was thought by many that voice recognition software would lead to the demise of the keyboard for word processing purposes but this has not turned out to be the case.

Other forms of data capture

* *Scanners* – These may be used with some of the other data capture methods and may be either hand-held or desktop devices which can read data in a variety of different ways. For example, most of us are used to flatbed scanners in which the sheet to be copied is placed on top of a glass screen under a flap and which works like a photocopier. A handheld scanner relies upon the user to move the scanner rather than a motorised belt scanning the image. In the publishing industry, drum scanners are used to capture detailed images.

A digital camera

* *Digital cameras* – These have transformed the whole world of photography. Once the camera has taken the photographs, it is then linked by a cable to the computer and pictures can be saved or downloaded to floppy discs, pen drives (pocket drives/memory sticks) or onto a CD.

* *Smart cards* – These look similar to any plastic card but as well as having a magnetic swipe function there is a processor embedded in the middle of the card behind a small gold electrical contact. Cards with chips can hold millions of characters of data, and these are becoming increasingly useful across a range of activities. For example, students in some universities have them. They simply charge the card up and use it for bus fares, food from the refectory, the payment of library fines and so on.

* *Sensors* – As automatic entry devices, sensors simply log data. Connected to computers the data is directly downloaded. Sensors may be used to log data such as traffic flow or river levels.

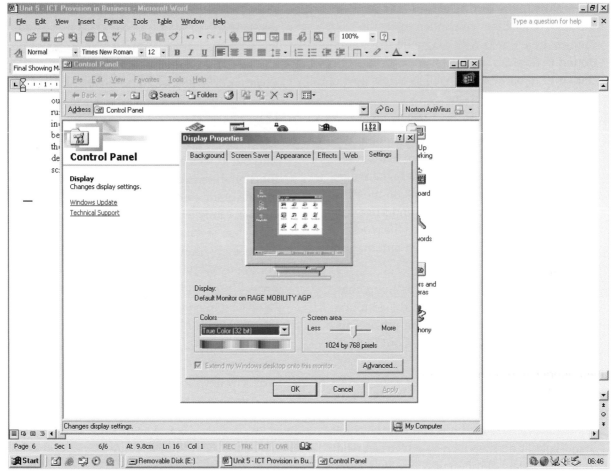

FIGURE 5.8 *Control panel screen shot*

Output devices

After data has been processed, output devices will make data available for the user in a variety of different forms, usually in the form of some kind of display or in some form of hard copy.

Visual display units (VDUs) / monitors

It is easy to take these for granted as output devices as they are nearly always turned on when the computer is running. VDUs come in an assortment of different forms and sizes and flat-screen varieties have now become much more common because of the space they save. The size of the screen indicates the length of the diagonal, so a 17-inch screen has a 17-inch diagonal. The resolution is determined by the number of dots of light, known as pixels, displayed on the screen. By accessing the display properties from the control

panel, a user can choose a different background or screen saver, and set the resolution.

Printers

There are many different printers and the printer a user will choose may depend upon a variety of factors. For example, users may look for:

* speed – different printers operate at different speeds

* colour – a colour printer will cost more to maintain as it needs more cartridges

* memory – printers have their own memory, the amount of which will affect the speed of the printer

* resolution – the resolution will determine the quality of the print

A laser printer

A graph plotter

∗ one sided/two sided – many modern printers offer a two-sided option which saves on stationery.

Laser printers offer speed and high-quality print for text and graphics. Ink-jet printers are also called bubble-jet printers. The print head consists of nozzles through which ink flows and these can also produce high-quality output like laser printers.

Graph plotters
Graph plotters draw accurate line diagrams on paper. They are used for plans, maps, line diagrams and three dimensional drawings. Plotters use pens to produce images which can be raised and lowered over a sheet of paper. They are used by architects for drawing property specifications and building plans and for computer-aided design.

Speakers
In the multi-media environment in which we live, speakers are very much an important part of the modern PC and many machines have them built into the hardware of the machine. In order for speakers to be used the machine will need a sound card.

CASE STUDY
Hardware developments in 2004
There are probably few markets that change in terms of products and innovation as quickly as that for computer hardware. The start of the year brought good news for laptop users, with the arrival of Vodafone's 3G Datacard heralding a new generation of telephonic uses. At the same time, Intel had other ideas for laptop users, with plans to bring wireless broadband to the masses allowing faster access to the Internet.

Intel also added 64-bit extensions to its Xeon range so that computers can compete with the functions of the sophisticated gaming systems. They also launched a much faster Dothan processor with a revamped manufacturing process and larger cache to make the chip faster, more efficient and cut down on heat generation. The Dothan processor is the next generation of Pentium processor.

Businesses got a little more choice when, at Linuxworld, HP launched its first Linux laptop, a laptop with a different operating system from that of Microsoft. IBM continued to grab the headlines when it built the world's fastest microcomputer. The company promises an even faster system next year.

1 Why does the market for hardware constantly change?
2 Explain why organisations change the hardware they use.

Voice output

Voice output is an electronic device that is able to generate spoken or printed text. It is an invaluable help for people who are unable to use natural speech to communicate effectively.

Robots

Electrical signals from computers can be used to control robotic devices such as a robotic arm.

Types of computer

There are three different types of computer. These are microcomputers, mainframe computers and mini computers.

Microcomputers

Microcomputers are the machines that you are most likely to come into contact both at home and at school. They include your desktop PC which may have the unit horizontally stacked on your desk with the monitor on top, or it may be in the form of a mini-tower. They are usually manufactured by brands such as HP, Compaq or RML, or by Apple, which has a different type of operating system.

There are a number of different smaller versions of the PC:

Personal digital assistants – There are a number of different makes of these small hand-held

A hand-held computer

devices which may be used as organisers. They are small devices that enable users to keep appointments, store the names and addresses of contacts and friends, and download email from the PC. They have a calculator and other special features.

Palmtop computers – These are small computers but are limited in applications. Their main advantage is their size. Data can be downloaded to and from a desktop PC and they can also be linked to mobile phones to send and receive email. In many ways they are smaller versions of laptops or notebooks with fewer functions.

Laptop and notebook computers – These are bigger than palmtops and have the same functionality as a PC. Batteries will last for several hours after which they have to be charged.

Mainframe computers

Mainframe computers are very large powerful computers capable of supporting a large number of terminals, normally more than 500. Banks, building societies and large utility companies make use of powerful mainframes.

Mini computers

Mini computers have a size, power and cost somewhere between microcomputers and mainframes.

Software

Many computer users take hardware for granted, particularly where the machines are provided by their school or college, or the organisations for

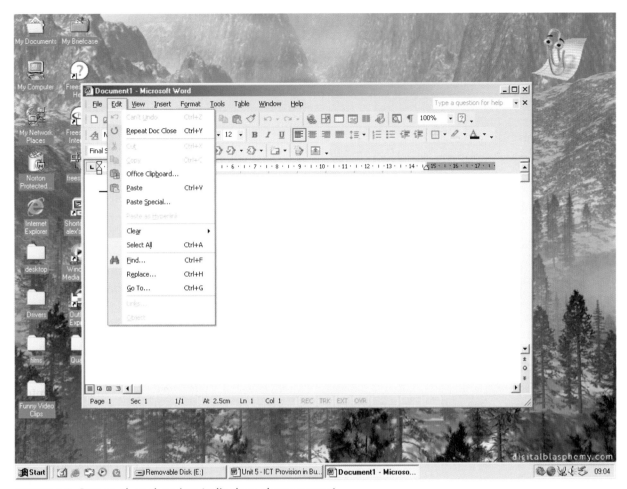

FIGURE 5.9 *Screen shot showing 'edit drop-down menu'*

which they work, but it is the software that helps users to meet their computing needs. Software is a very general term used to describe all of the programs that are run on computer hardware. There are basically three general categories of software: systems software, applications software and general purpose software.

Systems software

The operating system is the program that directly controls the hardware and provides a way in which other applications and general-purpose software can work, for example Windows XP or ACC Linux. Essentially the operating system is the interface between the user and the computer's hardware.

Applications software

Applications software is designed to perform a particular type of application. It could be payroll, accounting, stock control or an appointments system. This software will be specifically developed for the applications of a particular organisation.

General purpose software

Common applications packages such as word processing, spreadsheets, desktop publishing, databases and presentation graphics packages fall into the category of general purpose software. Sold as a package they can be adapted by individuals within organisations for their own purposes and functions. Some of these packages will be part of integrated suites of software such as Microsoft Office, Works or Lotus SmartSuite. For example, basic versions of Microsoft Office include Word, Excel®, Access, FrontPage® and PowerPoint®.

Features of software packages

There are a number of common features which apply to many software packages.

Editing capabilities – Most packages will have functions such as copy, cut, paste, delete, insert, undo, select all and so on. These save the user time.

Search facilities – Software packages usually include a search and find facility to make life easier for the user. For example, pressing the Control and F keys enables you to find and replace words within a large body of text.

Object integration – One of the key features of many packages is the ability to integrate files and objects within a file or document. This may include graphics, text, charts, graphs, slides and so on.

Data portability – This is the ability to transfer data from one software package to another, for example by copying and pasting.

Spreadsheets

A spreadsheet is a table of numbers that can be organised and altered on a computer according to preset formulae. Spreadsheets, as we will see, are particularly useful for forecasting and financial modelling, as they show the effects of financial decisions without the need to repeat the calculations manually.

A firm will make a forecast of all the money coming in and going out over a twelve-month period. The spreadsheet can alter the inputs to calculate the effect, for example, of lowering a heating bill by a certain amount each month. The computer will automatically recalculate the columns to change the heating figures, total cost figures and cash flows for each month. In this way a manager, accountant or other user of a spreadsheet can quickly carry out business calculations such as introducing and finding out the effect of minor changes of variables.

A spreadsheet presents the user with a series of rows and columns. Above each column are letters of the alphabet and each row is numbered. The box created where a column meets a row is called a cell and the cell reference is made up from its column letter and row number. So, B3 would be in the second column on the third row down.

Cells in a spreadsheet may contain:

* text to provide column titles or labels that help the spreadsheet user to understand the significance of other data

* numbers or values as they could appear as a currency or a percentage

* formulae that enable spreadsheets to make calculations, for example A1 + B2 will add together the values found in these two cells.

There are many formulae used in spreadsheets. For example the following formula A2+B3*C3/D1 will tell the spreadsheet to add the value of A2 to the product of the values in B3 multiplied by C3 divided by D1.

One term used within the spreadsheet is *function*. The SUM function adds up all of the values between two cells. By putting three values into a box and highlighting the three cells as well as the cell below these and pressing the sum function represented by Σ it is possible to add the three cells together. If the columns are C1, C2 and C3 you can see that the spreadsheet has added them together and this can be represented by =SUM(C1:C3) (see Figure 5.10).

Word processing

At its most basic, the function of a word processor is to manipulate text. Its great advantage is that it allows the user to make unlimited changes to text on screen before the final document is printed out.

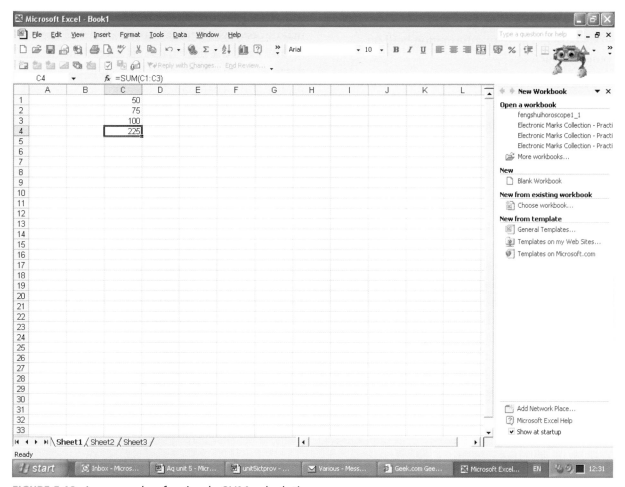

FIGURE 5.10 *An example of a simple SUM calculation*

Word processors make life easier for the writer in a number of ways:

* new text can be put on screen while existing text moves to create space for it

* blocks of text can be moved around on the document that is being created

* the text can be spaced out to fill the whole line

* a word or phrase can be searched for and removed or replaced by another word or phrase enabling a mistake which is repeated throughout the document to be corrected in a single operation

* a header or footer can be added to the top or bottom of the document.

There are, of course, numerous other functions, many of which you will probably be familiar with.

For example, you can use different styles and fonts, insert graphics into text, use a spellchecker, thesaurus, bullets, borders, tables, numbers, word count and even auto summarise. Files can be imported into a word processor and then mail merge facilities can be used to provide a list of names and addresses to personalise letters.

Another feature of word processing is the ability to create or use templates with preset text styles, margins and formatting for a range of business purposes.

Theory into practice

Make a list of the sort of activities for which you use a word processor. What functions of the word processor do you use most often?

Databases

A database is a store of information held on a computer such as:

* a list of customer accounts held by a bank or building society

* a record of members of a church congregation and their addresses held by a parish priest

* a record of tickets sold by a football club for various matches

* a list of students attending courses in a university listing their activities and their course registration details.

The main difference between a computerised and non-computerised database is the speed with which data can be accessed. Information that might have taken hours to find in some form of paper archive can be accessed in just a few seconds with a computerised database. Databases also have the capacity to undertake really complex activities. For example, every time a customer makes purchases from a supermarket and uses a loyalty card, the information is logged into a database from where it can be used to build a profile of the customer. Police databases are used to build up profiles of crimes and criminals.

The essence of a database is that data can be accessed and analysed in a number of different ways, depending upon the needs of the user. For example, a homeware store that wants to record the account details of all its customers will set up a database file. The database file is a collection of records and each record includes the fields into which the appropriate data will be entered. The fields stay the same for each record, such as

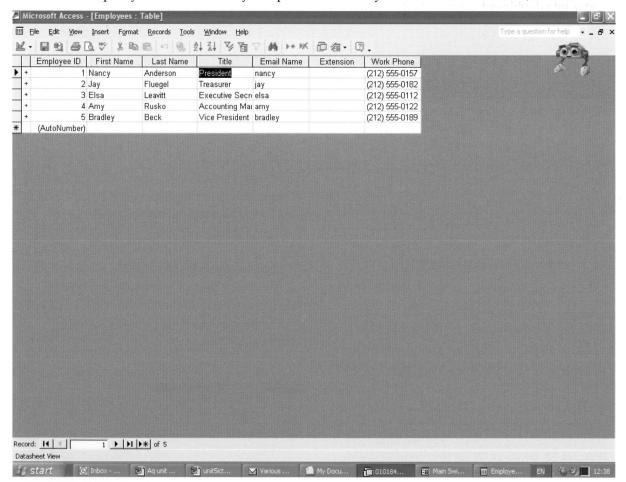

FIGURE 5.11 *Database records*

address, value of goods supplied, payments received and balance of account. If a customer rings up asking for the state of their account, the computer can be programmed to produce the appropriate information and display it on screen.

Accounting software

The widespread use of computers by all types of organisations has seen many organisations opting to computerise their book-keeping systems. There are a number of advantages of using computerised accounting packages:

* computers help to improve the control of funds coming into and going out of an organisation and make this control more effective

* they improve accuracy, particularly where large amounts of data are entered into accounts (they take away much of the tedium of data entry into double-entry accounts)

* accounting data is, by its very nature, arithmetical, which makes it well suited to being recorded and maintained by computer

* computerised book-keeping systems can supply reports and account balances much more quickly, such as trial balance, stock valuation, payroll analysis, VAT return, etc.

* they help to provide managers with a readily accessible view of how the business organisation is functioning

* many reports can be produced quickly and easily in a way that is not possible in a manual system because of time and cost. For example, it is easy to go through the sales ledger to find out all the customers who have not paid their debts (aged debtors) and send them reminders to do so.

Computer programs for financial accounts usually follow the same system of ledger division into general and personal. In doing so, the system provides an element of continuity with past

---

CASE STUDY

Sage Line 50

Sage Line 50 is the UK's best-selling accounting software. It is an integrated package designed to provide users with the opportunity to make the best use of their accounting data. The package makes all facts and figures readily available so that managers can quickly analyse their trading situation and solve problems or seize new opportunities. The package handles sales and purchases, stock control and order processing. It also generates invoices, produces statements, creates reports and can be used to create sales letters. There are a number of elements to the system, including the following:

* *Sales ledger* – This shows who the customers are, what and when they buy and how much they owe and for how long.
* *Purchase ledger* – This enables the users to get the best value from their suppliers and puts them in a strong position to get better discounts and higher credit levels.
* *Nominal ledger* – This brings together all the transactions and balances from other

ledgers to create a chart of accounts to suit specific user requirements.
* *Financials* – This enables Sage Line 50 to deal with management accounts, VAT returns and budget analysis.

A key benefit of using Sage Line 50 is that it integrates with all other office software. For example, data from the system can be transferred into spreadsheets. Information can also be integrated into mail-merge and marketing databases.

There are single user or network versions of Sage Line 50. The networking option allows more than one user onto the system at any one time.

1 Why does a package such as Sage Line 50 mirror the workings of a book-keeping system?
2 What are the advantages of using such a package?

---

practices. Commercially available accounting software is usually described as an 'integrated package', covering a range of accounting activities. For example, an accounting package will:

* update customer accounts in the sales ledger

* update supplier accounts in the purchases ledger

* record bank receipts and payments

* print out invoices

* make payments to suppliers and for expenses

* adjust records automatically.

Many packages offer more than just the control of each of the ledgers. Some may also provide for payroll, stock control production planning, electronic data interchange (EDI) and financial planning. These can be integrated with the rest of the accounting system.

An integrated accounting system means that, when a business transaction takes place and is input into the computer, it is recorded into a range of accounting records at the same time. For example, if a sales invoice is generated for a customer:

* the customer's account will be adjusted with the invoice total

* the sales account will increase and VAT will be applied

* stock records will change.

Project planning

As people increasingly work on one or more project teams, applications for computer software in projects are being produced. Computer programs allow projects to be broken down into a number of interrelated stages called activities. First the activities are defined and the time taken

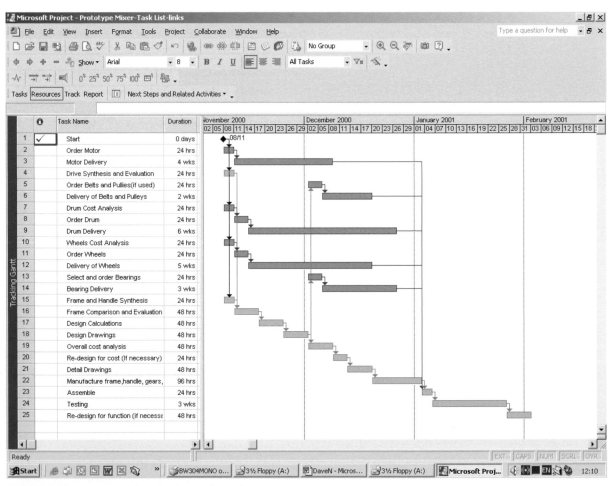

FIGURE 5.12 *An example of Microsoft Project*

by each is estimated. Then the way in which the activities depend upon each other is defined. The computer calculates the total time for the project and shows the activities that must be completed on time in order for the project not to be delayed.

For example, in the case of a project to build a new office the activities and times might be as follows:

1	Prepare land and build foundations	30 days
2	Build walls	30 days
3	Build roof	15 days
4	Install equipment	30 days
5	Equip office	20 days

Activity 1 must be done first, then activity 2, followed by activity 3. However, activities 4 and 5 – although they come after activity 3 has finished – can be done at the same time. Therefore the total time for the project is only 105 days (30 + 30 + 15 + 30), not 125 days. The computer output will also show that Activity 5 is not critical: that is, it can start late or take longer than planned without delaying the project.

Many organisations use packages such as Microsoft Project that not only help to calculate the path organisations should use to finish the project on time, but also have charting tools that show how the project is progressing.

Networking resources

Today, in nearly all cases, computers will be networked. Networking involves linking together two or more computers to allow facilities and information to be shared. A network could comprise just two machines or it could involve sharing information between millions of people. A network has the effect of decentralising information and communications so that managers and employees have more information upon which to base their decisions. A computer network may be specially developed for almost any type of organisation or application. Terminals may be just a few metres apart or they may exist in completely different parts of the world.

The benefits of using a network are that:

* resources and files can be shared by many people
* one copy of software can be purchased together with a user-licence and this can be shared across a network
* internal communication can be enhanced using an intranet that shares information across an organisation
* external communication can be enhanced by using email, electronic data interchange (EDI) and websites
* access to the Internet provides commercial opportunities for organisations and also allows research to be carried out
* users can be shut out from accessing data not relevant to their particular post or department.

Although there are many advantages of using a network, it can also bring its own problems:

* if a network goes down, even for a short period of time, it can cause chaos as so many people are dependent upon it for their work
* file security is a major concern as there may be hackers, unauthorised users and viruses which can cause data to be lost, misappropriated or damaged, with serious consequences for organisations
* if a file server goes down, then a network becomes unusable
* networks need to be managed well and require a high level of technical support, with constant development for its evolving needs
* a network needs to be supported with appropriate hardware otherwise it will run slowly or even crash if it becomes overloaded
* dependence upon a network might mean that if there are network difficulties, time, money and resources could be lost or damaged.

Local area network

A local area network (LAN) may be used to connect computers within a single room, building or group of buildings on the same site, without the use of telecommunicatiions links. LANs may be linked to a file server, which is a permanent data store that provides files and software for other PCs and also acts as a storage base. A hub is a form of device that links and networks computers. Computer games often connect their machines together using a hub, so that they can compete with each other in the same room or the same house.

Wide area network

A wide area network (WAN) may be used to connect computers on different sites by making use of telecommunications. The great benefit is that WAN networks extend the use of the computer beyond the office by using a modem (modulator/demodulator), which converts computer signals for transmission over the telephone lines before reconverting them again. In most circumstances, LANs are more usually connected to WANs through a gateway.

Modems are used because telephone lines are primarily used for speech transmissions and not for computers. Waves travelling along lines are analogue waves, where sounds and images are converted into corresponding variations in electrical voltages or currents. However, the digital revolution has seen the creation of new formats that enable the transmission of video and voice signals.

Email

Electronic communications such as email have become very widely used in the workplace as an alternative to written communications. Communicating via email requires the user to have an email address provided by an **Internet service provider**. Writing an email is done by using email software such as Outlook Express. Once connected to the Internet or the network the user can send their written message which is

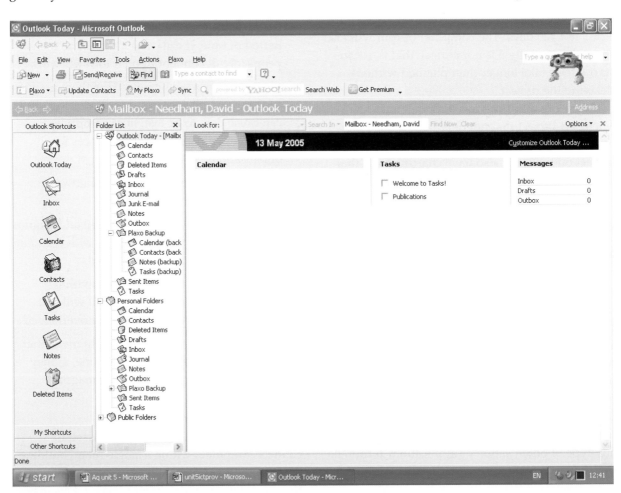

FIGURE 5.13 *Many people use Outlook to write emails*

Key terms

Internet service provider (ISP) – A company that provides access to the Internet, usually for a payment.

placed in a mail box on a main computer. As soon as the receiver of the message logs on to their system they will be able to access their email and read the message that has been sent.

To reply to an email, the appropriate software will have a button that can be clicked to send a reply. Once this is clicked, all the user has to do is to write their reply; the email address is automatically added.

Anyone who is connected to the Internet has the capability to use email with the following advantages:

* it is faster than ordinary mail and quicker to write

* emails are cheaper than letters and traditional correspondence and the sender does not have to go to a post box

* the message does not have to be printed

* a message can be sent to groups of people at the same time

* email programs have an address book for managing email addresses

* mailing lists enable email users to distribute emails to relevant groups of people

* files, including word processing files, spreadsheets or pictures, can be attached to emails

* it is more environmentally friendly as less paper is used.

CASE STUDY

Broadband

Broadband is a way of accessing the Internet with higher bandwidth allowing transmission and downloading times to be more than 40 times faster than that of a standard telephone line. Broadband can be delivered either over an existing telephone line or using cable and wireless networks.

Broadband has the potential to transform how people and businesses operate. With broadband, users are online all the time, which saves time and does not involve constantly dialing up and logging on. Broadband users have high-speed access to digital information. For businesses this means:

* being able to develop business opportunities electronically over the Internet and the World Wide Web
* developing ecommerce services such as on-line ordering and payment systems
* systems are developed to include all parts of an organisation wherever they are, so that information can be shared

* possibilities to take goods and services on-line to a global marketplace
* creating different ways for people to work, and providing them the opportunity to access information quickly, even from home.

Broadband services can be delivered in different ways – over an ordinary telephone line or private network, via a cable connection or across mobile and wireless networks. BT offers ADSL broadband services over a customer's existing BT telephone line, separating voice and data signals so you can continue to make calls when you are online.

1 **Why might businesses want to have broadband?**
2 **How might broadband create new opportunities for organisations, sometimes irrespective of size?**

There are a number of problems which may occur with email:

* some people do not read their emails frequently enough
* there is always the danger that somebody intercepts and reads somebody else's mail
* there may be bogus messages or viruses attached to emails
* it is important that credit card details or passwords are not written in emails
* sometimes individuals get overwhelmed by the number of emails that they receive and may miss important ones
* some people still do not have email
* junk emails can be a nuisance.

The Internet

The Internet came into being in the last quarter of the twentieth century. It was born in 1969, the year of the Apollo moon landings. For a number of years it was used mainly by computer buffs or 'Netties' who wallowed in their own brand of computer jargon, but today, it has become widely accessible to a broader group of users.

Today, the Internet is providing a magnet for most of the world's major businesses, many of whom have spotted opportunities for advertising and communications to open up a whole new world of ecommerce. Net shopping is becoming increasingly important across a wide range of areas of buying and selling. The World Wide Web (WWW) is just a part of the Internet. It is the part where graphics, sound, video and animation which are known as 'hypertext' are used as well as text. In other words it is the multi-media part of the web. To use the World Wide Web, special software is needed such as Internet Explorer or Netscape.

Most organisations have their own websites. A website allows World Wide Web users to browse in and out of websites, learning about organisations and their objectives and functions as well as their services. Websites are often written in Hypertext Markup Language (HTML) and many include a counter to record how many visitors they have had.

Unless organisations are a large business or have a file server permanently linked to the Internet they usually use the services of an Internet service provider (ISP) who will provide a permanent connection to the Internet. Examples of ISP providers include AOL, BT and CompuServe.

The Internet is also an excellent medium for sources of information. For example:

* **search engines** such as Google can be used to search for a whole variety of topics simply by inserting helpful words or research terms
* there are specialist engines for academics such as Google Scholar that can be used to search for articles related to specialist education-related topics
* organisations can use the Internet to search for information about competitors
* there are many specialist search engines, such as Emerald Fulltext, that provide business journals in fulltext format which saves having to deal with paper copies
* the Internet can be used as a form of market research in itself, so that those browsing a site can be asked to fill in and submit a questionnaire
* newsgroups on the Web are text-based discussion groups for people who have similar interests
* chat rooms allow people to talk to others from around the world without leaving their home. However, there are many dangers associated with chat rooms which have been well publicised
* there are a huge number of services available over the Internet, for example it is possible to

access radio stations as long as a PC is equipped with a sound card and speakers

❋ downloading where legally undertaken has become a popular activity for many computer users, who can access music, pay for it and transfer it to a number of media such as an MP3 player.

❋ buying and selling on the Internet has become increasingly popular with many people doing their shopping on the Internet, such as purchasing books or food

❋ huge amounts of information such as encyclopaedias, dictionaries, newspapers, magazines, and so on, can be accessed

❋ it is even possible to use the BT website to search for telephone numbers.

Electronic Data Interchange (EDI)

Many organisations today use a system called electronic data interchange (EDI). This links the activities of organisations to their banks, allowing them to pay payments to their suppliers electronically. In the past, all transactions were conducted on paper, which involved invoices, advice notes and statements as well as cheques. EDI cuts down on paperwork. With EDI, organisations receive electronic invoices from their suppliers requesting payment. These are checked against a purchase ledger and then the computer sends the details to the bank's computer so that an electronic payment can be made.

Ecommerce

Whereas ebusiness refers to how organisations use information and communications technology (ICT) within their businesses to improve their operations, ecommerce refers more to how organisations use ICT for trading purposes.

According to many surveys, and despite what is happening to many economies around the world, the statistics tend to show that ecommerce is booming.

You only have to look at a range of websites to see how organisations trade. There are now electronic banking facilities, and a whole range of products and services can be purchased over the

Web from a variety of different types of businesses, both large and small. eBay has been successful in allowing individuals to trade their own products, and one of the most popular ways of buying books today is from Amazon.

Although we hear of dot-com millionaires and of some fairly dramatic success stories associated with ecommerce, there are a whole range of issues associated with ecommerce with many different ramifications which are only now being fully considered. It is argued that ecommerce is gradually changing the way in which we shop and this may mean the demise of many more traditional retailers. Shopping as a family, and physically leaving the home to do so, may be a thing of the past in a few years and could lead to city centres becoming deserted. Dealing with machines rather than people also reduces the chances for interaction. In the same way that the television as a new form of technology changed the way the family interacted when it was introduced in the 1950s, today many people use their computers in the evenings for socialising, interaction with others via MSN Internet Services and for shopping.

On the other hand, if ecommerce is successful it will employ many people within the distribution system serving the requirements of customers. Programmers and those who can set up websites will be in huge demand and those with mobility problems will be able to shop more successfully from their homes. The net result should be greater choice and a much more varied and distinct market-place, with buyers able to buy from organisations across the globe.

FIGURE 5.14 *Amazon website page*

Theory into practice

Working in groups, discuss the barriers that a distinctive organisation local to you might face if it wanted to undertake some form of ecommerce activity. Make a list of the barriers and identify both the benefits of such a move as well as the costs. Finally, decide upon whether you would recommend that this business undertake ecommerce activities.

5.2.3 Benefits / drawbacks of introducing ICT provision

Benefits

There are many reasons why businesses might look to introduce ICT proposals into daily working practices. These include:

* increased productivity

* reduced waste

* improved speed and quality of communications

* improved decision making

* potential for working from home.

Increased productivity

Productivity measures the quantity of outputs that can be produced from a given quantity of inputs:

$$\text{Productivity} = \frac{\text{Outputs}}{\text{Inputs}}$$

You can see from the formula how the effective use of ICT in a business can increase productivity. For example, it can increase:

* *Labour productivity* – The quantity of outputs that can be produced from a given quantity of

labour. This is because by working with computers humans become far more efficient. For example, by using computers, this book was written and edited much more quickly than it would have been in the past. The same file can be edited several times until the final copy is in a form ready for printing. At the printing stage, computers can be used to manage the production machinery to control the mixing of the inks and to make sure that there are no errors in printing the final copies and binding the books.

The productivity of capital – Modern computer-based technology is far more efficient than in the past. You will have probably seen adverts on television showing modern car plants in action where many of the production processes are carried out by factory robots which are controlled by computers.

The main advantages of computers that make them efficient are:

They are extremely fast – For example, computers used to make weather forecasts can make over a million calculations a second. Computers can be used for international dealings, for instance by stockbrokers and international banks where large amounts of data need to be processed very quickly. Modern banking operations provide us with a fast and accurate service using computers. For example, during banking hours hundreds of thousands of customers are using bank services every hour, requiring changes to be made in bank records.

They are very accurate – Computers only do what they have been programmed to do, so providing the programming is accurate then the computer will do what is expected of it. For example, computers which monitor the weight and quantity of ingredients going into products can make sure with almost 100% accuracy that the weight and quantity is of the required standard.

Computers can work for 24/7 – Computers work every second of the day, for seven days a week. They don't need to have rest phases so they are able to increase the productivity of business and manufacturing operations to close to 100% capacity.

Computers can store large quantities of information in a small space – Computers are able to increase efficiency by condensing lots and lots of information into a very small storage space. Imagine if all the records of businesses had to be kept in paper form. There simply would not be enough storage space and the information would be very difficult to retrieve. Computers are able to find information through a very quick search, as witnessed for example by the development of Internet search engines.

Online efficiency benefits

Having a website enables businesses to become far more efficient and thus improve productivity. An online presence can be seen as a highly efficient tool that can be used in a variety of ways to make businesses work better, as shown in Figure 5.15.

One of the main benefits of an online presence to an organisation is the way in which it enables online order tracking. As a consumer you may be aware of how this process works. For example, you may have ordered a book from an online bookstore and it is due to be delivered. Each day you can check online where your order has got to, and when it is expected to arrive. Many parcel delivery services offer the same service.

From the business point of view there are many benefits in the integration of supply chains. The supply chain includes all the steps involved in bringing goods to the final consumer.

Having enough stock (or inventory) of a product to satisfy customer demand, while not holding too much stock that is sitting idle and getting old, is the goal of every business. To optimise the inventory levels in the total supply chain, trading partners need to work together to fully understand the volume and type of inventory held along the chain and future demand, to make sure that production takes place at the right time and is available when required by the consumer.

Modern electronic data interchange systems enable companies at all stages in a supply chain to

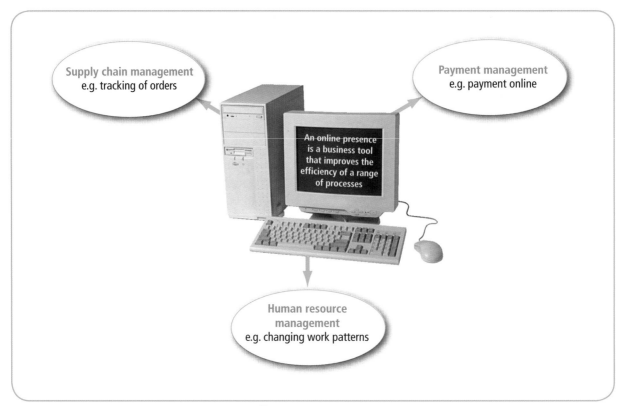

FIGURE 5.15 *An online presence improves efficiency in a business*

view the same information. The overall effect of EDI is a reduction in costs in a range of industries.

Online payment systems often mean that businesses which trade electronically are able to receive payments more quickly and more securely, with a reduction in bad debts (non-payment) because customers are expected to pay immediately by credit card or other means of electronic payment.

Online transaction processing involves settling payments as they occur. When you buy goods in your local supermarket and pay with a debit or credit card, the supermarket contacts the bank electronically for instant payment for the goods. This instant payment increases the supermarket's efficiency by providing a ready cash flow.

By trading online many businesses are free to change location to a low-cost area. For example, you wouldn't expect to find an Amazon book store in a high-street location.

Ebusiness has also made it possible for businesses to reorganise their human resources. For example:

* IT specialists, such as systems designers, systems developers and information systems managers have been given far more importance in organisations

* home working has become increasingly common for those people who work primarily with computers and the telephone and who do not need to be located in expensive high-street offices

* in many workplaces the layout and structure of the workplace is built around a computer network (for example in banks and insurance companies)

* people in workplaces are far more reliant on computers to manage and support their work online

* increasingly work involving ebusiness activity is being out-sourced by companies to places where labour costs are cheapest. In 2003, 2004 and 2005 we have seen many of the UK banks and even BT outsource call-centre work to India.

Search engine efficiency benefits

Search engines illustrate the power of ICT in increasing the productivity of business. A search engine gives you access to instant business information, such as the state of the economy, about what rivals are doing, about prices in different **market**-places, about exchange rates, what is happening on the stock exchange and thousands of other bits of information. If this information is used well it can help a business to drive down its costs.

The main players in the market are regularly increasing search technology to improve the services that they offer to users. So far Google has been able to dominate. Google's major innovation was in searching out web pages according to their popularity and inter-relationship, not just according to key words. The results are therefore more likely to be what the customer needs. Today we have a new (yet already established) word in the English language: 'googling'. To 'google' means to search for information on the Internet using a search engine.

Reduced waste

The use of ICT enables modern businesses to cut out a range of wastes including:

* *Time* – ICT applications enable time to be saved on a range of operations, including:
    * accessing records from a database
    * making calculations using a spreadsheet
    * making important calls using mobile phones

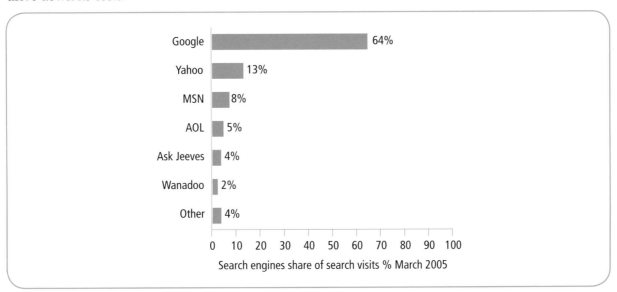

FIGURE 5.16 *Search engine share of visits*

- creating presentations using software such as Microsoft PowerPoint.

- *Cost* – ICT systems are able to drastically reduce business costs, for example by networking company information systems to avoid wasteful duplication. ICT control systems are used in controlling production systems to cut waste to a minimum.

- *Effort* – By simplifying work operations it is possible to cut out a lot of effort. For example, an email can be copied to thousands of work colleagues.

- *Energy* – ICT can be used to cut down on a lot of environmental costs such as energy consumption. Individual computers are very economical in their use of energy and can be used to minimise energy consumption, for example by controlling heating and lighting systems in a business.

Improved speed and quality of communications

The speed and quality of communications of computer use in modern businesses is an important aspect. For example, this chapter can be saved in a computer file and then emailed to the publisher. The publisher can then email it to an editor who will copy edit the manuscript. Once this is complete the copy is then sent to a designer who will build in the pictures and diagrams using a desktop publishing package. The final copy can then be sent electronically to the printer who will use the files to enter the completed manuscript into the printing process. This takes months off traditional printing processes enabling the reader to enjoy relevant and up-to-date information.

It is not only the speed but also the quality of communications that can be improved, for example:

- word processing packages enable the accurate creation of documents such as letters and emails

- video conferencing enables face-to-face conferences between distant locations

- *Wi-Fi* mobile and Internet connections enable links between individuals allowing them to

Video conferencing cuts down on travel expenses

check and verify information, take orders and clarify issues

- order tracking systems, for example related to B2C websites enable customers to communicate with suppliers to find out how their orders are progressing.

Improved decision making

The use of ICT enables business people to make 'better decisions' because:

- they have access to more timely, more accurate and more detailed information

- they have access to decision-making tools which are available using ICT packages. For example, Microsoft Project provides a range of useful features that enable decision-making tools such as Gantt charts (see page 267) to be produced.

Decision makers are able to pool and analyse a range of relevant information that is accessed through appropriate research techniques.

Potential for working from home

Businesses are able to cut costs by enabling their employees to work from home for some or all of the week. There are many jobs where work can be done as easily from home as from a centralised workplace. Home workers can be linked into a company's Intranet system where they can access all the resources they require such as shared databases. Home working can lead to much higher levels of motivation among staff who are freed from the hassle of wasting time commuting to work and who are able to combine work with family commitments and an enhanced lifestyle.

Many home workers will need to spend part of the week at Head Office, but these times can be reduced to the essential meetings and other activities where they need to be physically in the same location as their team. Essential ingredients of home working are:

* fast access to the Internet (e.g. broadband services)
* sophisticated mobile phones
* fax machines
* other facilities depending on the nature of the business, for example, digital cameras for design work.

Drawbacks

Introducing ICT can, however, bring with it a number of drawbacks. These drawbacks include:

* high cost of introduction
* loss of efficiency during the introduction phase
* alienation of staff who are 'computer phobic'
* hardware and software upgrading costs
* staff training expenses.

High cost of introduction

Introducing a new ICT system can be a very expensive business. Firstly, an organisation has to invest in the hardware and software. The hardware and software needs to be appropriate to the scale of the business and needs to be up-to-date. In the modern world of ICT, new computers become out-of-date almost as soon as they have been developed. Most firms today will depreciate their computers over a very short period of time (two to three years). When investing in hardware and software it is essential to make sure that all of the components are compatible.

A business also has to invest in systems. Usually a business will first employ a *systems analyst*. Businesses and service organisations need effective systems matched to their needs – as their

needs change so their information systems must change too. Working in close co-operation with the client, a systems analyst examines existing information systems, confirms their suitability, recommends changes or may produce a specification for a new system. A systems analyst defines the problem, works out a solution, costs it and produces outline designs for the new system for others to build.

The specification will then be passed on to a *systems designer* who designs the system, including hardware and software.

Loss of efficiency during the introduction phase

One of the problems of introducing a new ICT system is that it may go through a number of teething problems in the early days leading to

> **Think it over...**
>
> In 2004, Sainsbury's introduced a very expensive new distribution system using ICT, for example for ordering new stock. However, in the early days there were a number of serious problems with the system, leading to empty spaces on a number of shelves in the supermarkets and to a loss of profit of millions of pounds. These problems have now been ironed out as users have become more familiar with the hardware and software.

problems for an organisation. It is therefore important for organisations to have a very efficient information systems manager. Information systems managers work in every size of organisation in every industry and service sector, usually with a staff of technicians, programmers and database administrators reporting to them. They install computer systems, ensure that back up systems operate effectively, maintain the hardware and software, and provide the IT technology systems of an organisation. This is a very important role because systems managers are responsible for the day-to-day running and efficiency of the system. They therefore have to have a clear plan well in advance of the introductory phase.

Alienation of staff who are 'computer phobic'

Today, most people have some familiarity with computers. However, there are still some older employees who have a phobia about computers. One of the reasons for this is that in the early days of ICT development, computers were a lot more complex to use and far more prone to error than today – leading to an ongoing 'block' about computers in a number of people.

When introducing new ICT systems it is important to be aware that some people continue to be worried about the development of new ICT based systems so sensitive training and ongoing development of computer and other skills is required.

Hardware and software upgrading costs

When developing new ICT systems it is necessary to build in plans to upgrade hardware and software in line with ongoing developments. Software upgrades can be developed in-house or bought as off-the-shelf software applications. Hardware upgrades may be required if the input and output devices are inadequate to support new software.

Staff training expenses

Staff training in ICT is an important cost that a business has to incur in order to fully gain all of the benefits of modern ICT to an organisation. It is important to keep records of the training that staff members have had in relation to the requirements of their job. Training should be designed to plug the gap between existing ICT skills and ICT skills required to do jobs well.

5.2.4 Contingency planning

Introducing new computer systems is not easy as every organisation has their own way of working and a variety of requirements that meet their needs, all of which requires considerable research and planning. In addition, before attempting to introduce a system to an organisation it is essential for some form of contingency planning to take place. This provides support in case the system does not work, and enables the business of the organisation to take place as usual despite its IT problems.

The case studies on page 245 illustrate that when proposals are made about the developments of ICT systems, there also needs to be a contingency plan. In other words, if the system when it is introduced does not work properly or meet the expectations originally developed for it, there needs to be some way of working that ensures that the replacement technology does not either harm or interfere with the running of the business organisation. At the same time, those who are proposing to introduce the new technology must make sure that employees within the organisation are ready for all the changes that are about to happen and that adequate training processes are in place as well as staff development activities.

So, with the high risk of failure or the likelihood of many teething troubles, why do organisations introduce new technologies? Change may occur because:

* the world of technology may have changed since the old system was introduced which makes the old system outdated

Computer investment disasters

The history of introducing computer systems is littered with disasters. For example:

* The Swanwick traffic air-traffic control centre cost £623m and was designed to replace a centre in West Drayton, near Heathrow. Almost a year after opening in 2002 it was still suffering problems including radio communications cutting out between the centre and aircraft, unclear computer screens and health and safety issues related to the computer system.

* The London Ambulance Service covers an area of just over 600 square miles and is the largest ambulance service in the world with a residential population of 6.8 million although it deals with a larger daytime population. The service has 2,700 staff and 750 ambulances. When its new computer system was introduced in 1992, the system failed, and ambulances did not turn up where they were needed. An inquiry found that the service was not ready for the implementation of the system. The software was not complete and had not been fully tested. The hardware had also not been tested under operational conditions and there were many problems with the transmission of data. Additionally, when the system was introduced there was no paper back-up.

1 Why were the systems above introduced?
2 What were the problems?
3 How might they have been avoided?

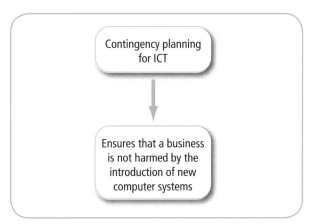

FIGURE 5.17 *The importance of contingency planning*

* the current system may simply be too expensive to maintain

* the old system may not respond as well to customer needs as the new system

* the current system may simply not be suitable for the purposes and activities to which it has been subjected. Changes in the workplace and the ways in which decisions are made and customer needs are met may dictate that the organisation needs to update the systems it uses.

Before a new system is introduced it is important to undertake some form of feasibility study. The purpose of this study is to identify any problems that the organisation might face; analyse whether it is worth proceeding with the new proposed technology and identify any problems that might arise if the new system is implemented.

The following areas of feasibility must be looked at:

* *Technical feasibility* involves investigating to see whether the technology exists to introduce the new system.

* *Economic feasibility* involves analysing the cost-effectiveness of the new system.

* *Legal feasibility* involves identifying if there are any conflicts between the proposed new system and legal requirements such as the Data Protection Act.

* *Operational feasibility* is concerned with whether the current procedures and way in which the organisation works would support the new technology.

* *Schedule feasibility* looks at how long the system will take to develop and work out a plan for the introduction.

Direct implementation

Making a decision about how to introduce a new system requires some thought. If the system is small or involves just a local network, some of the decisions might not be so critical.

The users may simply go for a direct implementation of the new technology on a particular date. So, one day the old system is running and then the next day the new system starts. Although this may be suitable for a small organisation, there are many risks associated with such a strategy for a large organisation. The issue is that the problems associated with the introduction of a new computer system usually occur shortly after the system is up and running. If too much reliance is put upon the new system the net result could be chaos!

Parallel systems

A more sensible alternative than direct implementation for introducing new technology is to have a period when parallel systems are used. This involves running the new system alongside the existing system. If the new system for one reason or another fails or does not meet up to expectations, the old system is still there to sort all of the problems out. Parallel running also provides a good opportunity to compare the operation of the new system against the running of the old system to see if the new system is better at meeting customer and operational needs and requirements. The real disadvantage with this,

however, is the duplication of effort required to manage two systems at once. The duplication of effort can put a huge strain upon personnel.

Staggered introduction

Another way of introducing new technology is to opt for some form of phased implementation, where a number of jobs or aspects of the technology are introduced separately. For example, one particular type of job or operation might be introduced first and then evaluated before introducing the next operation. Staggered introduction enables a system to break down tasks into smaller activities that can be implemented separately. For example, a few customers' accounts could be processed using the new system while the rest remain on the old system.

Pilot conversion

Another form of phased implementation is that of pilot conversion. With this system, the new technology is used within one part of the organisation first, such as a particular factory, branch or office so that the effects of the new technology can be properly evaluated.

Training and support systems in crossover period

Training staff in new technologies is critical for the success of any information and communications system, particularly where changes are being made to the system so that staff can overcome any problems and issues associated with the crossover period between the older technologies and the new technologies.

The introduction of new technology is likely to require the updating of skills. An initial training course might be provided for staff so that they can understand the way in which the new software and hardware works. There may be an opportunity for staff to use the new software and hardware so that they can accustom themselves to the way in which each operates. As the training evolves, staff should be able to understand some of the issues that might arise when the new technology finally goes live and the training should help them to deal with some of the day-to-day issues and problems that arise.

An important part of the implementation of any system is to evaluate and review how the new system is performing. Minor errors or technical details may need to be dealt with. Clerical procedures might need to be amended. It is usually only when a new system is running that those working on the system are able to identify all of the faults, problems and issues that arise.

5.2.5 Research

As we have seen earlier in this text, research is important as it provides you with information and feedback that you can use to construct your own recommendations for change. For this unit you are required to construct an ICT proposal showing how you would either introduce ICT provision to a start-up business or update ICT provision in a business that is looking to update its ICT provision. You need to consider the benefits that ICT provision could bring to your chosen business when producing your ICT proposal. In your research for this task you will need to gather information on the needs of the business, the needs of individual functional areas and the needs of individual employees for your proposal. Gathering research information about your selected business may not be easy, and you may need to discuss your ideas and thoughts with friends or family before you decide whether to choose a business that is starting up or one that is updating its provision of ICT facilities. Remember that selecting the right business is important in providing you with appropriate data.

You need to carry out both:

* secondary research, and
* primary research.

Secondary research

The starting point of your research should be to undertake some reading. This is known as secondary research. This research will help you to find out about the sort of ICT provision that companies use in order to become and remain

competitive. With ICT provision, it is important to remain up to date about all of the changes in the area as the range of software and hardware is constantly refined and updated. You may want to have a look at some of the ICT magazines in the library of your school or college or use the Internet to find out what organisations say about their ICT provision.

Primary research

Your primary research should focus on your selected business.

Having conducted secondary research, the next step may be to find somebody that is an expert in the area of ICT – this is known as primary research. Primary research will include speaking to someone who has responsibility for ICT provision in your organisation or one similar to the one you are studying. Using some form of semi-structured interview, where you have a range of questions and some space for answers, find out more about how information and communications technologies are used in the workplace. What changes does the person you are interviewing expect to take place in the future? You may also want to find out about how changes in ICT impact upon people in the workplace and might even prepare a questionnaire so you can find out about their opinions and attitudes.

5.2.6 Presentational skills

ICT enables us to present and communicate ideas in much more interesting and effective ways than in the past. For example:

* we can produce attractive PowerPoint presentations with graphics, charts, pictures and text
* we can produce posters and displays to communicate our findings
* we can produce attractive handouts using a desk top publishing package to support our presentations
* we can even access the Internet to draw attention to a website as part of a presentation. For example, in developing an ICT proposal

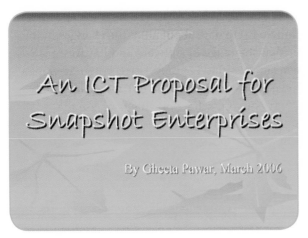

FIGURE 5.18 *An example of a PowerPoint slide*

we could examine an existing website or web page to draw attention to ways in which the business we are studying could improve its web presence.

As this unit is concerned with information and communications technology in business, an important aspect of your learning is that you should use ICT to process information that you collect from your research activities and store this information using ICT in a form which helps you to analyse the information in appropriate ways. You should then use ICT to enhance the display and communication of your final presentation. By using these skills you are employing important modern business processes.

For the assignment for this unit you need to present your ICT proposal to your teacher and your peers. Therefore, it is important that you understand how to deliver an effective presentation which will include considerations of:

* the use of appropriate business terms e.g. database, spreadsheet, internal and external customers, markets etc.

* the application of knowledge and understanding to the chosen ICT proposal

* the use of visual aids, and other techniques, to engage the audience

* the structuring of the material so that the presentation may be followed easily

* clarity of expression and confidence with the stimulus material that is being used.

Appropriate business terminology

As your presentation is about how a particular business can introduce ICT or improve its existing ICT you need to relate the ICT to particular aspects of the business. For example, most businesses will use ICT for their marketing activities by keeping databases of customer records, purchases made by particular customers, etc. Keeping such a database helps the business to focus better on meeting customer needs. Similarly you can show how businesses can use ICT for creating budgets, producing accounts, processing orders, keeping records of stocks etc.

Knowledge and understanding

When you prepare your ICT proposal you need to apply it to the business you have chosen rather than just talking generally about the benefits of ICT for business. For example, if you are studying a specific stationery business you can show how it uses a stock control system to make sure that it has enough (but not too many) of the items that customers require in stock.

Visual aids

In your ICT proposal, you need to use a variety of appropriate visual aids, such as posters, PowerPoint presentations, handouts, company logos, actual examples of company products etc.

Clear structure

Ensure that you have a clear structure to your presentation. You should start with a short and clear introduction setting out the nature of the business and the ICT challenge for the business. The middle section should outline the nature of the proposal in discrete sections. For example, you may want to look at ICT applications in each of the key functional areas or you may want to create a structure by type of application (hardware/ software, different types of applications etc). You will also need a section for recommendations for improvements. Finally you need to sum up the key aspects of the proposal.

Clarity of expression

You need to express your ideas in a clear way that captures the attention of your audience. You also need to speak with confidence and enthusiasm. You will be able to do so if you know your material thoroughly. The following notes should help you to make an effective presentation.

How to make an effective presentation

Everybody is nervous when they give a presentation and it is often because they are worried about whether they are able to give a good presentation. The rules of making a good presentation are very simple:

* prepare well
* don't use too many visual illustrations
* don't speak too quickly
* face your audience, look them in the eye
* smile and look relaxed
* imagine that you are in the audience – what would you like to hear?

You may feel embarrassed about giving a presentation, but if you take your time and present your findings in an interesting way, then people will enjoy your presentation.

Preparation is the key. You need to know in what order you are going to put over your points, and what messages you are going to put across.

In a 15-minute presentation don't use more than eight slides. If you have too many you will rush through your material and it won't make sense. Having just a few helps you to talk things through in a clear and simple way.

If you speak too quickly your audience will switch off within two or three minutes; they will start looking bored, and you will find it very difficult to give an interesting presentation. If you find yourself talking too fast, slow down and you will quickly find that your audience switches on again.

People are interested in presenters who look them in the eye. They are not interested in speakers who avoid eye contact. Try to engage as many people in the audience as possible with your eyes. Give them a little smile and they will usually smile back: often they will nod to show that they are interested in what you are saying.

Perhaps the most valuable suggestion is that you should imagine that you are sitting in your own audience. What would you like to hear? What would make you sit up and listen? Try not to talk like a textbook; talk as if you were giving some important information to your friends that you want them to understand.

People tend to think that if they give a PowerPoint presentation using a computer, they are automatically giving a brilliant presentation. Of course, PowerPoint is fantastic in the right hands, but remember that the centre of the presentation should always be the presenter and the way that she or he links together the talk, illustration, use of video, visuals and so on.

Presentation skills checklist

The following checklist will help you prepare and give your presentation:

Plan and organise the presentation
Set out your objectives (e.g. to explain an ICT proposal for a given organisation)
Use appropriate terminology
Set out the main idea and a clear conclusion
Set out your introduction clearly
Think about your audience, their interests and their level of knowledge
Brainstorm some main ideas
Plan handouts, visuals and use of PowerPoint
Keep a clear thread linking main points

Prepare for the presentation
Practise
Check the equipment
Set out your notes and handouts in a clear order

Develop the visual aids
Make them clear and easy to look at
Choose appropriate types of charts (e.g. bar chart, line graph etc)
Have clear titles
Talk to your audience, not to the visual (don't turn your back)

Avoid being nervous
Take deep breaths
Move during your presentation
Smile
Maintain eye contact

Deliver your presentation
Be aware of what you say and how you say it
Speak with a strong clear voice, and don't speak too quickly
Be animated, clear and enthusiastic
Use eye contact to make the presentation conversational and personal
Place yourself at the centre of the stage
Use a pointer, but not too often. Often a modern projector will have a laser pointer for use with PowerPoint

Questions and answers
Prepare for questions and practise the answers
Ask for questions by stepping forward with hand raised
Watch the questioner and listen carefully
Repeat the question to make sure everyone has heard it
Keep the same bearing as in your presentation
Use eye contact and scan the whole audience

5.2.7 How to judge viability

A viable proposal is one that will work in practice. To be viable the proposal needs to be:

* relatively easy to put into practice. It should be technically feasible and not too complicated.

* suitable for the resource base of the organisation. For example, there would be little point in suggesting systems that are too costly for a small organisation, or one that will perform a lot of functions that are not required (wasting resources).

* one that people in the organisation can be trained to use. There would be little point in developing a proposal that people couldn't work with because they lack the skills (and couldn't be trained to develop these skills).

* implemented within a given time period. There would be little point in installing new systems that became out of date before they were fully operational.

* relatively simple, well organised and easy to explain.

* one that clearly improves performance.

Having developed a proposal it is important to audit it and this means that you must try to assess how or whether the ICT proposal would work and what might influence how it would operate. It is essential to evaluate the relative strengths of the proposal you have developed and then try to think or appraise what would be necessary to fine tune or further develop it. For example:

* will the negative impact of introducing the ICT provision be outweighed by the positive gains for the business?

* what are the implications for employees working in the business and how will they respond to the changes?

* will the proposal improve communication between different departments of the business or slow things down, particularly when your proposals are first introduced?

* is your proposal financially and operationally sound?

To evaluate your ICT proposal, you may want to:

1 Find out the reactions of employees to key areas of the proposal. This could mean making a short presentation to selected employees or presenting a report and asking for feedback.

2 Find out whether the proposal is sustainable. Do you know somebody who is an expert in ICT who may be able to provide you with feedback?

3 Find out how the proposal might impact upon the different departments and functional areas of the business.

4 You may want to use a series of different media to show how your proposal might work.

5 It may be possible to set a series of objectives for your proposal and to show how well your proposal has met each of these objectives.

6 By looking at ICT literature it may be possible to find out more about some of the difficulties and issues associated with introducing new systems. As part of assessing the viability you might want to comment upon how well the systems you suggest could overcome such problems.

KNOWLEDGE CHECK

1 Give a brief definition of the term 'Information and Communications Technology'.

2 What is the difference between B2B and B2C links? Give an example to illustrate each of these.

3 How might a database help an online book seller? Give three main ways.

4 How might the finance department of a large retailing organisation benefit from ICT?

5 What is 'hardware'? What is the central processing unit of a computer?

6 Describe two input devices that are commonly used in ICT. In each case explain how they operate.

7 Describe two common forms of data capture. Explain how they might be used in a bank for customer service purposes.

8 What qualities should a business look for in selecting a printer for communicating by sending letters to customers?

9 What is a personal digital assistant? How might it be useful for a salesperson?

10 Explain the difference between applications software and general purpose software.

11 Describe three types of calculations that an accounts department might make using a spreadsheet.

12 How might a computer application be helpful in planning a building project?

13 What is meant by networking? How does this help members of a team to work together more effectively?

14 What is the difference between a LAN and a WAN? Explain how a WAN might be useful for a large company.

15 Why has email become so important in business? List six key benefits.

16 What is an Internet search engine? Describe one search engine that you think is particularly effective and state how it is useful to business.

17 What is EDI? How can it be used for making payments?

18 How can ICT increase the productivity of a business?

19 Explain four types of waste that ICT can help to reduce.

20 What is a parallel system? How might it be used for contingency planning?

Resources

There is a wide range of textbooks aimed at Advanced Level Business candidates. The list below is not intended to be exhaustive nor does inclusion on the list constitute a recommendation of the suitability of the resource for the specification.

Awad, E., *Electronic Commerce from Vision to Fulfilment*, Pearson, London, 2001

Buckley, P. and Clark, D., *The Rough Guide to the Internet*, Rough Guides, London, 2004

Cawson, A, *The Top 200 Websites on Ecommerce*, Kogan Page, London, 2003

Lawson, J. et al, *BTEC National: IT Practitioners*, Heinemann, Oxford, 2003

Matthewson, J., *E-Business – A Jargon Free Practical Guide*, Butterworth Heinemann, Oxford, 2002

Penrose, B. and Pollard B., *Complete A–Z, ICT and Computing*, Hodder & Stoughton, London, 2003

Websites

Some useful websites are listed below. These addresses are current at the time of writing. However, it needs to be recognised that new sites are being launched on the Internet on a regular basis and that older sites may change or disappear.

www.tt100.biz (The Times 100 – business case studies)

www.dti.gov.uk/bestpractice (Government advice on achieving best business practice)

www.marketing-online.co.uk (Resource for marketing professionals and students)

www.yahoo.com (Yahoo search engine)

www.google.co.uk (Google search engine)

www.freeserve.com (Freeserve search engine and news and information service)

www.btopenworld.com (BT's mass market Internet division)

www.webtrends.com (Web analysis)

www.kelkoo.com (Shopping information)

www.manutd.com (Manchester United site)

www.lastminute.com (Last-minute travel and entertainment)

www.amazon.com (Amazon main site)

Magazines

E-Business Review
Net Profit
Computer Weekly

UNIT 6
Running an enterprise activity

This unit contains eight elements:

6.2.1 Setting aims and objectives

6.2.2 Building and developing an effective team

6.2.3 Time management

6.2.4 Required resources

6.2.5 Need for regular meetings

6.2.6 Possible constraints

6.2.7 Research and analysis

6.2.8 Potential future changes to the enterprise activity

Introduction

Have you ever wondered what it would be like to run your own profit-making enterprise activity and what skills that you would need to do so?

As you study this unit, you will help to organise and run, as part of a team, an enterprise activity of your choice. You will produce a report on your chosen activity.

Your report will show that you understand the considerations that need to be taken into account when planning any kind of enterprise activity. You will then show how you and your team dealt with these considerations when planning and running your own enterprise activity.

Your report also needs to contain evidence of your research and analysis, as you investigate the success of your activity from a number of viewpoints, including:

- stakeholder views (stakeholders are individuals and groups who have an interest in decisions made by the business e.g. shareholders and customers)
- how the team interacted as a whole
- your own individual contribution.

Finally, you will need to show evidence of making reasoned judgements as you discuss changes that you would make to your enterprise activity to improve the performance of your group, and your own contribution, should the enterprise activity be run a second time.

There are a number of activities throughout this unit to reinforce your learning.

6.2.1 Setting aims and objectives

If you think of the meaning of the word 'enterprise' or 'individual initiative' it is usually interpreted as a small business, either a 'service' or 'creative' business. Big companies, particularly those engaged in manufacturing, are just 'there' – no one quite knows how. The fact is that with very few exceptions, every big company began as a small company, often with one enterprising individual at its head.

Small may be beautiful, but in business the great thing about being small is that one day you may become big. For example, you will all be familiar with the Glastonbury Festival which takes place in the summer each year. This started out as quite a small pop festival taking place in a farmer's field. Today, the farmer has a highly sophisticated business operation selling tickets (which are instantly snapped up) at very high prices. The event has to be highly organised to meet tough health and safety requirements, to keep top artists happy and to make sure that people who live around the festival site are kept happy.

CASE STUDY

The following examples are well-known large companies which began with one individual.

William Lever started work in the family shop when he was sixteen, and then decided that he could make soap as well as anyone else. The result of his enterprise is Unilever, now one of the world's largest companies making soap powders like Persil and Ariel and well-known ice creams such as Magnum.

Shell (the oil and gas company) began because Marcus Samuel over 150 years ago thought he could sell oriental shells to local people in the East End of London. When Marcus passed on his business to his sons they continued to trade with overseas countries and branched out into transporting illuminating oil to the Far East. The business flourished, and in 1897 the Shell Transport and Trading Company was formed.

Anita Roddick set up The Body Shop from a small industrial unit in Littlehampton because she was not happy with the way that the big cosmetics companies were charging such high prices for cosmetics and their attitudes to beauty and the environment.

Find out how another famous company, such as lastminute.com was set up, and what its aims and objectives were.

The Body Shop started out on a very small scale from the idea of Anita Roddick

The Glastonbury Festival

This unit enables you to set up a small enterprise, but your enterprise ideas may enable you to develop the skills to set up your own successful enterprise, either large or small. One day you may be able to organise events like the Glastonbury festival. If you do so you will undoubtedly have to work in a team. This unit involves working in a team and analysing your own strengths and weaknesses as a team worker as well as the ingredients of successful teamwork.

All businesses start from an original idea. Many new business ideas have 'come out of the blue' to inventive people. Examples of this are the Sony Walkman and the Dyson Dual Cyclone vacuum cleaner.

When Bob Geldof first organised the Live Aid concert, he was moved to do so by the plight of starving children in Ethiopia which he had seen on television. He organised one of the best remembered concerts of all time that was transmitted to millions of people across the globe. From this start he has gone on to organise a number of important fundraising events, each of which has been better managed and organised than the previous one. His concern for humanity led him to develop a range of enterprise skills.

Other enterprising ideas have resulted from careful work over a period of time. Examples are the development of the ballpoint pen, the photocopier and the dishwasher, as well as the work of charities such as OXFAM whose 'enterprising product' is to provide famine aid and disaster relief wherever it is required.

Theory into practice

Establishing a good idea for a business should be one of the first steps that you take in setting up and running an enterprise activity. There are many ways of coming up with a bright idea. Some of these are listed in the table below:

Ways of coming up with a bright idea	Your ideas (working with a small group of students). Perhaps one (or more) of these ideas can provide the basis for an enterprise activity.
Spotting a **gap in the market**	
Improving on an existing good or service	
Listening to people and finding out what they want or need	
Using a special skill or talent that you have	
Developing a hobby	
Combining two or more existing products or services	
Setting out to solve a particular problem	
Developing an idea that lends itself to ecommerce, such as selling via a website	
Organising an event	

Study the table and then working with two or three other students see if you can identify and develop ideas that could be made into a thriving business.

CASE STUDY
Anything Left-Handed

Anything Left-Handed is the name of a small but high profile shop in Soho (London). It deals in a range of items including left-handed golf clubs, left-handed carrot peelers, left-handed tools and equipment and many other items. Talk to a left-handed friend and you will quickly get an idea of which items of everyday use they have problems with. Anything Left-Handed trades in three main ways:

* by selling to customers who visit the shop
* by mail order
* through its website www.anythingleft-handed.co.uk.

The business was set up by a husband and wife partnership, Lauren and Keith Milsom, who are both left-handed.

The business currently has a turnover of £400,000 and employs four staff. Key issues for the business at present are on devising ways to encourage more customers to use the website and to make purchases once they have accessed the website.

FIGURE 6.1 *A web page taken from the website of Anything Left-Handed*

1 Do you think that Anything Left-Handed is a good idea for a new business?
2 How does the website open up new opportunities for the business?
3 Can you identify an enterprising idea which involves something novel like selling products for left-handed people?

Aims

You need to understand that any enterprise activity which is hoping to be a profit-making success needs to have, at its core, a primary *aim*. An aim is the end purpose that the business is trying to achieve. Examples of aims include:

* to make a profit
* to be the market leader (to make more sales than rival businesses)
* to break even over a period of time
* to create an enjoyable activity or event.

Organisations will write down their aims and seek to communicate these aims both within the organisation and to external groups such as lenders.

Mission / vision and values statements

Often the aim of the organisation is supported by a **mission**, vision and/or **values statement**. The mission and vision are quite similar.

The mission sets out the *purpose* of the organisation, for example a leading supermarket chain may set out its mission in a statement such as 'We will deliver the best value for money to our customers by finding out what they want and delivering it to them in the ways that best meet their needs.'

The mission of the organiser of a pop concert may be 'to provide a fun occasion that can be enjoyed by music fans and where entertainment is provided in a safe and happy environment'.

A **vision statement** is more future oriented and sets out what the organisation is seeking to achieve, for example a food manufacturer and distributor might have a vision that 'We will become the World's Number 1 Food Company.'

The vision and values of Manchester United

Manchester United organises different types of events

Manchester United provides a good example of an organisation that runs events. Each week when it has a home game at Old Trafford, business managers and administrators at the club have to organise the allocation of tickets, liaise with safety stewards, organise the cleaning up around the ground after the event etc.

Manchester United is not only concerned with organising football events. In the summer, the stadium will also be rented out for pop concerts and other events. The way that the club organises these events is determined by its vision and values.

Manchester United states that:

'Our values underpin our vision to be the best football club in the world both on and off the pitch. We aim to achieve this through our corporate values, which are:

United… with our fans in our commitment and passion for the club.

Non-discriminatory… in making Manchester United accessible to all, irrespective of age, race, gender, creed or physical ability.

Innovative… in our ambition to be "first to the ball" at all times.

Team orientated… in our desire to work together with the same dedication displayed in every game by our first team squad.

Excelling… in our aim to be first class in everything we do.

Determined… in our pursuit of success while being accountable for our actions.'

1 **Does Manchester United's vision provide a clear picture of where the club is hoping to go / what it is trying to achieve?**
2 **What do the values tell you about the sort of club that Manchester United is and what it stands for?**
3 **How will the vision and values help to guide actions at the club?**

A **values statement** sets out what a company believes in and the principles that govern the way it behaves. Just as you might have values of being honest, reliable and ethical in your dealings – so too a company might establish a similar set of values.

Themes

You can see that the aims and vision of an organisation cover a range of themes such as:

Profile raising, for example 'to be the best football club in the world', 'to become the supermarket of choice' etc.

Financial, for example 'to become the most profitable business in our sector', 'to have the highest return on assets' etc.

Objectives

The general aims of a business can then be broken down into more specific **objectives**. The business objectives are the stepping stones which a business uses when working towards an overarching aim. For example, the aim of a charity might be to raise money to assist people with special needs, whilst the objectives for the charity would set targets for fundraising.

CASE STUDY

Scenario

Super Supermarkets has set itself the aim of becoming the leading supermarket in the United Kingdom and to be the supermarket of choice. In order to achieve this aim in the next five years, it has set itself some objectives.

* to increase turnover by 5 per cent per year for the next five years
* to open ten new stores a year
* to refurbish all of its existing stores.

1 How might these objectives help Super Supermarkets to achieve its aim?

2 Identify two other objectives for Super Supermarkets which would help it to become the leading supermarket in the United Kingdom and to become the supermarket of choice.

3 Identify the aim of one other organisation and list the sort of objectives it might have to achieve its aim.

Theory into practice

Working with a small group of students brainstorm ideas for an enterprise event, for example organising the marketing, sales and financial activities associated with the school or college play or a music concert or a discotheque. Alternatively you may want to focus on running a small business enterprise over a period of time, such as selling stationery, or running the school tuck shop. At this stage, simply brainstorm ideas by coming up with the first ideas that come into your head. All you need to know is that the activity needs to be carried out by a small group of students – typically between 5 and 12 members, and that it needs to be relatively easy to manage. See if you can come up with at least 20 ideas.

Once you have generated your ideas, you will need to evaluate them. Questions to consider will include those in the chart on the right.

Each of the items listed in the chart could act as a **constraint** on the event making it unrealistic. It is important to consider each of the items as many small businesses fail because they have not sufficiently considered the constraints.

However, you should not be too despondent. There are lots of good ideas that you can put into practice such as organising a Christmas Fayre or running a car washing scheme. If you are setting up and running an enterprise over a period of time, good ideas might include producing personalised stationery, buying and selling stationery for sale in a school shop, providing website support to businesses and many other ideas associated with ecommerce. The list is endless, but you need to make sure that you choose a suitable activity that helps you to meet the requirements of the assessment for this unit.

Once you have established a business idea which you feel is workable, you can decide on the aims and objectives of the business enterprise. Your aim might be to run a profitable and successful enterprise producing Christmas, Valentine and Easter Cards.

You could then back up this aim with some SMART objectives (see page 260) related to, for example:

Is there a market for the event?	
Do we have sufficient interest in running the event?	
Do we have the skills required?	
Is there enough time available?	
Would we be able to raise enough finance to make the idea worthwhile?	
Would we be able to charge a high enough price to cover our costs?	
Do we have appropriate premises to run the event in?	
Would we be able to compete effectively against the existing competition?	
Are there health and safety regulations that prevent us from running the event?	
Do we have access to the appropriate equipment required to run the event?	
Do we have access to the right sources of advice to help us with difficult issues associated with running the event?	

* raising a given sum of capital by selling shares by a given date
* carrying out a specified amount of market research to find out what consumers want
* producing set quantities of cards for different peak periods, to pre-established quality standards.

Remember that the objectives you set should each help to achieve the aim of running a profitable and successful enterprise or a profitable and successful event.

In setting objectives you need to make sure that they are SMART:

* **S**pecific – clear and precise
* **M**easurable – wherever possible attach numbers to them
* **A**ttainable – possible to achieve
* **R**ealistic
* **T**ime related – have a time frame.

Having **SMART objectives** enables you to:

* communicate a clear direction to everyone in the organisation
* have clear stepping stones to measure progress
* have a time frame for achieving your targets.

6.2.2 Building and developing an effective team

People are the most essential part of the successful running of an event. Therefore, it is important, when building a team, that individuals' strengths and weaknesses are taken into consideration from the start.

Roles

Most teams contain a number of roles that are played out by individuals during the course of a business activity. The main roles include:

* leader
* facilitator
* innovator
* negotiator
* activator.

The above roles are the main roles that will be required to organise an event or enterprise activity. Of course, there is some overlap between these roles, and in different situations individuals lean towards different roles. However, for the sake of the team it is important to allocate team roles to specialists in your team.

Theory into practice

In his book, *Management Teams: Why They Succeed or Fail* (Heinemann, 2004), Robert Belbin identified eight roles required for a well-functioning team. These were based on his studies of how teams work in practice:

1 **The chairperson** (leader), who co-ordinates the efforts of the team to make sure that it makes best use of resources in achieving its goals. The chair gives direction to others.

2 **The shaper**, who sets objectives and priorities and drives the team towards successful completion of the task.

3 **The plant**, who comes up with new ideas and plans.

4 **The monitor evaluator**, who is able to analyse problems and evaluate progress.

5 **The resource investigator**, who is outgoing and will explore and report on ideas and developments from outside the group.

6 **The company worker**, who is an administrator rather than a leader, and good at carrying out agreed plans.

7 **The team worker**, who supports the team, helps to keep it together and tries to improve communication between members.

8 **The finisher**, who keeps activities moving forward and plays a major part in seeing the project through to the end.

1 Why do you think it is important to have a variety of team roles in an effective team?

2 Which of Belbin's roles do you most usually adopt when working in a team?

3 Which of his roles would you most like to adopt when working on an enterprise activity?

Leader

The **leader** needs to be decisive and have the ability to inspire others. Leading a team means taking responsibility for others and seeking to help them to fit in and give their best. The leader must lead all members of the team, so an important skill is that of being considerate to the needs of others, while at the same time being prepared to give clear and decisive instructions. The leader should not be frightened to make decisions that are unpopular with individuals in the team but which are in the team's interest. The leader has ultimate responsibility for making sure that the event is a success.

Facilitator

The **facilitator** is responsible for helping the team to work effectively, which may involve informing members about meetings, organising rooms for team activities and generally helping the activities to run smoothly. The facilitator makes sure that resources are available for enterprise activities such as providing an **agenda** for team meetings. Facilitation involves enabling others to perform their team roles well. The facilitator will therefore have a good understanding of the objectives of the activity and the needs and requirements of the various team members. They will definitely need to be well organised.

Innovator

Enterprising teams need one or more individuals that will come up with exciting new ideas. When there are problems they will come up with innovative ways of solving them. An **innovator** is a creative person who doesn't always look for tried and tested solutions but will come up with something new. Innovators need to be encouraged by leaders and facilitators to come up with new ideas, although some of these ideas may be impractical.

Theory into practice

Identify the team role that you typically take by identifying three of the following fifteen characteristics that you most strongly associate with when working in a team. When working in a team, do you:

1 Get frustrated when nothing is getting done, so try to inspire others by getting on with tasks that you see as being important?

2 Feel confident when you are providing the means for others to carry out work activities?

3 Feel confident in your own ability to direct others and to make tough decisions?

4 Enjoy yourself when bargaining and haggling with others in order to get good deals?

5 See yourself as a creative person, able to see new and exciting solutions to problems?

6 Like to report ideas and suggestions to others so that they can make decisions?

7 Like to carry out administrative tasks which enable the group to function better and to meet objectives?

8 Enjoy setting targets and goals and then directing others towards achieving these goals?

9 Feel confident in setting up and creating good deals which help your team to get ahead of rivals?

10 Come up with enterprising and new ideas?

11 Like to roll up your sleeves and get involved with moving things forward rather than sitting about discussing things?

12 See yourself as someone who others respect and are thus able to influence them and direct them to take decisions that favour the whole group?

13 Enjoy solving disputes where individuals have different interests?

14 Like to experiment with new solutions to problems which most others would not think of?

15 Like to be busy engaging in practical tasks and encouraging others to join you?

You will probably feel that at different times you may lean towards all of the characteristics outlined above. However, there are going to be some which you lean towards most strongly. If you chose:

✳ 2, 6 and 7 you see yourself as a facilitator

✳ 1, 11 and 15 you see yourself as an activator

✳ 3, 8 and 12 you see yourself as a leader

✳ 5, 10 and 14 you see yourself as an innovator

✳ 4, 9 and 13 you see yourself as a negotiator.

Negotiator

A **negotiator** helps a team to get the resources it requires in a suitable form (and of course at the lowest possible cost). The negotiator handles tricky situations where there is disagreement within the team to keep team members with different interests happy. The negotiator also plays an important role in negotiating deals and contracts – in this case in terms of organising an event. For example, the negotiator may take responsibility for buying-in resources for the enterprise, booking rooms, agreeing payment terms etc.

Activator

It is all very well having decision makers, facilitators, and negotiators in a team but you also need one or more individuals who are prepared to get the ball rolling by getting things done and encouraging others to get involved. The **activator** leads by example, by showing others what needs to be done and actually doing it. However, the activator can't work alone or you wouldn't have a team. The activator therefore works with others in getting actions carried out, and seeing that the event actually takes place. An activitator needs to be an outgoing, practical and determined individual.

Teamwork advantages

There are many advantages to be gained from working as a team on an enterprise activity, including:

* it is possible to share the knowledge and skills base of the team – everyone can contribute
* having a team working together reduces over-reliance on key individuals
* team members can learn from each other
* everyone has a part to play and this helps motivation because everyone has a stake in the success of the event the team is organising
* members of the team are able to build respect for each other from seeing the contributions that each makes over time, for example in negotiating, activating, innovating etc
* teamwork approaches encourage innovation (the generation of new ideas) because people are allowed to be creative rather than being told what to do.

CASE STUDY
ASDA

ASDA calls the team members that work for the organisation 'colleagues'. ASDA expects all colleagues to:

* wear name badges at all times
* use first names for everyone in ASDA
* treat others with respect
* communicate relevant information to relevant colleagues
* offer help to others
* ask for help if needed
* give praise and recognition to others
* treat people equally
* listen to and respect others' ideas and opinions
* own problems, don't leave them for someone else
* give extra help to new colleagues
* be open and approachable to colleagues and customers
* treat others as you would like to be treated yourself.

Which of the characteristics of teamwork used by ASDA could you employ in team building in your enterprise team?

Responsibilities

It is not just roles that will be played out by individuals. A number of responsibilities also need to be assigned to ensure a successful enterprise activity takes place. Examples of these responsibilities include:

* planning
* reporting
* recording
* promoting
* selling
* producing.

Planning

Planning lies at the heart of successful enterprise activities. The starting point of planning involves:

* examining the objectives to be achieved
* identifying the time constraints (how long have you got?)
* creating a plan that enables you to meet the objectives in the time available.

Individuals with responsibility for planning must be:

* well organised
* able to set out a clear and well-structured planning document
* able to communicate the plan to others.

Leaders and facilitators should be involved in the planning process because they have an overall responsibility for co-ordinating the various activities of the organisation.

The sorts of plans that need to be created include:

* a document setting out the aims and objectives of the enterprise

* a **timeline** setting out when various activities need to be carried out
* a document setting out who is responsible for what in the organisation – this should be a brief document allocating roles to various team members
* an income and expenditure **budget**. A budget is simply a plan set out for the future in numbers (in this case money that is expected to come in and go out of the enterprise). The budget should start out with cash raised to set up the enterprise, for• example from selling shares in the enterprise. It should then show expected income, for example from selling tickets, and expected expenses, such as paying wages to team members and the cost of supplies etc.

The above plans can be included in a masterplan which also sets out details of:

* marketing activities that will be carried out, such as preliminary market research
* how finance for the business will be raised, and repaid
* how the activity will be organised
* other resource requirements of the team, for example, physical and human resources.

A masterplan for organising an enterprise activity may therefore involve the following headings:

Name of the organisation

Event to be organised

Team members

Aims and objectives of enterprise

Timeline showing activities leading up to event

Explanation of roles of team members

Budget of income and expenditure, shown at regular intervals:

	Period 1	Period 2	Period 3	Period 4	Period 5	Period 6 etc
Starting balance						
Income						
Share issue						
Ticket sales						
Other income						
Total income						
Expenditure						
Wages						
Purchases						
Heating & lighting						
Venue hire						
Total expenditure						
Closing balance						
Marketing plan						
Financial plan						
Description of organisation of activity						
Other resource requirements						

Reporting

Another important responsibility is that of writing *reports* about enterprise activities. These reports will be prepared for company meetings which might be held at four week or six week intervals.

The reports help to:

* communicate information within the team

* provide a basis for checking on progress

* provide a means of communicating information to those outside the business, for example those who are providing finance or those whose facilities are being used for the organisation of the event.

Think it over...

Your reports can also provide a basis for preparing evidence for the assignment report that you will need to produce for this unit.

Reports should include:

* an account of progress towards meeting the objectives of the enterprise which can be compared with the timeline (see page 267)

* a report on additional resources required to meet objectives and time constraints

* a financial report setting out actual income and expenditure, compared with budgets. Financial reporting should identify whether the business is going to meet its original profit objectives.

Individuals responsible for reporting should have good communication and ICT skills. Typically reporting will be overseen by the team leader and will be the responsibility of the facilitator of the team. Reports should be word processed and sent to team members before team meetings take place.

Recording

Whilst reports need to be produced periodically, records need to be kept on an ongoing basis. Those responsible for keeping records therefore need to be well organised and diligent. Records can't be kept in a disorganised way because you will soon lose a sense of where the business is at a particular moment in time.

Examples of records that need to be kept include:

* records of what was discussed and agreed at meetings

* records of all money received and spent by the enterprise

* records of orders placed and orders received.

Modern recording systems have been improved through the use of information technology. For example, a simple spreadsheet can be used to record income and expenditure by an enterprise. Word processing packages and emailing can be used to send out records of meetings.

Promotion

Promotional activity involves letting the potential market know about our event or products and services that we hope to sell. Promotion involves identifying the best possible channels for getting

our message across, for example posters, email, bulletin boards, newspaper advertisements etc.

Good promotions are ones that are noticed. This requires:

* good communication skills to get the message across to the audience

* good creative skills, for example to make advertising interesting and eye-catching.

The best promotions will be those that persuade the most customers to purchase tickets to our events or want to buy our goods and services – thus enabling us to achieve our objectives for the enterprise event.

Selling

Products, services and events rarely sell themselves and will normally require a lot of hard selling. Sales people need to have a fairly 'thick skin' because they have to be prepared to put up with rejections and lack of interest.

Selling involves persuading the customer that what we have to offer will give them the benefits that they are looking for. Selling involves being able to communicate through a variety of media, for example through a website, by email, by talking to people on the phone etc. Modern sales people therefore need to be confident with a range of media.

Producing

The basic ingredient of any successful event is good production. If your enterprise event involves selling products to consumers, for example at a Christmas Fayre, they need to be well made. If the event involves putting on a play, a concert, or a disco then production needs to be first class.

For example, if you are putting on a disco, you don't want to find that the disc jockey is double booked, or that the equipment can't be brought in through the doors leading to the dance floor, etc.

Production therefore involves attention to detail. An important word here is 'quality'. Quality means 'fitness for purpose'. The goods or event must be fit for the purpose that the audience or consumer expects. If you organise an evening reception at a local restaurant you don't want to find that your party has to queue in the cold

Theory into practice

Examine the table below. Team roles are shown horizontally, and responsibilities vertically. Discuss with other members of your team which of the roles best combine with particular responsibilities. You can then choose team members to take on particular responsibilities and roles. However, you should remember that you may have to take on different roles at different times rather than sticking rigidly to a specific role and responsibility.

It is particularly important that team members take on the responsibilities outlined, although some of the activities will involve inputs from all team members. For example, the leader and facilitator will have a major responsibility for planning but all members should be involved in planning at team meetings.

Responsibilities	Leader	Facilitator	Innovator	Negotiator	Activator
Planning					
Reporting					
Recording					
Promoting					
Selling					
Producing					

outside the restaurant waiting for other diners to finish. If you are producing Christmas bags, you don't want the bottom to fall out of them when items are placed inside.

Those responsible for production therefore must both have an eye for detail and the ability to get the tasks required completed. They must have a can-do approach, once they know what is expected of them.

6.2.3 Time management

Businesses need to plan their time carefully when running an event, so as to maximise available resources, both human and physical. Time-management techniques that a business may use are:

* timelines
* Gantt charts
* diary
* ICT packages.

Timelines

A timeline is a very simple yet highly useful visual tool that can be used to plan an activity. All it is in effect is a line showing the number of days/weeks etc until the preparation of an event has to be completed.

For example, if you are organising a summer concert which involves booking a venue, booking a band and erecting a marquee at a given location. The ideal timeline may look like the following:

Each of the vertical bars represents a week leading up to the event. Each of the numbers represents an activity to be completed by a specified date. In Figure 6.2, activity 14 represents the event, activity 13 represents the erection of the marquee and the installation of the groups equipment. Activities 10, 11, and 12 represent the

busy period just before an event takes place when there are progress review meetings and checks to make sure that the marquee erecting company has everything in order, that the venue has been confirmed, that security is confirmed etc. Activity 1 may represent the original planning stage. Activity 2 and 3 represent ongoing planning and review meetings at which responsibilities for carrying out the plan are established. Activity 4 represents team members actually booking the venue, the marquee, and the band. Activity 5 represents a review meeting on progress and activity 6 represents checking that plans are in order. Activities 7, 8 and 9 represent review meetings to check that all the activities of the enterprise group are running to order – the finance, the marketing, the selling of tickets, organisational aspects etc.

Gantt charts

A **Gantt chart** is a very useful tool for project planning. It was first devised by Henry Gantt and is widely used in modern project planning. A Gantt chart is a more sophisticated version of the timeline and is used to make sure that activities involved in project planning are carried out on time. It is therefore an ideal tool to use in the time management of the planning of an event.

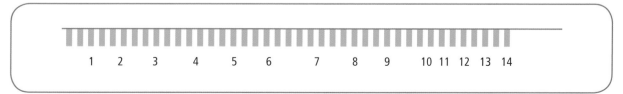

FIGURE 6.2 *Example of a timeline*

When you plan any event, there are some stages in the plan that can be carried out at the same time (simultaneously). There are other stages which must be carried out in a sequence (sequentially). For example, one member of your team could take responsibility for hiring a venue, and another member for hiring the band. These activities can be carried out simultaneously. In contrast, you could not put the canvas onto the marquee before you have erected the poles that will support the canvas. These activities are therefore sequential.

To produce a Gantt chart:

* make a list of all the activities that need to be carried out to complete a project, for example to organise an event

* allocate a reasonable amount of time required to carry out each of these activities. For example, booking a band to perform at the event could take anything up to a week (of course if you are lucky you might be able to do it in a day).

Let us assume that you have identified a number of activities that you want to carry out in organising a disco which you want to take place at the earliest possible date.

Before you go ahead you want to do some marketing to find out whether there is sufficient demand for the disco. This will take you three days to construct a questionnaire, five days to carry out the questioning and three more days to analyse the results. These activities are sequential.

Assuming that the results are favourable, you will then have a meeting to get the go ahead of the team to approve the project. The meeting can then decide to approve the proposal and to allocate responsibilities for organising the event. A number of activities can be carried out simultaneously, for example organising the venue (allocate three days), booking the band (allocate seven days), and getting the tickets printed (allocate 14 days). Although these activities can be carried out simultaneously, you will not be able to carry out the next stage, which is selling the tickets, until they have been printed in 14 days' time.

You may then want to allocate 28 days to selling the tickets. The concert can be organised

for the day after the last ticket has been sold. You may want to confirm the booking of the band and the booking of the hall once the tickets have been printed (these activities can be carried out simultaneously and will only last one day). On the day before the concert you can set up the hall and hopefully you will have planned a good event.

All the above information for organising a disco can be set out in a Gantt chart. The Gantt chart is a set of horizontal bars representing time periods needed to carry out activities. Each activity is given a letter as shown in the table below.

Letter	Description of activity	Time (days)
A	Construct questionnaire	3
B	Questioning	5
C	Analyse results	3
D	Meeting	1
E	Organise venue	3
F	Book band	7
G	Print tickets	14
H	Sell tickets	28
I	Confirm booking of band	1
J	Confirm booking of hall	1
K	Set up hall	1
L	Disco	

We can illustrate the Gantt chart for the activities described above in the following way:

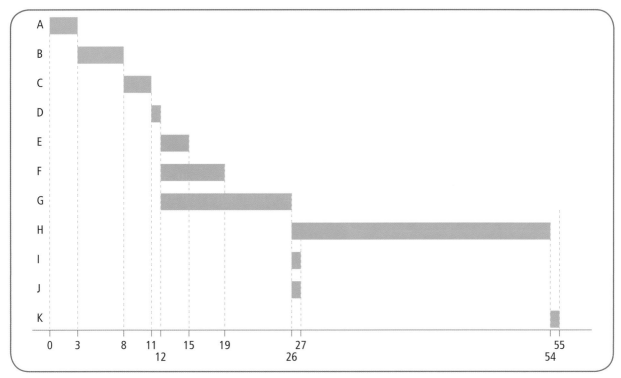

FIGURE 6.3 *An example of a Gantt chart*

You can see that activities A, B and C are sequential so will take 11 days in total. B can't start till A has finished. C can't start till B has finished. In contrast, E, F and G can be carried out at the same time – so together should only last 14 days.

When you produce a Gantt chart, place it where it can be seen easily. This provides a good communication tool letting everyone in the team know where you have got to in organising and preparing for the event.

Gantt charts lend themselves to inspection. For example, a project manager can inspect a Gantt chart and a project at any time, for example every 7 days on days 7, 14, 21 etc. The manager can then see whether the project is on time because the chart shows all the activities that should be taking place on that day.

For example, the Gantt chart in Figure 6.3 shows the following:

* on day 7 the project should be at the stage where market research questioning is taking place.

* on day 14 the venue should already be organised and the project should be at the

stage of booking the band, and the tickets should be being printed.

Diary

Another simple time-management technique is the keeping of paper based or electronic diaries. Each member of your team should keep a diary setting out key activities they need to perform and when.

Diaries can be linked to what is called an **action plan**. At company meetings the chair and facilitator can take responsibility for the setting and monitoring of action plans. The action plan sets out who in the team needs to do what and by what date. Each member of the team can mark in the actions that they are responsible for in their diary.

Actions	Who is responsible	Completion date
Book the band	JS & KW	23 June
Book the venue	JS & PD	23 June
Organise hire of marquee	PD & SS	30 June
Ring printers	DL	22 June
Organise agenda for next meeting	YT	30 June

JS's diary would then have the following entries for 23 June.

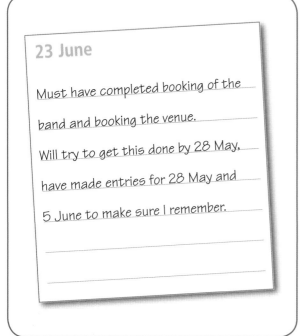

23 June

Must have completed booking of the band and booking the venue.
Will try to get this done by 28 May, have made entries for 28 May and 5 June to make sure I remember.

ICT packages

Nowadays there are a number of ICT packages that enable event managers to keep a good control over their time.

Examples of these are electronic diaries which you can keep on your computer. You can automatically call up your diary each day to check on phone calls that you have to make and tasks that you must complete that day.

There are other excellent ICT packages such as one which helps you to draw Gantt charts which is available on Microsoft Project. Microsoft Project identifies for you the critical path of a project (those activities which if delayed will lead to the delay of the project itself).

6.2.4 Required resources

In order for a business to run an activity, it requires a range of resources. Examples include:

* human – building the team needed to meet the business objectives
* time – a schedule as to where and when resources will be allocated
* physical – the space to carry out the activity, equipment needed, raw materials to be used, packaging, display units and marketing materials
* finance – the cost implications of running an event.

In your assignment you will need to show in your report the thought that you have given to planning out resource requirements.

Human resources

Teams need building, they don't just arise. An American writer (B.W. Tuckman, *Development Stages in Small Groups*, 2000) identified a number of stages that are involved in the building of a real team. From his own observations he noted that a team goes through a number of stages:

1   **Stage 1: Forming**: A number of individuals come together. They are simply that – a loose collection of people with no clear sense of

purpose. The group begins to develop some sort of agreement about the issues that need addressing. For example, you form a group to run an event but initially no roles and responsibilities are worked out.

2   **Stage 2**: **Storming**: The group begins to exchange ideas, but there is as yet little structure or anything like a real team, and there are no clear plans to take the team forward. However, any disagreements start to be managed constructively. The group starts to choose members to take on roles and responsibilities to organise the event. However, there is some tension about who should be doing what and individuals haven't got used to taking on a role.

3   **Stage 3: Norming**: The group begins to share ideas and is beginning to take on the characteristics of a team. A leadership pattern emerges with more clearly defined roles and responsibilities. Individuals begin to take on responsibility for carrying out their roles and there is greater clarity about objectives and targets. Things work to plan, records are kept, and team meetings are organised.

4   **Stage 4: Performing**: A clear, organised pattern is established, based on mutual respect, the sharing of ideas and the drawing out of clear plans and proposals from all members of the team. Every member is therefore able to make the best possible contribution to the team process and to make sure that the event is a success. The implementation of action plans is in full swing.

We now have a high-performance team, with well-organised meetings, and the responsibilities of planning, reporting, recording, promoting, selling and producing are all being carried out efficiently.

Team building involves understanding the processes that lead to good teamwork. These include:

✳ encouraging everyone to contribute

✳ listening to others' views

✳ having shared goals and objectives

✳ having some form of team leadership

✳ encouraging each other

✳ working hard to achieve team aims and objectives

✳ rewarding team effort.

Time resources

People often underestimate the importance of time in project management. We have already looked at the importance of using time-management techniques.

Another useful approach to using time effectively is to create a schedule as to where and when resources will be allocated. This could look like the following:

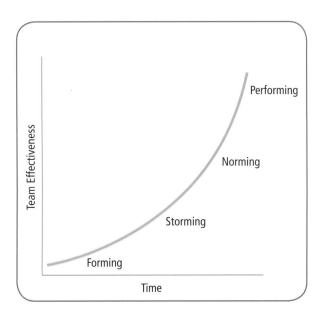

Time when resources are required	Human	Physical	Finance
May 12	Whole team for team-building exercise		
May 14			Raise capital through share issue (£200)
May 16		Purchase computer scanner (£50)	

Physical resources

If you are organising an event you will need a physical space to run it in – a venue. You will need to hire this space. You may also need to hire equipment such as speakers for a disco. If you are organising some form of manufacturing activity, then you may need to buy some machinery, raw materials and packing materials.

You need to identify the relevant resource requirements for your organisation, set out when they will be purchased, and when they will be delivered and paid for.

Finance resources

Finally, you must consider the cost implications of running an event. It is important to work out fairly detailed costings of what are referred to as the overheads of the event.

For example, in running a disco, overheads will include:

* cost of printing tickets
* cost of venue hire
* cost of equipment hire
* cost of hiring a disc jockey
* cost of security.

All of these need to be covered if you are going to make a profit. In running an event you should therefore calculate a break-even quantity – typically the number of people required to attend the event to cover costs. Usually businesses are reluctant to carry out activities if they only break even from them. They want to see that budgeted sales are considerably higher than the break-even point.

To calculate the break-even point of your event:

* do some costings to work out the total overhead cost of running the event – don't underestimate this as it is better to overestimate than to underestimate

* work out how much you want to charge for the event, for example the price you will charge for people to buy a ticket to the disco

* calculate if there are any variable costs associated with each person that attends the event. If this is not possible simply calculate break even assuming the variable cost is zero.

Break even is calculated using the formula:

$$\text{Break even} = \frac{\text{overhead}}{\text{contribution}}$$

The contribution is calculated by deducting variable costs per ticket sold from the cost of entry. For example, if you charge £2.50 for entry and the variable cost is 50 pence then the contribution is £2.

If the overheads of running the disco are £150 – then you will need to sell 75 tickets to break even. Of course if you have planned to sell 150 tickets then you will make a profit of £150.

Theory into practice

Explain how your team went about planning the physical resource and financial requirements of organising your assignment event or activity. Include any break-even calculations that were made. Once the enterprise activity is completed, evaluate the effectiveness of the work that your team carried out to ensure that the resource requirements of the event were met.

6.2.5 Need for regular meetings

When planning a possible event, businesses may hold a series of meetings where stakeholders come together to discuss key issues. The need for regular meetings may be affected by a number of internal and external factors. This may mean that a team has to adjust their initial plans if circumstances change radically. The stages involved in successful meetings are:

* preparing for the meeting
* running the meeting
* implementing the decisions of the meeting.

In a team-based situation, meetings will be an important part of running an enterprise activity. Meetings enable the team to:

* establish clear objectives, targets and goals
* plan activities together
* communicate the contents of plans
* present reports on progress
* monitor progress against targets, for example comparing progress with a budget, with a Gantt chart or a timeline

* create new action plans and to enter responsibilities into diaries
* celebrate the success of the enterprise.

Preparing for meetings

In preparing for meetings you could use the following checklist to establish objectives for the meeting:

Will the meeting involve:	What form will this take?
Establishing objectives and targets	For example, in the early days this may include establishing the aims of the enterprise activity and later on setting sales targets etc.
Planning activities together	For example, planning out budgets, sharing ideas about the master plan, planning the event etc.
Communicating the contents of plans	For example, when part of a plan has been prepared by someone with a role in the enterprise they can explain the detail of the plan at the meeting.
Presenting reports on progress	Individuals with roles and responsibilities can explain the actions they have taken.
Monitoring progress against targets	For example, examining where you have got to on a timeline or Gantt chart.
Creating new action plans and making diary entries	For example, establishing an action plan for selling tickets – each member of the group could put in their diary what their responsibility is.
Celebrating the success of the team	For example, opening a tin of chocolates to celebrate the successful planning of an event.

Running a meeting

Nearly all employees at all levels in an organisation will spend some time attending meetings.

Meetings can be called for a variety of purposes:

* to generate ideas by drawing on the knowledge and skills of a range of specialists, for example those with various roles and responsibilities in our enterprise team

* to arrive at shared decisions – sometimes an individual does not have the authority to make a decision so he or she might call a meeting in order that a team can make decisions

* for investigative reasons, for example, to find out why tickets aren't selling as well as intended, or to check why spending is over the budgeted figures.

Some meetings are simply informal gatherings in which no formal records are kept. In contrast, a formal meeting may involve lots of procedures and set ways of doing things. The features of a formal meeting are as follows:

* the meeting is called by a notice or agenda

* conduct in the meetings depends on the organisation's formal rules

* decisions are often reached by voting

* there are formal terms and expressions used in the meeting

* the proceedings are recorded in **minutes**.

> **Key terms**
>
> **Minutes** – a record of what was said in a meeting.

Memos

Before a meeting is held, it is helpful to send a memo (memorandum) to participants asking for issues which they wish to discuss during the meeting and what decisions they want to make about them. In organising team meetings for your enterprise activity the facilitator of the meetings should send out this memo well in advance of the meeting – either in paper form or in the form of an email.

A memo is a very short document which would look like Figure 6.4.

> **Memo: From Jane Briggs to team members**.
>
> The next meeting will take place on 21 May. If you have any items that you want to be put forward at the meeting please send them to me by 14 May at the latest so that I can put them on the agenda.

FIGURE 6.4 *An example of a memo*

Notice / Agenda

Formal meetings must be conducted according to legal requirements or to a written constitution. It is usual to give notice of the meeting to every person entitled to attend, according to the rules and regulations. The notice issued should specify the date, time and place of the meeting. (See Figure 6.5.)

> **NOTICE OF MEETING**
>
> **Disco Event Management Enterprises**
>
> The monthly review meeting of the Enterprise will be held in the business suite on 21 May 2005, at 7.30 pm. Any items for inclusion in the agenda should reach me no later than 14 May 2005.
>
> Amanveer Dhatt

FIGURE 6.5 *An example of a notice*

A notice of meeting will be accompanied or followed by an agenda, which is a list of topics to be discussed at the meeting. It will normally be sent to all those entitled to attend the meeting so they can consider the topics in advance of the meeting (see Figure 6.6 on page 275).

A chairperson has certain duties and powers in a meeting. He or she makes sure the meeting is properly constituted, keeps order, works through the agenda (preventing irrelevant discussion) and gains the views of the meeting by putting motions and amendments to those attending.

Often, a chairperson will have a special copy of the agenda (known as the chairperson's agenda). On this copy, further information is provided for the chair's guidance and space is left on the right-hand side for notes to be made.

AGENDA

Disco Event Management Enterprise

The monthly review meeting taking place on 21 May 2005 at 7.30 pm will cover:

1 Apologies for absence

2 Minutes of the last meeting

3 Matters arising from the meeting

4 Reports:
Chair's report
Financial controller's report
Marketing and sales managers' report

5 Proposed action plans for coming period

6 Proposal to increase price of tickets

7 Any other business

8 Date of next meeting

Charles O'Donnel

Charles O'Donnel
Enterprise Administrator

FIGURE 6.6 *An example of an agenda*

Shortly before the time a meeting starts, the chairperson makes sure there is a quorum. This is the minimum number of people required for the meeting to go ahead, according to the rules. The chairperson should make sure everyone has an agenda and that all new members are introduced.

The secretary then states whether any apologies have been received for absence, and reads through the official record (the minutes of the last meeting). If the minutes have already been circulated, it will be assumed they have been read. Members are asked to approve them as a correct record of the last meeting and, if necessary, the secretary will amend them before they are signed by the chairperson.

At this stage any matters arising from the previous minutes will be discussed. For example, if the last meeting suggested that certain individuals should carry out certain actions, these may be mentioned.

The chairperson then works through the business of the meeting, according to the agenda. If reports are to be read (again, circulated reports are assumed to have been read), the writers of the report may be asked to speak briefly. If a motion is proposed, the chairperson will ask for a proposer and a seconder, this will allow for discussion of the motion and will make sure all sides are heard. The chairperson will then call for a vote. The chairperson usually has the casting vote if the voting is tied.

Any other business is normally limited to non-controversial issues because, if it is felt that something deserves further attention, it must be put on the agenda for the next meeting. At the end of the meeting a decision may be made about the date, time and place of the next meeting.

Minutes

While a meeting is taking place, the secretary records the proceedings with a series of notes (the minutes). These should provide an accurate and clear record of what has taken place at the meeting and are usually written up in the past tense immediately after a meeting.

The secretary will usually have a folder containing agendas and minutes from previous meetings. It is important that such documents are kept as they provide a permanent record of issues that have been discussed and decisions that have been sanctioned. (see Figure 6.7 on page 276).

Some useful advice about making contributions to meetings is:

* scrutinise agenda items before you attend the meeting to see which areas particularly interest you
* research areas of interest and obtain any relevant reading materials
* plan out, either in your mind or by making notes, what you might want to say
* listen to what others have to say before speaking yourself
* timing is important – make sure the point you make fits into the discussion
* do not ramble on
* be tactful and do not deliberately upset someone

MINUTES OF MEETING

Disco Event Management Enterprises

Minutes of the periodic review meeting held on 21 May 2005 in the Business Suite

Present: Janine Jones (Chair), Amanveer Dhatt (Facilitator), Charles O'Donnel (Company Secretary), Mohammed Praven (Marketing Manager), Belinda Grey (Sales Manager), Yang Li (Production Director), Chris Chan (Creative Director), Chris Choi (Finance Director)

1	Apologies	Apologies from Paul Smith, Gerry Burbage
2	Minutes	Minutes from the last meeting were taken as read and approved
3	Matters arising	At the previous meeting, Belinda Grey had understated sales at that date. They were recorded as 14 when the figure should have been 21.

4	Reports	Janine Jones reported that the master plan, which sets out clear objectives, resource requirements, budgets, sales targets and detailed plans for the event has now been completed. The master plan was circulated and Janine identified the main targets and areas that needed to be covered in preparing the event.
		   Copy of report circulated to all members.
		
		Chris Choi circulated the budget for the event. Document enclosed. He explained that figures for sales were based on market research information and on sales to date. He outlined the main items of expenditure. The figure for the cost of hiring the venue has increased by ten per cent.
		
		Mohammed Praven and Belinda Grey together presented the marketing and sales report. Mohammed did a presentation setting out the results of the market research indicating that demand for the disco was likely to be for 200 attending the event. He said that this was based on interviewees ticking the 'definite' box when asked if they would attend.
		   This was supported by Belinda Grey who reported that advanced ticket sales had risen to 150.

5	Proposed action plans	Amanveer Dhatt introduced an action plan to cover key areas of the master plan including team-building exercises, purchase of physical assets, monitoring of the budget and sales and marketing plans. Copy of the action plan enclosed. Individuals diarised their responsibilities for specific aspects of the plan.
6	Proposal to raise prices	Mohammed Praven indicated that given current demand for tickets it might be possible to raise the price of tickets. Belinda Grey said that this would not be fair to those who had not already bought tickets. The general feeling of the meeting was that if the disco proved to be a success, a second event could be organised, with higher prices being charged.
7	Any other business	Chris Choi asked that all members of the team should examine the budget to see if they could identify any areas of weakness before the next meeting.
8	Date of next meeting	It was agreed that the next review meeting would take place on 14 June.

Charles O'Donnel

22 May 2005

FIGURE 6.7 *Example of minutes of a meeting*

* be assertive
* make your contributions clear and well communicated
* be ready for opposition to your ideas by trying to anticipate the response you might receive to the points you are making.

Implementing the decisions of meetings

Decisions will be made during the course of a meeting and wherever possible these should be logged in action plans. The chair and facilitator have an important role to play in ensuring that the decisions of the meeting are communicated in the form of minutes and action plans to those who attended the meeting. Action plans should be clearly laid out. During the meeting, team members should enter their responsibilities (in terms of the action plans) in their diaries.

Implementation then involves carrying out the decisions of the meeting.

Theory into practice

Keep a record of the meetings that you have while planning for and implementing your enterprise activity. What were the main areas discussed? What went particularly well at the meetings? What went badly? How could the meetings have been improved?

6.2.6 Possible constraints

Businesses find that all events are subject to a number of constraints (factors which may limit their success or prevent objectives from being achieved). Some of these constraints are internal and others external to the business. You need to demonstrate knowledge and understanding of a range of constraints. These constraints include:

* finance, e.g. budgetary constraints
* legal constraints
* time constraints
* skills constraints

* equipment constraints
* competition constraints.

You need to show how you dealt with the constraints that impacted on your chosen enterprise activity.

Financial / budgetary constraints

Finance is a scarce resource for all businesses. This is particularly the case for a new venture. How can you convince lenders or shareholders (if shares are issued) that your enterprise will be a success and that they will get their investment back with interest (or in the form of dividends for shareholders)?

At the outset you need to be able to convince investors that you have a good plan. You need to produce a clear and concise version of your master plan to show to investors including budgets and details of resource requirements.

Key financial constraints involve having enough financial resources at the start of your enterprise. This means that to start out with you have to be careful about your expenditures, rather than frittering capital which may be needed later. It also means having enough cash flow to pay your bills. If you are running an event you will need to have cash to pay for such things as the printing of advertising and promotional materials. You will need to pay for the printing of tickets. You may have to put a deposit down on the venue that you want to hire or pay a deposit to the disc jockey.

Careful planning/budgeting is therefore essential to deal with financial constraints. You need to be cautious in spending scarce financial resources.

Legal constraints

Legal constraints will limit what you can and can't do right from the start. In conjunction with your teacher/tutor you will need to examine relevant legislation, for example Food Safety laws if food is being served, and Health and Safety laws to ensure the safety of individuals attending an event. In conjunction with your teacher you will need to have a risk assessment carried out for any event that you want to organise.

Time constraints

Time may prove to be the biggest constraint. If your project is too ambitious, then the event may never take place. For example, if you want to organise an event in 60 days' time, then make sure that you can complete all the necessary planning and organising within 40 days. Try to give yourself 50 per cent more time than you think you require.

Think it over...

Did you know that in 2004 Diarmuid Gavin, a well-known television gardener, received a lot of sponsorship for the garden he prepared for the Kew Gardens flower festival. Unfortunately, he fell behind in planning for the event. When the judges came to judge his garden he was still administering the 'finishing touches' so the garden fell short of expectation. He hadn't allowed himself the 50 per cent extra time to complete his project.

Skills constraints

Most businesses suffer from skills constraints. They don't have enough people with the right skills to perform all the tasks required to the necessary standard. Make sure that you have the people with the right skills to help the organisation of your event to be a success. If you don't have the right skills yourself you might be able to hire someone with those skills. For example, if you are running a disco, it will be well worth hiring a professional DJ. If you try to do it yourself you could end up with lots of angry customers.

Equipment

Running an enterprise activity well involves having the right equipment, at the right time, in the right place. For example, when you run a disco, if you are missing an essential cable then you might not be able to operate.

In the run up to the event make a checklist of all the equipment you will need. If there are bits that are particularly crucial then you might need to have reserve stores that you can call upon.

Competition

The competition will always be a constraint on the success of your business. For example, if you run

Use the following checklist table to record how
you dealt with constraints that impacted on your
chosen enterprise activity.

What are the constraints? Describe them using the headings provided.	Explain how you will deal with these constraints.
Finance	
Legal	
Time	
Equipment	
Skills	
Competition	

a disco next to a nightclub make sure that your
disco is sufficiently different to attract the number
of customers you require to make a profit. You
will need to consider how your prices compare
with those of competitors as well as the range and
variety of your event to ensure that it is ahead of
the competition.

6.2.7 Research and analysis

To be able to research and analyse whether your
profit-making enterprise activity was a success,
you need to take into account as many different

views as possible. You need to carry out both
primary research and secondary research.

You need to use this research and further
analysis to help you to comment on the success of
your event, how the team interacted as a whole
and your individual contribution to the activity.

Primary research

Primary research may include the following:

* surveys with the participants who took part in
  your enterprise activity

* questionnaires to other group members on
  how they felt the group interacted throughout
  the activity

* face-to-face discussion with a group member,
  getting them to carry out a SWOT analysis on
  your contribution to the activity

* discussions with other stakeholders, e.g.
  suppliers.

An important part of your analysis should be a
review of the contribution of other members of
your enterprise team to the overall success of the
activity.

Questionnaires

In the course of time individuals will grow into
their roles, while others may find it difficult to
maintain their roles and others may grow to take
on the roles that are being vacated. You need to
monitor this interaction between group members
as part of your research and analysis.

On at least two occasions during the running
of your enterprise activity carry out research by
asking other team members how they felt the
group interacted. You could do this in the form of
a questionnaire or as a discussion. The following
questions may be included in your questionnaire:

* Who do you see as being the leader of the
  group and what responsibilities do they have?

* Who do you see as being the facilitator in the
  group and what responsibilities do they have?

* Have the roles changed at any times during the
  running of your activity and if so why?

* Have you been happy with the roles and responsibilities you have taken on board? Explain why.

* How have the roles that individuals have taken affected the interaction of the group?

SWOT analysis

Another useful activity you could carry out to find out about team interaction and your own role in the team is to get group members to produce a SWOT analysis of an individual's performance of a role and/or the way they have carried out their responsibilities.

For example, assume that Dalvinder has been chosen by the group to be their leader, to take on responsibility for creating and implementing the masterplan and for running team meetings. Group members have produced a SWOT analysis on Dalvinder's leadership role (see page 281).

The SWOT analysis is a useful evaluative tool of a team member's role and responsibilities. Individuals can then identify ways in which they can:

* build on their strengths

* reduce or eliminate their weaknesses

* seize opportunities

* rise to the challenge of threats.

Secondary research

Secondary sources of information that you can use to evaluate your enterprise might include:

* reports in school magazines and newsletters about your enterprise activity

* coverage in the local press

* reports written about the activity by external sources, for example by your teacher.

Team dynamics and interaction

Secondary sources that are useful in evaluating the effectiveness of the team and your role in the team include Belbin's and Tuckman's books and papers listed at the end of this unit.

By studying theories which are included in this text and in other specialist texts on team building you will get a better idea about how teams work, the problems in forming and maintaining team interactions and other aspects of working together on enterprising activities.

Wherever possible you should relate these theories to what happens in your enterprise activity. For example, Tuckman found that initially groups that come together for an activity do not work as high-performance teams. They need a period to settle down and to share objectives and targets. Of course, what happens in your organisation may not match Tuckman's concept of the development of a high-performance team. Your team may never gel together because of personality clashes and lack of clear direction.

Self analysis

Additionally you will want to evaluate your own performance in contributing to the team and the enterprise activity. Here is a useful checklist which can be used to evaluate your own performance:

Name:

Roles and responsibilities in the enterprise:

* List of what you consider to be your main strengths in contributing to the team and to making a success of the enterprise.

* List of what you consider to be your main weaknesses in contributing to the team and to making a success of the enterprise.

* Having considered the areas of strength and weakness, identify areas for development in the future. Make a list of these and what opportunities exist for helping with your development.

* Ask your teacher / tutor to write a comment identifying what he or she sees as your main areas for development and the opportunities that you might want to take to engage in this development process.

Create a questionnaire for members of your group to fill in to evaluate the success of your event. The questions on the right can be used to start you off.

You can then extend the questionnaire to cover other aspects such as planning, etc.

As well as using a questionnaire on members of your group, you may also want to evaluate your enterprise activity with others that have supported the enterprise. For example, if you have an outside business adviser working with your school or college, you could also provide a questionnaire for them to fill in. In constructing the questionnaire, provide opportunities for the outside adviser to suggest areas for improvement.

Having participated in our team enterprise activity it would be helpful if you could take a few moments to give us some feedback on how effective you feel specific aspects of the activity were:

1   The setting and communication of clear objectives.

2   Did you understand the objectives of the enterprise activity from the outset?

3   How were these objectives communicated to you?

4   What improvements could have been made in the setting and communication of these objectives?

SWOT analysis

Name: Dalvinder

Role: Leader with responsibility for creating and implementing master plan, and for running team meetings.

Strengths: You are hard working and respected by others in the team. You have turned up to all the meetings and created with the team a master plan including a clear set of objectives. You are always prepared to encourage other team members. You communicate clearly, and in an authoritative way. We all know what is expected of us in planning to run the disco on time and how many tickets we are expected to sell. You have liaised well with others in the team including the marketing manager and the venue organiser.	**Weaknesses**: You don't listen to everyone's views – sometimes you put them down and we have noticed that one or two members of the team are demotivated which is why they sometimes don't turn up. You need to tell Shona that she needs to record information about the accounts more thoroughly because the financial side of the business is a bit disorganised. Sometimes you spend too much time on marketing activities rather than leaving the responsibility to Steven.
Opportunities: As you grow in experience of the leadership role you will be able to give a clear sense of direction to the team. When we meet a business manager from a local company next week you will have the opportunity to discuss ways of improving your leadership style and then put this into practice at ongoing meetings. Going out to meet people outside the organisation e.g. the sales director at the venue, etc will enable you to develop your leadership role in a wider environment.	**Threats**: At times one or two stronger characters in the team challenge your leadership role. This is particularly when we are falling behind schedule on the timeline and when financial records are not available or are not well structured. Next week we have AS exams and this will lead to a fall in attendance at team meetings.

6.2.8 Potential future changes to the enterprise activity

For a business, it is important that its activity is constantly monitored and appraised to make sure that, if the event was to run a second time, changes could be made to improve the experience. You need to discuss your own enterprise activity and suggest suitable changes that you would make, should it be run a second time.

It will be helpful to hold a discussion among team members to identify potential future changes. Important contributions can be made at this meeting by inviting a business adviser from outside the school or college who has some knowledge of how the event was organised and run to provide important insights. Alternatively you could use your teacher/tutor as a business consultant.

Clear aims

Was there a clear aim provided at the onset with objectives showing clearly how the group would work towards achieving their overall aim?

To show evidence of this for your assignment you could include in your report the documents setting out the aims and objectives of your organisation. You can comment on how clear they are and how appropriate they are. You can give your own personal views as to how useful these aims and objectives were in giving your organisation a sense of direction. You could also provide examples of where the team failed to work towards the aims and objectives or where the aims and objectives helped the team to focus on what they needed to do.

Viability

Was the enterprise viable? Should it have been reduced in scope to ensure that it could have been managed more easily?

You need to show how effective the market research was in giving an idea of the overall market and whether the market was sufficient to make sure that the event was managed successfully. Useful evidence is whether you succeeded in meeting sales targets. How realistic was the original idea? Was the business successful enough to employ the number of people who were involved in the enterprise? You should comment on whether the organisation was too ambitious or whether it was not ambitious enough. Often small enterprises suffer because they try to do too much and overstretch their resources (for example by trying to organise too big an event given time and financial constraints). Can you give examples of when resources were used well or when resources were overstretched, for example not enough time to do particular tasks well? Was the choice of the event to manage feasible or were there too many problems in making it a success?

Profit

Was a profit made, and if not, what measures could be put in place to ensure this happened in the future?

You can use the profit and loss account to show the anticipated profit and the actual profit and the budget to analyse where differences occurred between what was planned and what actually materialised. You can use this as evidence to show how in future the event management could be more successful. You may need to look at how the market research data was originally collected and how the results of this research differ from what happened in practice. This could give indicators of how to improve market research. Studying variances between anticipated and actual costs can give ideas about how to keep better control over costs. Comparing actual revenues with anticipated revenues can give ideas about how to improve marketing activities and sales plans.

Interaction

Did the group interact well and were roles and responsibilities clearly defined with everyone working towards a common purpose?

There are a number of tools and tables in this textbook (see pages 261 and 266) which give you ideas about how to evaluate the way in which you and other individuals in your group contributed to team activities. The sections on Tuckman and Belbin team theories (see pages 260 and 270) can also be useful information when providing evidence of how successful your team was and how team interactions could be improved in the future.

Record of discussions

It is important that you make a record of the discussions to improve on past experiences, to provide you with evidence for your assessment activity. Each member of the discussion forum should go into the discussion with a sheet of paper set out under the following headings (shown opposite). Prior to the meeting everyone should write down some comments in the relevant sections and then add to these with comments from other group members.

Ideas for potential future changes to an enterprise activity:

Was there a clear aim or could the clarity have been improved? If so, how?

Was the enterprise viable? How could it have been made more manageable?

Did we succeed in making a profit? Was it what we budgeted for? How could we have improved the profit figure?

How well did we interact? Were roles and responsibilities clearly defined? Were we all working towards a common purpose – in other words were we a high-performance team?

KNOWLEDGE CHECK

1   What do you understand by the terms
    a) enterprise, and b) an enterprise?

2   Give three examples of aims that a small enterprise might have.

3   Distinguish between the mission and vision of an organisation.

4   Give examples of values that an event management enterprise might have. Give four values.

5   Set out a list of SMART objectives for a small event management enterprise.

6   Identify four types of roles that are required in a high-performance team. Show how these roles are essential for the team to work effectively.

7   Based on your own experience of working in a team make a list of six benefits of teamwork.

8   What are the key areas that need to be planned in setting up an enterprise and / or running an enterprise activity? Who are these reports for?

9   What is a Gantt chart? Set out a Gantt chart for a project in which Activity A must take place before all other activities and takes 5 days. B and C follow immediately after A and take four days each. Activity D must wait for the completion of B and takes 6 days. Activity E must wait for the completions of B and C and takes 12 days. Activity F can start when B is completed and takes 6 days. Finally Activity G follows on from F and takes 6 days.

10 Draw a diagram to illustrate the stages involved in the creation of a team. Briefly describe each stage.

11 Set out a formula for break-even. If the fixed costs of running an event are £250, the price of tickets to the event are £5 and the variable cost per ticket is £4.50, how many people need to attend the event for it to break even? Show your working.

12 Describe the purpose of the following in relation to meetings – minutes, notice / agenda, the role of the chair.

13 Describe two major constraints on running a successful enterprise activity. In each case show how these constraints can be dealt with to create a successful event.

14 What sorts of primary research would it be helpful to carry out when preparing to run an enterprise activity?

15 What should be the relationship between marketing and sales in preparing an enterprise activity?

16 What sorts of activities should a 'negotiator' be assigned in team management for organising an event?

17 Describe a situation in which the objectives which are set out for running an enterprise activity are not SMART.

18 Why do you think it is important to have a variety of team roles in an effective team?

19 Why is it important to keep diaries when organising an event?

20 How does budgeting help in the process of event management?

Resources

Reference sources

Useful reference sources include:

* talks by local entrepreneurs about planning for business success

* talks by events managers about the processes and problems of managing an event

* materials from banks, building societies, the FSA and other organisations, including those connected with enterprise activities

* access to business-type activities such as Young Enterprise, The Prince's Trust, company schemes or challenges to young people.

Textbooks

Books that have been written about group interaction and dynamics, including:

Belbin, M.R., *Team Roles and Work*, Heinemann, Oxford, 1996

Belbin, M.R., *Beyond the Team*, Heinemann, Oxford, 2000

Belbin, M.R., *Management Teams: Why they Succeed or Fail*, Heinemann, Oxford, 2003

Tuckman, B.W., Developmental sequences in small groups, *Psychological Bulletin* 63, pages 384–99

Websites

You can also carry out some useful Internet searches to find out about activities of businesses engaged in **event management**. Simply use the key words 'Event Management'

For example, at www.event-management-uk.co.uk you will find Event Management UK, which is a directory of sites related to providing event management solutions.

UNIT
7

Financial providers and products

This unit contains five elements:

7.2.1 Customers of financial services

7.2.2 Financial service providers and products

7.2.3 Research into the financial services market

7.2.4 Constraints affecting the provision of financial services

7.2.5 Potential effect of future changes to customer circumstances

Introduction

There are probably few products or service sectors that have undergone quite so much change as the market for financial services. The purposes of the **Financial Services Act** of 1986 were to regulate the conduct of investment business, to increase competition and to improve consumer confidence. The result of this and more recent changes such as the **Financial Services and Markets Act 2000** mean that today, instead of a consumer automatically thinking:

'If I want a way of paying for goods and services I should go to a bank; if I want some insurance I should go to an insurance company; if I want a mortgage I should go to a building society; if I want a loan I should go to a bank',

they now have the choice to buy financial services or accept different types of advice

from a range of institutions, with more services and prices. The clear lines between the various institutions have now gone forever. This unit provides the opportunity to better understand the complexities of the market for financial services both for individuals and for business activities.

Your evidence for this unit will be based on a scenario from OCR accompanied by a set of financial circumstances for your customer who is running their own business, either a new business or one that is looking to change direction.

You will research possible financial packages for your customer and decide which is the most appropriate package to meet the specific needs of your customer. You will then produce a financial package that includes material informed by your research which meets their needs on a personal and business level.

There are a number of activities throughout this unit to reinforce your learning.

7.2.1 Customers of financial services

Two of the most important factors that have changed the financial services sector beyond recognition have been the need to provide **customers** with more choice and financial institutions with more competition. Although the Financial Services Act of 1986 changed or deregulated the market for financial services by taking away many rules and regulations, it also imposed further regulations.

This changing consumer environment has seen:

* a developing awareness by **consumers** that they can go to several different kinds of institutions to buy products and services

* professional financial advisers helping consumers deal with fine distinctions between various services

* institutions trying to take advantage of all of the changing regulations and opportunities

* the use of **direct mail** and promotions targeted at different consumer needs

* new technology for financial services and products within the market-place.

The result is that there are now more institutions and services competing for both business and personal customers.

From an increasingly early age it is easy to realise that you need to become a customer of some form of financial institution. You may have been left some money or may simply want either to save some money or keep it in a safe place. You may want to transact electronically. All of these needs mark you as a potential personal customer for some kind of financial institution.

The purposes of financial institutions can only be achieved by attracting customers to their financial services and products. The problem is that even though such organisations depend upon their customers, customers now have significantly more choice than they used to in the past.

The lifestyles of many customers have changed significantly over the last 20 years. Today, people have more possessions, own their own homes, take holidays overseas and buy new cars. In many families, both partners are working with two incomes coming into their house. Alongside this rising standard of living, customers need to match their changing lifestyles with the sort of services they want from financial institutions.

Expectations have increased, and consumers have developed more financial needs to be satisfied. For example, few individuals are today paid in cash. We have also steadily moved towards a cashless society with the use of plastic cards dominating the way in which personal customers pay for their goods and services. Where cash is required many customers use cards in

Automatic Teller Machines (ATMs) to get cash out. More people own their own houses and so need mortgages and more people are also listening to financial advisers who may advise upon buying shares, pensions or other securities and financial products.

The result has been that customers are increasingly thinking about how to use financial services not just for today but also for the future. With direct mail bombardment as well as advertising, the average person on the street seems to know a lot about financial services and how those services might fit with the lifestyle and future needs they may have.

Direct mail → Targets householders → Reaches potential customers in their homes

To compete in this increasingly complex market-place, organisations have to use market research and their knowledge of customers to constantly adapt and fine tune their products for their customers. They need to understand consumer needs not just for today, but also what their needs are for the future and build products that meet such needs in an appropriate way.

So far we have been talking about the needs of personal customers, with the potential to reach nearly 60 million people across the United Kingdom. However, **personal customers** are not the only customers of banks. Businesses also need banking services. So, when we come to analyse different types of bank customers, we need to take into account the needs of both these types of customer.

CASE STUDY

Abbey attempts to increase its market focus

In 2003, as a result of market research, Abbey set about simplifying its products to provide a range of easy to understand products and services. This initiative followed on from Abbey's attempt at diversification into other financial products and markets that had resulted in substantial financial losses for the company, then trading as Abbey National plc. The most important change involved taking a new, critical look at this over-complex market.

Abbey uses a range of methods to communicate with its personal customers including:

* letters to all customers written in a simple, intelligible language
* new literature, cheque books and cards
* new advertising built around the theme 'turning banking on its head'.

Abbey has set out to transform banking practice by adopting a customer-led approach rather than a product-led approach. A key part of Abbey's strategy is to continue to research and develop new tangible products and services, which actively demonstrate its commitment to 'turn banking on its head'.

1 Why did Abbey use market research?
2 How did it try to communicate with its customers?
3 Why might an approach based upon understanding customer needs and being more customer-led improve how they operate?

The needs of personal customers

Personal customers form the largest group of customers for most high-street banks, building societies, independent financial consultants and insurance companies as well as most other financial institutions. These customers have a variety of needs including:

* social
* physical
* security
* long term and short term.

Social needs

When personal customers open an account or develop an arrangement with a financial institution they want access to their services. In fact not only do they want to access the money in their account, they also want all of the benefits of having an account that enables their use of finance within their lives to become easier. For example, in the modern world in which we live, people do not want to carry large amounts of money. They might not want to have to visit either their branch of a bank very often and want to have different ways of accessing their money. This means they want flexibility, for example, they want to have the convenience of accessing a range of services, get specialist advice when they need it and not have to go chasing to lots of different organisations in order to receive it. Flexibility enables individuals to be able to access services with the minimum of fuss, such as at ATMs, access to cash over the counter at supermarkets and services that enable them to shop either in this country or overseas but also to be able to consult the bank to meet more complex needs and requirements.

Physical needs

Financial institutions also provide us with physical needs throughout our lifetime. Personal customers develop a whole range of service requirements at various points in their lives. For example, as partners start to live together during their 20s or 30s or get married, they may want a mortgage on a property. The majority of people within the UK now live in owner-occupied houses. To protect their investment, they may invest in insurance in case anything happens to that property. They may want to sell their property when they move and may want to buy a larger property.

Physical needs may also include taking out life assurance in case anything happens to either partner and a pension plan designed to meet their physical and financial needs even further ahead in time.

Security needs

Personal customers want products that provide them with security. At the most basic level and, particularly as we move towards a more cashless society, they will not want to carry large sums of money either in their wallets or purses. Instead they will want a range of services, perhaps different forms of plastic cards which enable them to access their services in a safe and risk-free way. Personal customers want other forms of security as well. For example, when they invest in a house, they want the reassurance that if anything happens to it or to the belongings in it, that they will be compensated.

They may also want to make the most of any surplus money they have by being able to purchase risk-free or low-risk investments. Personal customers will also want to have some form of security involved with their investments. For example, unless they want to be speculators in stocks and shares, they may want advice from their bank upon how to invest their surplus cash more safely in some form of interest-bearing activity that gives them a good return on their investment.

Long term and short term

Most financial services can be classified either as long term or short term. For example, a short-term service may be a bank account that a customer has. The money might come into that account at the end of each month and the customer might take money out to pay for short-term needs such as food, clothing or paying for living expenses. Longer term needs provide the personal customer with a way in which they can deal with and prepare for the future. For example, buying a property is usually one of the biggest purchases that a personal customer will ever make. Financial institutions will provide the opportunity for customers to take out mortgages that enable them to do so. Similarly, many personal customers will want to prepare for old age and, as they do so, financial institutions may provide them with advice and help with personal pension arrangements.

The needs of business customers

Although there is another group of bank customers such as clubs/societies, churches, local authorities and charities, the other large group of bank customers is business organisations. Although there are not as many business customers as personal customers, they provide banks with a considerable amount of trade and one of the most profitable areas for banking activities.

There are three main types of business customers which you will have looked at throughout your course:

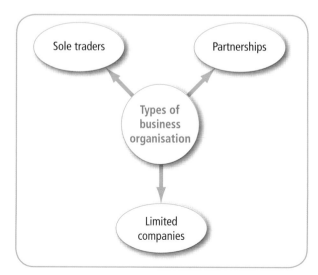

FIGURE 7.1 *Types of business organisation*

* *Sole traders* – These are generally very small locally-based businesses, run by a single owner and might include small retailers, farms, professional services and so on. The owner contributes most of the finance for the business, will take all of the risk and will receive all of the income and profit. There are few legal requirements for sole traders.

* *Partnerships* – Often when sole traders expand their business, they do this by taking on a partner. Partnerships are governed by the Partnership Act of 1890 which defines a partnership as 'the relation which subsists between persons carrying on business in common with a view to profit'. Partnerships may simply comprise two partners and are usually limited to 20 partners. There are many different types of partnerships, one of the most common is professional partnerships between dentists, doctors, estate agents and solicitors.

* *Limited companies* – As business organisations evolve their owners may want some form of limited liability. This means that the owners might want to protect their liability for debt within the company to the amount of shares they hold, enabling them to protect their personal assets. Limited companies are controlled by the various Companies Acts and are either private limited companies or public limited companies. Private limited companies allow the owners to raise capital through the issue of shares, although these cannot be advertised to the public. Public limited companies are usually very large business organisations. The public can buy shares in these companies on the London **Stock Exchange**.

Banks distinguish between personal customers and **business customers** as business organisations require different types of services because they have different needs, as shown below.

Start-up capital

When small businesses start up for the first time, owners need the funds to invest in new premises, equipment, motor vehicles etc. These are known as the fixed assets of the business. They will also

NatWest Special Offers

Look at the special offers NatWest is making for new businesses and answer the questions below:

'Special offers for start-ups and established businesses

We offer a range of special offers designed to help start-ups get started and to help established businesses get more out of their banking service. Our free Business Software is designed to help you think through business ideas, complete a business plan and run your business day to day.

Starting up in Business

With NatWest you can take advantage of a wide range of benefits and services to help you bank in the way that's right for you. These include:

* free banking for up to 18 months

* discounted account fees for a further 6 months

* choice of a local Business Manager or telephone-based business banking

* committed business overdraft

* NatWest business card

* business savings accounts

* free online guidance via our Starting up guide

* free businessline and NatWest online banking, our telephone and PC banking services

* free business review, whether you bank with NatWest or not.'

1 What is a start-up business?
2 How might a small business owner use the free business software?
3 Why do banks specially target small businesses?

Think it over...

The first **building society** is said to have been founded in Birmingham in 1775. The original societies were set up to help small groups of people invest in buying land upon which they could build houses for their members.

need stock and will have shorter term financial requirements that enable the business to be managed on a day-to-day basis. This will be its working capital.

Very few new business owners will have enough money to invest in everything that they need and so will have to produce some form of business plan that they can take to financial institutions who may be able to help them with their investment requirements. Starting up is a particularly important time for these businesses and it is essential that they have enough capital to meet their requirements as they start to trade. Financial institutions provide a variety of different ways in which they can provide assistance with the start-up needs of businesses. According to Gary Jones, author of *Starting Up*, (1998) 'one of the most common mistakes made by potential new businesses is getting wrong the total money/capital requirements for efficiently starting up and operating their new venture – you cannot afford to make such a mistake'.

Organic and external growth

As businesses grow their needs are constantly changing. Some businesses may grow organically. This means that as the business develops and its sales increase, it may need to invest in more plant and machinery or buy other premises to meet the needs of its customers. Clearly, to finance such growth they may want to go to their bank and access the provision of other services. For many businesses, the quickest and easiest form of growth is to buy another business. This form of external growth can be costly, but it does enable the organisation to expand very quickly.

Finance / day-to-day working capital

Managing a business organisation in a way that enables it to meet its short-term debts is particularly important. Businesses that cannot meet their short-term debts lack what is called 'liquidity' and may struggle to survive.

Banks provide a number of services that help businesses effectively manage their working capital. Working capital is the difference between a business's current assets and its current liabilities. Current assets include the cash that can be used to pay bills in the short term, near liquid money such as people who owe the business money (debtors) and all of the stocks that can be converted in the short term to cash. Current liabilities are creditors who send their bills to be paid. The difference between the current assets and current liabilities determines how quickly bills can be paid.

Current assets are either in the form of cash or items that could soon be turned into cash and current liabilities will soon have to be paid for with cash. It is said that a prudent ratio of current assets to current liabilities is 2:1, although most businesses operate with a lower ratio than this. A business that is not very good at managing its working capital will be unable to innovate, take advantage of credit facilities or buy in bulk. At the same time, their creditors may take action to ensure that payments are made upon time.

Overseas business

Businesses of all sizes are increasingly looking to international markets in order to develop business

FIGURE 7.2 *Cash and liabilities*

opportunities. At a very simple level, business owners might look for overseas travel services that enable them to go overseas and meet foreign customers. As they begin to undertake business transactions with overseas customers, they may want help with documentation for exporting products such as Bills of Lading and Waybills and they may also seek some form of payment system enabling the overseas customer to pay for products and services. It is very important that there is a secure way of paying for products overseas where buyers and sellers may have limited information about each other.

Financial requirements

Managing financial requirements is much more difficult for a business than it is for a personal customer. The account of most personal customers will simply have a large sum of money coming into the account at the end of a month, and then a gradual drip feed of money from that account during the month, until the receipt of income from the salary goes back into it. This is not the case for business customers who have a significantly less predictable movement of income and expenditure. In a business, amounts that come in and go out will depend upon investments and when customers are willing to pay. Sometimes businesses have to wait a considerable time for customers who have been sold goods on credit to make payments. As a result, business customers are much more likely than personal customers to need to access business services to provide support for their uncertain receipts and payments.

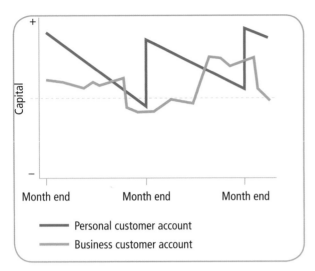

FIGURE 7.3 *Typical movement in the account of a personal and business customer*

Security needs

The customers of financial institutions will have a variety of security needs that have to be met. For example, retailers may need to transfer large sums of money or may want to make a deposit of money outside banking hours and need a secure way of doing this. They will want to insure the business to make sure that in the event of a burglary or some other shock event that the business is able to continue. They may also need advice with investments that are low risk. Businesses may also have important documents or valuables that they may not want to store on their premises and would like to have stored in a vault.

Access to funds

Most businesses, at various stages during their development, will want access to funds and for this access to be flexible and tailored to their needs. Financial institutions will provide a range of different ways of helping businesses to develop from business development loans for the expansion of a business to franchise finance that helps a business owner to purchase and run a franchise.

Support services

There are many different ways in which financial institutions tailor services to particular businesses. Different institutions will develop packages to meet the requirements of particular groups, such as farmers, or specialist professional partnerships including investment management, to help with cash flow, to support share dealing, for overseas requirements and so on.

Looking at all of the needs of both personal customers and business customers helps us to understand that in the rapidly changing market-place for financial services, it is essential for financial service organisations to understand the needs of their customers and provide services that meet these evolving needs if they are to be successful. The net effect is that the range of services provided by these types of organisations has increased dramatically in recent years as each attempts to develop and retain its market position.

7.2.2 Financial service providers and products

With the increased competition of recent years, there are now a huge range of different types of financial service providers making up a complicated network of financial institutions, most of which have slightly different functions and activities.

At a simple level it is important to remember that financial institutions are themselves business organisations and will make profits by charging interest to borrowers at a higher rate than they pay to their lenders.

As a result it is probably best and most appropriate to think of a financial service provider as an intermediary. A financial service provider is an organisation that borrows funds from lenders

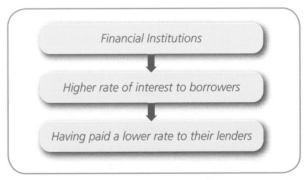

FIGURE 7.4 *The basic purpose of a financial service provider*

and then relends them to borrowers on terms which benefit the supplier and the receiver of those funds. In other words, all providers link borrowers and lenders (linking those who have surplus money and do not wish to spend it immediately with those who do not have surplus money and wish to borrow).

Financial providers have:

* access to deposits and so have an availability of funds for borrowers

* operate on a large scale

* minimise the risk of loss if the borrower does not repay the loan because they have large reserves and lend to many individuals and organisations.

Providers of financial services

Banks

In every high street of every town and city we see banks. There are different types of banks, but the banks that we instantly think of are the **retail banks** that we see in the high street such as NatWest, Lloyds TSB, Barclays, HSBC, Bank of Scotland and The Royal Bank of Scotland. The distinguishing feature of all of these banks is that they have large branch networks with an emphasis upon lending to individuals and business organisations. They are all large institutions and some notable mergers in recent

years have seen some of these become even larger. As a result of their large branch network these banks have always had a tradition of dealing face-to-face with large numbers of customers. These banks are associated with a huge number of services that broadly include:

* payments services

* deposit services

* lending facilities.

All of these services are focused upon individuals and businesses. Almost every retail bank offers a slightly different range of services each designed to meet the financial needs of their customers. For example, banks are the traditional providers of cheques as well as loans and savings facilities, but in today's more complex and competitive business environment, they now provide a whole host of new services for different groups of customers such as businesses, young people and students.

At the heart of the banking system is a very different bank, the **Bank of England**. Founded by Royal Charter from William III on 27 July 1694, its initial purpose was to finance a war against France. The Bank of England was nationalised under the 1946 Bank of England Act. The Bank of England does not deal with personal customers in the same way as retail banks:

* it is the sole issuer of English banknotes

* it is the banker to the main banks themselves

* it banks accounts for the government

* it lends money at short notice to the money markets

* it manages the gold and foreign currency reserves

* it influences monetary policy.

The Monetary Policy Committee of the Bank of England meets every month to set the base rate of interest for the economy in order to meet inflation targets.

Another form of bank that will have business customers is merchant banks. The main work of merchant banks includes direct lending both to large companies and governments and issuing of new shares and stocks on behalf of companies and local government.

If you walk around large city centres, as well as seeing retail banks you will very likely see foreign banks such as the Allied Irish Bank, Bank of China, National Bank of Dubai, The Bank of New York and the State Bank of India. Although originally located in the UK to cater for customers who have both business and private interests in Britain, they have increasingly developed a wider range of services for various groups of customers that have brought them into competition with other parts of the banking system.

Building societies

With 63 building societies in the UK and with total assets of over £240 billion, building societies are important providers of financial services. According to the Building Societies Association 'about 15 million adults have building society saving accounts and over two and a half million adults are currently buying their own homes with the help of building society loans. In recent years building societies have diversified and a number now offer, among other services, current accounts, credit cards, cash machines, travel money, unsecured loans, various types of insurance and estate agency services.' Today, building societies are the main competition for banks, providing a similar portfolio of products and services for personal customers.

The key distinction between a building society and a bank is based upon its ownership. Building societies are 'mutual organisations', whereas banks are public limited companies with shares listed on the London Stock Exchange. This

A high-street building society

effectively means that in building societies most people who have a savings account or a mortgage are members of the building society and have certain rights to vote and receive information as well as to attend and speak at meetings. Each member has one vote, regardless of how much money they have invested or borrowed or how many accounts they may have. Each building society has a board of directors who direct the affairs of the society and who are responsible for setting its strategy. As societies do not issue shares and do not have shareholders wanting dividends/ profits, they tend to run on a lower cost base and their services are very competitive in the market-place. Building societies are often related to the local area in which they started up such as the Darlington Building Society or the Cumberland Building Society, while other building societies cover the whole country such as the Nationwide or the Britannia Building Society.

In recent years there was a trend towards demutualisation, which saw some building societies change their ownership structure and become banks, such as the Woolwich, the Halifax and Abbey National.

> ### Key term
> **Stock Exchange** – main securities market for stocks and shares within the UK.

Insurance companies and insurance brokers

Insurance companies have always been a regular competitor for personal savings, traditionally by offering life insurance, which has been a major competitor for the savings of personal customers. At the same time insurance companies have traditionally offered insurance for:

* property
* motor vehicles
* personal accident and sickness
* transport
* marine and aviation.

Perhaps the most famous name in insurance is Lloyd's of London. The origins come from a

CASE STUDY

The Association of British Insurers
According to the ABI,

'Although many types of insurance seem complicated, the basic principles are straightforward. Insurance companies assess the risk of any eventuality and the potential downside associated with it. Then, based on past experience and their own expertise, insurance companies calculate the "premium" that a customer needs to pay to provide "cover" against injury or loss. When the insured event happens, the company pays out the agreed level of "claim".

Overall, the total premiums must cover the total claims which may need to be paid out. To help ensure that costs are kept as low as possible, and that customers' needs are met, insurance companies also invest in the stock market and elsewhere.

The main types of insurance are:

* general insurance
* life and pensions
* health and protection.'

General insurance

'General insurance plays a vital role in the modern economy. It lets individuals and businesses minimise the impact of unexpected and unwelcome future events and helps them organise their lives and businesses with greater certainty. The insurance industry pays out £74 million per working day in general insurance claims.'

For example, general insurance would include motor insurance as well as household contents insurance.

Life and pensions

'Life insurers offer valuable financial protection in the event of your early death if members of your family are dependent on your earnings, as well as a variety of ways of saving for the future. The industry pays out almost £222 million per working day in pension and life insurance claims.'

Pensions are a way in which individuals can invest in life after work. Life assurance can provide a family with security if the main income earner has an early death.

Health and protection

'The insurance industry offers peace of mind by providing ways of paying for private medical care for curable or short-term illness or injury. It also enables you to plan for old age and to protect your financial assets, but still pay for appropriate levels of care. There is a range of policies designed to provide a monthly income if you are unable to work due to sickness, accident or injury, until you are able to re-join the workforce.'

Many people today invest in their future by taking out health insurance, to ensure that they have access to private medical care if the need arises.

1 What is an insurance premium?
2 Why might an insurance premium differ between one customer and another?
3 Where do insurance companies invest?
4 How might insurance companies compete with banks?

---

meeting place in London where wealthy individuals would sign their names under each other at the bottom of an insurance contact, together with the amount of risk they would accept, so that each became an underwriter. Today, Lloyd's is a unique institution, providing a market place for those seeking to insure large amounts underwritten by syndicates.

In recent years, competition between other financial service providers and insurance companies has intensified and there has been considerable overlap in activities. For example, a number of assurance companies have bought chains of estate agents and entered the markets for mortgages.

Within the insurance market there is a clear division between retailing and wholesaling. Some insurance companies simply specialise in the wholesale area of the market and these tend to include life assurance companies. Other organisations and individuals, such as insurance brokers and personal financial advisers are the final retailers of the products to the end customer. One recent development has been the use of call centres by organisations to sell products such as life assurance and mortgages to the public.

Credit agencies

When providing their customers with credit, organisations need to take reasonable care to ensure that their customers can meet the payments and financial commitments placed upon them. In order to do this they may attempt to gain a status report from a credit agency. The agency will provide full customer details, financial results, payment experience of other suppliers, county court judgments, registered lending, etc. and a recommended credit rating.

Financial service providers might from time to time ask their customers for a 'status enquiry'. The purpose of the enquiry is to find out whether customers can meet their financial commitment.

Finance houses and factoring

These are lending organisations such as Lombard North Central and Mercantile Credit that have become known for small-scale lending on consumer goods and also for loans for business organisations. Rather than attract funds from the general public in the form of accounts, finance houses raise money on the wholesale finance market where funds are placed with them from around three to six months.

Finance houses will offer:

* unsecured loans from one to five years for personal customers. Finance houses are generally prepared to take greater risks than banks and this is reflected in the higher rates of interest charged for loans.

* secured loans on properties

* **hire purchase** whereby items are bought by instalments, with the goods belonging to the lending institution until they are fully paid for

* **leasing** in which the lending organisation retains ownership of the item, receives payments over a period such as two years and then takes back the item and sells it on to recoup the costs

* **factoring** where the finance house will manage a business's invoices and debtors and collect and retain the money owed to a business. Effectively the factor, the finance house, will buy the book debts of the business. They may pay 80 per cent of the value of what is owed to the business so that the business can have the money straight away. They help the business to deal with all of its short-term financial commitments. The finance house is not doing this for nothing. The cost of factoring varies and will depend upon the sales of the organisation, but will usually be between 1 per cent and 5 per cent of turnover.

Think it over…

ProShare (www.proshare,org) is now owned by the Institute of Financial Services (ifs), a leading UK based provider of financial education. As a school of finance, the ifs provides for the formal learning needs of consumers and those employed within the industry, both in the UK and in key markets worldwide.

Stockbrokers

Many investors want to buy and sell securities on the London Stock Exchange. **Stockbrokers** can be found in all cities and many towns across the UK. Stocks and shares are the main way in which public limited companies raise capital. A share is a part of a company's issued capital. Investors will hold a number of shares and receive dividends from the distributed profits to which they are entitled. As well as receiving dividends, the value of shares might change due to influences on the stock market, so the value of stock constantly fluctuates.

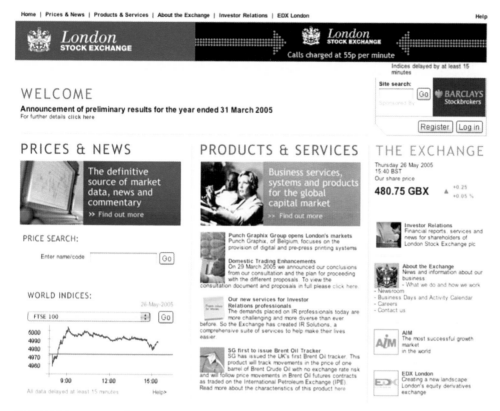

WELCOME

Announcement of preliminary results for the year ended 31 March 2005
For further details click here

Site search: [Go] BARCLAYS Stockbrokers
Sponsored By

[Register] [Log in]

PRICES & NEWS

The definitive source of market data, news and commentary
>> Find out more

PRICE SEARCH:

Enter name/code [   ] [Go]

WORLD INDICES:
26-May-2005
FTSE 100 [ ] [Go]
5000
4990
4980
4970
4960
9:00   12:00   15:00
All data delayed at least 15 minutes   Help>

PRODUCTS & SERVICES

Business services, systems and products for the global capital market
>> Find out more

Punch Graphix Group opens London's markets
Punch Graphix, of Belgium, focuses on the provision of digital and pre-press printing systems

Domestic Trading Enhancements
On 29 March 2005 we announced our conclusions from our consultation and the plan for proceeding with the different proposals. To view the consultation document and proposals in full please click here.

Our new services for Investor Relations professionals
The demands placed on IR professionals today are more challenging and more diverse than ever before. So the Exchange has created IR Solutions, a comprehensive suite of services to help make their lives easier

SG first to issue Brent Oil Tracker
SG has issued the UK's first Brent Oil tracker. This product will track movements in the price of one barrel of Brent Crude Oil with no exchange rate risk and will follow price movements in Brent Oil futures contracts as traded on the International Petroleum Exchange (IPE). Read more about the characteristics of this product here

THE EXCHANGE

Thursday 26 May 2005
15:40 BST
Our share price

480.75 GBX ▲ +0.25
+0.05 %

Investor Relations
Financial reports, services and news for shareholders of London Stock Exchange plc

About the Exchange
News and information about our business
- What we do and how we work
- Newsroom
- Business Days and Activity Calendar
- Careers
- Contact us

AIM
The most successful growth market in the world

EDX London
Creating a new landscape London's equity derivatives exchange

FIGURE 7.5 *A page from the London Stock Exchange website*

Many of the other financial service providers will have some form of share-dealing activity or department which they might offer to their customers.

Independent financial consultants

Just about every town will have an office of independent financial advisers (IFAs). They are not linked to any insurance company, unit trust company, financial service provider or other product provider and are considered to be 'independent'. As a result, they are able to look at an overview of the whole market for financial services in order to tailor the most suitable products and services for customers.

IFAs vary considerably in size from self-employed individuals to large companies. Many of the smaller self-employed IFAs join together with others in order to provide training and other facilities, so that they can satisfy the strict regulatory requirements for providing independent financial advice.

> **CASE STUDY**
>
> **The Association of Independent Financial Advisers**
>
> The Association of Independent Financial Advisers includes 70 per cent of IFAs within the UK. The AIFA's role is to:
>
> * ensure that IFAs have their views properly represented to the government and regulatory authorities
> * supply members with regular information and relevant publications
> * provide a forum where IFAs can share views
> * get specialist advice on matters such as compliance, training and regulations.
>
> 1 Why might an IFA want to join the AIFA?
> 2 Could joining such a professional association influence the independence of their advice?

Retail outlets

Money shops were set up in the early 1970s and are more usually located in high streets and open during normal retailing hours. Many of these were set up by American banks seeking to get into the UK high street by offering a simple and approachable way for individuals to bank. Most money shops offered a basic range of banking services often meeting needs in different ways, within comfortable and informal offices and were able to appeal to a range of private individuals. They were simply an alternative method to banking. These shops have been trying to win a place in the market and making banking easy for their customers.

Today, even some of the supermarkets provide financial services. For example, Tesco now offer loans, credit cards, mortgages, travel money, savings products and a variety of different forms of insurance.

Financial companies

The term 'financial companies' is used to describe joint stock companies that provide a broad range of financial products and services for their customers financial needs. Each of these companies provides a different range of services that may include almost anything from helping customers invest their money, supporting investments in property to providing services relating to events within people's lives such as funding private education, wealth management and retirement planning.

Financial service products

Deposit accounts

Deposit accounts seem to have been retitled 'savings accounts' by most financial service providers, who seem focused upon providing a range of opportunities for individuals to use such accounts for the purpose of saving. So, if you look at various websites, although you may not find anything called deposit accounts they still exist under a different guise, such as Barclays 'Reward Saver Account'. They can be opened with as little as £1, give instant access to a customer's money, and reward customers who make fewer withdrawals with better interest rates. Different groups of customers save for different reasons, so what banks have essentially done is to divide up the market for deposit accounts, replacing the name 'deposit' with something that sounds attractive for each group of savers and then provide a range of benefits or services attached to each type of account related to the needs of the users.

FIGURE 7.6 *A page from the financial part of Tesco's website*

Although each deposit or saver account will differ a little, their features tend to be as follows:

* passbook/paying-in book to provide a personal record of transactions

* customers can invest either large or small amounts into their account (most bank tellers will provide customers with advice on which is the best account for them, and it is usual for many customers to change the sort of account they have according to the options available from the bank and their changing circumstances and needs for different services)

* unlimited age range allowing the services to be used by young and old alike

* the payment of interest either half-yearly or annually

* access to funds, depending upon the account, at a variety of levels such as instant or seven days notice. Different types of deposit account might include:

    a) regular savers accounts with higher rates of interest for those who save fixed amounts every month

    b) higher rate deposit accounts to cater for customers who retain a large amount over a minimum period within a deposit account

    c) term deposit accounts with higher rates of interest over a particular period such as six months or a year, with restricted access to the deposit

    d) young savers accounts, providing young people with the opportunity to save with the bank, receive interest and also a range of basic banking services.

Theory into practice

Although you may not have a bank account, discuss how you save and plan your income and expenditures. How could a financial service provider help you with this process?

Current accounts

Current accounts are the accounts that provide the user with cheques as well as a vast range of other services offered by the financial service provider, some of which will be discussed shortly. Again these may vary between institutions both by range and type of service, but a current account provides the user with instant access to their money.

A cheque is an unconditional order in writing drawn on a banker and signed by the drawer, requiring the banker to pay on demand a certain sum of money to the order of the named person known as a bearer. A cheque:

* is unconditional – payment will not depend upon certain conditions being met

* must be in writing using a pen or biro

* must be signed by the drawer, the person paying the money

* will be paid when it is presented to a bank

* must state an amount in words and figures

* must be payable to somebody.

It is usual for a current account holder to also have a card, traditionally known as a cheque guarantee card. These cards greatly increase the use of and flexibility of a current account. For example, cards may be used to guarantee cheques

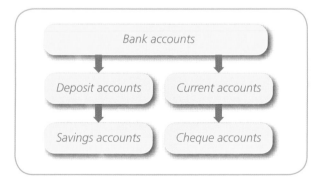

FIGURE 7.7 *Saver accounts*

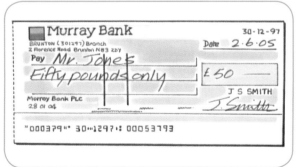

FIGURE 7.8 *A sample cheque*

Cash convenience on the high street

up to a specified amount such as £250. Most retailers will not accept cheques without a card number on the back.

These cards also act as debit cards. This means that the card rather than the cheque can be used to buy goods and services. The customer gives the card to the seller who swipes the card through an electronic funds transfer terminal (EFTPOS); the customer types in their personal identification number (PIN) and the transaction is complete.

These cards may also be used at ATMs and also for getting cash-back alongside purchases at retailers such as supermarkets.

Overdrafts

Managing finances is not easy and it is quite possible for a personal customer to have an unexpected expenditure in any one month. One of the easy ways of meeting such an expenditure is to take out an **overdraft**. An overdraft is when a customer takes money from a current account that is not in the account, leaving them overdrawn. An overdraft may be set up for a small charge and interest charges are applied to the amounts overdrawn for the period of the overdraft. Some student accounts have an overdraft facility attached which may incur only a small charge or there may not be a charge.

It is usual for customers to arrange an overdraft limit with their bank and it is considered to be a flexible form of borrowing as many accounts may swing from being in credit to debit and back again. Overdrafts are, however,

repayable on demand and should really only be used to meet a short-term cash shortfall.

Loans and mortgages

Broadly speaking, there are two sorts of loans provided by financial services organisations:

* personal loans
* business loans.

Personal loans

Personal loans were originally introduced by the banks but are now also provided by organisations such as building societies. Customers often want to purchase new cars or go on a holiday and find it difficult to save up for such an expense. A personal loan is a good way of buying the goods or receiving the service now and paying for them over a period of time. Personal loans generally have the following features. They tend to:

* be unsecured
* have a fixed rate of interest calculated upon the original loan
* be paid back in equal instalments
* be offered with life insurance
* have an extra charge for sickness or unemployment insurance.

All loan agreements must show details of the total charges. This should include the total amount of the loan, the charge for credit, the total amount of repayment, the monthly payments and the Annual Percentage Rate (APR).

Business loans

Business loans provide a particularly important source of business for financial service providers. Banks will lend both small and large amounts to a whole variety of different types of organisations from sole traders through to public limited companies. These loans may be to buy property, machinery, other businesses or may simply be for research and development.

Mortgages

Traditionally, providing **mortgages** has been the role of the building society. This has changed in recent years as there is now competition by a whole range of financial service providers to sell mortgages. Mortgages are long-term loans secured upon properties that enable those who want to become property owners to buy the homes in which they want to live. They may vary from just a few thousand pounds to hundreds of thousands of pounds and may last for up to 25 or 30 years. A mortgage repayment scheme would depend upon the age of the property, the income of the borrowers and the length of the repayment period. The amount that a bank will advance to customers may vary, but may be 90 per cent or even the full amount of the purchase price. There are a number of different types of mortgage:

* *Repayment mortgages* – the customer pays off interest and capital so that at the end of the term the mortgage is cleared.

* *Endowment mortgages* use an endowment policy to provide life insurance and save funds to repay the loan at the end of the term (usually 20–25 years). If the investment performs badly, a customer could face a shortfall at the end of the mortgage period.

* *Individual Savings Account (ISA) mortgages* work on the same principle as endowments, but use an Individual Savings Account as the loan repayment method. Again if the investment performs badly, customers could face a shortfall at the end of the period.

* *Pension mortgages* work on the basis that pensions (both private and company) provide tax-free cash on retirement. At the end of the mortgage term the loan is paid out of a tax-free lump sum.

Savings facilities

If we do not spend all of our income upon goods and services, we may want to save what is left over. People save for a number of reasons. For example, they may be saving for a holiday or for the family. Given the rapidly changing and increasingly more financially stringent market for students, many individuals save so that they can afford for their children to go through higher education. Some people also save because they feel that having saved money they have become wealthy.

CASE STUDY

The 10 key points for home buyers

A number of experts in the field have suggested that homebuyers should ask the following ten questions when deciding whether or not to take out a mortgage:

1 How much can I afford to borrow? This deals with such questions as 'what will the cost be each month?' and 'what fees will I have to pay?

2 How can I tell which mortgage rate is best for me?

3 What is the best type of mortgage for me? This deals with how to understand the jargon, such as 'what do fixed rate, variable rate, discounted or low-start, and flexible mean?' and 'will this mortgage suit my circumstances now and in the future?'

4 How should I repay it? 'Why are you trying to sell me an endowment policy or a pension or an ISA?', 'why is it best for my circumstances?' and 'what commission are you being paid?'

5 Can I make lump-sum payments to reduce the size of the loan?

6 Are there any redemption penalties?

7 Does this mortgage come with compulsory insurance?

8 What other charges will I have to pay?

9 What happens if I can't pay?

10 What about the small print?'

1 In a crowded market-place for financial products, why might mortgage customers need advice?

2 How might this advice help mortgage customers?

3 Look on the Internet for details of mortgages from at least one financial service provider. What does this website help you to find out?

As we saw when we looked at deposit accounts, banks and other financial service providers offer a range of opportunities for individuals to save depending upon their particular needs. Such services depend upon:

* access to funds
* the amount they wish to save
* the rate of interest they wish to access
* their age and time of life.

Credit cards

Credit cards are separate from a bank account. Holders of credit cards, such as a MasterCard, are given a credit limit on their credit card account, for example for £5,000. Goods or services can then be bought at any retail outlet that displays the credit card stickers and most retailers will accept most types of credit card. The customer signs a copy of a receipt or enters their number in the chip and pin machine and is given a receipt for the purchase.

Every month the cardholder receives a statement from the credit card company outlining the month's purchases, together with the total amount outstanding. The customer does not have to pay this amount but may simply pay the minimum amount that needs to be paid. In other words, they can pay the full amount or spread the payments over a number of months. Where the full balance is not settled, the customer is charged interest on outstanding balances and this provides the credit card company with a source of income. The companies also receive a source of income from retailers who make use of the cards.

Insurance

Most financial service providers give their customers access to insurance facilities of one kind or another. They do this either through their own insurance subsidiaries or through traditional insurance companies, with discounts for their customers. Insurance can be either Life insurance or **General insurance**.

Life insurance, as we have seen, may be offered with personal loans or with mortgages. However cover may also be offered for illness, accidents and unemployment. There are also a number of other plans such as assurances that offer a fixed amount either in the event of death or at the end of a fixed term, and these can be used as a form of savings plan.

General insurance covers a wide range of needs and risks such as:

* house insurance, covering any damage to a house
* contents insurance, insuring the contents against fire, theft or flooding
* car insurance, from third party to fully comprehensive
* travel insurance, providing medical cover as well as cover for cancellations and loss of luggage.

It is not only individuals that require insurance (known as personal insurance). As well as investing in general insurance policies such as for vehicles and property, business organisations also require insurance such as:

Employer's Liability Insurance

This covers employees who are involved in an accident, disease or injury caused or made worse as a result of work, maybe because of employer negligence. This insurance does not automatically cover volunteers and there is no obligation to do so, but it is good practice to extend the policy to cover them.

Public Liability Insurance

This protects the organisation for claims by members of the public for death, illness, loss, injury, or accident caused by the organisation's negligence. This covers both employees and the public who use the organisation.

'The UK insurance industry:

* is the largest in Europe

* is the third largest in the world

* employs 348,000 people, a third of all financial services jobs

* accounts for 17% of stock market investment

* pays out £222 million per working day in pension and life insurance benefits and £74 million per working day in general insurance claims.

772 insurance companies are authorised, by the UK or by an European Economic Area member, to carry on insurance business in the UK.

568 of these can carry on general business only (such as motor, household and commercial insurance), 159 are authorised for long-term business only (such as life insurance and pensions) and 45 are composites (can do both).'

Source: Association of British Insurers

Professional Liability Insurance

This covers the organisation for claims arising from loss or injury caused by services provided by the business negligently or without reasonable care.

Pensions and investments

Pension funds have grown enormously over the last 50 years. Pension funds provide employees with an income when they retire. They receive payments from both employees and employers and then invest them on their behalf, eventually paying pensions to employees upon retirement. It is hoped that the investments in the securities market are successful in providing surplus funds to meet the current and potential retirement needs of employees and past-employees. Sadly, in recent years this has not been the case. Many pension funds have not had sufficient return upon their investment to cater for such needs and with people living longer, this has meant that many employees are having to rethink retirement dates or think about how to cope with a smaller

CASE STUDY

Working until we are 70

Workers may have to work until they are 70 to help solve the looming pension crisis, the Organisation for Economic Co-operation and Development has said. Improved life expectancy is stretching pension funds and systems. By 2050 it is anticipated that the number of workers for each pensioner will have fallen from four to just two. Systems in Spain, France, Germany and Italy could all face significant shortfalls by 2050 partly due to a dramatic fall in fertility, especially in southern Europe, where the average woman only has 1.3 children, far below the replacement rate of 2.1. That means that there will be even fewer workers in the future to pay for pensions.

1 What does this indicate about the main cause of the pensions crisis?
2 How is this likely to change the working lives of those currently in work?
3 Are there alternative solutions to solve this crisis?

Working longer to cover pension shortfall

pension. Pension funds may be managed by a financial service provider.

International facilities

Financial service providers tailor a range of services both for personal and business customers. Individuals can use both their cheques and cards overseas as well as their credit cards. They can also obtain traveller's cheques, foreign currency

CASE STUDY

Charity Commission for England and Wales

The Charity Commission for England and Wales provides the following advice for charities on electronic banking.

1 What is electronic banking?
'The term "electronic banking" or "ebanking" covers both computer and telephone banking. Using computer banking, a charity's computer either dials directly into its bank's computer or gains access to the bank's computer over the Internet. Using telephone banking, the charity controls its bank accounts by giving the bank instructions over the telephone. Both computer and telephone banking involve the use of passwords which give access to the charity's accounts.

Using these methods, banking transactions can be actioned 24 hours a day. Computer banking allows a charity, for instance, to view recent transactions, print out statements and transfer funds between accounts and make payments. Many banks also have the facility for a charity to set up, amend or cancel standing orders. Electronic banking also allows payments to be made to the charity, i.e. acceptance of credit card donations. Most charities that use electronic banking will also continue to use some of the elements of more traditional methods of banking, such as a chequebook.

Electronic banking services differ between the different banks and building societies. If trustees decide that they want to use electronic banking then they should shop around for the most suitable package for their charity.

2 What is the Charity Commission's view about electronic banking for charities?
'With changing bank technology more and more charities are likely to consider moving away from paper-based banking methods; many charities have already done so. Broadly speaking our view is that the trustees of a charity will be justified in deciding to use electronic banking if:

* they can identify overall advantages for the charity in doing so
* they put in place adequate financial controls
* they have, or can acquire, the necessary legal power.

It is important that any decision to adopt electronic banking be made with the benefits and advantages to the charity in mind. It is not right to move to electronic banking just because it seems fashionable or because the charity's bank wants it to change (the motive for this might be to help the bank to reduce its own costs, rather than to provide a better service for the charity).'

3 What are the advantages of electronic banking?

'* For trustees who give their own time to charities it means that they can carry out charity banking out of working hours in the evenings and at weekends. Trustees are able to carry out transactions 24 hours a day, 7 days a week and will no longer be restricted to bank opening hours.
* Trustees can instantly see what is happening with the charity's money rather than waiting for statements to be sent.
* There is no time spent queuing or journey time to travel to and from the bank for trustees or employees of the charity.'

1 What is electronic banking and how does it differ from other forms of banking?
2 Why might charities adopt it?

and travel insurance from their financial service provider. This is a clear example that instead of visiting several different organisations or companies before going overseas, an individual only has to visit one.

For businesses overseas, services are significantly more complex as they often involve foreign trade and payments facilities. Financial service providers may have branches overseas or work with other organisations in other countries. Banks will handle all of the overseas documentation an exporter might need such as for shipping and transport. There are also many different ways in which they help with payment facilities.

Factoring

Many financial service providers have a factoring service. Imagine that a business has a liquidity or cash flow problem and needs to pay some creditors, people to whom they owe money, quickly. They are owed money and have many debtors, people who owe money to them, but are having to wait to get payment themselves. They can go to a factoring agent or company. This company simply buys their book debts. For example, they may pay for 80 per cent of the debts and advance the business the value of the debts to be collected.

Banking facilities

The range of facilities provided by financial organisations today is vast and will vary from business to business. Although these businesses may be called 'one-stop financial-supermarkets' for financial services, each one uses its marketing activities and knowledge of the market to tailor specialised products to its customers in order to try and lead the market in a particular way. As well as all the facilities already mentioned, banking facilities may also include:

* storage of money, deposits and valuables for safekeeping

* money transfer, which involves the encashment of cheques for their own customers as well as the transfer of funds from their own customers' accounts to accounts in other branches, banks

and other providers. This may involve payments through 'standing orders' – customers authorise the bank to make payment of these fixed amounts on regular dates, and 'direct debits' – where the customer authorises a third party to take money out of their account, with the amounts and dates varying according to the needs of the third party

* acceptance of deposits from customers

* providing savers with a rate of return

* a range of accounts and associated services

* loans and other advances

* insurance

* share dealing and investment management

* night safes

* executor and trustee service where the financial service provider has a department in which staff are experts in wills and the administration of estates following the death of a customer

* investment management.

With greater emphasis upon electronic banking, many services today have been complemented by using the Internet to provide some form of home banking or other facilities.

Most of the above services will be available to both business and personal customers. Clearly it is businesses and not personal customers that will make more use of night safe facilities, factoring and many of the international services.

> **Think it over...**
>
> Barclays has over 20 million customers and employs more than 78,400 people worldwide.

Sources of business finance

Running a business and keeping it solvent is not easy. A business organisation needs to constantly monitor its financial needs for the short, medium and long term in order to make sure that it is able on the one hand to meet its debts and pay bills and on the other to plan ahead through processes of investment. To be able to do this they need to

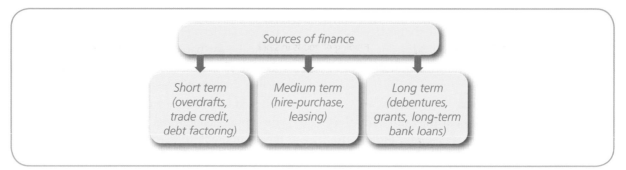

FIGURE 7.9 *Sources of finance*

think about and review all of the sources of finance that are available for them.

Short term

Working capital is the difference between current assets and current liabilities. Current assets are either in the form of cash or items that can be turned into cash and current liabilities will soon have to be paid for with cash. Working capital is often considered to be the portion of capital that 'oils the wheels' of business. The dangers to a business organisation of insufficient working capital are:

* a business with limited working capital will not be able to buy in bulk and could lose the opportunity to gain trade discounts

* cash discounts will be lost as the business will avoid paying creditors until the very last possible opportunity

* it will become more difficult to offer credit facilities to customers and by shortening the credit period, customers may go to alternative suppliers

* the business is unable to innovate

* the financial reputation of the business as a good payer might be lost

* creditors may take action – as cash becomes squeezed a business may be put in a position where it has to finance its short-term activities by overdraft, trade credit and debt factoring. This might mean that its future is dependent upon the actions of creditors

* overtrading can take place which means that the business is expanding and developing and taking on new contracts but has not got the

short term funds to finance and develop such business opportunities.

Overdrafts

Overdrafts are probably the most flexible form of borrowing that can be used in the short term to meet a range of debts. The bank provides a limit allowing the customer to draw up to that limit and this allows bank accounts to move from being in credit to debit and back again as the customer manages how much they want to borrow within this prescribed limit. An account in credit would have money in it while an account in debit would be overdrawn. The overdraft takes into account the uncertain business environment in which many organisations exist, allowing for the different timings of money coming in and going out.

Trade credit

By far the majority of business organisations both buy and sell their products through a process known as **trade credit**. For example, a business might buy goods and when they receive them they will get an invoice. By paying the invoice 30 days after its receipt they have gained a credit period. Similarly, they may sell goods, providing their customer with a similar amount of credit and then have to wait for that customer to pay them. This is sometimes known as the 'operating cycle'. It can be measured by looking at the time period between:

* the purchase of raw materials and the receipt of cash from debtors

* the time cash is paid out for raw materials and the time cash is received from sales.

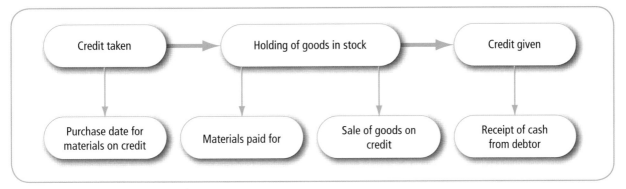

FIGURE 7.10 *The operating cycle*

For example:

A business buys raw materials on two months' credit and holds them in stock for half a month before issuing them to a production department from which they come as finished goods. These are then held on average for one and a half months before sale. Debtors take three months to pay. The operating cycle would be:

	Months
Raw materials credit from suppliers	(2.0)
Turnover of stock of raw materials	0.5
Turnover of stock of finished goods	1.5
Debtors' payment period	3.0
Operating cycle	3.0 months

A critical form of short-term finance for a business must come from managing this cycle efficiently. So, by reducing the period between the time cash is paid out for raw materials and the time cash is received from sales will provide funds that will help an organisation to meet its working capital requirements. The real problem with this is that it could be unpopular with creditors and it may well affect future sales.

Debt factoring

Debt factoring is also a way to reduce problems in the short term of having to meet debts. A factoring service will advance up to 80 per cent of the value of credit sales as they are made, which enables a business to settle many of their short-term financial problems. The factor will charge as little as 1 per cent to 5 per cent of the sales turnover for this service. Some factors will not only do this but will also be prepared to manage the administration and control of debtors on behalf of a business arising from credit sales.

Medium term

In the medium term a business will have more time to look at and review its asset structure to make sure that it is resourcing the business properly and will look for new and different ways in which to source finance. Imagine that a business wants to replace its machinery and equipment or the fleet of vehicles it has is ageing rapidly.

One way of meeting such medium-term requirements is through hire purchase. With hire purchase, monthly payments are made for the hire of an asset, which then becomes the property of the customer after the final payment. The benefits of using hire purchase in the medium term are that:

* short-term methods of finance such as overdrafts and trade credit are not strained

* it is easy for the organisation to budget as the hire purchase agreement depends upon equal instalments

* contracts are simple, easy to set up and flexible.

Rather than enter hire-purchase agreements and 'purchase' machinery and equipment for their use, many organisations enter into leasing and this method of meeting requirements has become increasingly popular in recent years. A lease simply involves paying a 'rent' to the owner of equipment for the use of that equipment. There are two types of leases. An operating lease is where the supplier of equipment or goods not only provides the goods but also agrees to service and repair them. A popular area for this sort of lease is for photocopying equipment. Finance leases are where the leasing company buys the equipment and remains the owner, but passes the equipment on to the lessee to use. The great advantage of leasing is that it does not use up liquid assets and there are no issues of ownership. Contracts can be tailor-made for a business's own requirements. The benefits of leasing are:

* it enables a business to have complete use of an asset without having to use risk or loan capital to finance it

* leasing payments are an expense charged to the profit and loss account before tax is assessed.

Long term

Sources of finance in the long term may involve substantial investment in a business organisation over an extended time period. It is very important that such long-term investments are carefully judged as the repayments or financing of such sources will have a considerable impact upon a business's costing structure for some time to come.

In any term or period of time there is a strong relationship between risk and interest rates. For example, longer term bank loans are higher risk as are small businesses and so both of these tend to have to pay higher rates of interest for services.

Financial services providers call loans advances and are willing to 'advance' a loan to businesses for a variety of different purposes. Before doing this they have to assess the risk. The principles of lending are usually represented by the mnemonic IPARTS. This is as follows:

I   Integrity – the integrity of the customer will generally determine whether the loan will be paid back or not.

P   Purpose – the provider will want to know what the loan is to be used for.

A   Amount – they will want to know that the customer has the right amount.

R   Repayment – the customer must be able to meet the repayment schedule.

T   Term – the longer the loan the greater the interest payments.

S   Security - most loans are unsecured. The American term for security is 'collateral'. Wherever possible collateral helps to reduce the risks for the financial services provider.

Theory into practice

Work in pairs. The first person must think of a purpose for a large loan for a business idea of their choice. The second person is going to act as a financial services provider who will interview the first person and so will need to construct a series of questions. Carry out a simulation with the first person being interviewed by the financial services provider. Assess in what instances they would provide funds for business ideas.

There are a number of different options for business organisations. *Mortgages* are long-term loans secured on a property as we saw earlier in this chapter. There is also a variety of different types of business loans available.

Debentures

Another form of lending available to large quoted companies on the Stock Exchange is a **debenture.** A debenture is an acknowledgement of a debt made to a company for a fixed rate of interest and which specifies the terms of repayment at the end of a period. It is a form of loan which is bought as a security on the stock market and is a loan because the buyer is then lending money to a business for owning that security. In the same way as stocks and shares, a debenture may be bought and sold. A debenture holder is not a company member or shareholder but a creditor. This means that interest payments are an expense to the company and are allowable against profits for corporation-tax purposes. Therefore, it can be cheaper to finance a company with debentures rather than to issue shares.

Grants

Depending upon the nature of the business and the area or market it services, there is a range of grants from different institutions and bodies that can be used as a key source of finance and these change frequently. There is a multitude of grants and schemes, and for many businesses it is useful to contact their local enterprise agency in order to find out more. The government is keen to develop inner-city areas suffering from industrial dereliction as well as to focus upon rural areas or areas which have high rates of unemployment. Where businesses create employment they may be eligible for grants, and grants and schemes may relate to particular groups of the population such as the socially disadvantaged. The key areas of government support include:

* research, development and innovation
* training and skills development
* the New Deal to back people in work
* best practice improvements
* businesses that stimulate people back into work, urban regeneration and or regional development
* young entrepreneurs.

The Prince's Trust is a major backer of young entrepreneurs

7.2.3 Research into the financial services market

The financial services are extremely important to the UK economy. As a result, they have always been heavily regulated by government. There are a number of reasons for this. It has always been necessary for regulation to:

* focus upon the degree and nature of competition within the market for financial services
* protect consumers of financial services
* encourage investors to enter the market for financial services
* ensure that financial institutions had the capital and resources to meet all of their commitments within this market
* preserve the reputation and development of this very important market.

Theory into practice

Working in a group, imagine that you are coming towards the end of your working lives and have a large lump sum to invest. What would be your aims for your investment? Discuss your fears. Think about the alternatives available to you to invest this large lump sum.

The market for financial services depends largely upon confidence. The biggest worry for all of the organisations within this market is that of **contagion**.

Contagion is where the collapse of one institution leads to debts within the financial services market which then causes some loss of confidence in other financial institutions which leads to their collapse as well. This loss of confidence for the banking sector as a whole is a real fear.

Another key feature of the financial services environment is the need to protect consumers of banking and financial products. It is important that as many people as possible contribute to the financial services environment, attracting lots of savers and investors. Many people who buy products from the financial services sector have little knowledge of the products that they are buying and yet may invest their life savings. It is important to ensure that they are not exploited by the market as well as by profiteers with little interest in the rights of consumers and so they need some form of protection.

The final key concern within the market is that financial intermediaries can meet their liabilities. A strong argument for controlling the market is to ensure that banks meet their commitments to their customers as well as to prevent financial intermediaries failing.

Recent changes and developments

Financial regulation within the UK has gone through significant change over the last 20 years.

Competition

Competition involves organisations that are looking to compete for the same customers in the same market. Before the government decided to regulate financial markets in the 1980s, in some markets there were few competitors. The aim of the government was to deregulate the financial markets. This meant that they aimed to allow other types of organisations such as insurance companies to compete in markets traditionally catered for by banks and also banks to compete in the insurance markets by providing insurance services. This increase in competition allowed organisations to diversify (to do something else and broaden their services away from traditional areas such as banking to provide other services in other financial markets).

Financial Services Act 1986

One of the biggest changes in financial services was the Financial Services Act 1986. This was an important piece of legislation and was seen as crucial for the protection of the investor. The Act came into force from 29 April 1988 and was aimed at:

* increasing competition
* regulating the conduct of investment business
* increasing consumer confidence in financial services providers.

A key aim of the Act was to set up a flexible system of regulation that inspired confidence not only to those working in the market but also to

---

CASE STUDY

The private pension row

In the early 1990s, legislation encouraged people to take out private pension plans. Some of the larger insurance companies saw this as an opportunity to persuade huge numbers of people to switch from their existing private pension schemes operated by their employers to private pension plans. In numerous instances they were misled by the insurance companies into believing they would be better off with a private pension plan when this was not the case. In fact, the situation was the reverse. There was widespread anger against these companies and the industry regulators fined many of the companies involved.

1 Why do consumers need protecting?
2 What does the case study imply about the need for regulation?

Think it over...

The death of the newspaper tycoon Robert Maxwell led to the discovery of massive fraud relating to the pension funds of the Maxwell companies.

investors. In doing so it established a new principal authority with the power to supervise the affairs of the City of London. This body, called the Securities and Investment Board (SIB), recognised a number of self-regulatory organisations (SROs), formed of investment practitioners, who were to supervise the markets. It did in addition recognise a range of professional bodies that were to supervise the market and maintain standards. The system did not work well and there was a certain amount of dissatisfaction so that by 1993 a report indicated that the objectives of the Financial Services Act were unclear, the system was too complex and a lot of fraud was unpunished.

Following the election of the Labour government in 1997, two major regulatory changes were announced. The first was the abandonment of the self-regulatory system, and the re-establishment of full regulation by the government. This regulation was to be administered by a single regulatory body, the Financial Services Authority. At the same time, it became the responsibility of the FSA rather than the Bank of England to supervise the banking system and the money markets.

Diversification

One of the reasons for all of these changes was that the financial and monetary system had become increasingly diverse. The difference between banks, building societies, insurance companies and so on were blurred and there were less distinct differences between them as competition for financial services had increased considerably. It was felt at this time that although having this diverse and interesting financial services sector was of benefit for the consumer, it did need focused supervision under the one authority.

The main result of these changes is a bit of a contradiction. On the one hand deregulation has occurred, particularly in the areas of banks and buildings societies, with many more organisations providing banking or similar services. On the other hand, many parts of the industry have become more regulated. The Building Societies Act of 1986 and the Banking Act of 1987 were passed alongside the Financial Services Act of 1986 in the belief that increased competition would be beneficial for consumers who would be spoilt for choice as the cost of many products fell.

Impact of technology

It was during the middle of the 1990s that many financial services providers realised that technology could have a significant use not just for reducing their costs, but also as a basis for improving their competitive abilities and market share. In fact, technology is probably the biggest single factor driving the changes in the financial services industry.

The industry has the ability to store vast amounts of data electronically, process it at speeds that are almost instantaneous and to communicate information electronically around the world. This has seen a huge growth in business involving volumes of information and data that would be impossible to process manually.

Perhaps the first significant step was what is known as 'real-time' systems. These systems enable customers' accounts to be checked in seconds. By having this 'real-time' information, accounts can be checked with balances through ATMs, by telephone and when customers enter the bank to undertake some point-of-sale service. It is also possible for many customers to access their cash either in ATMs or at supermarkets and other retail outlets. Electronic services have allowed many banks to reduce the number of tellers they employ and close down smaller branches.

The use of technology is not simply down to account handling. Computer programmes can be used to assess loan applications with their own impartial scoring systems. Within a banking context, instead of loans having to be vetted by bank managers, these can now be undertaken by administrative staff.

Technology has also:

* allowed attractive graphics to be used in the design of publicity materials and has helped banks to send mail shots to targeted customers

* enabled financial service organisations to use databases to manage customer relationships, with access to detailed information about customer accounts

* enabled organisations to use the Internet.

Internet-centred organisations, products and services

In recent years, customers of banks have looked for different ways of both managing and accessing their accounts. Since the onset of banking businesses such as Egg, the floodgates were

CASE STUDY

PayPal

PayPal is faster than sending cheques or postal orders and is a form of electronic funds transfer payment where financial information is kept private and secure enabling users to use eBay and other websites. Individuals who sign up for a PayPal account make no payment although there are transaction fees. There are three different kinds of account:

* **Personal account**
  This account is for customers who want to shop online and helps them to make secure payments on eBay and other websites.

* **Premier account**
  This account is for both buying and selling so that secure payments can be made on eBay and other merchant or trading websites.

* **Business account**
  This account supports organisations that want to develop online business.

1 Why might an individual wish to use PayPal?
2 To what extent do PayPal and other secure exchange mechanisms have the power to transform the ways in which customers both trade and pay for goods and services?

opened and now just about every major bank and building society as well as some supermarkets have been in a rush to expand and develop online services.

To bank online requires special software for customers to put onto their PC and this has to be changed every time the bank upgrades its services. Electronic banking services enable customers to check balances, transfer money between accounts, order chequebooks, download information into money management packages and make transfers by direct debit or other electronic means.

Customers simply access their account from their own PC which is connected to the bank's intranet via a modem and a telephone line. The greatest benefit is that it enables individuals to access services 24 hours a day and 7 days a week from anywhere in the world with a computer terminal. Many of the services offer a range of financial planning tools for customers to use.

Given the nature of this industry there is also an ever-expanding range of services becoming available either through the web or using digital TV. The next development in technology will allow customers to access and manage their accounts using their mobile phones.

Just about all of the banks and building societies have got in on the act. Barclays, for example, offers a small business service providing a range of services such as money transfers, bill payment and account checking. Royal Bank of Scotland offers a payroll service for managing staff payments. Bank of Scotland offers a messaging facility designed to cut out the need for branch visits or telephone enquiries and Alliance & Leicester uses Girobank to offer competitive rates and banking through local Post Offices.

The main worry is security. Although banks use a strong form of encryption and multi-level passwords to protect personal data, there is a worry that data could be hacked. The UK Deposit Protection Scheme protects money transacted through electronic banking.

Undertaking the research

From the outset it is important to get some kind of feel for the financial providers and services

market. Entering a new business sector must at the very start involve listening to people to find out how they operate, what they do and what services they provide and this can be a very steep and very difficult learning curve. You might want to pick up some leaflets from your local bank or building society. Find out:

* what sort of accounts they provide
* how they meet the needs of business and personal customers
* about the range of different services they provide.

Your assessment involves you using your information from a past customer to produce an appropriate financial package to meet your customer's specific needs. To match such needs with appropriate products you need to know as much as you can about the customer as well as all the products and services that are available. Don't forget, in suggesting the package and making realistic judgements you also need to think about how you might, if you were a financial service provider, handle and monitor all of the services you are providing for that customer.

Business plan

Being able to read or understand a business plan is essential if you are thinking about the requirements of a financial provider's client. A business plan will:

* provide a clear sense of direction for owners and managers so they know where they are going
* provide a means for managers and other interested parties to check on progress in meeting targets
* provide a means of controlling the business – i.e. keeping to plan
* help to raise finance. Outside parties such as banks need to be able to see that an organisation is well planned if they are to have confidence in it, for example to provide loans.

If you are shown a business plan as part of your research you will see that it contains:

* *A contents page*
* *The owner* – Information about the owner or owners and their background. This section may contain some referees.

CASE STUDY

Scenario – Setting up a geophysics company

Richard, Peter and Shirley used to work for companies that processed and interpreted geophysical software. Though they enjoyed the benefits of being involved in a high-tech industry, they felt that they were simply earning money for others and wanted to make a more individual contribution to their work that would be more challenging, stimulating and creative. They clearly needed to satisfy a number of essential questions:

* Where could they obtain business premises?
* What were their financial needs?
* What equipment would they need?
* Would there be enough work?
* What about the competition?

In order to answer these and many other questions, they carefully researched their ideas and put together a sensitivity analysis to indicate the levels of risk they might face. They also looked at their predicted costs, sales and overheads as well as the capital expenditure required before they started trading. From their analysis, the indicators pointed to the viability of their ideas and so they constructed a business plan.

1 **If you were assessing the services to provide for Richard, Peter and Shirley, what questions would you like to ask them to find out about their needs?**
2 **What would you expect to see in their business plan?**
3 **Discuss the range of services that you might provide.**

* *The business* – This will contain the name and address of the business and then some description of the product/service being offered.

* *The market* – This section will describe the marketing objectives, the market research that has been undertaken and also details of the competitive environment.

* *The marketing mix* – This describes the range of ways the organisation meets the needs of customers.

* *Physical resource requirements* – This will identify what premises, equipment and motor vehicles the business requires.

* *Human resource requirements* – This will identify the staffing requirements.

* *Costings* – The plan should give some indication of the cost of producing a good or service.

* *Financial forecasts* – This should include a forecast trading and profit-and-loss account as well as a forecast balance sheet.

Interviewing is a form of primary research

in to see the representative you need to construct some form of questionnaire. The interview has little basis for credibility if you do not have a structured or semi-structured questionnaire ready to use.

Many of the research methods depend upon the use of a questionnaire. Earlier in this book we said that a questionnaire is a systematic list of questions designed to obtain information from people about:

* specific events

* their attitudes

* their values

* their beliefs.

It is important to get your questions together and make sure you are prepared. A good questionnaire will result in a smooth interview, giving you a precise format to follow and ensuring that you obtain the information you require in a format that is easy for you to analyse later. Remember that a badly designed questionnaire will lead to poor results and may lead to you making inappropriate decisions about the financial services you advise.

Be careful when you conduct the interview to ensure that:

* the results are not biased

* there is a starting point and focus for your questions

* your questions are appropriate for the respondent and the task you are undertaking

Theory into practice

All business plans will have a different structure and most financial service providers will have their own suggested structure and some even have business planning software. Ask for a business plan template for a small business at a local bank.

Primary research

Any information that is original and is obtained by you as you undertake the research within the organisation can be referred to as **primary data**. Primary research in this instance is specific to your needs and will, as we can see, involve a range of different methods. As you prepare for your assessment the likelihood is that you will use one or more of these methods.

Face-to-face discussion

Perhaps the starting point for finding out more about the sort of services you would recommend to your customer is to interview a representative from your chosen adviser. However, before going

* you do not ask too many questions
* your questions relate directly to your information needs and requirements
* your questions are logically sequenced and are not confusing or ambiguous.

Remember that your questions may be open or closed. You may want to ask some closed questions early in the questionnaire to find out more about the activities of the respondent within the financial services market-place.

Questioning relatives and friends

Your primary research may include conducting interviews with family and friends to find out about how they have used financial service providers to meet their needs. Again, this is not an informal talk and if you do not construct a questionnaire beforehand, as well as think about how to record data, your results will lack validity. So, construct a questionnaire making sure that the questions precisely relate to the requirements of your assessment and then arrange the interview. Given that these are family and friends, you may want to make the interview more formal to illustrate how important it is for you to have an appropriate and usable response.

Leaflets and booklets from financial providers

There are so many different financial providers in the market-place today with so many different services, that there is a huge amount of information from the organisations that you can collect. Although the information is in itself secondary data (it is there and collected by somebody else) your interpretation and the comparisons you make from the information you collect involves an element of primary research as well.

Surveys on competitors

There is a whole range of surveys of financial services from many different providers. Information may have been published in financial magazines or appeared in *Which?*, the magazine published by the Consumers' Association or on the Internet on different websites. With so much information available today, it has never been

---

CASE STUDY
Moneyfacts

The Moneyfacts survey of 2005 listed the following providers of mortgages as the best value based upon total annual interest repayment on a £100,000 standard variable rate mortgage:

1 EGG
2 HSBC
3 First Direct (at 95%)
4 Intelligent Finance
5 Nationwide
6 Skipton
7 West Bromwich (borrowers of 5 yrs & more)
8 Co-operative Bank
9 Direct Line
10 Standard Life Bank (at 95%)

1 Who is this information for?
2 How might customers use it?

---

easier for consumers to shop around and to have so many choices.

Secondary research

Internal sources of secondary data

Financial services organisations may have a considerable amount of internal information kept in databases and classified in a variety of ways about customer types, segments and trends.

A lot of internal data is simply constructed from information held within the organisation. It might come from customer accounts and records and may note customer occupations, the sort of services associated with particular postcodes and occupations and so on.

External sources of secondary data

There is also quite a lot of external secondary data that may be available. For example, as you construct a report and think about the requirements of customers you may refer to the external environment that the organisation is in by looking at the websites of competitors and also using the Internet to find out other information about them.

You may also use newspaper articles by looking through the archives of the BBC as well as current newspapers and textbooks you may find in the library of your school or college.

7.2.4 Constraints affecting the provision of financial services

When consumers or customers use the financial service markets, they are hoping to invest in the market to provide some benefits that they will gain from in the future. In the environment of financial services, no matter how secure the institution or particular products look, there is always an element of risk, with the risk higher with some organisations and products than others.

There are a number of different criteria that the consumer can use in order to assess and make comparisons between different products and services.

Risk

A consumer must consider all of the risks attached to some products. As we saw in the case study on pensions (see page 310), sometimes it is easy to accept advice but just forget about all of the risks. Clearly there are higher risks in some products than others. Investing in securities on the stock exchange is likely to be much more risky than placing money into a building society and receiving the benefits of interest rather than dividends. However, because of the risk factor on the stock market, if an investor makes a sound investment the rewards could be significantly higher.

Customers will want to know about the risks they take when they are offered different services by banks. Some may want products that provide certainty, usually with lower rates of return, while others may want to accept some degree of risk in return for higher rewards.

Convenience

It may be possible to shop around for financial services to tailor them to your precise needs but some customers may look for convenience to suit their needs rather than the best deal. Despite the growth of Egg and other electronic banking services, many customers still want the convenience of going to their own branch of the bank rather than the convenience of the Internet. It is important when thinking about developing a financial package for a customer to consider how they access and use their services.

Speed of service and payback

Increasingly, customers are looking for better customer service. However with some financial service products the pay-back period and speed of service is not as fast as with others. For example, to get higher rates of interest with a deposit account there may be restrictions upon how quickly money can be drawn out.

Flexibility of the finance

Different services have different features and benefits which mark them out within the diverse market for such products. For example, overdrafts are perhaps the most flexible form of borrowing, particularly in the way they can simply be accessed when a shortfall takes place. This is in strict contrast to borrowing for which the applicant would have to fill in a form or in a business situation may have to produce a business plan and undergo a series of meetings and interviews. It is important that the form of package recommended fits the circumstances, purposes and requirements of the customer.

Availability of advice

The notion of the traditional bank manager seems to have disappeared in recent years, with many financial service organisations meeting the information needs of their customers through their use of call centres. Electronic banking runs on a significantly lower cost base than a branch banking organisation and these types of banks may offer very little advice. These movements are in strict contrast to the growth of personal financial advisers, many of whom visit their clients' homes regularly to talk about what help they could provide with their changing financial needs. Some customers may want advice and others may not.

Clarity and impartiality of information provided

Under the Financial Services Act of 1986 those working in the financial services sector should:

* know their customers so that any advice is based upon the customer's personal financial circumstances

* provide the best advice so that only services appropriate for that customer are recommended

* explain the risks to the customer so that they are aware of the dangers arising from the investment

* provide the customer with the best terms available

* maintain records of the advice given to customers and the reasons for that advice.

Each of these areas is extremely important when thinking about how to provide a package for customers. They each provide an opportunity for you to evaluate how well you are meeting the needs of your customer.

One important factor when dealing with complex information is to make sure that customers understand exactly what they are investing in. Information should be both objective and clear. In constructing a package for a customer it is important to think about how to provide them with appropriate information.

Ease of use

This may be another deciding factor. Sometimes financial and even what might seem like simple

banking services can be difficult to use. Think about your customer's needs and how they may use the package of services you recommend.

Value for money

Competition between financial service providers in recent years has meant that financial service providers have to sell their products at competitive prices. However, providers continually seek to give better deals and win more custom. When you make recommendations, consider how much a customer would be prepared to pay, and whether there are cheaper offers from competitors.

Status and size of business

Different organisations will have access to different banking services dependent upon their status and size. For example, very large businesses will be able to borrow at significantly better rates than small organisations because they are viewed as a lower risk whereas smaller organisations may be considered as a higher risk.

Statutory legal constraints

Financial Services Act

The Financial Services Act 1986 (see page 310) has been mentioned many times within this part of the book as a particularly significant piece of legislation. Before this Act there had not been any comprehensive law governing the provision of financial services within the UK. As we have seen, the Act set up the Securities and Investments Board (SIB) alongside a number of self-regulatory organisations (SROs), formed of investment practitioners to supervise the markets. It also recognised that the professional bodies of lawyers, accountants, insurance brokers and so on could maintain standards where their members participated in markets.

There were some problems with this approach to regulation and so following the election of a new government in 1997, the self-regulatory system was abolished and the Financial Services Authority (FSA) was established with the FSA taking over the responsibility for the supervision of the banking system and money markets.

Today, as a result of the updated Financial Services and Markets Act 2000, the FSA is the regulator of the financial services industry and has four main objectives. These are to:

* maintain market confidence
* promote public understanding of the financial system
* protect the consumer
* fight the different kinds of financial crime.

Organisations authorised and regulated under the Act include:

* banks
* building societies
* insurance companies
* friendly societies
* credit unions
* Lloyd's
* investment and pensions advisers
* stockbrokers
* professional firms offering certain types of investment services
* fund managers
* derivatives traders.

Trade Descriptions Act 1968

The purpose of the Trade Descriptions Act is to impose criminal liability on traders who falsely describe their goods or services. For example, if somebody says something in the description of a good or service that is not true, then the organisation could be prosecuted. This is particularly relevant to the area of financial services.

The Act states:

'Any person who, in the course of a trade or business
i) applies a false trade description to any goods; or
ii) supplies or offers to supply any goods to which a
false trade description is applied; shall, subject to the
provisions of this Act, be guilty of an offence.'

In establishing the requirements of the act it is important to define the terms used. The first term that needs defining is *in the course of trade or business,* which sets the criteria for who can be prosecuted under the act. The act is intended to penalise only dishonest businesses, so a private seller cannot commit an offence under the act.

The second term to which we should refer is the concept of *applying a false description.* Oral statements or advice given by a personal financial adviser can constitute the application of a false trade description as can the supply of goods which were requested under a description if they do not correspond with that description.

Think it over...

The British Bankers' Association has Business Banking Codes which are voluntary codes which set standards of good banking practice for banks and building societies to follow when they are dealing with personal or business customers in the United Kingdom.

Ethical constraints

Codes of practice

A **code of practice** is a voluntary agreement by a trade association that agrees the standards of business it expects from its members. By having a code it is hoped that standards of behaviour improve so that customers get a better deal. The Office of Fair Trading (OFT) is a government department which keeps a watch upon trading matters in the UK and aims to protect both consumers and those in business against unfair trading practices. The OFT encourages trade associations and industry representative bodies to draw up codes of practice that organisations within those industries should follow. The purpose of these is to raise standards and also to identify special ways of dealing with complaints and other issues.

Key term

Code of practice – a voluntary agreement constructed by a trade association for its members.

Professional associations / watchdogs

There are a whole range of professional and trade associations representing the interests of their members and of customers across the financial services industry ranging from the Association of British Insurers, to the Law Society, the Building Society Association and the Council of Mortgage Lenders. These organisations, although aimed at protecting their members are also involved with consumer protection and have the ability to take action and control the members and the ways in which their members might operate.

Financial Services Authority (FSA)

Formerly the Securities and Investments Board, the Financial Services Authority (FSA), has a range of supervisory duties over financial providers and their activities, as we have already seen within this part of the book. The main role of the FSA is to consolidate the supervision of organisations across the financial sector into a single and controlling agency.

Ombudsman

There are a number of different **ombudsmen** across the financial sector including insurance, banking and building societies. An ombudsman is somebody who acts on the behalf of customers, particularly where customers are not happy about particular services. The purpose of an ombudsman is to act as a fair and independent arbiter between customers and financial service providers when customers feel that they have justifiable complaints about how they have been treated or the services to which they have been exposed. Most of the ombudsmen are prepared to take on a justifiable case once the internal complaints procedures of the individual organisations concerned have been exhausted.

The Bank of England

Previously, the Bank of England supervised the banking system. If there were any problems, issues or worries within the system, the Bank of England was a steadying hand ready to intervene to ensure that the interests of customers were met.

The Bank of England Act of 1998 transferred responsibility for the supervision of the banking sector in the UK from the Bank of England to the

The Bank of England

Financial Services Authority. The aim of the government in doing this was to bring the supervision and regulation of the whole financial services sector under one roof. The Bank of England still has a huge influence on the financial services sector with interest rate control as part of the UK government's monetary policy. The bank alters the rate of interest in the discount market by making funds available as the lender of last resort. The Monetary Policy Committee of the Bank of England meets monthly to decide upon the announcement of the base rate.

7.2.5 Potential effect of future changes to customer circumstances

Personal needs

As we travel through our life-cycle from youth to old age we require a different range of financial services. Everybody's need for financial services changes as they move through their lives.

Financial services providers tailor specific accounts for young adults at university or starting work. After leaving university or in their early 20s, many individuals will have very different needs, and may want to buy their own property. They may also start 'nesting', to use a marketing word, and start living with their partners. At this stage they may want personal loans and mortgages.

When or if children arrive their financial requirements may change again. This may be a very difficult time financially. It could involve reducing from two incomes to one income or one full-time income and a part-time income, or the two incomes could remain but then the partners may be burdened by the cost of child-care arrangements. To accommodate a growing family, they may change their property requirements from an apartment to a house, and then as the family grows they may require more space.

Once the children have left school, there are other commitments. One of the huge financial commitments of parents today is towards their children when they go to university. Despite student loans and in a world of top-up fees, this may be an expensive time for parents. After their children have graduated and entered the world of work, it may be time for the parents to think more about retirement and again require a new range of services. For example, they may want to set up a range of savings accounts. In the past, in order to prepare for retirement they may have invested in a private pension plan.

Business needs

Businesses also go through a life-cycle. When they first set-up, they require start-up capital. As the business develops it may require a range of different banking services that allow it to expand and develop. Increasingly, many businesses are looking to expand through online services and this opens up a whole new prospect of trading within a different context.

One key threat to many businesses is a change in market conditions. Such a change may have a huge impact upon the services it requires.

KNOWLEDGE CHECK

1 Name the two main types of customer that financial services organisations cater for.

2 Identify four physical needs that cause customers to require financial services.

3 Explain the difference between a private and a public limited company.

4 What is start-up capital?

5 Explain what is meant by organic growth.

6 Define the term 'working capital'.

7 What was the purpose of the Financial Services and Markets Act of 2000?

8 What does the Monetary Policy Committee of the Bank of England do at its monthly meeting?

9 What is the main distinction between a building society and a bank?

10 What does ABI stand for?

11 How does life assurance differ from general insurance?

12 Use an example to describe what is meant by factoring.

13 What is the difference between a current and a deposit account?

14 On a cheque, who is the drawer?

15 Describe the purpose of an endowment mortgage.

16 Explain how a credit card works.

17 What is meant by the term 'electronic banking'? Use examples to support your answer.

18 How does an overdraft differ from a loan?

19 What is the operating cycle?

20 Why do companies issue debentures?

Resources

Lipscombe, G. and Pond, K., *The Business of Banking* 3rd Edition, Chartered Institute of Bankers, Canterbury, 2002

Stanic, V. and Boyle, D., *Developing People and the Corporate Culture in Financial Services*, Woodhead, Cambridge, 1999

Gandy, A., *Banking Strategies: Beyond 2000*, CIB Publishing, London, 1999

Minghella, L., *Blackstone's Guide to the Financial Services & Markets Act 2000*, Blackstone, London, 2001

Websites

Some useful websites are listed below. These addresses are current at the time of writing. However, it needs to be recognised that new sites are being launched on the Internet on a regular basis and that older sites may change or disappear.

www.natwest.com
www.tescofinance.com
www.hsbc.co.uk
www.prudential.co.uk

ASSESSMENT EVIDENCE

Your evidence for this unit will be based on a scenario from OCR accompanied by a set of financial circumstances for your customer who is running their own business, either a new business or one that is looking to change direction. The case study supplied by OCR will require you to look at both the personal needs of customers as well as their business requirements.

You will research possible financial packages for your customer and analyse these to decide which is the most appropriate package to meet the specific needs of your customer. You will then produce a financial package for your customer that includes material informed by your research and which meets their specific needs, both on a personal and business level.

The financial package that you recommend to your customer must contain evidence of:

* your understanding of the different financial needs of individuals and businesses, as well as the financial providers and products that are available. You also need to understand the constraints that might impact upon the provision of financial services

* being a package that is directly applied to the needs of the given context

* research into financial services and providers and an analysis of the data you have gathered

* reasoned judgements as to whether you consider that the effectiveness of your financial package could change given the differing circumstances that your customer might encounter.

Remember that it is important to provide reasoned and realistic judgements as part of your report. Try to use evidence to support your actions and support this evidence with logically-based arguments.

UNIT 8

Understanding production in business

This unit contains eight elements:

8.2.1 The role of the production department

8.2.2 Operational efficiency

8.2.3 Organising production

8.2.4 Ensuring quality

8.2.5 Stock control

8.2.6 Health and safety

8.2.7 Research into production

8.2.8 Potential production improvements

Introduction

This unit involves the exploration of a real business, focusing mainly on the activities carried out by the production department and issues concerned in the production process of a particular item, for example the manufacture of a book, a batch of cakes or biscuits, a particular type of garment or sports equipment etc.

You will learn about production from studying production activities based on real settings. This involves investigating how the item that you have chosen is produced in a **manufacturing** business.

Modern automated production in a car plant

You will produce a written report containing visual images of how your chosen business produces a particular item. This visual and written report will be informed by your research into your chosen business context and analysis of the strengths and weaknesses of production in its current form.

This unit is assessed through your portfolio work. The mark on that assessment will be the mark for the unit.

There are a number of activities throughout this unit to reinforce your learning.

8.2.1 The role of the production department

The primary role of the production functional-area within a business is to transform **inputs** into **outputs**. Converting inputs into outputs (finished goods and services) enables the business to satisfy the needs of consumers.

We can illustrate this process by taking the example of the **production** process for dog biscuits:

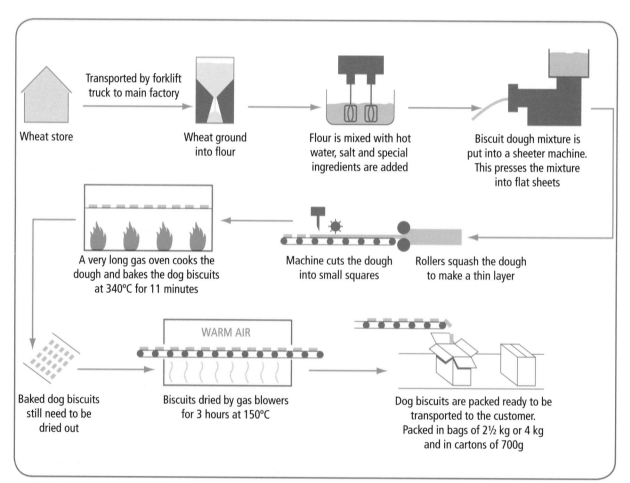

FIGURE 8.1 *Inputs needed to manufacture dog biscuits*

Set out and complete the following table using the illustration to find appropriate answers:

Inputs	Processes	Outputs
Wheat	Grinding the flour	?
Hot water	Mixing with ingredients	
?	?	
?	?	
?	?	
?	?	

FIGURE 8.2 *Inputs, processes and outputs in the production of dog biscuits*

The production process involves working with two types of resources. **Transformational resources** are those that carry out the processes including the people that work for the company (production workers) and the machinery and equipment, for example mixing machines. The **transformed resources** are the raw inputs that are converted into more valuable outputs. For example, the wheat is ground into more valuable flour.

The transformed inputs should become more valuable at each stage of their transformation. **Adding value** to a product simply means making it more desirable to the final customer (so that customers are willing to buy more products, at higher prices). We can measure the value added to a product at each stage of production. For example, the dog biscuit manufacturer buys in each month £100,000 of ingredients from suppliers (wheat from farmers). The manufacturer then produces and sells £250,000 worth of biscuits to retailers. The retailers sell all these biscuits to end customers for £300,000.

We can calculate the value added at each stage of production:

Output price – input price =	Value added
250,000 – 100,000 (manufacturer's value added)	150,000
300,000 – 250,000 (retailers' value added)	50,000

When we add together:

The value added by farmers	£100,000
The value added by the manufacturer	£150,000
The value added by the retailer	£50,000

You can see that the value added at each stage of production totals £300,000.

List the sorts of transforming resources and transformational resources that would be used by

✳ a farmer

✳ a manufacturer of dog biscuits

✳ retailers.

Identify the inputs, processes and outputs in the production of a specific product or related set of products in a manufacturing company.

Identify the key transformational and transforming resources. Explain how the business adds value in the process of production.

Operations managers

We use the term '**operations**' to describe all those **processes** and methods by which an organisation uses its resources to produce something or to provide a service. For example, in a factory, operations are the processes used to turn raw materials and other inputs into finished products. In a restaurant, operations take place when food is

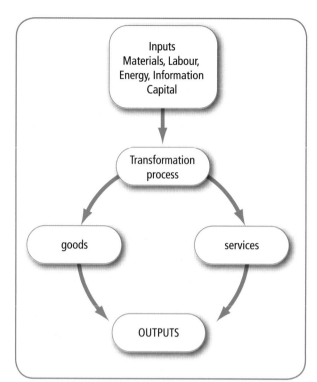

FIGURE 8.3 *Transforming inputs into desired goods and services*

prepared in the kitchens and served to customers at the tables. Banking operations are concerned with converting given inputs into desired financial products.

In any type of organisation, operations managers will be responsible for controlling and co-ordinating the organisation's resources, such as finance, capital equipment, labour materials and other factors. Timetables and schedules are needed to show how these resources will be used in production.

Figure 8.3 shows how **operations management** involves successfully transforming inputs into desired goods and services.

Typical activities carried out by production managers include organising, planning and supervising:

* product research to identify new products and new processes for manufacturing existing and new products

* the production process e.g. the links between the various stages of production and the organisation of the production line (where appropriate)

* the setting up of a production line to produce a particular product

* the maintenance of the production line

* the speed and flow of the production line

* the ordering of equipment and raw material

* other production management activities such as setting out production targets and monitoring whether these targets are being achieved.

Organisations such as Cadbury's and Nestlé – manufacturing confectionery, The Body Shop – manufacturing and selling cosmetics, and Virgin – manufacturing and selling a large range of items including Cola drinks, rail travel and air travel, all depend upon the management skills and manufacturing skills of their operations managers and skilled employees.

Operations managers need to be able to organise operations to produce products that satisfy consumers. You may hear the expression that production is at the 'sharp end' of business activity. In other words, if production does not produce the right goods then the organisation will fail. Targets have to be met and standards kept up. Failure to meet targets and standards can be disastrous (especially when customers lose patience because of poor **quality**).

Production management involves controlling and co-ordinating the use of manufacturing resources such as manufacturing employees, physical plant and machinery, raw materials, parts, etc. Timetables and schedules will need to be set out to show how these resources will be used in production.

Efficient production sets out to:

* keep costs to a minimum

* keep quality standards as high as possible

* meet the needs of customers

* maximise the use of plant and equipment

* keep down the level of stocks to the minimum requirement.

The types of operations which an organisation carries out depend in a number of ways on what it is that they are processing. The table on page 327 gives examples of different operations which

Mainly processing materials	Mainly processing information	Mainly processing customers
Oil refinery	Accountancy firm	Hairdresser
Chocolate manufacturer	Market research company	Leisure Centre
Construction company (e.g. building houses)	Government Statistical Office	Hospital
What other examples can you think of?	What other examples can you think of?	What other examples can you think of?

focus on processing material, information or customers.

You can see that the first two types of organisation focus on efficiently converting inputs to output. This is a very technical process. The third type of organisation is more likely to place most emphasis on service and face-to-face customer relations.

The five Ps of production

The production function concentrates on 5 Ps:

* product
* plant
* people
* process
* programme.

We can illustrate this by taking the example of Jamie Oliver's London restaurant:

The product: It is essential to provide a good or service that clearly meets the needs of consumers (in this case the diners in Jamie's restaurant) and that can be provided for them at the right place, at the right time and for the most attractive price.

Jamie wants his customers to go home to feel that they had a good meal in an enjoyable atmosphere at a value-for-money price.

The plant: Companies always need some form of plant or base for manufacturing. The location, size, design, safety and layout of the plant are all very important. Managers need to think carefully about how parts and materials are to be delivered, and how finished goods will be delivered to customers. The layout should make it easy to co-ordinate the various activities that will take place there. Jamie's restaurant is therefore located in a convenient and vibrant part of London. It is designed to secure healthy and safe practices in the kitchens, where meals can be prepared in batches and individually to meet the needs of clients. Each day, fresh deliveries are made, which must then be stored in the right temperature conditions until they are ready for producing into exciting recipes.

The people: The success of any production process will depend on the people involved. The quality of people depends on how much is invested in them. Training and development are vital.

Jamie Oliver takes pride in personally training and developing young people to work for him. He believes in giving young people a chance to make a success of working as chefs. His personal involvement and concern (working extraordinarily long hours) has won him the admiration of many observers.

The process: Different organisations will have different sets of operations depending on the nature of the product they make, the type of plant and equipment employed and many other factors. Process management sets out to:

* identify the key processes – if these are carried out well this will lead to customer satisfaction and high financial returns

* understand how processes work

* identify who in the organisation should be involved in these processes

* continually seek to improve these processes.

For Jamie, the challenge then is to create the processes – the ordering of new ingredients, the creation of menus, the organisation of the cooking, the delivery of food to tables etc. As a perfectionist he is continually seeking to improve on these processes.

The programme: Progamming is mainly concerned with timetabling the use of resources. To meet orders successfully, the organisation will need to plan and control activities carefully. Successful programming involves, purchasing, stock control and **quality control**.

Entrepreneurial managers like Jamie Oliver need to pay careful attention to creating systems which timetable the delivery of materials, the starting of cooking meals the time taken to cook meals etc to ensure maximum benefit to the customer.

How production interacts with other functional areas

Most manufacturing businesses are divided up into a number of functional areas or specialisms.

For example, a business manufacturing biscuit tins might be divided into the **functions** shown in Figure 8.4. Each of these areas interlinks with the other areas.

Where a manufacturing company is split up into a number of production units a **factory (or operations) manager** will have overall responsibility for the management of factory-floor operations. This involves close liaison with functional specialists from human resources, finance and accounts, marketing and sales and other departments such as administration and information-technology management.

Production / human resources

The human resources (HR) department in an organisation is broadly concerned with recruiting, selecting, training and motivating people in the workplace. The human resources department works very closely with production to seek to employ the right people with the right skills to carry out operational activities. Although HR will organise training courses, production specialists will need to carefully specify the requirements of such courses, for example developing skills with operating modern high-tech computer controlled machines. HR and production must also work closely together to design the payments and rewards systems and other ways of motivating employees to create high levels of motivation and hence high-quality production.

Human resources and production must also work closely to guarantee the health and safety of employees. For example this will involve jointly designing training courses for new production-line employees to make sure that they operate in a

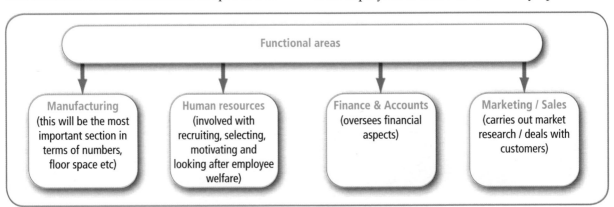

FIGURE 8.4 *Functional areas in an organisation*

CASE STUDY

Producing a ballpoint pen

We can better understand the relationship between the various functions of a business by taking the example of ballpoint-pen manufacture. A ballpoint pen typically involves a number of elements as shown in the diagram below.

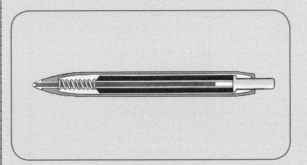

Each of the elements of the pen is made separately. For example:

* the ball will be made of a metal like tungsten carbide which is added to a fatty substance, heated and rolled between two flat surfaces to create a perfect ball
* special tools are then used to encase the ball in a brass housing (the ballpoint)
* the grip is made separately – today many pens include a moulded rubber grip
* inks are made separately and contained in the cartridge which is assembled to contain the ballpoint – assembled cartridges are run through a centrifuge to eliminate possible air bubbles
* a small spring is placed around the cartridge (in many cases)
* an end stopper holds the parts in place.

Assembling the pens involves a continuous process of feeding the components and assembling them along a fast moving production line. The speed and the processes along the line are controlled by computer systems.

At the end of the assembly line the pens are sorted and packed ready for shipping to retail outlets such as supermarkets.

Look at the following table and discuss how the processes involved in manufacturing ballpoint pens may integrate the production department with the human resources, finance and marketing departments.

Production / human resources	
Matching staffing levels to the level of production	An important aspect of planning is to make sure that you have enough line workers for the level of output that you want to produce. Production managers will plan production schedules based on expected sales of the product. This involves liaising with human resources. For example, if the demand for your ballpoints is rising over time then you may need to recruit and select more employees with the right sorts of skills, such as computer programmers, quality controllers etc. Also, if the number of ballpoints needed varies on a day-to-day basis, production managers and human resource managers will need to liaise about staffing levels and plan staffing hours.
What skills are needed to meet the operational needs of the business?	The manufacture of ballpoint pens involves a variety of skills ranging from work which involves only a few skills, such as operating a forklift truck to highly skilled operations, such as computer programming and machine-maintenance work. Production and human resources must work together to recruit the right types and right numbers of skilled workers and to train employees so that there are enough people in the right places.
How does the company motivate its workers to produce a quality product and to maximise productivity?	Ballpoint manufacturers continuously work to improve the quality of each product line. They are most successful when their employees are alert and vigilant at all times and constantly seeking to ensure high quality products. They therefore need to be motivated by financial and non-financial rewards. Human resources managers are best placed to advise operations managers and supervisors about the sorts of work practices that will best motivate employees to focus on quality and to enjoy and take pride in their work.

How is workers' health and safety ensured?	Health and safety is one of the most important aspects of operations. Human resource managers typically take responsibility for health and safety issues and training within an organisation. Health and safety needs to be given a major emphasis, from the induction of new employees to instilling safe ways of working in training activities. Human resources and production work together to make sure that legislation such as the Health and Safety at Work Act is properly applied. The Act is concerned with maintaining or improving standards of health, safety and welfare of people at work. It protects other people against risks to health and safety arising out of work activities and it controls the storage and use of dangerous substances and emissions into the air from certain premises. Employers have a general duty to ensure the safety, health and welfare at work of their employees. This is particularly important for production-line workers where accidents are more likely to happen. The premises, the plant and machinery must all be safe. All employees need to be trained by HR in safe operational practices. All employees have a duty of care to ensure that they do not endanger themselves or anyone else who may be affected by their work activities. HR and production will work together to ensure that employees use equipment and dangerous substances in accordance with the training they have received. Risk assessments are required to make sure that all operations are safe.

Production / finance

Production costs need to be controlled to enable the business to keep prices down and to make a profit.	The production department and the finance and accounts department need to work closely together to work out ways of minimising costs. Typically this will involve a costing exercise. This involves working out how much it costs to produce different quantities of the various components of the biro including the ball, the casing etc. It is then possible to work out the cost of producing different levels of output of the pen e.g. 100,000 a week, 200,000 a week etc. The finance and accounts department is responsible for working with production managers to identify ways of cutting down costs, e.g. by identifying processes that do not add value to production and then cutting them out where possible. This enables production to lower the costs of producing each individual pen.
The need to cost each aspect of the work in order to determine prices, wages and profit or loss.	Managers need to know how much it costs to produce each individual pen and the revenue that they receive from it. In this way they can see how much each item adds to profits. Those items or activities that are not profitable may need to be cut out. By knowing how much it costs to manufacture a pen, then it becomes possible to set an appropriate price. It is also possible to determine a suitable wage for production-line workers. Armed with this information, finance and accounts specialists are able to see how much an individual item contributes to profit (or loss). Finance and accounts specialists can then help production to focus activity on the most profitable lines.

Production / marketing

The need to build in the requirements of the customer into every aspect of their work.	The guiding principle of any form of production should be 'first find the customer'. There is no point in providing what the production department considers to be a brilliant new ballpoint that nobody wants to buy. Production research and marketing research therefore need to work very closely together to get the product right. Market research identifies the types of product features, colours, grips, functions that each pen can perform etc and will estimate the numbers that can be sold. Production research will work out whether it is feasible to make the numbers required in the ways required. For example, recent research has shown that there is a demand for ballpoint inks that have a nice smell. Production research then involves finding ways of making these pens while keeping costs reasonable.
The need to ensure that the quality of the final product meets the expectations of the customer	Marketers are able to find out what customers expect. This information is communicated to production managers who must create the quality systems and production methods that guarantee this quality. Failure by production to achieve the standards identified by marketing can lead to lots of unsold products.
The need to produce the product / service at the right price at the right time for the customer	Pleasing customers involves getting the marketing mix right. We have already discussed the importance of getting the product right. However, marketing and production must also make sure that they get the product in the right places at the right time. For example, the demand for ballpoints rises in the summer just before the school exam period. It is essential to get the right numbers into suitable outlets such as supermarkets and corner stores for students to be able to buy them. Marketers also provide useful information about the right pricing points for ballpoints and other items. Fortunately, because so many ballpoints are bought and used it is possible to produce them on a very large scale at a low cost. However, more specialist pens are produced in smaller quantities and are therefore more expensive.

FIGURE 8.5 *Linkage between different departments in the manufacture of ballpoint pens*

way that protects their safety, the safety of work colleagues (and of course of the consumers of end products). HR and production work together to make sure that when new production processes are developed, careful attention is paid to guaranteeing the safety of the new processes used.

Production / finance

The finance and accounts department is responsible for securing finance for a business, recording financial transactions and providing managers with important information such as details of production and raw material costs. Production and accounts must work closely together to seek to secure the most appropriate supplies (e.g. raw materials) and equipment to create an up-to-date and efficient production line. An important aspect of working together is to calculate costs of production. By developing a clear idea of how much individual items cost to produce it is possible to calculate the profitability of each item. Accountants can help production managers to identify ways of cutting costs, for example by increasing the scale of production, by changing raw material suppliers, by altering production techniques etc.

Theory into practice

Carry out some research to find out about the role of the production department and ways in which production and human resources, finance and marketing are integrated in a real organisation. An excellent source of research information will be through primary research in the form of face-to-face discussions with a speaker from a production department. Perhaps your teacher can arrange for you to visit a manufacturing company. You could prepare a questionnaire for a visit to the production department.

You may also be able to collect your information by examining a website dedicated to the explanation of the production of a particular type of product – however this is likely to be less fruitful than primary research. In planning your research consider the sorts of factors which are listed in the left-hand columns of Figure 8.5 on pages 329–330.

Production / marketing

The marketing department is concerned with identifying customer needs and requirements. Market research and product research go hand in hand and these two departments work very closely. For example, market research helps to provide good ideas for product modifications to make them more customer focused. Production is able to provide prototype products for marketing to test the market on small groups of customers.

8.2.2 Operational efficiency

The term **efficiency** relates to maximising the outputs that you can achieve from your inputs. An efficient business therefore will:

* achieve high levels of good quality outputs from its inputs

* minimise waste.

An important aspect of operating in an efficient way is to produce an efficient level of output.

Both large and small scale producers are able to operate in an efficient way by focusing on organising their transforming resources so that they can get the most from their inputs.

The term *scale of operations* refers to the size of operational activity. Large producers are able to benefit from economies of scale. **Economies of scale** are the advantages that are gained from large-scale production enabling the producer to produce individual items at a low cost per unit.

Think it over...

At the Jaguar plant in Castle Bromwich, the speed at which the production lines run is determined by the level of demand for the cars (mainly from America). If demand increases, the production line goes faster and it slows down when demand falls. This ensures that cars are produced just-in-time to be delivered to customers. No cars are left waiting to be sold, in which case they could possibly be damaged and they would waste valuable space in storage depots.

Some manufacturing businesses operate on a small scale whereas others operate on a very large scale. Can you think of other examples to complete the table?

Examples of small-scale producers	Examples of large-scale producers
Producers of handcrafted products such as furniture	Mass producers of flat-pack furniture
Makers of speciality products, e.g. specialist magazines for a very small audience	Mass market magazine publishers
Local manufacturers, e.g. a local bakery	A national mass production bakery
?	?
?	?

An obvious example of economies of scale is in ballpoint pen manufacture. Well known ballpoint manufacturers like BIC are able to produce very large outputs of high-quality pens at relatively low **unit costs**.

Examples of economies of scale available to BIC include being able to:

* afford and employ the best quality mass production machinery

* employ and train specialist production-line employees

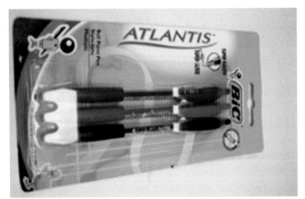

BIC benefits from economies of scale enabling it to produce very large quantities of pens efficiently

* invest in quality control procedures to minimise waste

* employ well-paid specialist production managers enabling high levels of efficiency.

Influencing factors

You need to understand the factors that influence the scale of operations in any manufacturing unit or in the production of a particular item.

Time taken for one item to be made on the production line

BIC biros can be made in a fraction of a second. (BIC produces 21 million stationery products every day). Ballpoint production lends itself to mass production techniques. This contrasts with other items which have to be produced far more slowly, for example wedding cakes. It would be unwise to mass produce high-quality wedding cakes. Can you think of other contrasting items?

Staffing levels on the production line

Large companies tend to have much larger workforces than smaller ones. The number of staff working on a production line therefore plays an important part in determining levels of output that can be produced. However, it is important to realise that some modern manufacturing plants such as breweries can produce very large quantities of finished product with a relatively low staffing ratio because a lot of processes can be carried out automatically. The level of production can be increased by changing staffing levels, for example by increasing overtime or taking on part-time labour at peak periods such as Christmas or when major orders need completing.

Output shown over a period of time

When examining output efficiency it is important to do this within the context of a particular time period. The longer the time period the greater the potential to increase the quantity produced. However, in examining efficiency it is best to compare outputs in a given time period, for example output per hour, day or week. For example, we could compare the efficiency of two firms in terms of output per hour. However, if one firm operates for more hours per week, for example by operating a shift system, it may be using its transforming resources more efficiently than another which operates 9–5, 5 days a week.

Maximum capacity level

Another useful measure of efficiency is the maximum **capacity** level over a period of time. The maximum capacity shows the maximum amount that can be produced by a given business, plant, or unit. This amount is measured when the organisation is fully staffed with all of its equipment working to maximum capacity. Firms with higher capacity are better placed to meet large orders than those with smaller capacity.

Actual capacity level

The reality is that most firms operate below their maximum capacity which can be regarded as a lack of efficiency. The actual capacity of a business (what the firm is actually able to produce) is below the maximum capacity level frequently because they lack key resources. On one level, this can be seen as a management problem as managers may not organise work processes as efficiently as they could be organised. Alternatively, the firm may lack other key

Key terms

A firm working to maximum capacity would be using all of its resources to their full potential. This is an indication of good management.

A firm's actual capacity is what it is currently able to produce. This is frequently short of maximum capacity because management has failed to make sure that it has the resources required to work at maximum efficiency.

resources, for example. sufficient numbers of trained workers to use its machinery and equipment to its full potential, lack of spares to maintain machinery etc.

Added value

It is important to have an understanding of where and how value is added during the production process. Adding value as we have seen is the process of making a product increasingly desirable to customers. For example, in the case of a ballpoint pen, value is created:

* by making the pen functional – it does what it is expected to do which is to help you to write clearly

* by making the pen attractive e.g. an easy to hold grip, ink that flows freely and improves writing

* by branding the pen – using a distinctive and well-recognised name like BIC makes it more desirable to the customer

* packaging the product in attractive and distinctive materials.

Any activity that adds value to the product helps to improve the product.

It is very important to identify where and how value is added to the product because knowing this information enables production planners to add more value and also to cut out activities that don't add value. Becoming more efficient therefore involves adopting more value creating activities and cutting out non-value creating activities.

Efficiency-based calculations

Calculating efficiency measures how well a business is doing in a particular period. Operations managers need to be able to measure efficiency. Common performance indicators for measuring efficiency include:

* labour productivity

* unit labour cost

* productivity

* capacity.

Labour productivity

Labour productivity simply measures the output produced by a given level of input (labour). There are two main ways of measuring output:

* output in terms of units produced (e.g. numbers of pens in an hour)

* output in terms of money values (e.g. £100,000 of pens).

In a similar way, input can be measured by:

* the number of employees (units of labour), this could either be the number of employees, or the number of hours they work

* the input measured in terms of money values (e.g. wage costs).

CASE STUDY

Tesco recently produced the following figures to show labour productivity:

	2000	2001	2002	2003	2004
Turnover (sales) per full time employee	155,042	159,678	163,443	160,157	162,459

The Tesco figures show an increase in labour productivity over time, although there was a decline in 2003.

The Tesco calculation involved measuring output in terms of the value of sales and the input in terms of the number of employees.

What other measures could you use to calculate labour productivity at Tesco?

Unit labour cost

A second way of measuring efficiency is to measure the labour cost of producing each unit of output.

For example, if we take the following figures for a business that manufactures shoes:

	January	February	March
Number of pairs of shoes made (units)	5,000	10,000	15,000
Wage bill (£)	100,000	250,000	450,000

In January the wage bill came to £100,000 and 5,000 pairs of shoes were made. This means that for each pair of shoes sold the wage cost was £20. (100,000/5,000) We refer to this as the unit wage cost i.e. the wage cost per pair of shoes.

In February the unit wage cost was 250,000/10,000 = £25 per pair.

In March the unit wage cost was 450,000/15,000 = £30.

This has clear implications for the business. Its unit wage cost is rising very steeply indicating that wages are potentially becoming a threat to the business. The business would either have to increase the price of its shoes to cover wage costs or reduce the wage cost per unit.

Unit labour costs in this country are regarded as very important. Unit labour costs are an important indicator of the competitiveness of a business. You should wherever possible keep your unit labour costs below those of rivals.

Productivity

Productivity simply measures:

$$\frac{\text{Outputs}}{\text{Inputs}}$$

We can measure the productivity of any type of transforming resource – for example, labour (see above), machinery and equipment, or even of the business as a whole.

Examples of calculations that could be made include:

$$\text{Labour productivity} = \frac{\text{Sales revenue}}{\text{Wages}}$$

$$\text{Capital productivity} = \frac{\text{Sales revenue}}{\text{Value of capital items}}$$

$$\text{Materials productivity} = \frac{\text{Sales revenue}}{\text{Value of materials used}}$$

If we wanted to work out a figure for *general productivity* we could use a formula like the following which takes into account a range of inputs and hence costs:

$$\text{Productivity} = \frac{\text{Sales revenue}}{\text{Labour} + \text{Materials} + \text{Overheads}}$$

Productivity needs to be measured in terms of what is relevant for a specific business. For example, at Tesco it is important to calculate how efficiently they use the space available to them. Hence they do a calculation of weekly sales per square foot.

	2000	2001	2002	2003	2004
Weekly sales per sq ft (£)	21.27	21.75	22.43	21.86	22.48

Capacity

Another way of measuring efficiency is in terms of capacity. This simply involves calculating the total output in a particular period of time if a business was using all of its resources efficiently. You can then examine actual rates of production in the same time period in order to see the extent to which the firm is falling short of its maximum capacity.

8.2.3 Organising production

Businesses organise their production methods in a number of ways including:

* job
* batch
* flow
* cell
* lean.

Businesses may use several types of production methods within a single facility.

Job production

Job production is the term used to describe a situation where an organisation produces one or a small number of items, for example a designer dress or hand-made suit. The product would normally be made on the producer's premises and then transported to the retailer's premises, although in some cases the product may be made on site, for example, the construction of a bridge.

The producer might work on several jobs at the same time for different groups of customers.

Firms operating in this way need to make sure they keep having orders for new jobs to replace the ones that are nearly completed.

One of the main advantages of job production is *customisation*. The product can be designed and made specifically with the customer's needs and requirements in mind and there can be ongoing discussion of the project as it unfolds.

The main disadvantage of job production is that it can be a very expensive process. For example, materials may need to be ordered in relatively small quantities for the job, designs created for a one-off process and trial and error can lead to costly labour and other expenses.

> **Think it over…**
>
> One of the most expensive examples of job production was St Paul's Cathedral. The architect Sir Christopher Wren had not built any other large buildings of this type before so he was effectively learning on the job.

Batch production

Batch production is where a number of identical or similar items are produced in a set or batch. The items need not be for any specific customer but are made at regular intervals in specific quantities. Batch production involves work being passed from one stage to another. Each stage of production is highly planned.

A simple example would be the production of loaves of bread in a bakery. Every day, 200 brown loaves, 100 white loaves and 500 small buns are produced. First the dough is made for the brown loaves. While this is rising, the dough for the white loaves is kneaded and so on.

A key feature of batch production is that, every now and then you have to stop the production process and reset it for a different product. Most manufacturing companies work in this way, as do most service organisations. For example, a cinema attendant at a multiplex cinema checks the tickets of a batch of cinema-goers waiting to see the latest Harry Potter film, he or she then checks the tickets of a batch going to see the new James Bond movie etc.

Batch production enables greater economies of scale than job production and enables a business to produce relatively large quantities of standardised items making it possible to meet the needs of a variety of customers.

Flow / line production

Flow production involves products or services passing down a line of production. The production process is a repeating one, with identical products going through the same sequence of operations. Car assembly lines are a classic example of line production. The work comes down the line to a team of workers who carry out set operations. Nowadays, humans have been replaced by robots in many continuous flow processes. Other examples of flow production can be found in chocolate bar manufacture, soft drinks manufacture and many other areas of tinned and frozen food production.

Line production produces identical products. The disadvantage is that many customers, for example mobile phone buyers, want their purchase to be made different or distinctive in some way. The great advantage of the line is that it enables mass production at a very low unit cost.

Continuous flow production takes line production one step further. Today, it is an advantage to be able to mass produce standard items such as Cadbury Creme eggs and bottles of shampoo. Continuous flow involves producing

for 24 hours a day, using automatic equipment in a standardised way.

An oil refinery, for example, works on a continuous flow basis, with petrol being refined around the clock. Modern breweries, paper mills and chocolate factories also use the continuous flow method.

In continuous flow, the whole operation is handled by machinery controlled by computers. Human labour does not touch the product. Continuous flow, therefore, does not apply in the service industries, which depend more on human labour.

Theory into practice

From the descriptions of the following six activities, can you identify whether the activities are using batch, job or flow production:

1 Fetching a batch of cakes out of the oven.

2 A production line of bottles.

3 Someone having their hair cut.

4 Chocolate bars going down a production line.

5 Sewing a wedding dress.

6 Processing a batch of cinema tickets (i.e. checking them in).

Cell production

In recent years what is referred to as cells have been increasingly used in production. A **cell** is a team of workers who have shared responsibility for producing a particular product or part of a product. Cell working has been widely adopted in the engineering and other manufacturing trades.

In the past, an engineering factory might be divided into a number of workshops each responsible for one stage in a production process. For example, in manufacturing car bodies, there might have been one shop which was responsible for cutting out part of a car body, then the sheet of metal would be passed onto the next shop where it was trimmed, then passed on to another shop where the metal was formed into a shape. This wasn't always highly motivating work and

CASE STUDY

Today many car plants are organised with workshops operating in teams or cells. Next to the production line they have rest areas with facilities for team meetings. When the production line stops they can have team meetings (led by a team leader) to discuss ways of cutting out waste. Cutting out waste does not mean that employees have to work any harder. Rather they are working smarter because they are not wasting time on activities which do not create value for them or the organisation. This leads to a more competitive business which is able to make more profits and to pay higher wages to its employees.

Just-in-time production is an important component of lean production and involves cutting out the waste of over stocking. **Just-in-time (JIT)** manufacturing is one of the strengths of the Japanese production system and is one that has enabled Japan to have a highly productive economy.

Just-in-time production is a very simple idea:

* finished goods are produced just in time for them to be sold, rather than weeks or months ahead
* the parts that go into a finished product arrive just in time to be put together to make the final product, rather than being stored at some cost in a warehouse.

The idea is to run a company with the smallest possible levels of stock and work-in-progress. Clearly, this needs careful planning:

* all sources of uncertainty must be removed from the manufacturing process

* there must be absolute reliability of production targets, supplies and levels of output achieved
* the time to set up machines must be reduced to a minimum so that components and finished products can be produced in small batches as and when required
* bottlenecks must be eliminated.

Using a JIT system requires a complete reorganisation of the traditional factory. Factories have usually been organised into 'shops', each working on a particular stage in producing a final product. With a JIT system the factory is reorganised so people are grouped together around the products they produce. They may need to have access to a family of machines, for example a lathe, a milling machine, a drill and a grinder.

1 A cell of workers involves people with different skills and specialisms working together. What do you see as being the principle benefits of organising employees into cells (rather than the old system of work passing down a line from one specialist to another)?
2 How can cutting out waste make production more efficient?
3 How can teams work together to eliminate waste?
4 What do you see as being the difference between working harder and working smarter?
5 Can you work smarter without working harder? Give an example to illustrate.

employees didn't have a sense of responsibility for the total product leading to a number of product defects (everyone could blame somebody else).

Organising employees into cells involves changing the way that workplaces are structured into areas called cells where the whole of the product is made by a team (cell) of workers. The main purpose is to increase motivation, sense of

responsibility and to raise quality, thus lowering costs and increasing profitability.

Lean production

Lean production means cutting out all the wasteful activities from the production process. For example consider the following set of operations:

Activity 1	25 seconds	Adds value to the product
Activity 2	15 seconds	Adds value to the product
Activity 3	12 seconds	Doesn't add any value
Activity 4	2 seconds	Adds value
Activity 5	39 seconds	Doesn't add value
Activity 6	2 seconds	Doesn't add value
Activity 7	60 seconds	Adds value

You can see from the chart above that there is a production process that lasts for 2 minutes and 35 seconds. However, for 53 seconds no value is being added to the end product. Lean production involves trying to cut out the waste. Finding out ways to cut out waste often involves bringing together teams of workers who are involved in the processes concerned and encouraging them to discuss ways of cutting out waste.

By cutting out waste in lean production it is possible to increase efficiency, leading to lower unit labour costs and higher productivity levels.

Theory into practice

Carry out some primary research, for example through interviewing a production manager or by means of a questionnaire to a manufacturing company, to find out:

* what are the main types of production method used in the business: job, batch, flow, cell and lean

* the advantages and disadvantages of the methods used.

Suggest ways of improving one of the production processes for a product of your choice or suggest how the firm might benefit from using a different production method, for example by introducing cell working.

CASE STUDY

Lean thinking

Lean thinking became popular in the West in the mid-1990s with the publication of a book called *Lean Thinking* by James P Womack and Daniel T Jones. They set out to show how production could be designed to meet the customers need for a product 'at a specific price at a specific time'. They started from the belief that what customers want is value for money.

They then set about identifying the key steps in providing this value, while cutting down on waste. Once you have decided on how to cut out waste the next step is to create the value-creating steps.

They argued that organisations need to be reorganised into product teams which focus on the customer. This enables companies to let customers pull the product from them as they need it, rather than pushing products on to a market that does not necessarily want them. From this stage it is a small step forward to mass customisation – mass producing products which at the same time meet individual customer needs through subtle yet clear differences.

1 What is the central focus of lean production?
2 Why do you think it is termed 'lean production'?
3 How does lean production enable organisations to become more competitive?
4 Why is it a continuous process?
5 What is the link between lean production and quality?

8.2.4 Ensuring quality

Businesses have different criteria to ensure quality. The criteria may be different from business to business and may include considerations of:

Fitness for purpose

Something is 'fit for purpose' if it does what the consumer or user expects of it. For example, if I want a very cheap sandwich because I am hungry, and buy one which is near to its sell by date for a reduction of 50p – then it is fit for the purpose that I required. Another day, I may want a luxury sandwich and pay a premium price for it in a coffee shop – that sandwich too is fit for the purpose.

Excellence in function, appearance and overall image

This indicates that an item does everything the user expects and delights that customer. For example, I may buy a pen to write a letter and find that it:

* works really smoothly and makes my writing look clear and exciting,

* has an attractive look – it is an item that I am proud to own, look at and display.

* has an excellent overall image – it makes me feel good about myself as the owner of that pen.

You will readily identify with this notion of excellence – think about some of the clothes and CDs that you have bought that really delighted you.

Freedom from faults and errors

Sometimes we are disappointed by items which are flawed in some way, e.g. a car that breaks down when it is relatively new, or a tap we have mended that continues to leak. Real quality occurs when there are no mistakes and the new item is 100% reliable. Can you think of items that you have purchased that have been free from faults and errors?

Durability with limited necessity for repair or replacement

Durability is a great feature of goods that we purchase. Think of items that you have that you love because they have gone on and on giving you value. Because we can rely on them they are often our most trusted possessions.

Value for money

Value for money does not necessarily mean cheap (although it can do). For example, an expensive pair of trainers may be considered to provide value for money because they give an air of prestige, are comfortable and cool, etc.

Value for money is all about providing a lot of satisfaction for each penny spent on the good or service. An expensive car therefore may provide more value for money than a cheaper one. People often use the expression 'you get what you pay for'.

In his widely acclaimed book *Thriving on Chaos* (1998), Tom Peters argued that consumers' perception of the quality of a product or service is the most important factor in determining its

Theory into practice

Use either primary research (interview or questionnaire) or secondary research (websites on the Internet) to identify how a particular business emphasises the following quality criteria for their product. Fill in the following table.

Quality criteria	Explain how the firm emphasises this criteria
Fitness for purpose	
Excellence in function / appearance / image	
Freedom from faults and errors	
Durability	
Value for money	

CASE STUDY

Aspects of quality

BIC pens provides a good example of a business with a strong emphasis on quality. The BIC Group's manufacturing expertise is based on a 50-year heritage in ballpoint pens. This means excellent performance every day, thanks to high-technology facilities and equipment, integrated production processes, well-trained employees and a rigorous quality control system.

The BIC Quality Department regularly checks products made throughout the world to ensure that the same high quality and safety standards are applied consistently in each location.

BIC's total quality commitment extends to all aspects of its business, including packaging and sales, giving retailers and distributors a world-renowned brand they can deliver with confidence to consumers.

Aspects of providing quality ballpoint pens include:

1 *Fitness for purpose.* When customers buy a BIC pen they expect to receive a writing implement that enables them to write notes, make out cheques and other writing operations. Products should do what customers expect of them. At one level this involves providing a reliable and easy to operate ballpoint pen, but it may involve additional features such as providing a steady grip, a reliable ink supply, good flow over the page etc.

2 *Excellence in function, appearance and image.* BIC provides a range of pens varying from the standard BIC crystal pen that we are all familiar with to newer more sophisticated pens such as the BIC crystal grip and BIC crystal gel pens. BIC pens are instantly recognisable in a market in which there is a lot of competition by their appearance and image.

3 *Freedom from faults and errors.* This is an important aspect of quality. Customers'

perceptions about the quality of a business are often more influenced by their memories of purchases that didn't meet the required standards than of products that worked well. 100% of the balls that go into the BIC ballpoint pen are checked for roundness and resistance and there are many other quality checks for BIC ballpoint pens such as checking for air bubbles in the ink cartridge.

4 *Durability.* Another aspect of quality that is important for many businesses is that of durability. A BIC biro is robust, and the ink lasts for a long period of time.

5 *Value for money.* Another criteria which is widely built into the concept of quality is that of having a reasonable price for the standard of product. For example, BIC crystal pens are very cheap compared with rival products. BIC is able to gain this advantage because it produces very large quantities enabling it to drive costs down. The BIC Group also owns Schaeffer pens. While these are very expensive compared with for example, a standard BIC biro, they are reasonably priced when compared with other upmarket pens. So when looking at value for money we need to compare the price with the standard for the product.

1 What do you understand by the term 'quality'?
2 Why do you think that BIC needs a quality department?
3 What do you think is meant by a total quality commitment?
4 Apply the concepts of fitness for purpose, excellence in function, appearance and image, freedom from faults and errors, durability and value for money to a product other than pens.

success. Quality as defined by the consumer, he argued, is more important than price in determining demand for most goods and services. Consumers will be prepared to pay for the best quality. Value is thus added by creating those quality standards required by consumers.

Nearly all businesses today (at least those that are successful) understand the importance of quality. However, different businesses set out different criteria for creating quality depending on the types of products and services they make, the types of markets they operate in and the values of the organisation and its leaders.

Quality initiatives

Businesses have a number of initiatives which they look to use to ensure quality is achieved at various points of the production process. These initiatives include:

* quality control
* quality assurance
* ISO (9000)
* TQM
* benchmarking
* kaizen (continuous improvement).

Think it over…

An interesting quote which highlights the importance of the customer in the quality process is that:

'We judge ourselves mostly by our intentions but others judge us mostly by our actions.'

How true do you think this quote is?

In the context of quality, consumers judge a good or service in terms of what they actually get, not what the producer hopes to provide.

Tom Peters (who we referred to earlier as an important writer on Quality issues) emphasises the important of what he refers to as **Total Quality Management** (TQM). This involves taking quality to new heights and involves three stages in the development of quality.

1   Quality control
2   Quality assurance (QA)
3   Total Quality Management (TQM)

Quality control

Quality control is an old idea. It is concerned with detecting and cutting out components or products that fall below set standards. This process takes place after these products have been produced. It may involve considerable waste as defective products are scrapped. Quality control is carried out by quality-control inspectors. Inspection and testing are the most common methods of carrying out quality control.

We can illustrate how quality control works by taking the example of a head chef working at a top restaurant. Prior to a business event being held at the restaurant, he or she will have prepared the recipes and tried them out. The staff will all have been briefed on how to cook the meals to the chef's recipe – how long to cook each item, how to present it etc.

On the evening of the event the head chef will not be able to supervise the production of each meal but will be able to make sure that they have been cooked to his specifications. The chefs will prepare the food and then it will be put on the plates ready for distribution to the guests. At this stage, the head chef will engage in quality inspection. He/she will check each plate before it leaves the kitchen. He/she will do this visually by looking at the presentation and also by testing samples to make sure they meet the requirements. Some meals he/she will throw in the bin as being unsatisfactory, others will be altered, for example by removing vegetables which are overcooked.

Inspection is important because it provides an opportunity to make sure that sub-standard products are not being supplied to customers, but it can lead to an awful lot of waste.

Quality assurance

Quality assurance occurs both during and after the event and is concerned with trying to stop faults from happening in the first place. Quality assurance is concerned with making sure products are produced to predetermined standards. The aim is to produce with 'zero defects'.

Quality assurance (QA) is the responsibility of the workforce, working in cells or teams, rather than an inspector (although inspection will take place). Quality standards should be maintained by following steps set out in a QA system.

To create an effective quality-assurance system requires a lot of training and the development of clear manuals and guidelines so that individual employees can learn the required processes at each stage of production. It is based on the process of 'empowerment' (giving power/ responsibility to individuals) at every level within the organisation, particularly within manufacturing teams. It replaces end of production line inspection as the primary means of ensuring quality. Every employee is now responsible for the quality of their work. For example, in a small company making sandwiches a production line might start with the first operative taking bread out of packets and cutting off the crusts, and then passing it along to the next operative who spreads a thin layer of butter, the third operative fills the sandwiches, the fourth packs the sandwiches, etc. With a quality-assurance system each operative is given the responsibility for guaranteeing the quality of their work. The first operative must treat the second as their customer and seek to supply them with materials that have zero defects. Not only are employees in such a system given responsibility for quality assurance, they are also empowered to identify ways of making improvements in their work.

Total Quality Management

Total Quality Management (TQM) is the most complete form of operations management. It is concerned with encouraging everyone in the workplace to think about quality in everything he or she does. Every employee sets out to satisfy customers, placing them at the heart of the production process.

Companies such as BIC and Tesco have been following this policy for a long time. It involves providing customers with what they want, when they want it and how they want it. It involves

FIGURE 8.6 *Moving to Total Quality Management*

moving with changing customer requirements and fashions to design products and services that meet and exceed their requirements. Delighted customers will pass the message on to their friends.

With a TQM approach, quality should become part of the **culture** (typical way of doing things) in the organisation.

By training staff to understand the importance of quality, they can then build it into everything they do, for example:

* trying to identify problems before they happen
* trying to please the customer without having to be told to do so by a supervisor
* thinking about how improvements can be made and then having the confidence to suggest them.

The staff are the best people to implement the systems because they know what is going well and what is going badly at grass-roots level. Involving ground-level staff in ensuring quality means they are more motivated – because they are involved in decision-making and because they have a better understanding of the quality objectives of their organisation.

Another major advantage of developing the quality culture is that inspection is cheaper to carry out. Improvement is a continuous process, and you do not have to wait for the problems to come to light at the end of the process.

Quality circles

Quality circles (QCs) are an important way of increasing participation in organisational activities. A quality circle is a study group of volunteers (5–15 people) that meets regularly to work on a variety of operational and employee problems. The quality circle will be made up of ordinary working employees and their immediate supervisors and managers. One supervisor or manager will usually operate as the circle's leader.

Quality circles do not deal with theoretical problems. They are concerned with putting ideas into action. This involves in-depth analysis, proposals for action and presentations to management on what could or ought to be done. There are four main components of a quality circle framework.

1 A steering committee (one per organisation), staffed by senior managers, will make general policy and set up the framework and resources for the circles to operate within.

2 The facilitator is there to support the process in each of the circles, as well as to provide an operational framework and guidance, if required.

3 The circles' leaders will often be the unit supervisors and they will stimulate discussion within their circle without dominating it. Leaders need to be familiar with problem-solving techniques and group dynamics.

4 The members of the circle. The circles meet during company time, perhaps for one hour a week. Problem-solving techniques employed will include brainstorming, graphs showing the frequency of problems, sampling of products and other tools.

ISO 9000

Reliable quality is a prime concern when deciding which supplier of a good or service to use. Leading retail organisations in this country like Marks & Spencer and Tesco extend their own quality-control procedures into their suppliers'

An ISO 9000 certificate

organisations to ensure reliability. A reputation for quality is important, but it can be established only over time. This presents problems for organisations tendering for orders from new customers.

The International Quality Standard **ISO 9000** certificate indicates to potential customers that the quality procedures of the certificate holders are reliable and, by implication, they are capable of delivering consistently the promised quality of the good or service.

To gain ISO 9000, organisations need to implement a range of quality management systems and procedures which relate to a range of aspects of how the organisation operates from checking on the quality of inputs, through creating quality processes and ensuring the highest quality of finished outputs. Managers are responsible for creating audits of quality procedures and for creating quality policies. Employees need to be trained in quality procedures. Once the systems are in place, the organisation will be inspected and its procedures examined before it is allowed to claim the standard. It will then be subject to periodic audits to check that it is maintaining the standards required.

For organisations wishing to develop quality systems, ISO 9000 provides a ready-made system for quality management.

Benchmarking

Benchmarking has been defined as 'the continuous process of measuring products, services and practices against the toughest

CASE STUDY
Nissan at Sunderland

Over 20 years ago (1984) Nissan and the UK government signed an agreement to build a car plant at Sunderland. The plant has been an ongoing success and introduced British workers to a new approach to quality management – known as kaizen. Nissan's aim was to create mutual trust and co-operation between all those involved at the plant in order to seek to best meet customer needs.

Nowadays, kaizen is a word much used in Sunderland. The literal translation of the Japanese word is 'continuous improvement'. The improvement is gained by slow and steady change and once achieved it is maintained at that level until the next improvement is introduced.

Nissan introduced quality circles in Japan in the 1960s and today there are thousands of active quality circles in the company. Such circles encourage contribution from a business's most important resource – its employees.

The kaizen programme at Nissan encourages constant quality awareness and is better suited to the needs of British workers than formal quality circles. Kaizen assumes the total involvement of all employees but recognises that participation depends on individuals genuinely feeling part of the Nissan team.

The company policy is that:

1 All staff have a valuable contribution to make as individuals, and this contribution can be most effective within a team environment.
2 Kaizen team activity helps develop leadership and presentation skills as well as enabling people to understand, acknowledge and learn from others.

Kaizen is only one way in which employees may participate in issues that affect their workforce. The kaizen philosophy may be applied anywhere at any time. Everyone is encouraged to participate in the activity and as members of a team, learn how to analyse situations logically and factually and discuss issues meaningfully and efficiently. People who contribute to the activity include:

* leaders – who receive special training in the kaizen process and then apply these skills to team activities
* members – who participate in the activities, often from the same work area
* specialists who assist a team with a particular project.

The kaizen process is designed to enable a team to move on from the stage of dealing with current problems or areas in need of improvement to a stage where sources of concern are dealt with in advance of their actual occurrence.

1 **Explain how and why kaizen activity or the process of participation through quality circles might motivate employees to contribute more to quality issues.**
2 **Explain how the kaizen approach is based on 'total quality'.**
3 **What organisational benefits can you see arising from 'kaizen'?**
4 **How will the customer benefit from dealing with organisations which adopt 'kaizen'?**

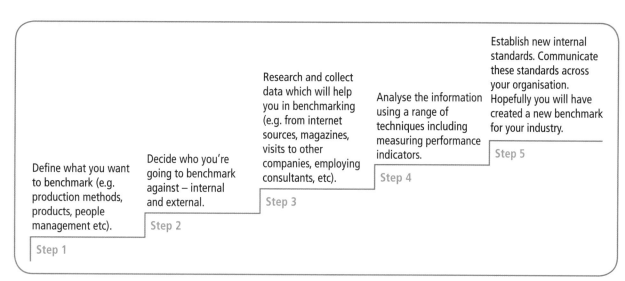

FIGURE 8.7 *Benchmarking can be seen as a series of steps.*

competitors of those companies recognised as industry leaders'.

Best practice benchmarking (BPB) is a method many organisations use to help them to discover the 'best' methods of carrying out processes which are currently being used and then to adapt these processes for use in their own organisation.

Organisations can benchmark internally, for example by examining best practice in another department or externally by looking at best practice in another organisation. Many organisations will set themselves the objective of becoming the 'benchmark for the industry' in which they operate.

BPB involves:

✴ finding out what customers consider excellent practice to be

✴ setting standards for business processes based on best practice

✴ finding out how the best companies create best practice and create standards within an organisation that meet or exceed the best currently available.

Recent research has shown that over two-thirds of major companies in the UK use benchmarking and that 90 per cent of these use benchmarking regularly to improve quality.

The benchmarking process can be seen as a series of steps – in which you seek to move up from Step 1 to Step 5. See Figure 8.7.

Kaizen

The Japanese word '**kaizen**' means continuous improvement. Typically it involves making small improvement steps all the time rather than major changes. Kaizen involves quality circles and the process of Total Quality Management (TQM). Kaizen processes are illustrated in the case study on the previous page.

8.2.5 Stock control

In an ideal world, in which businesses know demand well in advance and suppliers always meet delivery dates, there would be little need for *stocks*. In practice, demand varies and suppliers are often late, so stock acts as a protection against unpredictable events.

Organisations hold stocks in a variety of forms:

✴ raw materials (for example supplies of tungsten carbide which BIC converts into the balls in its ballpoint pens.

✴ work-in-progress (components of ballpoint pens that are in the process of being assembled)

✴ finished goods (completed ballpoint pens)

✴ consumables (items such as oil for servicing machinery in a BIC plant)

✴ plant and machinery spares.

Efficient production management involves making sure that you order enough stocks of items to keep your production line running in the most desirable way. For example, BIC will need to order tungsten carbide from metal suppliers on a regular basis in line with fluctuations in its use of this metal. It will need to order sufficient supplies of plastic and the chemicals that go into producing its inks.

If it is running short of any of these items it cannot expect instant delivery. The time taken between when it orders new stocks and when they are delivered is called the *lead time*.

The aim of any stock-control system is to provide stocks that cater for uncertainties but are at minimum levels thus making sure that costs are kept low without reducing service to customers.

Balancing stock levels is essential. Having too little or too much stock can be harmful to a business. High stock levels represent money lying idle, whereas low stock levels might mean that the business cannot fulfil its orders.

Buffer stocks (a stockpile) can be built up as a protection against stocks running out owing to unexpected variations in demand. A minimum level will be set below which it will be hoped that stocks will not fall, although this may depend on the lead time between placing an order and its receipt.

Figure 8.9 shows an ideal situation in which stocks never fall below the set minimum level or go above the set maximum level.

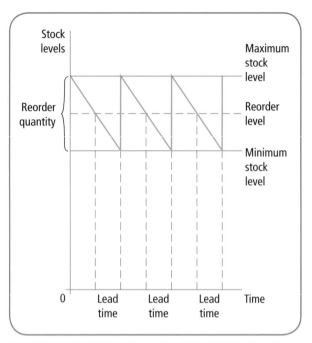

FIGURE 8.9 *Maintaining stock levels*

Stocks are replenished just at the point at which the minimum stock level is about to be breached. In reality, delivery times, reorder quantities and rates of usage will vary and either a continuous or periodic review system will monitor and control the levels.

At regular intervals, stock is counted and accurately recorded so that trading results can be calculated. The physical counting of stock can be time-consuming and it is inevitable that inaccuracies will creep in. After stock is counted it is checked against records so that discrepancies can be investigated.

Problems of low stocks	Problems of high stocks
Difficult to satisfy consumer requirements	Increased risk of stocks becoming out of date (obsolete)
Potential loss of business	Potential loss of business
Potential loss of goodwill (what people think of the business – their loyalty and willingness to buy from it)	High storage costs
Ordering needs to be frequent and handling costs rise	Stocks tie up working capital (ie money that is required to pay the daily bills of the business)

FIGURE 8.8 *Problems with high and low stock levels*

The following information relates to the stock-control system of two businesses. Read through the data and then answer the questions by drawing graphs to show:

* maximum stock levels

* minimum stock levels

* the reorder quantity

* the reorder level.

1 A business starts the year with a stock of 1,000 which is its maximum stock level. It uses up 100 units of stock per month. The minimum stock level which it is prepared to hold is 600 units. The lead time between ordering stock and having it delivered is one month. Draw a stock chart for this business (assuming that when it reorders it orders a sufficient quantity necessary to return it to the maximum stock level).

2 At the end of December it was noted that there were only 800 units left at the ABC business. ABC uses up 200 of its units every month. The minimum stock level allowed by managers in the company is 600. The lead time to replenish stock is 1 month. However, managers do not like to hold more than 1,000 in stock because stock dates very quickly. When should new stock be ordered? How many should be ordered? Draw a stock chart for the next six months starting from the 1 January.

It is important in stock management that there is a *rotation of stock*. A useful basis for this is 'first in first out'. In other words you get rid of your oldest stock first.

Market traders have always practised first in first out. They put their oldest stock nearest to customers, so that they don't incur the wastage (loss of profit) from their stock going off.

It is important to rotate stock because:

* old stock goes out of fashion

* old stock of perishables goes off.

However, you must bear in mind that getting rid of old stock to customers goes against 'quality

The Japanese use the term '**kanban**' for any form of sign or signal that someone who uses stocks sends to the stock provider asking for new supplies. This could be a buzzer, a bell or a visual signal that new stocks are required. With a kanban system the emphasis is on the user of stocks to ask for fresh supplies when they are needed. One of the earliest kanban systems occurred in a factory fitting small springs into a mechanical device. The operatives had to fit three springs. However, sometimes they forgot how many they had put in, so that for example they might only put two springs in. A kanban system was therefore created where workers were given plastic bowls with three springs in. When they had completed fitting them they put out the bowl as a kanban that they wanted another bowl with three more springs. This helped to cut mistakes to zero.

principles' that place the customer at the heart of things. If you sell old stock then you may lose customers. The most efficient business therefore is the one that stocks those items that customers will buy when they are freshly bought in. Good stock management is therefore a very important skill.

Stock control in this country has improved enormously as a result of the adoption of 'just-in-time' (JIT) approaches. JIT is now used in many different industries ranging from chocolate manufacturing to constructing motor vehicles.

The great thing about JIT is that much less storage space is required and there is much less wastage of scarce resources because stocks, parts and finished goods are only delivered just before they are required for use. The traditional 'just in case' (JIC) approach relied on having lots of spares in stock. These spare supplies were often damaged, went out of date, got lost and sat there taking up space.

Examine the stock control processes in an organisation of your choice. Explain whether the organisation typically uses a JIT or a JIC system. What are the advantages of the system that it uses? What are the disadvantages compared with using the other system?

The distinction between 'just in case' and 'just-in-time'

The traditional British method of holding stocks has been termed 'just in case'. In other words you hold surplus stock just in case you need it to make up orders, for example to cope with a sudden surge in demand. Just in case is quite a costly and messy business. The more stock you hold, the more difficult it may be to sell it as it may get damaged, go out of fashion or go out of date.

The alternative Japanese approach is that of just-in-time. Supplies, components and other stocks are supplied to manufacturing processes just in time for when they are needed. The production-line employee that needs stocks signals to supplies by pressing a buzzer or giving some other form of signal that they will shortly need fresh supplies. These are then delivered just in time from the factory stores. Production can therefore take place in a much smaller area and in a much cleaner and better-organised workplace. This should help to reduce costs and increase **efficiency**.

However, the weakness of just-in-time is if there is some sudden disruption to supplies, such as a natural disaster or some man-made cause such as a strike. In such situations it doesn't take long for production to have to shut down completely.

1 **What situations (e.g. types of manufacturing) can you think of where just in case is more appropriate?**
2 **In what situations is just-in-time more appropriate?**
3 **Which system do you think is likely to be more efficient – just-in-time or just in case?**

8.2.6 Health and safety

Businesses have to adhere to a number of legal requirements in their production process. Some of these requirements relate to reducing levels of pollution, but the main legislation attempts to protect workers involved in production and relates to health and safety issues.

Businesses today have a responsibility to make their workplaces as safe for their employees as possible. The British health and safety laws are rooted in the Health and Safety at Work Act (HASAWA) 1974 and the Management of Health and Safety at Work Regulations 1999 (the Management Regulations). These Acts outline the duties which employers have towards employees and members of the public and which employees have to themselves and to each other. There are numerous other Acts specific to certain workplaces. It is necessary, therefore for a particular employer to familiarise themself with any laws specific to their industry.

The responsibilities imposed by the HASAWA are not just upon employers. It also imposes obligations on the employee with regard to responsibility for Health and Safety. Section 7 (a) requires all employees to take reasonable care for their own health and safety at work and that of others who may be affected by their acts or omissions (what they do not do). Section 7 (b) requires all employees to co-operate with the employer in carrying out their health and safety responsibilities. Section 8 requires all employees not to interfere intentionally or recklessly with, or misuse, anything provided in the interests of health, safety and welfare.

What employers are required to do under the Health and Safety at Work Act 1974 is to look at what the risks are in their particular workplace and take sensible measures to tackle them.

The key requirement of employers is to carry out a *risk assessment* in their workplace and record the significant findings of the risk assessment. Following this assessment, the employer should then:

* appoint nominated employees to implement the health and safety measures identified as necessary by the risk assessment

* set up emergency procedures

* provide clear information and training to employees.

The Management of Health and Safety at Work Regulations 1999 covers standards of care in a number of areas:

* the maintenance of the workplace and of equipment, devices and systems
* ventilation, temperature and lighting in indoor workplaces
* cleanliness and the handling of waste materials
* room dimensions and space
* floors and organisation of traffic routes
* windows and transparent doors, gates and walls
* ability to clean windows safely
* escalators and moving walkways
* sanitary conveniences
* drinking water
* accommodation for clothing and facilities for changing clothes
* facilities for rest and to eat meals.

The regulations suggest that one of the company directors should be appointed health and safety director to oversee these matters for the company. They also make it clear that a safety officer or adviser should be appointed.

You can see from the above requirements of the Health and Safety at Work Act and related legislation that safe production can only take place within a framework of abiding by laws and regulations.

Theory into practice

Research ways in which the Health and Safety at Work Act affects the production of your chosen item. Carry out primary research by interviewing the production manager or safety officer of the company, or giving them a questionnaire with answers to complete. You can carry out secondary research by examining websites – for example by using the search terms 'Health and Safety', and your chosen product or industry.

The law requires that employers and employees shall operate in a safe way and that appropriate risk assessments are carried out in relation to the production process. There are additional requirements in relation to the cleanliness and handling of waste materials.

8.2.7 Research into production

The assessment for this unit asks you to produce a written report containing visual images of how your chosen business produces a particular item within your chosen business context.

To produce a realistic and appropriate report, you need to carry out different forms of research.

Primary research

Primary research may include face-to-face discussions carried out with a speaker from a production department. Your teacher should be able to organise this for the whole of your group. In addition, it may be possible for groups to use personal contacts to interview someone from a production department and other functional areas of a local business by using questionnaires or surveys.

An ideal way of carrying out the primary research for the activity is for your teacher to arrange for you to visit a plant where operations are taking place. Before going on the visit you need to be clear about the sorts of areas that you want to find information about. Set out these areas in a set of questions, for example:

* How many people are employed in production activities?
* Is production split into a number of sub-sections? If so, what are they?
* What are the main processes involved in the production of a specific item?
* How can these processes/activities be set out in a flow chart?

* What are the main resources used in the production process (raw materials, human, machinery, plant, etc)?

* How is quality managed within the organisation?

* How efficient is the production of the product you are examining?

* What current problems are encountered in the production of a specific product? (Perhaps you can look at these in terms of the five Ps of production.)

During your visit or following the visit your teacher may be able to arrange for you to spend some time with someone responsible for production in the company who will be able to answer your questions.

Secondary research

Secondary research includes information gained from textbooks, the Internet and other relevant reading material. Very useful information for this research will be a company annual report which outlines key operational areas and in addition any materials provided about the company's products and production processes (including quality systems).

You will score higher marks for relating your research into the production of a specific product made by a real business and to the production processes of that business.

The following chart gives a summary of some of the most important areas to research:

1 The role of production in a particular business. The role of the production department in organising the production of a specific product.
2 How the production department interacts with other departments such as finance, marketing, and human resources in organising the production of a specific product.
3 How a specific product is produced and whether it is produced efficiently.
4 Ways of measuring the efficiency of production, e.g. important performance indicators such as wage costs per unit.

5 How production is organised, e.g. job, batch, flow etc., in relation to your chosen product.
6 What aspects of quality your business emphasises (e.g. fitness for purpose).
7 What initiatives are used to ensure quality (e.g. TQM, benchmarking etc) of your chosen product.
8 How stock is ordered in your chosen business and for your chosen product.
9 How stock is managed, e.g. just in case or just-in-time. Is it possible to use diagrams to illustrate the stock-control system for your chosen product?
10 How does the Health and Safety at Work Act affect the production of your chosen product?
11 Does any other legislation affect the production of your chosen product?

8.2.8 Potential production improvements

When making informed judgements on possible improvements to the business's production process, you need to ask the following questions:

1 Could improvements be made to the way in which the production function is organised in order to improve the production of the selected product?

   Look at the organisation of the production function in terms of the way it is organised to take responsibility for a range of products that the company makes – could this be better structured to give more attention to the needs of your product?

2 Could the way the production department interacts with other departments such as finance, marketing, and human resources in organising the production of a specific product be improved? For example, does the interaction with human resources lead to enough workers with the right skills being trained to maintain high-quality production? Does liaison with finance and accounts help to give an accurate **costing** of the product? Do marketing and production work in such a way as to provide products which are customer focused?

3 Could the specific product be produced more efficiently?

Here you will need to consider the 5 Ps of production and how well they are organised.

4 Could production be organised more efficiently e.g. by different methods such as job, batch, flow etc. in relation to your chosen product?

5 How could initiatives to ensure quality (e.g. TQM, benchmarking etc) be improved for your chosen product?

Perhaps here you could draw on some of your reading into initiatives used by other businesses to show how your business could make use of best practice that is applied in other companies.

6 Could the processes for ordering stock for your chosen product be improved? For example, is there enough information about stock levels to inform the timing of ordering in new stocks so as to minimise waste? Is there room for ordering stock in greater quantities to gain discounts? How well organised is stock ordering?

7 Could stock management be improved, e.g. by changing the system from just in case to just-in-time?

8 Could health and safety aspects related to the product be improved? Assuming that risk assessments and other requirements have been met, is there scope for making improvements to health and safety procedures, e.g. by reorganising production methods or layout?

9 How could the production process be improved to give more focus to the customer? Remember that quality is all about fitness for the consumers' purpose. Emphasis on this should provide a useful conclusion to your evaluation.

KNOWLEDGE CHECK

1 What is the relationship between inputs, processes and outputs in the production process? Use an example with which you are familiar to illustrate your answer.

2 What is meant by adding value in production? Explain how value is added in the provision of three different services e.g. retailing, banking, and hair dressing.

3 What is 'operations management'?

4 What are the 5 Ps of production in relation to the manufacture of a specific product, e.g. the production of chocolate bars?

5 What is meant by operational efficiency? How can it be improved?

6 What are economies of scale? Illustrate them with reference to the operation of a large hotel chain.

7 What is a 'unit cost'? How can unit costs be lowered?

8 What is a 'capacity level'? How could the capacity level of a production plant be increased?

9 How would you measure labour productivity in a supermarket?

10 Explain one way of measuring capital productivity.

11 What is the difference between job and batch production? Give examples to illustrate your answer.

12 Give examples of industries that would use flow production techniques.

13 What is cell production? What are the advantages of cell production?

14 How does lean production help business enterprises to be efficient?

15 Explain the difference between the terms 'quality control' and 'quality assurance'.

16 What are the three stages in the development of quality? Explain the difference in each case.

17 Why might firms seek to achieve ISO 9000.

18 What is 'best practice benchmarking'? How would this help a firm to achieve an advantage over rivals?

19 Explain the following terms in relation to stock control – 'lead time', 'minimum order quantity', 'buffer stock'.

20 Describe the main problems associated with low and high stocks. How does just-in-time help to deal with these problems?

Resources

The emphasis in this unit is on applying businesses concepts in a practical context which means you will need to research how a product is made in an actual organisation. The following resources will be helpful:

* visits to manufacturing businesses and interviews with employees. These need to be planned well in advance. For example, visits to Cadbury's World near Birmingham need to be booked by your teacher up to six months in advance of the visit

* talks by well-informed employees about the production process

* business materials, for example, the Times 100 (www.tt100.biz) provide a good case study on the production processes at Coca-Cola

* case studies produced by your teacher

* national and local newspapers often provide materials which examine production-related issues.

Books

Many general business texts provide a section on production and operations management.

Examples of books which deal directly with operations management include:

Harrison, S., Swift, A. and Gellespie, A., *Operations Management* (2002), London, Hodder and Stoughton,

Vidler, C. *Operations Management* (2001), Oxford, Heinemann

Websites

Some useful websites are listed below. These addresses are current at the time of writing. However, it needs to be recognised that new sites are being launched on the Internet on a regular basis and that older sites may change or disappear.

Typing 'production' or 'operations management' into an advanced search engine such as Google will give you a list of many potential areas that can be investigated.

www.tt100.biz provides lots of up-to-date case studies many of which are about production and operations management.

www.geocities.com/TimesSquare/1848/japan21 Kanban production system from Japan.

www.tutor2u.net has an extensive area on business studies and there is a link for production related issues.

All of these can be accessed through www.learn.co.uk

Glossary

Action plan a short to medium term plan setting out a series of actions that need to be completed by particular named individuals by particular dates.

Activator someone who is able to put plans into action.

Added value making a good or service more desirable to the consumer. The added value can be measured by deducting the input value from the output value.

Agenda a document setting out a list of topics to be discussed at a meeting.

Annual General Meeting under company law, the directors of a company must present a report to shareholders each year at an annual general meeting; at this time shareholders have the right to ask questions and in some cases can vote to replace directors.

Applicant a person applying for a job.

Appraisal interview between a manager and employee to agree targets for the future.

Arithmetic mean total of values divided by the number of values.

Automation production processes that are controlled by machinery and information devices such as equipment rather than by direct human control.

B2B business-to-business interaction or communication through the medium of the Internet.

B2C direct links between businesses and consumers through the Internet.

Balance sheet a snapshot of a firm's assets, liabilities and sources of capital at a moment in time.

Bank loan loan from the bank for a specific purpose for which interest is charged.

Bank of England central bank.

Bankruptcy where a business or person is taken to court to prevent further trading.

Batch a quantity of similar or identical products that is made at the same time. Typically one type of batch will then be replaced by an alternative type of batch. The original type of batch can then be produced again at a later stage using the same or similar processes.

Benchmarking the continuous process of measuring products, services and practices against the toughest competitors of those companies recognised as industry leaders.

Board of Directors Senior directors of a company who have been appointed to direct company activities.

Body language communication involving sending signals by the ways in which we position and use our bodies e.g. through hand signals, gestures, facial expressions, crossing of the arms etc.

Brand symbol, image or sign associated with a particular product or service.

Break-even analysis comparison of a firm's revenue and its fixed and variable costs, to identify the minimum sales level needed to break even; it can be shown on a break-even chart.

Break-even point the level of output at which total revenue equals total costs.

Breaking even making sure costs are covered.

Browsing viewing the Internet by entering it through a web viewing program such as Internet Explorer.

Budget a financial plan for the future that is set out in numbers.

Building society a mutual organisation providing a range of financial services for personal customers.

Business customer a business such as a sole trader, partnership or joint-stock company that is a customer of a financial services institution.

Business plan an organised document that enables a business to prepare for the future and forecast all of the events and actions it takes within the context of a range of forecasts.

Candidate individual who has applied for a job and will continue with the recruitment process.

Capacity the quantity that a business, production line, or a manufacturing process is able to produce assuming that resources are fully utilised.

Cash-flow forecast a technique for estimating the future bank balance of a company and anticipating overdraft requirements.

Cell a team of workers, using pooled equipment and resources working on the production of a complete product or most of a product in a given space.

Closed questions questions that limit the range of responses and often obtain a yes or no answer or a number.

Code of practice this emphasises the commitment of an organisation to its customers and will attempt to show how any elements of dissatisfaction or issues can be resolved; also a voluntary agreement constructed by a trade association for its members.

Company any type of business that has a legal separate identity from its members; most companies are limited and most are registered under the Companies Act.

Constraint a limiting factor.

Consumers people who use/consume a product.

Contagion the collapse of one institution leads to debts within the financial services market which then cause some form of loss of confidence in other financial institutions which leads to their collapse as well.

Contribution the money contribution that each unit of an item sold makes towards paying off the fixed costs of a business; for example, if the variable cost of producing a chocolate bar is 10p and the chocolate bar is sold for 40p, each bar is contributing 30p (revenue variable cost; 40–10 = 30).

Costing financial activities involved in calculating how much it costs to carry out various activities and the costs of various elements for example in a production process. An example would be the calculation of the wage cost of producing a particular unit of production.

Creditor a business or person that the firm owes money to.

Culture the typical pattern of inter-relationships and way of doing things in an organisation.

Current assets   items that a business owns that can be turned into cash in the short term, such as stock or debtors.

Current liabilities   things that the business owes in the short term, such as goods bought and not paid for, or loans borrowed that must be paid back.

Curriculum Vitae   (usually called a CV) is a summary of your career to date.

Customer perceptions   the general public will have an overall impression of the level of service they expect an organisation to provide.

Customer satisfaction   a product's performance relative to a buyer's expectations.

Customer service   a process that provides time and place benefits for the customer pre-transaction, during the enjoyment of the product and post-transaction.

Customers   people who buy a product.

Database   a computer program for storing data and records.

Debenture   an acknowledgement of a debt made to a company issued as a security on the Stock Exchange for a fixed rate of interest and which specifies the terms of repayment at the end of a period.

Debtors   people who owe money to a business.

Demographics   characteristics of people such as age, gender, marital status, etc., which are used by marketers to segment the market as a whole.

Development   the process of identifying and then finding opportunities to meet the needs of individuals within an organisation.

Direct mail   mail sent though a media such as the post and targeted at customers.

Discrimination   treating individuals less favourably than others on account of factors such as gender and disability.

Diversification   spreading interests over a variety of products/activities.

Dividend   payment to shareholders out of company profits.

Economies of scale   the lowering of unit costs that arises as a result of producing larger outputs or selling increased quantities of a product. The advantages that larger businesses have over smaller ones.

Efficiency   maximising outputs from quantities of inputs.

Electronic commerce (ecommerce)   buying and selling using the Internet as the medium for making transactions.

Electronic data interchange (EDI)   a network link that allows customers such as retailers to pay suppliers electronically without the need for invoices and cheques, thus dramatically reducing the time, paperwork and costs involved.

Empowerment   giving responsibility to staff lower down the organisation so that individuals are given power to make decisions, rather than being told what to do.

Encoding   putting an advertising or promotional message into a form that provides meaning for customers and consumers.

Ethics   moral principles or rules of conduct generally accepted by most members of a society.

Event management   the key processes involved in organising an event.

External constraints   influences outside the control of an organisation.

External customers   these may include individuals from different organisations working in business-to-business markets (B2B) as well as individual customers.

External written communications   communications sent outside an organisation.

Facilitator   an individual whose role is to enable others to work smoothly towards achieving set objectives by providing them with the means to do so.

Factoring company   an organisation that buys a business's debts and can manage short-term finances

Financial Services Act   1986 Act that aimed to increase competition. It has now been overtaken by the Financial Services and Markets Act 2000, which, amongst other things, has concentrated regulatory power in the hands of the Financial Services Authority (FSA).

Financial Services Authority (FSA)   the single financial regulator in the UK. In order to do business in the UK most financial service firms must get permission from the FSA. The FSA regulates banks, building societies, insurance and investment firms and independent financial advisers. The FSA is also responsible for Lloyd's Insurance Market and its powers today cover general insurance advice and mortgage lending.

Fixed cost   a business cost that does not vary with the level of output or sales.

Flow production   system whereby raw materials and products flow down a line in a continuous way. Continuous flow production in some case takes place 24/7.

Focus groups   small groups of customers who are able to discuss their needs in some depth.

Forming   the stage in team development where individuals first come together.

Functions   the components or departments of a business involving some form of specialism, e.g. marketing, production, accounts, human resources.

Gantt chart   a chart set out in horizontal bars showing the sequencing of activities that need to be carried out and how long each will take.

Gap in the market   an opportunity to provide a good or service where there is little or no competition.

General insurance   covering a range of risks such as for property, motor insurance and travel insurance.

Hire purchase   goods are bought in instalments so that after a period of time they are owned by the buyer.

Hit   a single request for a file on a website; each transaction involves a separate hit.

Human resources department   department dealing with the management of policies and procedures relating to the people who work for an organisation; it covers areas such as payroll, sickness monitoring, grievance and disciplinary procedures.

Indirect discrimination   setting out a requirement which on the face of it may appear to be non-discriminatory but which is in fact more difficult for some groups of people to meet than others.

Induction   sessions introducing new staff to the work and work environment in an organisation.

Innovator   someone who comes up with bright and exciting new ideas and solutions to problems.

Inputs   what goes into the production process e.g. raw materials, human labour, capital equipment etc.

Insolvent   not having enough funds to meet pressing liabilities (debts).

Integrated accounts 'package'   accounting system running across a business organisation taking into account budgeted areas and departments that use the system.

Intention-to-buy   expressing a likelihood of purchase.

Internal constraints   controllable influences within an organisation.

Internal customers   within an organisation these would include all colleagues, ranging from support roles such as delivering post within the organisation, to jobs at the top of the organisation.

Internal written communications   communications within an organisation.

Internet   an internationally linked set of computer networks with a common addressing scheme.

Internet service provider (ISP)   a company that provides access to the Internet, usually for a payment.

Interviewing   the process of asking questions and giving tests to candidates in order to select the most suitable person to fill a job role.

Intranet   network within an organisation providing an internet-like framework with limited and exclusive access.

Investment   two principal meanings in business. 1. Sums of money invested in a business for which investors expect to receive a return. 2. Purchase by the business of an item that contributes to further production, e.g. a machine or tool.

ISO 9000   an international standard for businesses. The standard can be met by introducing a quality management system and a range of quality guaranteeing procedures.

Job analysis   a study of the tasks that are required to do a particular job.

Job application   details supplied to an employer typically in a job application form by someone seeking a post with an employing organisation.

Job description   the list of working conditions for a job e.g. pay, hours and duties.

Job production   a one off or one of a small number of production jobs to manufacture a set item e.g. a motorway bridge, a suit of clothes etc.

Just-in-time (JIT)   providing components, raw materials or finished products just-in-time for them to be used in production, or just when the consumer wants to use them.

Kaizen   making continuous steady small step improvements in production processes and activities.

Kanban   any form of signal from someone involved in manufacturing to a previous stage in the production process or to stores indicating that more stocks or supplies are required.

Leader   an individual with responsibility for giving direction and a sense of purpose to others.

Lean production   eliminating waste to concentrate on value adding activities.

Learning   is generally defined as 'a relatively permanent change in behaviour that occurs as a result of practice or experience'.

Leasing   the user pays for the use of an item and makes payments but does not become the owner of the item. After a period the leasing company will take back the item and sell it.

Liquidity   how quickly a business can turn its assets (anything it owns that is valuable into cash).

Manager   is someone with responsibility, usually for others, for making decisions and for managing resources.

Manufacturing   making things e.g. ball point pens, chocolate bars etc.

Margin of safety   the difference between a selected level of output and the break-even point.

Market   the whole situation in which products and services are traded by buyers and sellers.

Market research   'the systematic gathering, recording and analysis of data about problems related to the marketing of goods and services'.

Market segmentation   dividing the customers within a market into groups, each of which has distinctive needs and expectations.

Market share   the sales of a product by a company expressed as a percentage of total sales in a market; if a company sells 20,000 products and the total number of those product sold overall is 200,000, the company has a market share of 10%. Often market share is measured in sales revenue i.e. in £'s rather than the physical number of units sold.

Marketing   'the management process responsible for identifying, anticipating and satisfying customer requirements profitably'.

Marketing mix   a series of variable factors such as the four Ps (product/price/place/promotion) used by an organisation to meet its customers' needs.

Marketing objectives   the targets that the organisation seeks to meet through its marketing activities.

Marketing plan   a plan that uses the marketing mix to identify and then meet consumers' requirements

Mass marketing   marketing to all potential customers within a whole of a market in a way that fails to take into account parts of a market.

Median   middle number in an array of figures.

Mintel   a market research company that produces detailed market reports on most industries and products.

Minutes   a record of what was said in a meeting.

Mission   sets out the long-term purpose of an organisation and helps to emphasise why the organisation is there.

Mode   a value that occurs more frequently than others.

Mortgage   long-term loan secured upon a property.

Motivation   the personal drive to achieve targets and get things done.

Negotiator   someone who bargains with others to get a better deal.

Non-verbal communications   communications based upon body language.

Norming   the stage in team development when team members begin to share common values and ideas.

Objectives   the specific ends that an organisation or individual seeks to achieve.

Office of Fair Trading   a government body set up to look after the interests of consumers and traders.

Ombudsmen   role undertaken on behalf of consumers to investigate complaints about practices.

Online payment   method of paying for products and services, typically involving secure credit card payment at a computer terminal.

Open questions   questions that provide the respondent with the freedom to answer in a variety of ways.

Operations   the processes which are involved in making goods and services.

Operations management   the management function of organising and controlling production activities.

Outputs   the end products of the production process e.g. ballpoint pens.

Overdraft   money taken from a current account that leaves the account holder in deficit with the bank. It is set up for a small charge and interest charges are applied to amounts overdrawn.

Overheads   costs that do not change when the firm sells more, and are not incurred by a specific department of the company, e.g. rent.

Percentages   figures expressed as an amount of one hundred.

Performance appraisal   a process of systematically evaluating performance and providing feedback on adjustments that can be made.

Performance indicators   ways of measuring the performance of something such as a business process or a manufacturing resource. Performance indicators typically involve measurement in numbers.

Performing   the stage in team development when there is a consensus view and everyone is working to achieve shared goals.

Person specification   list of attributes needed by a person to perform a job, such as personality type or experience.

Personal customer   member of the general public who is a customer of a bank.

Personal digital assistant (PDA)   a very small personal computer that can fit into a pocket: data is input using a small keyboard or a pointing device.

PEST analysis   analysis examining political, economic, social and technological factors.

Planning   creating clear systems and direction for the future, often involves paper planning.

Positioning   placing a product within the overall market e.g. at the 'no frills' end or at the 'luxury' end of the market.

Post-sale surveys   aspect of a customer care programme used as a means of identifying the levels of satisfaction experienced by customers who have recently made a purchase.

PowerPoint   a Microsoft computer program for producing professional-looking and versatile slides for display on a computer during a presentation.

Pressure groups   these may be set up to fight a specific issue, such as the closure of a plant or the increased traffic on a road as a result of a local business.

Price-maker   organisation that has the freedom to set prices within the market.

Price-taker   organisation that sets prices at the market price dictated by market forces.

Primary data   data collected first hand for a specific purpose.

Primary information   information an organisation compiles by its own efforts perhaps commissioning a specialist market research agency.

Primary research   original research to find out information e.g. by asking questions and interviewing people.

Probability   likelihood or chance of achieving predicted outcomes.

Processes   all those activities which are involved in converting inputs into finished final products.

Product knowledge   the ability of staff to deal with any queries or issues that arise about products or services on offer.

Product life-cycle   key stages in the life of a product e.g. launch, introduction, growth, maturity, decline.

Production   activities involved in converting inputs into outputs by planning and organising processes.

Profit   the difference between revenue and cost.

Psychometric or aptitude testing   tests designed to check that a candidate has the right sorts of personality characteristics (psychometric) or the right sort of approach or is suited (aptitude) to fit a particular job role.

Quality   fitness for purpose. Exactly meeting customer requirements.

Quality circles   these provide a valuable opportunity for employees to meet together and think of ways in which they can improve the ways in which they work and how they meet both internal and external customer needs.

Quality control   checking to make sure that given quality criteria have been met and that the product is of a given standard.

Questionnaire   systematic list of questions designed to obtain information from people about specific events, their attitudes, their values and their beliefs.

Rank order scale   questions that ask respondents to express preferences.

Real-time systems   online banking providing instant banking information upon customers' accounts and finances. Regulate investment business and increase the confidence of consumers in financial providers.

Recruitment   the process of attracting, and finding employees to apply for posts being offered by an organisation.

Resources the means of supplying what is needed.

Responsibility accounting providing departmental areas with the responsibility and freedom to act within the confines of a budget.

Retail bank high-street bank or joint-stock bank.

Revenue the value of sales (in money terms) that the product is likely to have achieved or has achieved.

Sale and Supply of Goods Act ensures that sellers provide goods that are of 'merchantable quality' that is, they must not be damaged or broken.

Sales value total sales value in pounds.

Search engine database or extracts from the web that can be searched to find references to the subject being researched.

Secondary information published data collected by another organisation and not specific to the project in hand.

Secondary research research using work already carried out by someone else for some other purpose.

Selection the process of choosing suitable candidates to fill a post being offered by an organisation.

Selection criteria requirements that must be met when choosing the best individual to fill a post.

Semantic differential scales market research technique with words describing opposites.

Shareholders part owners of a company who own shares in it.

Shortlisting involves drawing up a list of the most suitable applicants from those that have applied for a post with an organisation.

SLEPT analysis Social, Legal, Economic, Political and Technological changes in the business environment that influence decision-making.

SMART objectives specific, measurable, achievable, realistic and time related objectives.

Sole trader single owner of a business.

Solvency ability to pay wages, supplier's bills and other obligations as they fall due.

Spreadsheet a computer program that allows the user to manipulate figures and perform complex mathematical tasks.

Stockbrokers people or companies that buy and sell securities on the London Stock Exchange.

Stock Exchange the main securities market for stocks and shares within the UK.

Storming the stage when teams are being formed and there are some disputes, misunderstandings and disagreements.

Strategy the long-term plans of an organisation, large plans involving substantial quantities of resources.

Suggestions box a way of collecting customer feedback.

Supervisors have responsibility for supervising a particular task or group of people.

Surfing clicking around the Internet by following links between pages.

SWOT analysis analysis of an organisation and its external environment to assess its internal strengths and weaknesses, and the opportunities and threats that exist in the operating environment.

Tangible physical item that you can touch and see.

Targeting developing strategies for particular segments.

Timeline a line show the planned sequence of events (can also be used to show past events).

Total Quality Management building in concern for quality at every stage in the production of a good and where everyone involved in its production shares responsibility for ensuring and improving on quality. Philosophy based upon quality that shapes relationships between suppliers and customers.

Trade association organisation set up to represent a range of businesses within an industry.

Trade credit credit obtained by selling or buying on credit.

Trade Descriptions Act this attempts to ensure that the description given of the goods forms part of the contract the buyer makes with the seller.

Training needs analysis a study to find out what training an individual needs to become a more knowledgeable and skilled worker in order to help the organisation to meet its goals.

Transformed resources those resources that are altered in the process of production e.g. tungsten carbide is converted into balls for ballpoint pens.

Transforming/transformational resources resources such as machines and people that change the transformed resources, such as materials in the production process.

Turnover the money value of sales made by a company, also referred to as sales revenue.

Undifferentiated marketing mass marketing to a whole market, without distinguishing between the parts.

Unit cost the cost of producing one unit of output.

Unit labour costs the cost of the wages that go into producing a particular unit of product, e.g. one biro.

Values statement a written document setting out the core values that an organisation believes in.

Variable cost a cost that increases with the level of output or sales, e.g. the cost of ingredients in producing chocolate bars.

Variance the difference between a budgeted (planned) figure and what actually materialises. For example, if actual costs are higher than budgeted costs this would be described as a negative variance.

Vision statement what the organisation is seeking to achieve long term.

Verbal communications speaking in a way that is acceptable to customers.

Website resource on the Internet containing pages that have been designed and published using HTML.

Weights and Measures Act this ensures that consumers receive the actual quantity of a product they believe they are buying.

Wholesalers organisation that links manufacturers and retailers within the chain of distribution.

Wireless Application Protocol (WAP) a set of standards that determine the way in which mobile phones and other devices connect to the Internet.

Working capital current assets less current liabilities.

Index

Page numbers in italics refer to illustrations and diagrams.

accounting
  financial 130–3
  management 132
  software 135–6, 231–2
  see also budgets; costing; finance
action plans 269–70
activators 262
'added value' 203, 325, 333
administration 12, 58
advances, banks *see* loans
advertising 40–3, 195, 213
advice, financial 317–18
after-sales service 176–7, 204
agendas 274–5
appearance, business premises 173, 200–1
appraisal, staff 86, 88–9
attitudes, consumer 15–16

Bank of England 144, 293, 320
banking
  electronic 304, 312–13
  facilities 110–11, 298–300, 305
banks 293–4
batch production 335–6
benchmarking 343, *345*
body language 77, *78*, 202
borrowing 110–12 *see also* loans
brands 8, 33–4
break-even analysis 120–6, *124*, *125*, 272
British Standards Institution (BSI) 195
broadband 190, 235, 243
budgets 114–15, 119–20
  constraints 277
  enterprise activities 263, *264*
  setting 116, 117
  variance analysis 117–18
  see also accounting; finance
building societies 290, 294
business
  accessibility 201
  classification 213
  decision-making 109, 113–14, 131, 153–7, 242
  efficiency 238–44
  financial needs 109–13, 289–92, 305–9
  growth 60, 291
  image 173–4
  objectives 60, 80–1, 109, 257–60
  ownership 102–9, 113–14
  performance monitoring 130–1
  use of ICT 210–19
business plans 290, 314–15
buyer-readiness *40*, 40

capacity 333, 335
capital
  owner's 110
  start-up 102–5, 289–90
  working 110, 291, 306

capital budgets 120
cash-flow forecasts 126–30, *128–9*
cell production 336–7
charities 107
codes of practice 180, 181, 191, 192, 319
collateral *see* security, of loans
communication 173, 201–2
  electronic 210–14, 242
  marketing 7–8, 39–40, *40*
competence 63
competition 4–5, 143, 146–7, 278–9, 310
competition-based pricing 38–9
complaints 176, 189–90, 200, 206
computers 219–38
constraints
  business 277–9
  financial services 317–20
  marketing 8–10
Consumer Credit Act (1974) 193
'consumer power' 183–5
Consumer Price Index (CPI) 143, *144*
consumers
  attitudes of 15–16
  behaviour of 19, 20
  protection/rights 181, 193, 319–20
  understanding needs of 3–4
  see also customers
Consumers' Association 183, 316
contagion 310
contingency planning 244–7
continuous flow production 336
contribution 121, 122
co-operatives 105–7
corporate social responsibility *149*, 150, 153, 156, 195
cost-benefit analysis 152–3
costing 121, 330, 331
cost-plus pricing *38*, 38
credit agencies 296
credit cards 302
credit control 131
creditors 110, 155–6, 291, 305
curriculum vitae (CV) 71–2, *73*
customer loyalty 26, 45, 46, 169–70, 177–8
customer needs 51, 170, 179–81, 185
'customer satisfaction' 16–17, 169–71
customer service 11, 16, 58–9, 169–79, 197–205
customers 155, 166–9, 194
  dealing with 174–6
  feedback from 185–90, 204
  of financial services 286–92
  see also consumers

data capture 222–3
data collection 185–90
data mining 216–17
Data Protection Act (1984/98) 194, 246
data storage 190–1, 214–15

databases 25, 57, 137, 215, 219, 230–1
debentures 110, 308
debt factoring *see* factoring
debtors 110, 111, 305
decision-making, business 109, 113–14, 131, 153–7, 242
demographics 32, 201
deregulation 286, 310, 311
diaries, keeping 269–70
direct mail 7, 43, 287
directors, company 154–5
Disability Discrimination Act (1995/2004) 93–4, 194
discrimination 93–4
distribution 46–9, *48*
diversification 310, 311
dividends 109, 296
Drucker, Peter 166, 348

e-commerce 49, 60, 212–14, 237–8
economic conditions, changes in 31–2, 140, 142–6, 148
economies of scale 35, 38, 146, 331–2, 336
efficiency
  ICT in business 238–43
  operational 326–7, 331–5
electronic banking 304, 305, 312–13
electronic data interchange (EDI) 211, 213, 214, 237
email 211, 234–6
employees 155
  disabled 93–4
  motivation 84–92, 179
  payment schemes 84, 86
  priorities of 197–8
  qualities needed in 59, 61–2
  responsibilities of 65
  working conditions 87, 195
employment
  ethical issues 94
  health and safety 82–3
  legislation 93–4, 149
empowerment 92, 155, 341
enterprise activities 254–60
  constraints 277–9
  meetings 273–7
  resources 270–2
  team building 260–7
  time management 267–70
environmental responsibility 152, 184, 195
equal opportunities 93–4
ethical issues 94, 148–51, 191, 319–20
evaluation
  customer service 203–5
  enterprise activities 282–3
  ICT proposal 250–1
  marketing proposal 51–2
  production process 350
  recruitment/selection 79, 96–7

event management 255, 259
exchange rates 144–5
experience, employment 62–3, 68, 72
experiments, market research 20–1

face-to-face discussions 94, 315–16
facilitators 261
factoring 111, 296, 305, 307
feasibility studies 245–6
feedback
    customer 185–90, 204
    interviews 76, 80
finance 11, 131
    enterprise activities 272, 277
    international 291, 303, 305
    legislation 132, 309–11
    management of 114–15, 291–2
    production costs 330, 331
    sources of 109–13, 305–9
    use of ICT 218–19
    see also accounting; banks; budgets
financial services 286–92
    changes in 310–11
    constraints 317–20
    new technology 312–13
    products 298–305
    providers 292–8
Financial Services Act (1986) 285, 286,
    310–11, 318
Financial Services and Markets Act
    (2000) 285, 293
Financial Services Authority (FSA) 293,
    311, 318, 319
fixed costs 120–1, 124
flow production 336
focus groups 24–5, 187
food, labelling of 185, 196
forecasting 17, 30–1, 135–6
franchises 108–9
fringe benefits 86–7

Gantt charts 267–9
government 156
    finance from 111
    statistics 26–7
grants 111, 308–9

hardware, computer 220–6, 244
health and safety 82–3, 180, 194, 330,
    348–9
Herzberg, Frederick 91
hierarchy of needs, motivational theory
    90
hire purchase (HP) 111, 296, 307
historic budgeting 119
home working 240, 242–3
human resources (HR) 12, 219, 240,
    270–1, 328–31

ICT 12–13, 133–5
    benefits 134, 238–43
    drawbacks 134, 243–4
    introducing 244–7
    IT operatives 57–8
    see also computers; Internet
ideas, for new products 5–6
independent financial advisors (IFAs)
    297

induction process 80–4
inflation 143–4
innovators 261
insurance 294–6, 302–3
interest rates 144, 145
intermediaries 47–8
international markets 217, 291
Internet 236–7
    banking 312–13
    market research 27, 217–18
    service providers (ISPs) 234, 235, 236
    see also broadband; e-commerce;
        websites
interviews
    aptitude tests 76
    body language 76, 77–8
    candidate selection 79–80
    feedback about 76, 80
    preparation for 74, 76–7, 77
    questions 74–6, 78
    techniques 77–9, 79
    see also appraisal, staff; market
        research
investments 110, 303
IPARTS (lending principles) 308
ISO 9000 (quality standard) 342–3

job production 335
jobs 56–9
    see also recruitment; selection process
just-in-time (JIT) systems 337, 347, 348

'kaizen' 344, 345
Kanter, Rosabeth 92

labelling, of food products 185, 196
labour budgets 83, 120
labour costs 334
labour productivity 334
leaders 260–1
lean production 337–8
leasing 111, 296, 307–8
legislation 140, 142, 149
    accounting 132
    charities 107
    consumer 181, 191–4, 319
    discrimination 93–4, 194
    employment 93–4, 194
    financial sector 309–11, 318–19
    health and safety 82–3, 194, 348–9
    non-compliance 194–7
limited liability 102–5, 289
liquidity (solvency) 132–3, 291
Lloyd's of London 294–5
loans 110, 111, 113, 300, 308, 312
loyalty, customer 26, 45, 46, 169–70,
    177–8

management accounting 132
Management of Health and Safety at
    Work Regulations (1999) 348, 349
managers 56, 58, 92, 198, 325–7
manufacturing see production
marginal costing 121, 122
market conditions, changes in 146–8
market position, analysis of 137–42
market research 13, 331
    companies 27–8

    and e-commerce 213
    interpretation of data 29–33
    planning 18–19
    primary 19–24
    secondary 25–8, 217–18
market segmentation 14–15
marketing 10–11, 16, 195
    constraints 8–10
    and ICT 219
    objectives 2–10, 51, 137
    and production 330, 331
    proposals 49–51
marketing mix 33–49
Maslow, Abraham 90–1
mass marketing 14
mass production 332, 336
'McDonaldisation' 183–4
McGregor, Douglas 92
McNealy, Roderick M. 170
media 27, 42–3
meetings, business 273–7
Mintel 27, 217, 218
minutes, of meetings 275–7
mission statements 197, 256
Monetary Policy Committee (MPC) 144,
    293, 320
money shops 298
mortgages 111, 288, 289, 300–301
motivation
    employee 84–90, 179, 337, 342
    theories of 90–2
mystery shoppers 185

negotiators 262
networks 211–12, 233–4
new technology 32, 133–5, 147, 243–6
niche marketing 14–15
non-verbal communication 202
not-for-profit organisations 107

Office of Fair Trading (OFT) 193, 319
ombudsmen 319–20
operating cycle 306–7
operations 11
    efficiency 331–5
    management 325–7
    see also production
order tracking systems 239, 242
organic growth 291
organisations 102–9, 289
    communication 7, 39–40
    culture of 87, 342
    external influences 31–2, 143
    functional areas 10–13, 328–31
    resources 8–9, 270–2
output-related pay 84, 86
outsourcing 240
overdrafts 110–11, 300, 306
owner's capital 110
ownership, business 102–9, 113–14

packaging 33–6, 48
partnerships 104, 289
payment schemes
    employee 84, 86
    online 240, 312
penetration pricing 37
pensions 289, 303, 310

Peppers, Don 170
percentages 30
performance related pay 86
person specifications 61–3
PEST analysis 31–2, 140
political changes 31, 140
positioning 15, 42
presentational skills 49–51, 57–8, 247–50
pressure groups 156, 183–4, 195–6
pricing 36–9, 204
primary research 19–25, 94–6, 247, 279–80, 315–16, 349
private limited companies 104–5, 289
product mix 35–6
production 11, 324–5
  efficiency of 326–7
  five Ps of 327–8
  improvements in 350
  links to other departments 328–31
  methods 335–8
  see also operations
productivity 238–41, 334–5
products
  branding 8, 33–4
  development of new 5–6
  features 34–5
  financial 298–305
  websites for 217
profit sharing 86
profitability 126, 131, 132–3
profits 109, 133, 282
project planning 232–3
promotion, job 60, 87–8
promotional mix 7–8, 39–46
psychometric testing 76
public limited companies 105, 289
public relations (PR) 43–5, 214

qualifications, job applicants 62, 68
quality 12, 177, 182, 189, 339–43
questionnaires 21–4, 95, 186–7, 188, 279–80, 315–16

Race Relations Act (1976/2000) 93
rating scales 22–3
record-keeping
  customer feedback 174
  enterprise activities 265
  financial 130–3
recruitment 59–60
  advertising 65–7
  ethical issues 93–4
  evaluation of 79
  job analysis 60–1
  job applications 67–73
  job descriptions 63–5
  person specifications 61–3
  see also interviews; selection process
relationship marketing 170–1
reports
  enterprise activities 264–5
  market research agencies 27–8
research 19–28, 94–6, 247, 279–81, 313–17, 349–50

research and development (R&D) 6, 11–12
resources
  business 8–9, 270–2
  manufacturing 325, 326
  see also human resources
'responsibility accounting' 114, 116
retained profits 109, 109
revenue 114, 334
risks, investment 17, 30, 317
Rogers, Martha 170

safety see health and safety; security
Sale and Supply of Goods Act (1979/94) 191
sales 178
  budgets 119
  channels 47, 47
  forecasts 30
  invoices 25
  promotions 45–6, 265
  revenue 114, 334
  use of ICT in 48–9, 219
satisfiers and dissatisfiers, motivational theory 91
savings accounts 298–9, 301–2
scale of operations 331–2
search engines 236, 241
secondary research 25–8, 96, 247, 280, 316–17, 350
Securities and Investment Board (SIB) 311, 318, 319
security
  businesses 292
  computer data 134, 233
  customer data 191
  of customers 180
  electronic banking 313
  of loans 308
segmentation 14–15, 170
selection process 67, 73–80
September 11th 131, 143, 147–8
Sex Discrimination Act (1975/86) 93
shareholders 154
short-listing 74–9
skimming 37
SLEPT analysis 140–2
SMART objectives 3, 18, 51, 260
social trends 32, 140, 152
software 226–38, 244
  accounting 130, 136, 231–2
  databases 25, 57, 137, 215, 219, 230–1
  spreadsheets 57, 125–6, 135–6, 218–19, 228
  word processing 228–9
sole traders 102–3, 289
solvency 132–3
special needs 168–9, 180–1, 204
spreadsheets 57, 125–6, 135–6, 218–19, 228
staff
  appraisal 86, 88–9
  induction 80–4
  training 89–90, 244, 246–7

stakeholders 153–7
start-up capital 102–5, 110, 289–90, 309
statistics
  calculating 29–31
  government 26–7
stock control 201, 216, 239, 345–8
Stock Exchange 105, 289, 294, 296, 297, 308
supervisors 56–7
suppliers 111, 155
supply chains 239–40
Supply of Goods and Service Act (1982) 193
surveys, customer satisfaction 21–4, 186–9, 204
SWOT analysis 32–3, 137–9, 141, 280

team building
  responsibilities 263–7
  roles 260–2
  stages 270–1
team working 199–200, 255, 262
technology 32, 133–5, 144, 147, 312–13
terrorism, economic effect of 147–8
Theory X vs Theory Y, motivational theory 92
time management 263, 267–70, 271–2, 278
total quality management (TQM) 178, 341–2, 343
trade associations 27, 195, 319
trade credit 306–7
Trade Descriptions Act (1968) 193, 319
training 89–90
  customer service 173, 198–9, 204
  ICT 134, 135, 244, 246–7
  induction 83–4
triple bottom line 148–9

unemployment 145–6
unit costs 38, 331, 332
unit labour costs 334

value for money 38, 203, 318
values/vision statements 256–7
variable costs 121
variance analysis 117–18
venture capital 110
video conferencing 211
voluntary organisations 107, 109

wages 84–5, 146, 334
watchdogs, consumer 183, 319
websites 211, 212–14, 217, 236, 239–41
Weights and Measures Act (1985) 193–4
Which? (Consumers' Association) 183, 316
wholesalers 47–8
word processing software 228–9
work measurement 86
working capital 110, 291, 306
working conditions 87, 195

zero budgeting 117, 119